REVOLUTION OF SPIRIT

RICHARD SHAULL

Revolution of Spirit

Ecumenical Theology in Global Context

ESSAYS IN HONOR OF

Richard Shaull

edited by

Nantawan Boonprasat Lewis

WILLIAM B. EERDMANS PUBLISHING COMPANY
GRAND RAPIDS, MICHIGAN / CAMBRIDGE, U.K.

© 1998 Nantawan Boonprasat Lewis

Published by Wm. B. Eerdmans Publishing Co.

255 Jefferson Ave. S.E., Grand Rapids, Michigan 49503 /

P.O. Box 163, Cambridge CB3 9PU U.K.

Printed in the United States of America

03 02 01 00 99 98   7 6 5 4 3 2 1

ISBN 0-8028-4591-6

Contents

v

Acknowledgments

FROM THE INCEPTION through the production of this Festschrift, many people and institutions have provided help and support. Without them this Festschrift would not have been possible. I would like to acknowledge the hospitality of Elsa Tamez and her institution, the Seminario Biblico Latinoamericano in San Jose, Costa Rica, where the majority of contributors met to discuss their essays and collaborated on the idea of the Festschrift.

Several friends and churches enthusiastically welcomed the effort to honor Richard Shaull and helped to finance the meeting in San Jose. Specifically, I wish to thank John Chapman of Southern Africa Desk, PCUSA, Margaret Flory, Annice and Steve Gregerson, David Gregerson, Nancy Johns, Paton and Judith Lewis, Margaret Lynch, Racial Justice Development Office of the Presbyterian Church USA, Paul Long and his congregation at Indian Hill Church, Cincinnati, Ohio, the late Bernard Quick, John Sinclair, Westminster Presbyterian Church, Minneapolis, and Robert Zeimes. Special thanks is also extended to Luther Tucker and the Mary Brady Tucker Foundation for their generous support. In addition much appreciation is given to Roderick Frohman, his staff at the Grace Trinity Community Church of Minneapolis and the Janthira Foundation for their active involvement in this project. I would also like to acknowledge Alvaro Perez of the Seminario Biblico Latinoamericano and Donald Lewis for their help in compiling the bibliography of Richard Shaull.

Dr. Thomas Gillespie, President of Princeton Theological Seminary deserves a special recognition. He greeted this project with enthusiasm and offered institutional support to the project, including identifying the publisher and providing a grant for this project. Fred Kirchhoff, Dean of

College of Arts and Sciences at Metropolitan State University, gave me encouragement and support to work on this project. Lastly, the editor owes a special thanks to Bill Eerdmans of Wm. B. Eerdmans Publishing Company, whose openness to and accommodation of the project helped to bring this book to its completion.

Introduction

NANTAWAN BOONPRASAT LEWIS

ESSAYS IN THIS VOLUME were written in tribute to Richard Shaull, colleague, professor, theologian, and mentor to many of us; and friend of the poor, oppressed, and marginalized. One of Dick's theological landmarks has been a call to recognize the end of Christendom and the challenge to find a way to speak prophetically in a new historical situation. This often means more than accommodating an adjustment to the way theology "used to be done." To Dick, acknowledging and accepting "the signs of the time" requires a radical change in the way we construct our world theologically. This is essential for us to prophetically bear witness to the messianic message in church and society. Also key to his thinking is that such theological construction is to be grounded in a concrete situation, wherever that might be. In most cases it means to discern the messianic message in the midst of social movements and people's struggles within one's particular context and social-political-economic milieu. This presents an ever-present opportunity to discover new frontiers and new ecumenical situations to fulfill God's mission.

In paying tribute to Dick Shaull, whose life and work exemplify this conviction, the essays in this volume were accordingly organized into three main parts which hopefully reflect Dick's theological approach and prophetic emphasis. Part one contains a series of theological discussions on critical issues facing people in different contexts and parts of the world. The essays in part two persuasively argue that new historical situations lead to new theological questions and interpretations. Part three concludes the volume by presenting the challenge and the need to create theological paradigms which address particular historical situations of people and speak to their struggles.

1

Richard Snyder begins his essay in part one with a reflection on his spiritual journey juxtaposed with his theological training and finds himself wrestling with the question of how to witness the messianic message in a time of social fragmentation and disorientation where the center no longer holds. In his search for resources to withstand the challenge, Snyder shares his insightful discoveries. Andrew Conrad's painful personal journey as a gay Christian raises critical issues concerning the community of faith and its ministry. María Marta Arís-Paúl sees her issue of struggle as one shared by Latin American and Caribbeans immigrants in the U.S. She puts forward issues and challenges confronting her community in this situation. Experiencing that the world and social structure are not what they ought to be, theologian Joseph C. Nyce explores two contrasted themes — the arrogance of beliefs and the openness of faith — to clarify his experience and to reconnect with the creative forces for a better tomorrow. As chaplain at a university in upstate New York, Nancy A. De Vries lives with an awareness that religions, including Christianity, exist on the fringe of the academic community. Sadly, this is an increasingly common situation for academicians in Christian studies in colleges and universities. It leaves many of us, including De Vries, with the challenging task of finding their prophetic voice from a peripheral location. Shifting the discussion to a global context, Douglass Sullivan-González highlights the ever-present relationship between theology and politics through an examination of the ethical dilemma a prominent and popular cleric, Francisco González Lobos, was confronted with during the mid-nineteenth century in Guatemala.

Identifying issues of struggles in one's particular historical situation often results in having to reframe and reconstruct new theological questions to speak to the situation. In her attempt to address a new situation in Latin America, that of the free market, Elsa Tamez looks at the concept of Christian freedom in Galatians in light of this new reality. After serving the Amity Foundation in China for over twenty years, Philip L. Wickeri feels compelled to examine a phenomenon of modernization and development in China and asks what a Christian perspective on modernization means for China and for the current ecumenical situation. His theological interpretation on this subject will surprise readers and indeed stretches one's previous understanding and assumption about mission in China today, as hinted by his quotation of Michael Walzer, "The promised land is not utopia; it is just a better place to be than Egypt"! From the Latin American continent, specifically Brazil, where Dick Shaull spent most of his missionary life, Dick's long-time colleague and companion in the struggle, Waldo Cesar, reflects on two extraordinary moments in the history of Protestantism in Brazil. The first happened in the mid-1950s and extended until the military coup of 1964, when both worked on a project called "Church and Society." The second moment is the present astonishing growth of the neo-Pentecostal movement in Brazil. This provided both Waldo and Dick an opportunity to work together once again to undertake an interdisciplinary research to understand sociologically and theologically the spiritual and material contribution Pentecostalism is making to the poor in their desperate situation in Brazil. Alan Neely's essay suggests a new historical situation is not limited to a social-economic-political milieu. Latin America is also going through a new historical situation religiously with John Paul II's declaration of the "new evangelization." Neely theologically assesses this new situation and its implications for liberation theology in the continent. He leaves the readers with an open statement regarding the future of liberation theology: "Basismo is still a force to be reckoned with by the church" and "unless history ends, the struggle for justice will go on. . . ."

Essays in part three present various paradigms of ecumenical theology. In his eloquent and provocative voice, Timothy Njoya raises new theological questions from his African context. With a discussion on the two types of Christianity at work in Africa — missionary Christianity and African experiential theology — Njoya enlightens us to "a radically new understanding of the dynamic interaction of conversion, incarnation, and creation." George Armstrong introduces a people's theology in New Zealand in a form of public liturgy. His discussion focuses on the intersections of Christian faith and the church with the prevailing political and economic conditions during the past fifty years. Kim Yong-Bock's essay explores the meaning of power and the *minjung* in the new situation of a global market economy. As Kim sees it, the *minjung* of Asia is yet to grasp the meaning of this new reality, its power and their own victimization. Thus there is a need to develop a theology of the sovereignty of the *minjung*. With reference to Apollo 8 and the space program, Bruce Boston discusses a revolution of human consciousness resulting from scientific development. The planetary age, Boston suggests, produces a case for a new theological paradigm to interpret the revolution of human consciousness that contemporary society is going through. Mark Taylor analytically examines the case of Protestant Mayan uprising in Guatemala in the nineties and how Mayans' mythic vision provides them with resources for revolutionary practice to resist and change. On the same thematic approach, Nantawan Boonprasat Lewis explores the history of struggle of Asian American women and the liberative trends that become their spiritual sources for survival and resistance to the forces of racism, patriarchy, and imperialism which specifically affect them.

The essays in this volume make a strong statement about theology in ecumenical situations and in a global context. Together they speak of a theology that engages in a dialogue with the context in which it participates, be they religious, cultural, sociopolitical, or economic aspects. The essays indicate that ecumenical theology is multicultural. God speaks many languages and through all cultures, races, economic classes, genders, and sexual orientations. No one theological framework is the norm and dominates others. Each context provides particular resources for the community to discern the messianic message. Although the essayists speak from their particular contexts with particular concerns, their concerns are framed within a context of global awareness and acknowledgment of mutual existence, interconnectedness, and interdependence of human life and environments.

It is with great pleasure that we, the authors herein, honor Dick Shaull with theological statements that exemplify Dick's life and work.

Profits from the sale of this book will be used to establish a fund for publication, in Latin America, of writings on spirituality and social transformation.

PART ONE

Critical Issues in the Struggle

Disabilities and Disorientations: Resources for the Struggle

T. RICHARD SNYDER

WHEN I FIRST MET Dick Shaull in 1962 he had just joined the faculty of Princeton Theological Seminary after many years in Brazil, and I had just returned from a year's internship in Rio de Janeiro. It was a transitional time in our society and in my own life. In lectures and private discussions he spoke of the end of Christendom, the challenge of a new way of doing theological work for the sake of radical change, and our roles in witnessing the messianic message in church and society.

In my own journey I have experienced both the drought and the refreshing waters of the messianic message. My world as a child was a protected one in every respect. Growing up in the suburbs of Philadelphia, I was sheltered from the harsh realities of poverty. With the end of WWII came a period of economic expansion and nationalistic dominance for the United States that easily lulled me as a young teenager into an uncritical acceptance of my culture's myopia. Every day in every way, things seemed to be getting better and better.

The fundamentalist religious faith of our family offered further assurances that all this was part of God's plan. Our nation had been called to fight the demonic, ungodly forces of communism and to point the way to a better life for all. (The "all," it seemed, was primarily defined as white folks.) Our particular brand of fundamentalism was of a dispensationalist mode, which meant that Scripture revealed a specific outline of the stages of history. We believed that we knew, within a reasonable margin of error, where civilization was headed.

The visceral politics of anticommunism and dispensationalist philosophy of history were joined with an equally uncritical view of the Bible

7

as a direct revelation from God. The Bible was considered plain in its meaning to all who would approach it with that basic preunderstanding. As such, I and most of those around me, were very sure about both our eternal state and the state of affairs of the world. Doubts were the stuff of those with too little faith. To doubt guaranteed that one would sink as Peter did when he tried to follow Jesus in walking on the water.

My years at Philadelphia Bible Institute and Wheaton College (Ill.) did little to loosen that tightly woven world. Doctrine was prescribed and deviation denounced. The casuistric code of behavior at both places (no drinking, smoking, dancing, card playing, or movies) reinforced my certainty that there was *one way*.

Fortunately, that was not the whole story. At Wheaton, I majored in philosophy and one of the unintended consequences of that study was to introduce me to the relativity of human truth claims. While the professors did their best to assure us that any ideas not consistent with a literal interpretation of the Bible were — by definition — untrue, a small appreciation for relativism began to creep in. Perhaps it would be more accurate to describe this new mood as a gnawing suspicion.

That suspicion was deepened as I was introduced to higher criticism in biblical studies and existentialist philosophy at Princeton Seminary, beginning in 1959. It was not until a year's internship in Rio de Janeiro, Brazil in 1961-62 that the tapestry that had been so tightly woven finally unraveled, leaving me with an unrecognizable mass of fiber.

There I encountered poverty and wealth in such stark contradiction that my myopia was shattered. There I met Western expatriates who considered the plight of Brazil's favela dwellers to be, at best, the result of their own indolence and stupidity or, at worst, the will of God. There I met Christians whose fervent anticommunism outdid my own, leading them to condemn all attempts at transforming the plight of the poor except through prayer and the expansion of capitalism which, in Darwinian form, would inevitably require some losers.

The dissonance between a loving God and the plight of the poor coupled with the laissez-faire response of so many Christians was more than I could handle. When I returned for my final year of study at Princeton Seminary, nothing seemed to hold together. I remember standing on campus, looking up the sky, shaking my fist and cursing God. The unraveling seemed complete.

This journey was not idiosyncratic to me, of course. Untold numbers had faced up to the enlightenment-rooted claims of historical criticism and found their personal foundations shaken. Even more had participated in the normal identity process that includes rebellion against the structures, values, and directives of our roots. My unraveling, however, involved more than either of those dynamics. It was more than just my personal orientation that was unraveling.

The entire culture was coming apart. The racist underbelly of our society was being laid bare by the civil rights movement. The imperialistic reach of our military industrial complex and our unquestioning patriotism were being challenged by the anti-Vietnam War movement. Male chauvinism and patriarchal control were being rejected by feminists and the role and structure of family life were being questioned as never before. The threat of nuclear annihilation led many to conclude that they would not live to see their old age. Even some who detested communism were now saying, "better Red than dead." And the death of God was announced and celebrated by many who saw nothing but illusion in traditional Christianity. Nothing — motherhood, the flag, not even God — was sacred. It seemed that there was nothing left to count upon.

Fortunately, that unraveling was not the final word. Several persons at Princeton Seminary offered me some new ways of looking at the world, the church, and my faith. Tim Kerr's courses in Christianity and the arts and literature invited me to approach theology in an intuitive, affective, and non-linear way. Several courses with Gerhard von Rad offered me a chance to experience the power of Scripture in fresh ways. And Dick Shaull's prophetic iconoclasm reassured me that it was possible to stand within the stream of Christianity and at the same time engage in radical doubt and questioning.

It was a long journey back for me. In some very profound ways it is still going on and I suspect it will until I die. For, even though I have found a center and faith that sustains me, the unraveling of our culture continues all around us.

Racism prevails, as witnessed by the ethnographies of Jonathan Kozol *(Amazing Grace),* the philosophical analysis of Cornell West *(Race Matters),* and the journalistic reporting of Ellis Cose *(The Rage of a Privileged Class).* The United States' imperialism has continued with its militaristic forays into Grenada, Panama, and the Persian Gulf. The second-class status of women has been reinforced with a rollback of abortion rights and the diminishment or elimination of social programs that provided a safety net to prevent them from falling into abject poverty. Perhaps the only piece missing is the death of God movement. Unfortunately, for many God has proven to be worse than dead; God has become uninteresting.

As if this bankruptcy were not sufficient, we now face two additional realities that reinforce the unraveling. We have discovered that our industrial grandeur has been built at the expense of the environment. As Chief

Seattle predicted, we are lying in our own waste. The second development, which has had even more visceral impact upon the so-called average citizen, has been the corporate downsizing, outsourcing, global "free" trade, and multinational corporate control that is out of control. For millions who may have been able to hold on to the promise of a better tomorrow despite the unfortunate "glitches" of racism, patriarchy, and militarism, the death of the American Dream is now coming home to roost.

If ever there were a time that the center was not holding, this is one of them. That is how I would characterize the present moment in time for western society.

To say that we are postindustrial is to understand that we are also postmodern. The confidence we had placed in human ingenuity, human capacity, and human control can be seen in both industrialization and in modernity's ideological structures. Just as industrialization and modernity share the roots of rationalism so, too, postindustrialism and postmodernism are mirror images of one another. They derive from the fragmentation of the same center, from the pulling up of the same roots.

The fragmentation is not simply experienced as the falling apart of an evil society. The fragmentation has affected the shape of the future, the eschatological project that calls us toward something new. We live in a time of apparent messianic drought when the promise is, at best, seen through a glass darkly — when there seems to be no way ahead.

And no wonder. Many of us who placed our hope in one or more of the democratic socialist projects have witnessed the fragmentation of these experiments in hope as well. Not only have the experiments in Eastern Europe and the Soviet Union failed, the more democratic expressions of it such as Allende's Chile, the Sandinistas' Nicaragua, Scandinavia, and France have either been driven underground or voted into marginality. Cuba's experiment has been starved by embargo and now, increasingly, China is capitulating to the logic of capitalism. For those of us who have hoped for some semblance of democratic socialism there are no prototypes left.

What many of us thought were bases for hope now appear shattered or at least moribund. And so we search for new resources. To seek resources for hope in a time such as this is to seek a center, not as a place, but as a way of holding the pieces together — however tentatively — in such a manner that patterns can be discerned and commitments can be made.

This has always been the way of faith, at its best. The wilderness wanderings of the slave band led by Moses evidenced this tentative re-weaving. Manna, clouds, pillars of fire were not the stuff of the promised land but rather the interim realities of a period of wandering. Interestingly, both the food provided and the signs for guidance for those wilderness wanderers were momentary. They were there when needed, but not forever. They were new every day and they moved as the people moved. They were not like the stones placed by the bank of the Jordan River as reminders and guides for future generations, nor were they like the temple that stood permanently on a hilltop. These pilgrim people were offered transitory signs that pointed to a hope beyond their limited experience but which could not be carried over even from day to day. They were offered a center that was new every morning but which at the same time provided continuity.

That is the nature of faith in a postindustrial, postmodern age. The hope we have is offered to us through signs that are fleeting at best. The assumed permanence of once-for-all rules, structures, and relationships gives way to epiphanies — the appearance of God in a stranger, in a cloud, in not-to-be-repeated events — each of which provide us with clues for our future. Within and among these fleeting signs there is a constancy that provides us with a foundation. The constancy or centering is provided by the narrative born in the midst of relationships of struggle and hope. It is found in the signs of a community that bear witness to its experience of abundant life.

For those who have grown accustomed to living with rational certainties, and who approach the future by seeking to control it, such transitory, tendentious, and tentative a base can seem insufficient. What happened to the rules, the Word of God, the orthodoxy, the structures that provided security in the past?

We are accustomed to fixed certainties. Industrialism offered us an essential structure for organizing our world, viz. bureaucracy. Bureaucracy has shaped not only our governments and industries but also our churches and even our personal relationships. Bureaucracy is designed to remove arbitrariness and surprise — to provide predictability. Similarly, modernity has offered us an essential structure for understanding our world, viz. rationalism. Rationalism has shaped our science and technology, our orthodoxy and worship, and our expectations of the possible. Rationalism has assured us that if we but put our minds to things, we can understand and control them. Both bureaucracy and rationalism have historically offered us an organizational and ideological centering that provides us with unchanging certainties.

Today, however, the center is not holding. We are being forced to search for new resources for organizing our lives and for finding meaning. We are at a crisis point in the human project. And because it is a crisis rather than a catastrophe, we have the opportunity to discover new ways of thinking and being that offer us resources for a hopeful future.

Where we turn for those resources, where we look for meaning and structure is the crucial issue. Where are the reservoirs of hope?

I have grown increasingly weary of doctrine that precedes or takes precedence over experience. It is not that I have no appreciation for theory — quite the opposite. Rather, it is a question of where we are to find the reservoir. Theory is helpful in pointing us toward the source of hope. But the hope is not to be found in the directions to the reservoir, it is to be found in the reservoir itself.

Another way to ask the question about reservoirs of hope is to ask, "where do we meet God?" Surely the source of the water is rooted in the creative and redeeming power of the God of the future.

That is why I find it impossible to begin with theory or doctrine. My own hope is grounded in experience, not in orthodoxy of any form. There are certain experiences for me that have consistently been the place of meeting with God — that offer me a center. Theory (doctrine) is but one form of our narrative about those experiences. Doctrine is simply theory that has been given the imprimatur of some authority. The rationality of theory and doctrine must be open to, shaped by, and corrected in dialogue with other forms of narrative that point to the experience of God's presence. In that spirit, I turn to two experiences that provide me with messianic hope, that serve as my reservoir. Limiting myself to two is not because these exhaust the ways I encounter the power of a messianic God but they represent several of the most fertile ways for me. They are: relationships of solidarity, and worshipful experiences that invite ecstasy. Together, these give birth to a utopian vision that leads me to a radical social analysis.

The first, and for me foremost, way we meet God is in relationships. Buber's restatement of the Gospel of John's preface, "In the beginning was the relation" says it well. In gospel terms it is, "God was *IN* Christ, reconciling the world to God's self."

The question then becomes, "what are the relationships and what is the nature of those relationships that are reservoirs of hope"? It is not just any relationships that give essential meaning to our life and provide us with a foundation of hope. I suggest that it is the relationships at the margins of life where God meets us. In a word, we meet God as we enter into solidarity with the oppressed.

It may seem strange to some to seek God at the margins of life, especially in the light of Dietrich Bonhoeffer's warning against the God of the Gap. He was concerned that those who sought God only at the point of their own extremities, only where their control and rationality could no longer suffice, were failing to experience the fullness of God. For him, God is to be found at the center.

I am speaking of a different marginality. The marginality I am concerned with is that created by the power arrangements of our world. Our world is filled with people who have been confined to the margins of power, benefits, and worth. They are the ones Jesus described as the "least." When viewed in this way, meeting God on the margins is not a shrinking possibility but an expanding one.

We can discover resources for hope as we join in solidarity with the *dis-abled.* The use of "dis" here is interesting. In street language, to "diss" someone is to show disrespect. Few things are worse than being dissed, for one's identity, honor, and dignity are all threatened. To be dissed is to be moved to the margins of the culture (whether dominant or sub). In our society, the *diss-abling* is done not only through face-to-face disrespect but through invisible structures of organization and logic that give rise to poverty, insecurity, obsolescence, and ostracization.

To speak of relationships at the margins is to point to relationship with those persons who have been *diss-missed* (their absence from the center of our lives goes unnoticed), *diss-carded* (their identity is not recognized), *diss-counted* (they do not appear in our census), *diss-abled* (their abilities are not recognized as worthy contributions to our commonweal). It is precisely in discovering the abilities, wisdom, and worth among those who have been *diss-abled* that hope is to be found.

Obviously I am using the word *diss-abled* to indicate something larger than simply those who suffer from some physical or mental incapacitation, but it certainly includes those who are traditionally labeled as the disabled.

To search for hope in such relationships, however, flies in the face of the inertia of our culture. C. Wright Mills suggested that one way to understand relationships in the United States is in terms of a pyramid of power. At the base are the poorest of the poor. In the middle is the largest group of people, often referred to as the middle class. And, at the very top are a few members of the military/industrial complex. I believe his analysis is essentially correct and that this pyramid of power relations has led us as far from the true reservoirs of hope as it is possible to stray.

For my purposes here, I am not as interested in exploring the nature of those at the top. Studies such as Domhoff's *Who Rules America?* offer detailed descriptions of the interlocking directorates, control of Trust Funds, old boy's networks, etc. that constitute the shape of power. An interesting point that is sometimes overlooked is how often the interests of the ruling class are intertwined in such a way that conspiracy is often unnecessary. There is a "naturalness" about the way the ruling class operates and the decisions they make, that follows an unwritten logic. There are certain things that just are or are not "done." There are conspiracies, of course, but some of the ruling class's decisions are unintended, the results of an inertia rather than intentional plot.

Nor am I interested primarily, at this point, in analyzing those at the bottom. This has been done by William Julius Wilson in *The Truly Disadvantaged,* Warren Copeland in *The Rich Get Rich and the Poor Get Welfare,* Jeffrey Reiman in *The Rich Get Richer and the Poor Get Prison,* and in Michael Harrington's classic study, *The Other America.*

My interest here is in understanding the nature of those in the middle; those who were labeled by Richard Nixon as the "silent majority," and by many sociologists as the middle class. The notion of the middle class is quite elastic in the United States. The self-definition of middle class by those who consider themselves part of it is important, for to hear people define their own place in society you would conclude that it encompasses all those who have incomes slightly above the poverty level to those making several hundred thousand dollars a year.

This elasticity is due in large measure to the fact that the category of middle-classness entails more than simply income level. It is wrapped up with education, job or profession, family background, ethnicity, elements of style, cultural activities, neighborhood, etc. And it is at this point that we find some important clues for understanding the current mood of the nation. It is a mood that I would characterize as the "upward gaze." People at the bottom, but even more so, people in the middle tend to identify upward, to set their sights on the small group at the top. Whenever someone from below makes it into that elite echelon there is great rejoicing in the schools, country clubs, and churches of the land for, once again, we have proof that there is always a chance.

This upward gaze can be seen in the lifestyles people emulate: the cars they drive or aspire to drive, the designer clothing they wear, the resorts and cruises they choose. It is testified to by the $150 basketball shoes worn by kids whose families have almost nothing. The voyeuristic fascination that millions have with the rich and famous has created an entire media industry of celebrity watching. And the gambling boom throughout the nation has fed the frenzy of upward gazing. "Hey, you never know." You too could be rich and powerful.

There are two deceits connected with this upward gaze. The first conceals the fact that it is an illusion. Despite the fact that a Michael Jordan can rise from poverty to enormous wealth and popularity, or that a Bill Gates can become one of the world's several richest men in a matter of a decade, more and more people are out of work or working for less. Many of our elderly are being forced to spend their last days as wards of the state, and the ranks of women and children living in poverty swells. The illusion that I can become that one-in-10-million success story is the stuff of fairy tales.

This illusion leads us into a false consciousness, an anesthetized state that substitutes the cheap world of unrealistic wishes for an honest confrontation with reality and what it will take to change things. And even if we should be able to afford the Lexus, build the second home, send our children to prep school, or retire early, what we have gained is only a little more of the power that we possess as members of that great middle. It is not the power at the tip of the pyramid.

There are several kinds of power operating within the pyramid. The primary power of those at the top is the power to decide. They are able to shape the basic options through such things as their control of the media, their investments, their decisions about closing or moving factories, their lobby power, their influence over policies, and their financial backing of parties and candidates.

The power of those in the middle is essentially the power to consume. Our choice is which internal-combustion-powered automobile to buy, but not how much will be invested in mass transit versus the automobile. Our choice is in which designer label to wear and how much to pay for it, but not whether our family should be subjected to massive advertising that is creating an appetite for the unnecessary. Our choice is in which channel to watch, but not how to place the resources of the media in the hands of the public for the sake of the commonwealth rather than for the sake of profits.

Part of the illusion is that in being granted more resources to consume, we are on the way up the pyramid. If we can move from a Chevrolet to a Mercedes, we must be making it. But it is absolutely critical that we understand what power comes with such a move. It is merely the power to consume more. Even the highly publicized sports heroes with their millions do not usually make it to the top of the pyramid, i.e., to the place of decision-making. They merely can buy more toys.

The first great deceit of the upward gaze disguises its illusory nature. The second is that it leads away from life, away from real fulfillment and hope.

In Philippians 2, the followers of Jesus have been offered a prototype for living, a way to walk, a revelation of what God intends.

So if there is any encouragement in Christ, any incentive of love, any participation in the Spirit, any affection and sympathy, complete my joy by being of the same mind, having the same love, being in full accord and of one mind. Do nothing from selfishness or conceit, but in humility count others better than yourselves. Let each of you look not only to his or her own interests, but also to the interest of others. Have this mind among yourselves, which you have in Christ Jesus, who, though he was in the form of God, did not count equality with God a thing to be grasped, but emptied himself, taking the form of a servant, being born in the likeness of humans. And being found in human form he humbled himself and became obedient unto death, even death on a cross. Therefore God has highly exalted him and bestowed on him the name which is above every name. . . .

The key word in the Greek text is *kenosis,* which means self-emptying. "He emptied himself." It is sometimes thought of a ridding oneself of all knowledge, power, desires, and will. But just the opposite is implied. It is not an emptying of everything but an emptying of a certain thing and the filling with another. It is the giving up of one desire for the sake of another.

The specific emptying called for is the ridding oneself of an exclusive or even primary focus on one's own position, well-being, and advancement. That is replaced with a humility, an identification with those at the bottom, a willingness to be crucified for the sake of the least of these, our brothers and sisters. It is the relinquishment of the false power gained through the upward gaze and the reception of the incredible power of the downward gaze.

We see in Jesus that the way to fulfillment is to claim the power of the downward gaze, the power of identification with those who are the recipients of the unjust power arrangements of the pyramid. It is important to recognize that the issue is one of making an option. Jesus had some choices. He was not born into the worst possible condition. He would have had far fewer options had he been born a woman, or even worse, a woman with a crippling disease. The issue was not how far down on the pyramid he was born but the direction of his gaze.

As a person with options, Jesus could have chosen the way of comfort and upward mobility. That is a central part of the temptation he underwent in the wilderness experience — "I will give you all these nations." Instead, he touched the untouchables, talked with the rejects, ate with the outcasts, and stood up for the marginal. Jesus self-consciously identified with those at the bottom of the pyramid.

The fundamental choice facing each person born is with whom we will identify. Our upward gazing society identifies with those at the top. Jesus identifies with the people at the bottom; his gaze was downward, toward the margins. But this marginality is only in terms of the unjust power arrangements. Jesus recognized that the marginals constitute the center of God's love, the center of life. And in that downward gaze we are told he found the strength to set his face to Jerusalem, in that downward gaze he was able to endure the cross, and in that downward gaze God has given him a name above every name. In the downward gaze Jesus comes face to face with the resurrecting power that is at the center, not at the margins of life. Jesus found a reservoir of hope in his relationships with those who had been *diss-abled.* So, too, can we.

Contrary to this, we are a nation and a people captive to the upward gaze. Even many at the bottom have swallowed the illusion. Perhaps we should stop looking upward to heaven, upward for God. Perhaps our hands of praise should be reaching downward, reminding us that the heart and mind of Jesus carried him to the base of the pyramid of power.

The downward gaze is far more than simply an abstract identification with or an empathy for. While it involves these, it also includes political struggle alongside. The downward gaze drives us toward alliances with the *diss-affected,* the *diss-carded,* the *diss-abled.* These alliances constitute a basic solidarity in which we are called upon to stand with, act with, and suffer with.

There is nothing magical about relationships of solidarity, as I have said elsewhere *(Divided We Fall: Moving from Suspicion to Solidarity).* Misinterpretation, mistrust, misunderstandings, and mistakes mark our path. But occasionally the confusion of Babel gives way to the communication of Pentecost, the dividing walls give way to hands that reach across forbidden space. When that happens, we are experiencing the power of God's Spirit, the power of the future breaking in upon us, the messianic stream flowing in the desert of our world. Those who have been dissed are given respect, those who have been outside are now at the center of our world, new relationships and structures are born, and new meaning is found.

When understood in this way, solidarity becomes not simply a political strategy but a path to salvation. It becomes a source of revelation, a means of grace, a way in which we meet God and experience the power of the messianic future.

A second reservoir of messianic hope I have discovered is in experiences of ecstatic worship. Let me clarify several points before going further. First, I am not referring to worship in general but to a specific kind. I find many worship services boring, empty, and even counter to the gospel. I do not mean worship in which the flag and country are the operational commitments with God as the titular head, or in which orthodox slogans substitute for critical and constructive thinking, or rote repitions lull us into false comfort. Nor does my use of the word ecstatic signify "feel good" religion in which the affirmation of possibilities is reduced to a psychological fix.

Second, the use of the word ecstatic should not be taken to mean only or specifically Pentecostal forms of worship. They are included, but the experience is not limited to Pentecostalism. The word "ecstatic" means joyous, or thrilled, often to the point of delirium. Delirium is a state often associated with high fever, eventuating in mental disequilibrium or "being out of one's mind." Ecstasy is the experience of being out of one's mind in such a way that the boundaries of rationalism can no longer prevent the emergence of feelings and insights previously precluded. R. D. Laing's psychotherapeutic insight that insanity is the only appropriate response to an insane world is fitting. In a society oriented to the logic of profits above people, disorientation is in order.

Such ecstasy can occur even in traditional Euro-American contexts. I vividly remember a concert held at St. Paul's Cathedral in New York City almost twenty years ago. Seiji Ozawa conducted the Berlioz Requiem in that massive European-style cathedral. At the climax of the concert thousands of people leapt spontaneously onto the pews, shouting and applauding for many minutes. Later I wondered when was the last time in that sanctuary that people had stood on the pews cheering. It was, indeed, an ecstatic experience.

But such is not my usual experience in church, and I say this as an active (perhaps even overactive) participant. I am a non-stipendiary Parish Associate at our little Presbyterian Church, preaching often, leading adult classes and film forums, counseling, and just being there. I love the people, the pastor, and the opportunity to serve. But seldom do I find myself leaping to my feet, overwhelmed by tears of joy, oblivious to the constrictions of propriety as I did that evening at St. Paul's. And our congregation is far better than many in which I preach or visit. We are small, informal, overrun by the joyful sounds and movement of children, and sometimes experimental. But like most "mainline" Protestant churches we emphasize order and rationality. Boundaries are not easily crossed. Presbyterianism's emphasis on an educated clergy and sermons that expound Scripture in rational fashion leaves little room for ecstasy.

In contrast, I have experienced other forms of worship that have the capacity to invite ecstasy. Pentecostalism offers a worship experience in which ecstasy is common. I believe that one of the reasons why Pentecostalism appeals to so many poor in our world is precisely because they understand, often in ways that are formally unarticulated, that the promises of rational human understanding and control are bankrupt. Movement beyond the limits of modernity and industrialism is being provided not only by postmodern theorists but also by practitioners of the ecstatic.

In some very important ways, many Pentecostals and other adherents of popular religions have not been so completely caught in the limitations of modernity and industrialization. They represent an experiential post-modernism and postindustrialism. They know that our political machines do not serve democracy. They know that the mysteriousness of life leaves our rationality tongue-tied. They realize that corporations are disinterested in human development. They experience the oxymoron of a legal justice system. They understand that truth is found in the body as well as the mind, in the feelings as well as thought. One of the central appeals of Pentecostal-ism is that truth and vitality are experienced beyond the bounds of human control and structuring. Tongues, healing, and visions are not simply "primitive" but also at the heart of our "post" experience. The mystery to which they point can only be captured in metaphorical and bodily language.

I know an Episcopal priest who regularly conducted healing services in New York City. He had occasion to visit Nigeria where he attended a healing service to which thousands of persons had come. Someone pointed out a woman who had walked one hundred miles carrying her dying infant. As they were vesting for the eucharistic healing service, he asked the Nigerian bishop, "How do you hedge your bets with a woman who has walked one hundred miles in the hope that her baby will be healed?" "You Americans, you don't understand," he said. "She has come here to expe-rience God's grace. If that grace eventuates in the healing of her child, she will be grateful to God. If it does not, she will still give thanks for the grace made available." My friend, the healer, understood that even at the edges of his own rationality, he was still controlled by the need to control, still dominated by the need to explain, still focused on making sure the outcome was acceptable.

This is not to suggest that communities can live without structures of control, even Pentecostals. But it is to claim that order and orthodoxy are not the only ways to hope and, in fact, may even be straightjackets constricting hope. The narratives of a community of faith must necessarily encompass a broader range than rational speech. Narrative must include music and body language such as anointings and washings, as well as nonrational speech forms such as poetry, metaphor, tongues, and silence. That is why I believe in many more sacraments than even Roman Cathol-icism admits. Seven is too few, and two is absurd.

I have had ecstatic experiences within many non-Pentecostal African American and Hispanic churches. There tears of grief and joy flow freely, music envelops the whole being, sermons address the emotions as well as the mind, prayer overflows the boundaries of control, and bodies give evidence of the movement of the Spirit.

When middle-class Euro-American churches attempt to emulate this ecstasy, it usually comes up empty. Perhaps that is my limitation, but I find such attempts by charismatic groups and praise groups barren. This probably relates to my earlier comments about class and the direction of a community's gaze. Often, hymns, gestures, and words that I find deeply moving when shared in a context of survival cause me great discomfort when utilized in the service of privileged communities. That is why hands raised in most "mainline" churches cause me discomfort. It feels too much like one more exultation over our good fortune. Most of us ought to be stretching our arms and hands downward. I cannot raise my hands in many churches.

It is important not to confuse my claims about ecstatic worship with simply a recovery of emotions or anti-intellectualism. A totally or even primarily emotive foundation will leave us blown by every wind. We are called upon to discern the spirits, to make judgments which necessarily involve analysis and theory. There is no escaping hard intellectual work if we are to be holy. But having been shaped by the rationalism of modernity and industrialism, I have become increasingly aware of the necessity for unloosing the straightjacket in which we have been bound. Ecstatic worship enables us to break beyond the boundaries and controls of modernity and industrialization in a way that opens us to the life-giving power of God's Spirit. In this way of being, we taste the messianic future, not merely describe or point to it, and in so tasting are offered food for the journey, resources for the struggle.

Increasingly, I have found this ecstatic resource also in solitude, or more accurately, in the community of nature. It is not true that I am alone, but rather that there are no people with me at some moments. But I am not alone — I am in relationship with other parts of the household of creation. I am beginning to understand what Martin Buber meant when he said that we are able to be in an I-Thou relationship with elements of nature, those elements that we have often considered either inert or purely functional.

One of the great joys of my life is sailing — single-handed. I relish the hours spent in total silence or, better put, hours without speaking words. It is not silence. The wind, the water, the fish, the seals, the dolphins, the occasional whale, the birds, my breathing, the flap of the sails and the groaning of the rigging are all part of the narrative of life. It is a narrative far richer than the rational narrative of modernity. It is a narrative far more complex than the functional narrative of industrialization. It is the sound of silence that opens me to the power of God's spirit. In those sounds I discover strength for the journey, resources for the struggle.

As is apparent from what has been said, I have discovered that the resources of hope are more broadly available than simply within my own communion or epistemological roadmap. Because the messianic future involves the entire cosmos, the resources for hope must be equally as expansive. We are at the threshold of a new ecumenism: an ecumenism that finds resources in people at the margins, in popular religions, and in relationship with nature itself as part of the household.

I am painfully aware of my own limitations when it comes to experiencing these resources. And I feel even more limited in articulating what I am haltingly discovering. But I am persuaded that in the struggle to discover and work for God's messianic future these resources are critical and life-giving.

A Journey of Faith: A Gay Perspective from the Late Twentieth Century

Andrew W. Conrad

In the twenty-seven years that have passed since I entered Princeton Theological Seminary to study ethics, a great deal has changed in the church and certainly in my experience. I came to seminary the product of a benevolent fundamentalism; I was comfortable with a "high" view of scripture and I found little coherent that could challenge it. While my experience as a Christian had been shaped in many different ways — a Methodist childhood, three years in Practical Bible Training School in Johnson City, New York, study at Barrington College in Rhode Island, two years at Dallas Theological Seminary, and a year at Gordon Divinity School (now Gordon-Conwell Theological Seminary), and the latter part of the sixties as an itinerant preacher in the Brethren assemblies in New England — there was little in my past to challenge me to consider the intact theology I professed in the light of my personal experience.

I was newly married, terribly serious, uncertain of my future goals (except that I coveted a life in higher education), and open to listening to something that would reopen the world to me. The judgments my religious past required that I make on the vitality of the sixties did not come easily to me, and the turmoil I experienced as I came of age politically prepared me to wonder if I had as much insight into the will of God as I had been ready to believe.

A decade later, I had left seminary to finish my Ph.D. in linguistics, was working through the difficult, but ultimately positive (for both of us) end of my marriage, striving to ensure the loving support of our two children, and on the brink of coming out publicly as a gay man. How could such change find expression? How was I, or anyone else, for that matter,

22

to understand a transformation so apparently profound that it seemed silly to talk about continuity of identity? "Making sense" of this all is, after all, the point. Sense does not simply appear; it is made. The understanding, the sense, I have begun to forge of that transformation has been the project of the last seventeen years, an unfinished process I interrupt with the writing of this interim report.

When a particular experience is being lived, it often seems *sui generis,* one of a kind. In retrospect, it may come to seem like a cliché writ large, and it may be easy to take that experience, write it in capital letters, and call it theology. In the high profile "comings out," from Dr. Mel White (whose experience seems to me something like mine) to Ellen, from Martina and k. d. lang to Steven Gunderson and Barney Frank, one finds parallels everywhere, at least in the public acknowledgment of gay sensibilities and orientation. But in 1980, I felt quite singular, quite alone. And there were no books around the libraries like John Boswell's or even Peter Gomes's to reassure this young Christian that being gay was no bar to some vital spiritual connection with a still emerging community of faith. The church was embarrassed by me (or so I heard), and I was embarrassed by it. So instead of being a Christian who was an in-the-closet gay man, I became a gay man whose Christianity was in the closet and I worked at nailing the door firmly shut.

The nails in that door were many. One was the notion of authority, an authority which if acknowledged seemed to condemn me. I had learned from my long study of the Bible that the truth was objective, "out there," expressed best in the Scriptures, and interpreted through a tradition of exegesis. My task was to read that tradition and the text, understand it carefully in conversation with my teachers, and conform my beliefs to what the text said. I was a "proof-texter," and certain proofs were heavily on my mind. How could I continue to claim a connection to the apostle Paul and his teaching when Romans 1 said what it said? If my understanding of authority was "right," I was in trouble. So I let go of that notion of authority, with no other one readily at hand to replace it. That took more than a decade to resolve.

Another nail in the door was my "understanding" of the Christian god, a god who needed to be bargained with, and who was to be feared, a consuming fire. I made deals with him, early on. Then I convinced myself that my being gay was a variation on a theme in creation, so I used the claim, "God made me this way!" to counteract my conflicted feelings about myself. None of this brought me a sense of serenity, and so I found myself less and less able to say I believed at all in anything that I could comfortably call "God" given my understanding of that word. For perhaps a decade, I could identify no spiritual agenda at all for myself.

More conflict came from my learned distrust of my own feelings and my interpretations of those feelings. I had long ago found that I was not interested in my own feelings so much as I was in what others might think of them. I remember well an early teacher of mine thundering from the pulpit at the front of the lecture hall, "What is important is the Truth, not man's attitude toward the Truth." I believed that (and thundered it a few times myself) and reminded myself that how I felt mattered little in the larger scheme of things. Deciding my feelings were important drove yet another nail into the door of the closet where my old faith found its crypt.

Still another was my fear of confronting old friends and compatriots (compounded by the negative experiences some tries at those conversations generated.) They would misunderstand, I feared. I later came to understand this fear as the lodging homophobia had inside me, as much as I tried to confront and defeat it. At any rate, I avoided those confrontations for a long time, simply by moving far outside the circle of friends I had lived in for years. I wrote some detailed letters, but finally stopped doing even that. I would simply close up the past and not deal with it.

But perhaps the first and foremost motivation for keeping that door shut was the sense that I had been betrayed by the tradition I thought had given my life meaning, and somewhere I felt that I had betrayed it. That mutual betrayal, an experience I have come to understand in conversation with many another gay man or lesbian with roots in the church, is a complex of feelings and understandings rooted in the rhetoric of rejection, the language of homophobia, which the church uses to dismiss us, language we have long ago internalized. Remaining close to the church and the community of Christians is simply too painful, and even if we do not early (as I did not) articulate what is happening in those terms, that begins to be the central articulation as time passes. So I simply dissociated myself from the church, abandoned any dialogue with the Christian tradition, put my Greek New Testament and my Hebrew Bible on the back shelf, and walked away. And what a liberating experience it was!

I felt new energy. All the effort that had gone into hiding, into shame, into apology, could go into projects, work, play, exploration. The whole world seemed open, at least a part of it about which I knew nothing. To be sure, there were shadows. My friendship with my former wife was strained. She was mourning the loss of her assumptions about what her life would be like, and she was mourning the loss of a relationship that had died, at least in its traditional form. I had no full-time employment, after three years on the English faculty at Princeton University; though free-lancing kept me busy and left me plenty of time to explore a new world and to make new friends, the income was irregular. The financial security of my children concerned me, but I was enough out of focus to miss the clues that were all around me of coming turmoil and disaster. Just as the energy of the sixties had to face the calamity of Vietnam, so the energy of my eighties was about to be threatened. I was becoming more and more aware of the way the political and the personal were embedded in one another, and my reaction to societal homophobia became defiant. A life of predictable choices given a heteronormative order was no longer possible for me. I was an outsider, and while I acknowledged little of the direct effects of homophobia at the time, I was marginalized as a gay man in a homophobic structure. And AIDS was rapidly overtaking all of us.

Finding order — a predictable income, meaningful work, a home, some stability, and a spiritual life — seemed at times more than I was going to be able to do. What had seemed ordered and challenging, now seemed chaotic and fraught with insurmountable obstacles. And I felt always the need to keep up a good front. My old friends in the church (including some of my family, I suspect) presumed that the job changing, the marginal jobs (night club manager — 3 months, deli man — perhaps 5 weeks, landscaper — too long, however short it was), the financial chaos, the moves, all these were "because" I was gay. So I struggled to keep on a happy face, and anyone who asked would hear a good story about what was happening, the change that was just around the bend. When I took a job part-time teaching GED preparation to inner-city adults in Trenton, I explained it as the reopening of my academic career and as a commitment comfortably in line with my earlier religious agenda. I couldn't say it was a job I could get at that point, that I needed the money, and that I liked doing it anyway. That would have required a self-respect I had left along the way when I charged into the eighties without a road map and without doing the personal work my ex-wife had wisely done.

During that period of time (my ex-wife and children were planning a move to Virginia), I became more and more aware of how marginal my life was. I lived on the edge with no clarity about what I wanted or how I thought I needed to get it. I was entangled in some unhealthy relationships, I was privately unhappy with my choices, and I felt quite helpless to make the necessary moves to become someone I at least knew, let alone liked. I understood the world as more and more closed. What had seemed open before, now presented little possibility, little hope. I felt hemmed in by circumstances I felt powerless to change. I had no reference point by which to establish my actions, no context in which to understand my choices, and no place in a community of self-acceptance where I could explore what the future held.

My decision to move to Trenton followed shortly thereafter, and set the stage for a process of growth that put into perspective my rootlessness, my inability to make decisions, my lack of self-respect, and my spiritual estrangement from my own life. I reasoned that I would need to live somewhere near the urban campus of the community college where I was working, and near the train station so I could easily get to Washington and on to Virginia to spend as much time as I could with my children. Important practical priorities were intervening in my belief system which until that year had kept me in denial about the disconnections of my life for fear I would think the problems were caused by my being gay. I was determined that no one think that (they did anyway), and more importantly, that I not think it (I did anyway). I was heading for trouble again, only because no one can live his life based on self-deception. I had learned it once, a lesson which brought me out of the closet, and now I needed to learn it again, and thereby find a place of spiritual renewal.

By 1990, nearly all the outward details of my life had stabilized. I had a circle of friends (some of whom had tested positive for HIV), I had a job I liked as director of the computerized learning center at the urban campus of Mercer County College, I liked the spacious second floor of the old Victorian house where I lived in Trenton. And I felt connected to my children, and to their mother, sustained by regular trips on the train to Virginia. But inwardly, all was not well at all. I felt like I lived in a dark space, where I felt cornered, completely without choices. The practical, outward settling of my life had not come integrated with any growing spiritual awareness, and I had filled that void in ways I now understand to be predictable.

The gay community into which I moved in 1981 was a community with values shaped by the harsh realities of institutionalized homophobia. The primary social institution (as in some places, it still is) was the bar. There was a fierceness about the pride expressed in the community, an in-your-faceness which left little room for quiet reflection. Our mood was defensive. We were attacked on all sides, accused of promiscuity by a society (primarily Christians) which refused to recognize our relationships. Many gay men I met were estranged from their families, or barely tolerated at holidays. Many men with children were barred by the courts from seeing them. And many people dealt with it by pretending it wasn't so by "partying" the nights and sleeping the days away.

My living arrangement in 1981 was not unusual. I lived with a vibrant, funny party guy who used his ample disposable income to stock the liquor closet, entertain enthusiastically, live hard and fast beyond his means, and take no prisoners. I came home in the afternoon to cheese, fruit, and crackers, candles, and music at 5:30 in the evening. Two cocktails, friends dropping by to join in, dinner for however many, wine, and then "out" followed, which meant prowling the bars looking for people to dance with, drown our meaningless sorrows with, and home, perhaps at 4:00 a.m. A weekend party might last all weekend.

There was always music in my house, and my books were in storage. I was never alone, and I was game for whatever turned up on a given day. One young man, turned out of his house by his family, showed up at our door with a new love, so he moved in. Soon we had five people overnight most nights. I was living a life I would simply never have imagined, not because I thought it was wrong or unhealthy, but because it was completely outside my experience. Alcohol was a major part of every day, and though I had never drunk before (and seldom, if ever, been drunk), I was now with many people who got drunk every day. I didn't notice that this had a negative effect; I was simply exploring a new world. I put my uneasiness aside and participated.

I look back on those days now with a bit of wonderment. The high drama, the conflicts, the distortions, all were the direct result of an artificial world, built by us to blind ourselves to the fact that the real world of relationships, commitments, responsibilities, and spiritual integration did not welcome us, and we felt powerless to make our own, denying even the reality that the world we lived in did not satisfy us. That is not an excuse; it is a fact, or a fact as we experienced it. As I moved slowly beyond that life, terrorized by financial disaster and the threat of AIDS, I began to understand, with considerable help, I might add, that I needed to make a responsible life for myself and that what others thought, however institutionalized that rejection might be, was a minor obstacle. What really stood in my way of my being who I could be and wanted to be was myself.

The trap of those days was related to a distortion of the Christianity on which I had been raised, which kept me stuck in negative behaviors with negative people, unable to free myself from "helping" relationships with addicts and alcoholics. These folks were in trouble, I reasoned, and I could help them, even if sometimes it appeared that I was becoming one of them. Anyone knows that all they have to do is stop using, and if they see that someone is kind to them, they will be encouraged and supported in stopping. I was wrong about that, and while many of the people I worked with would have seen little disturbing about my outward life, there was plenty wrong inside and I had not a clue what to do next.

All this is to say that the beginnings of self-understanding and self-acceptance I have experienced since mid-1990 are the result of my taking an honest look at those behaviors and by getting involved in a group of like-confused people who learned together what the "care of a higher power" is about. In June of 1990, I discovered that, beyond the bar, there was another social center for gay people, and that was the programs of recovery from addictive behaviors called twelve-step programs. A friend of mine who noticed he had a problem with alcohol after his third arrest for drunken driving had joined Alcoholics Anonymous. I was in the habit of having dinner with him and several others every Sunday evening, a dinner of good food, abundant alcohol, and convivial conversation. I used several of those evenings in a row trying to convince my newly sober friend that he was not an alcoholic; he finally responded by taking me to an Al-Anon meeting, a gathering of family and friends of alcoholics who work to understand a bit about addiction and their relation to the alcoholic behavior that has come to play such a significant role in their lives. What a revelation that meeting was!

I had come to believe what I suppose others believed, that my problems were directly the outgrowth of my being gay. Instead I learned that being gay had nothing to do with it. I was living in an addictive context, a scene so intensely filled with control fantasies, fears, obsessions, and a resulting loss of self, that I had lost touch with my own spiritual life. Had I remembered it, I would have found little to help me there since I had read that tradition to mean much of the negative stuff I had a decade or more earlier nailed into a new closet. I was so wary of god-talk, for fear of falling back into the traps set by my past, that when I began to work on the twelve steps, I avoided using the word god at all, and I am still not comfortable with it. Recognizing, however, the traditions in Christianity which see god in the despised and rejected, among the poor and the outcast, let me at least begin to think about a god whose presence in my life was no threat, but was a comfort and a guide. The third step asked me to turn my life and my will over to the *care* of god as I understood god, so I set about "making sense" — I inverted god-language and began to speak of the will of god as I understood *her.* I relaxed into her care, *and* I read Peter Gomes. Gradually I began to feel loved, to feel accepted, to feel cared for. Gradually I began to count less on the approval of any system or anyone, and more on the approval and coherence I felt coming from a new spiritual core.

I know now that the center of my life is a safe place. I know something about my limits and my strengths. And I know that as my life has begun to be stable and productive, and as my relationships have begun to have commitment and responsibility again at their core, I am comfortable in my faith in the future, in my sense of a spiritual energy and presence, and I've even found some ease at trying to read again historic texts of the Christian faith. As I've said to many of my friends, "I'm not yet certain that I am a Christian; I am certain that I'm a Protestant!" That claim simply affirms that I have no intrinsic sense of the authority of any system of god-language, of ecclesiastical tradition, nor of an organized religious community. But I do have a focused, centered sense of my own life and its place in a larger redemptive scheme, and I find language emerging from time to time which comforts me in the midst of the plague we call AIDS that has devastated the gay community and that guides me in the transitions of my life.

So now instead of putting on a front that my life is OK, I *am* OK. I have a career which includes productive work I enjoy and which keeps me secure. I live in a stable home, a place where I am safe to be who I am and what I am. I enjoy a mature and satisfying loving relationship with two delightful adults who happen to be my children. And my friendship with my ex-wife seems extraordinarily uncomplicated though it does provide both of us with a challenge of understanding now and then. And I meet regularly with groups of other outcasts, primarily gay and lesbian, as we work together to keep our perspective clear and to reassure one another that life can be more than we had come to believe.

And as all this moves forward, I hear the language of my past resonating in strange ways and at odd moments. When I listen to the rhetoric of people calling themselves Christian railing against gay and lesbian people, or people with AIDS, I remember other language, language of communion, language reassuring me that god is love, and the language of invitation, "Come unto me, all you that labor and are heavy-laden, and I will give you rest. . . ." Or I hear that "justice will roll . . . like a mighty river." I remember to whom vengeance belongs, and I remember that John in Patmos saw the holy city descending. . . . I remember that the truth makes us free, and that the grain of wheat that falls into the ground and dies bears fruit. I remember such language standing in the memorial service of a beloved friend, gone to AIDS, and I know that somehow there is a connection between my past and my future and that that connection "makes sense."

Additional Resources

Boswell, John. *Christianity, Social Tolerance, and Homosexuality: Gay People in Western Europe from the Beginning of the Christian Era to the Fourteenth Century.* Chicago and London: The University of Chicago Press, 1980.

A book of extraordinary erudition by the A. Whitney Griswald Professor of History at Yale, this book documents the relatively recent emergence of a doctrine of homophobia in the church. A revolutionary and eye-opening book.

Boswell, John. *Same-Sex Unions in Premodern Europe.* New York: Villard Books, 1994.

Boswell, whom *The New York Times* called one of the preeminent authorities on the Middle Ages, finds and translates medieval church documents solemnizing same-sex unions. His clarity and scholarship demonstrate clearly that the contemporary hysteria about same-sex marriage has no basis in the self-understanding of the medieval church.

Bouldrey, Brian, editor. *Wrestling with the Angel: Faith and Religion in the Lives of Gay Men.* New York: Riverhead Books, 1995.

A lively and enlightening collection of essays, this volume demonstrates the wide variety and vitality of the spiritual lives of contemporary gay men.

Doty, Mark. *Heaven's Coast: A Memoir.* New York: HarperCollins Publishers, 1996.

This memoir documents the loss of Doty's lover to AIDS and in so doing makes an articulate and moving case for the homes gay men make for themselves and the spiritual resources Doty found along the way.

Gomes, Peter. *The Good Book: Reading the Bible with Heart and Mind.* New York: William Morrow, 1996.

Gomes writes with the fervor of the preacher he is (pastor to The Memorial Church at Harvard and Plummer Professor of Christian Morals at Harvard College), arguing that no reading of the Bible is adequate which uses its language and its narratives to alienate groups of people from the Bible. He writes of the wrong use of "hard texts" to push women away, to relegate black people to the back pew, and to drive homosexuals out of the church. A fresh, brilliant, careful, thoughtful meditation on an important topic.

Odets, Walt. *In the Shadow of the Epidemic: Being HIV-Negative in the Age of AIDS.* Durham: Duke University Press, 1995.

Odets's work has revolutionized approaches to HIV-negative gay men in finding group support for their staying negative, for understanding their "survivor" status and accompanying guilt, and for thinking our way into the future. An eye-opening book.

White, Mel. *Stranger at the Gate: To Be Gay and Christian in America.* New York: Simon & Schuster, 1994.

White, a former writer for Billy Graham, Jerry Falwell, and Pat Robertson, chronicles his remarkable transformation and emergence as a spokesman for gay Christians. He is now national minister of Justice for the Metropolitan Community Churches, an open, accepting union of congregations of Christians. He lives with his partner, Gary Nixon, in Dallas, Texas.

Latin American and Caribbean Immigrants in the U.S.A.: The Invisible and Forgotten

MARÍA MARTA ARÍS-PAÚL

FORTY YEARS OF Latin American and Caribbean immigration to the United States have caused a new phenomenon in the history of the Americas that is being lived and experienced by large numbers of our peoples all over this country. It is a complicated phenomenon to understand and address unless we see it from a theological perspective. As peoples of faith, we might want to understand this experience as another one of God's moments of intervention in human history. The phenomenon that I am talking about is the meeting of Spanish-speaking peoples of the Americas in one country, in one of the dominant societies of the world. Together we have to love, live, and work in this, our adopted country. This is a first in history. Our struggle is for survival as whole persons, as families, as members of the larger society, as members of a community of faith.

My thesis is that our struggle has many facets, and in relationship to that, I ask the following questions: One: Are we able to identify as a group, claiming our similar roots of colonial oppression, deep spirituality, common language? Two: Are we able to identify the reasons for our immigration and claim them with honesty and openness? Three: Can we go through a process of adaptation to the culture that exists here, adjusting to new values, learning the language, claiming our power, all this without assimilating? Four: Can we identify the gifts that we bring to this society? Five: Can we retain our deep spirituality as part of a community of faith without succumbing to the prevalent "isms" of this culture, especially materialism and consumerism? Six: What is the response to our immigration of the people in this country, most of whom are immigrants or children of immigrants themselves, and how does their response affect us? Seven: What is the

31

response to our immigration of the people we have left behind in our countries of origin, and how does that affect us? Eight: What is our hope for the future?

This essay is based on my personal immigration story and the stories of those members of the Latin American and Caribbean communities among whom I have worked. It is based on my experience working for ten years with people in prison in the Department of Corrections of the State of New York, as well as working for thirteen years with Latin Americans and Caribbeans in a theological education and training program for Hispanics in the Episcopal Church in New York City.

I need to look at my own long process of acculturation and adaptation to understand the larger picture of Latin American and Caribbean immigration to this country.

A major issue for my own survival has been understanding and learning about my own internalized oppression and the part that I have played in the patriarchal systems in which I have participated or been involved.

I want this to be my own voice and my own perspective. Women's voices are seldom heard or taken seriously, and when they are, it is often because we have molded what we speak or write to the patriarchal model. What occurs then, is that our own voices do not emerge. What emerge through us are the voices of the "fathers."

My immigration story spans over a forty-six year period. I am a Guatemalan woman, a Central American, a Latina, a "Hispanic." It has taken me most of these past four decades and a half to understand my immigration to the United States. As a young girl in Guatemala, I was sold, and I bought into, the concept of the "American lifestyle." My upper-class friends and I spoke in English to each other much of the time in high school. We wore blue jeans whenever possible. Our favorite music was popular swing and rock, and our favorite movie stars came out of Hollywood. Some of us believed that life was better in the United States and we aspired to live in this society in order to have a better chance of fulfilling our dreams. I wanted a college education. There were perhaps one or two women studying at the university in Guatemala City when I left. I remember one who wanted to be a physician. She was considered an oddity and she was called "queer," "lesbian," "strange," and even "ugly" because she had dared to cross that barrier, dared to break the rule that said women were not to study to be professionals because we were to be exclusively wives and mothers. First, our fathers determined our future. If a father was missing, it was our brothers who told us what to do with our lives, and once we were married, we belonged to our husbands; it said so in our new names. My mother's maiden name was Marta Paúl. She married my father, Enrique Arís. Upon their marriage she became Marta Paúl de Arís. That "de" means "belonging to" or "property of."

I had dreams of becoming a philosopher and/or a healer, so I came to this country to study when I was sixteen. I thought that I was coming for a period of a few years, but I stayed a lifetime. My journey became an immigration story and a spiritual quest.

In 1950 I was a passionate sixteen-year-old Roman Catholic girl in search of my spirituality which did not seem separate from the rest of my experience, even then. I was in the process of leaving the Church that I knew but did not understand, while living with all the taboos I had been taught. What a moment to be set adrift in the current of a new culture and an unknown secularity! Not only did I experience profound culture shock, I also had to sort out large issues of personal morality and social ethics. This was a society where young women had more freedom of sexual expression than I was used to, and where climbing the social and financial ladder was a common goal among those with whom I related. I felt quite alone and unable to speak about these issues with anyone. That was the moment of rupture with my roots and my community. It was a new beginning, the birth of a new person, but I did not know it then.

For the first fifteen years of my life here I tried to assimilate. I learned to speak English almost without an accent. I brought with me the privilege of my Spanish ancestry: my white skin, my affluent life-style, and a good bilingual high school education. I was able to go to a top women's college in New England and that was a major struggle for me. That is where I had my first encounter with discrimination. I experienced, in terms of classism and racism, a movement downward, from "upper class" to "second class." My speaking was problematic — that Spanish accent; my writing was problematic — that strange syntax; my sense of timing was and still is problematic — always late according to the dominant culture's clock.

During our college years I married my childhood sweetheart, who was from El Salvador. He became an engineer and then a naturalized United States citizen. We were able to bring up a family of six children and live in affluent suburbs on the East Coast and in the Midwest. But I still considered myself a Guatemalan and carried within me a deep struggle to understand my identity and my place in this society. For many years I thought that soon I would go home and live in Guatemala once again. But whenever I was there, people who did not know me would ask me where I was from, as my accent had changed when I spoke Spanish. I had picked up a mixture of Spanish phrases and intonations from other "Hispanics" in New York, Boston, and Chicago. I also had adapted some of my thinking in order to live in this society, and this was a cause for conflict with my family and friends back home.

My children grew older and I was able to continue my studies, which led me into the fields of theology and psychology. I had joined the Episcopal Church years earlier and now began to look towards the ministry as my vocational choice. I attended seminary and was ordained a transitional deacon and then a presbyter in the Episcopal Church of the United States of America, the second Latin American woman to be ordained in the denomination. As a member of the clergy within the institutional church, my journey has been a painful one. Ordained Latina women have experienced rejection by both the Anglo and the Hispanic communities among whom we have worked. More rejection has come from men than from women, but it is more painful when it comes from the latter. I have been rejected because of my gender, my class, and my leadership role within the church. It seems that those of us who have become bicultural and bilingual leaders threaten many who know only one culture and one language.

Through my work as a prison chaplain, as a pastor and counselor, and as a theological educator, I have come to understand that I am only one of thousands upon thousands of "Hispanics" who have come to this country in search of a better way of life even though our stories are all very different. I had thought that my journey was an individual one. Now I know that it is part of a larger picture. From a theological perspective, I believe that this large immigration of our peoples to this country is part of God's plan for the future of this society. As it has happened to me, it has happened to the majority of Hispanic immigrants. We came for what we thought would be a short time, to study, to work, but we have stayed and brought forth a new generation. As a woman of faith I cannot understand it in a different way. It is a call, like the call to Abraham, to leave our land, our families, everything that was familiar and comfortable, to move to a new land and become a great nation. This connects with the journeys of all other immigrant groups, past and present. But I believe that recent immigrant groups do not want to lose their cultural heritages and so our differences seem more obvious.

This is such a big story that as I participate in it I cannot truly see it all. I get small glimpses. But I know that my life here is not about assimilation. Neither is it for other Latin Americans and Caribbeans. It is about acculturation in a society where we move and live among many cultures including our own other "Hispanic" cultures. Our life here is about making a difference in this society. It is about our gifts, our values, our language, and our cultural traits being useful. It is about teaching as well as learning from others in this amalgam of cultures. It is about contributing to the spiritual life of our community. Personally, I want to help ease the pain of exile, the pain of acculturation. I want to be a bridge between cultures and a healer where healing is needed.

As long as I was in the process of assimilation I was on a lonely journey. Even becoming a member of the Episcopal Church with my husband and my children was another step to assimilation. It was after I became an ordained Episcopal priest that I began to recognize my own community and work towards my liberation and theirs.

We are called "Hispanics" in this country and we are considered one group because we have the Spanish language in common. But there are nuances and meanings that separate us, even in the language, as we speak to one another. What we truly have in common is our deep spirituality and the experience of five hundred years of colonial oppression. This experience of oppression has a direct connection with our immigration and with the way in which we then survive in this foreign country.

The Spaniards came to the Americas to colonize and conquer. From the beginning the understanding was that the peoples living on this continent were savages, therefore ignorant "infidels" who needed to be saved from eternal damnation. The conquest occurred with the use of two weapons, the sword and the Bible. This story is similar for all indigenous peoples in North, Central, and South America. The sword was used to kill, torture, and subjugate. The Bible was used and interpreted to diminish and control.

Over time the Spaniards mixed with the Indigenous. Africans were brought over as slaves and the races continued to mix. At present, the peoples who have migrated to this country are truly a mixture: some of us have African, Indigenous, and European ancestry; some have Indigenous and European ancestry; others have African and European or Indigenous ancestry; others have only Indigenous ancestry; very few of us have only European ancestry. We vary in the color of our skin and in the class system in which we were brought up in our country of origin. Many of us are bilingual before we even learn to speak English, because we speak an indigenous language along with Spanish. And I believe that all of us, for better or worse, have, deep inside ourselves, internalized oppression that says to us that we are not as good, not as smart, not as attractive, not as able, as the dominant white Anglo-Saxon group.

The church almost always identified with the people of Spanish descent who were members of the ruling classes in Latin America and the Caribbean. It preached a gospel that taught about the cross here on earth and the resurrection in the afterlife. It taught about a male God who is all powerful, all knowing, and distant. It taught about Mary, the mother of

Jesus as the all-suffering virgin, "good" woman, who was wife and mother, submissive to the male will.

Certainly the God that the upper classes have worshiped is a very different God from the one that the people of conscience and the "conscientized" poor have been able to know and love. The latter know this God through their own discernment after reading the Bible together, and reflecting about their own lives in light of what the gospel says to them. The God of oppressed peoples is the one who walks with us on our journeys, hears our cries and sees our tears, suffers when we suffer and does not punish us for being human.

I belong to the Episcopal Church. I perceive it as a church that identifies itself with the dominant groups, who in this case are the dominant white, affluent Anglo-Saxons. My impression is that African Americans are few and only tolerated, Asians are token, and Hispanics are still within the church's concept of "mission field." It worships a male God, as liturgical language announces wherever one goes to worship on Sundays, in spite of the efforts of a few to begin the usage of inclusive language. Women have been ordained to the three orders of deacon, priest, and bishop, but in practice we continue to be diminished if we do not follow the patriarchal model in all that we do and say. For the most part, seminaries are still teaching the hierarchical model of ministry and the lone ranger model of priesthood. It is important, I think, to look at the mutuality and participatory models which we women would generally advocate, where the community of faith works as equals, designating as a group, those within the community who are to perform the different tasks and responsibilities necessary for the life of the church, including those who are to be ordained.

Twenty years ago, just after the Episcopal Church began ordaining women, some clergy leaders with vision in the Diocese of Connecticut got together to discuss the fact that there were many Hispanic people appearing at Sunday services in our churches in the metropolitan areas around New York. Many of them were becoming active members, especially those who could speak English and were trying to be leaders in their Spanish-speaking communities where there was much need for pastoral care. It was decided that an institute for the training of lay leaders in the Hispanic community would be established. Seven or eight Hispanic lay leaders began to study in what was called the Instituto Pastoral Hispano. Here they would learn about the Episcopal Church, study the Bible, and be taught some church history to understand the difference between the Episcopal and the Roman Catholic Church.

It became apparent almost at the outset, that most of these Hispanic leaders had deep vocations to the ministry and most of them wanted to be

ordained to the priesthood. They did not all have the educational background nor the financial resources to go to seminary, so a program of study
was established at the Instituto to provide adequate training for people to
meet the necessary requirements for ordination through the regular canon
established by the Church for this purpose. This is where Dick Shaull and
I began our seven-year collaboration in teaching and administration at the
Instituto Pastoral Hispano. We had both been invited by the then Executive
Director of the Instituto, Enrique Brown, to work together as a team. Dick
was our Academic Director and because of his extensive connections with
the world of liberation theology in Latin America, we were able to benefit
from powerful teaching, not only by Dick, but by theologians of liberation
who came to the Instituto from Puerto Rico, Brazil, Costa Rica, and other
places. The Instituto, by then, had moved to New York City and had been
enlarged to become an inter-diocesan program which served the whole
metropolitan area of New York, Connecticut, and New Jersey.

The Instituto Pastoral Hispano became for me a microcosm of the
phenomenon mentioned above of Latin American and Caribbean peoples
coming together to live, love, and work together. As a theological education
and training program, it encompassed a very thorough curriculum which
was geared to the total person. The students had an opportunity not only
to take academic courses, but were provided with practical experiences in
ministry in different settings, as well as seminars geared to encourage them
to have a dialogue about the effect of the program on their spirituality and
daily life concerns.

Instituto students and faculty became a community. We spoke and
studied mostly in Spanish, we practiced the pedagogical method of learning
put forth by Paulo Freire, Brazilian educator, which aims for a non-hier-
archical circle of people in the classroom, in dialogue, where we are all
teachers and students and where we practice mutual respect. We studied
Latin American liberation theology and ways in which we could begin to
do our own theologies of liberation from the perspective of our lives and
experience in this country.

The dream that we had at the Instituto was one of empowerment. We
hoped to give the church our best leaders in order to bring the fullness of
our cultural background and spirituality to the community of faith. Dick
Shaull taught us and encouraged us to become the subjects of our own
destiny as people in exile, as immigrants who are treated in most cases as
non-subjects or objects of derision and ridicule. We did not have enough
time to do that. Apparently, seventeen years was not enough time to bring
our project to fruition. At the end of our seventeenth year, the eighth year
of my leadership as Executive Director, we were told by the hierarchy that

funds had dried up, and the program ended. Our Hispanic community does not yet have the cohesion nor the resources to put together theological education programs that can be validated within the larger institutions of learning.

We graduated twenty-four students during the years that the Instituto was in operation. Most of them are out in their local Hispanic communities serving in different capacities. There are eight presbyters, three deacons, and many lay leaders doing the work of ministry, but wherever I go now, and listen to them, I hear frustration, isolation, and despair. The Hispanic community is not an integral part of the church yet, perhaps it will not be in my lifetime. Within our own communities there is division, power struggles, deception, antagonism, and blatant sexism.

In our Instituto community we had represented the following countries of origin: El Salvador, Costa Rica, Guatemala, Honduras, Nicaragua, Panamá, Mexico, Colombia, Argentina, Chile, Paraguay, Ecuador, República Dominicana, Puerto Rico, and Cuba. We also had Newyoricans (people of Puerto Rican descent born in New York). In this amalgam of Latin cultures, how could we erase from our very genes the historical differences among us? We tried to learn about each other, to listen to our different perspectives, to ignore our class differences and to combat the everpresent sexism. While we sat in the classroom circle we almost believed that we were achieving a new frontier. We discussed our internalized oppression, we debated the meanings of "liberation," we looked to Scripture for answers to our existential situation. We laughed together and cried with each other in moments of vulnerability. We spoke in Spanish while agreeing that we had to learn English so that we could function within the larger church body and society. But when the moment of truth arrived, when someone got ordained or got a paid church position, the differences among us emerged, judgments and criticisms were hurled, alliances were made to bring down the one who seemed successful.

I believe that these are all survival mechanisms. We seemed to have a safe space within our Instituto community, but it was not safe out in the larger church, as it was not safe in the larger society and we had not worked long enough to rid ourselves of our internalized oppression. There was a lot of vying for power within our Hispanic community. People allied with each other according to nationality, race, and gender. The majority of us still believed that we were second class. Instead of helping one another to have a voice within the church, we silenced each other so that finally no one could be heard or seen. Our internal and everpresent conflict vexed the hierarchy, and we were ignored. Because of the weak front that we presented, we did not receive respect. How difficult it is to be open and honest when one is invisible! How difficult it is to act with integrity when one is ignored! How difficult it is to remain calm and compassionate when one is shunned or rejected!

So, the new clergy began to work in isolation, following the pattern that is already established in the institution. We had a diocesan Hispanic network in place, which was trying to give form to our work together. The clergy did not support each other, the majority competing for leadership and constantly at odds with each other. We involved our lay leaders, many of them women, but they were not accepted, they were mostly ignored by the male clergy. Alliances formed, nationalism came forth, gender battles were unending, class issues were covertly handled to stir up antagonisms. It was not possible, as far as I could see, for us to be supportive of each other. We needed the compassion of other "minority" communities, like the African American community, but that did not happen, and to this day we continue to be divided.

I believe it took me a couple of decades to identify the reasons for my immigration to the United States. As I was growing up I could see the big cultural chasm in my country between the lives of the upper class, those of Spanish descent, to which I belonged, and the lower classes which at that time included Ladinos, those of mixed Spanish and indigenous races, and indigenous. There was also the gender gap, the double standard between men and women. Because I felt very oppressed as a young woman I could understand that there was also great oppression in the areas of race and class. I did not know what to do about that, I felt helpless and very sad and did not want to accept the theology of suffering which was being preached from the pulpit to me. This theology of suffering taught by the clergy of the Roman Catholic Church at that time, presented suffering, any kind of suffering, as something to be desired by humanity. It was important to imitate the lives of Jesus and of Mary, his mother, which were portrayed as lives of suffering and pain. The main emphasis was on the cross, suffering, and death on the cross. Resurrection was presented in a hushed and nebulous way, and it belonged to the afterlife. I feared this theology of hopelessness and as it happened, at that moment, I left my country and I left the church. I came to a new land fleeing from oppression and was eager to be a part of a different society where I thought women and other oppressed peoples had the opportunity to live fully empowered lives.

As the daughter of the oppressor in Central America I did not suffer the same oppression that the poor of our countries experience. As a woman, my destiny was determined by patriarchy. This is what I was fleeing, and I was fortunate that I could leave my country without the threat of torture or execution. I had enough to eat, so I did not leave because of hunger or malnutrition.

Many of the people with whom I have worked in New York had no choice about their immigration. Many have fled the poverty they lived in their countries; many others have fled political and military repression and terrorism. They have come, often knowing the part that the government of the United States has played in helping the oppressive systems they have fled, systems that enforce a type of regimen that keeps a few people in power and affluence, and the majority in repression and poverty.

Most of us have found that this society continues the patriarchal model in its institutions. Also, those who are poor continue to be poor, in spite of their ability to purchase cars and television sets. We experience discrimination because of our surnames, the color of our skin, our gender, our accent when we speak, and our lack of educational degrees, among other things. But if we decide to live in this country, we must stop being victims and that means that we need to begin to believe in ourselves. Our differences do not make us inferior; on the contrary, our differences help others to look at themselves and question their way of life from a new perspective. We need to seek empowerment by becoming educated, learning the language, supporting each other, and unlearning our internalized oppression. This cannot be done in isolation nor in the ghettos.

Acculturation is very difficult when people continue to feel oppressed. They find it almost impossible to have a positive attitude toward learning the language and accepting values that are different and seem antagonistic to old traditions and customs. These are some reasons that often keep our Hispanic communities in ghettos where they try to duplicate the lives they lived back home in their countries of origin.

The duplication is also about values and customs which worked in the country of origin but which in this new environment seem to alienate the immigrant within the larger society. These traditions are usually held by the older generation as a way of security. But the younger generation is trying to adapt and fit into the larger society, and changes occur which are difficult for everyone to accept. Frustration and generation gap emerge. This can break up families. The family is all important in the Hispanic perspective, so people need to find a way by which dialogue occurs between individuals in the different generations. Hispanic therapists and counselors are available to do this work and more people should avail themselves of their services to begin to understand these new dynamics that are occurring in our communities.

We women suffer from the effects of machismo and negative marianismo, which are deeply ingrained in our culture. Machismo presupposes the power of men over women; and negative marianismo enforces the docility of women, our dependence and passivity, our obedience and even our lack of self-respect. Like the portrait of the Virgin Mary which the church has painted for us, we are to be obedient, "good," virginal, a passive wife and mother.

Men are also socialized into believing that they are superior to women, that they are always in charge of the family, that the whole responsibility of sustenance and support is on their shoulders and that the double standard is perfectly all right. Our culture permits the male to be autonomous and independent; not so the female. But the reality of the matter is that women now want to make choices and decide how we want to live our lives. There is more separation and divorce among married couples and there are more single mothers. Women are more and more becoming professionals with the ability to earn our livelihood. We are less dependent and more autonomous. But as Latinas, we want to keep those cultural traditions that enhance our identity and our self-esteem. We want to keep good relationships within the family, and we want to preserve the extended family whenever possible.

One way to preserve our language, our music, and our historical memory as Hispanics is to maintain a link with our countries of origin, however we can do that, and another way is to claim our voices, speak and write about our struggles in this country, say who we are. Some of those voices, thank God, are already being heard!

We are people who live in the moment and who live fully in our bodies. We are passionate about what we love and hate. We show our emotions readily and cherish our connection with others. We are generous with what we have and ready to be of service when someone needs our help or support.

We are present to the task at hand and cannot be rushed until we are finished. We are relaxed about time. Our internal clock is very different from that of the Anglo. The external clock does not rule us. Sometimes we wait until tomorrow to do what could not get our full attention today. Our inner pace is slower than the outer pace of the society. I have often felt guilty or ashamed by my sense of timing, until I realized that it is something that I cannot change. I have learned to adapt and plan more carefully so that my schedule is more in tune with my surroundings. But I consider our laid-back attitude as a gift to this society which seems to be moving more and more at frenetic speed, especially in the cities.

Our sense of family and community is vital for the survival of our cultural heritage. We feel very closely connected with all our blood relatives even though we may not get along with everyone. This poses great difficulty for us because the very fact that we have moved to this country often means that we become separated from our parents, siblings, and extended family. We like living in multi-generational circles where the care of the children and the elderly is a given. Some of us are losing that richness here as we live in more isolated conditions and more often in the prevalent configuration of the nuclear family.

When we gather with friends and family we always share a meal with music and dancing. Our music and our dancing are gifts to a society that in large measure gathers to talk, is mostly a verbal society, in some sense disembodied.

Our culture is imbued with spirituality. We cannot conceive of our daily lives without God's presence in every moment. We are passionate about the way we love God, Jesus and Mary his mother, and our common vocabulary is filled with religious expressions. I believe that this is a gift to this secular society. My hope is that it does not erode as we adapt to the rhythm of consumerism. I hope that our church will not become the mall, as it seems to be for so many people.

Materialism is seductive. It seems to me that one of the more difficult things to do in this country is to live a simple life with only the necessities. The abundance of material things confuses us and soon we begin to think that we need all the things that we want. We begin to believe that we are not somebody until we can own everything that our money can buy.

Those of us who come from extreme poverty, of course, find that being able to own things is as important as eating and sleeping. And we all should be able to live a comfortable life with the essentials. But consumerism takes us a step further. Consumerism teaches us that we cannot live happy lives until we have everything that is available in stores, in malls, advertised on television. And so, we decide to join the shoppers and spend what money we have on all those things that we believe will make us happy, starting with a television set in every room of our house or apartment, every gadget there is for home and car, and the car itself.

Buying things forces us either to have to work very hard to earn the money to pay for these things, often needing to have two jobs, or it leads us to a life of crime which will illegally procure us the money that we think we need. In New York City I know of many women who have two jobs to maintain a way of life and barely survive. It is a very hard life. I also know that almost fifty percent of the population of New York State prisons is made up of Latino men. They often do their time hoping to come back out on the street and not get caught the next time. What blatant examples of alienation these are!

Coming from a background of oppression, one of the things that confuses us when we come to this country is the notion of freedom. We confuse being free with doing only what we want. We forget about responsibility and moral principles. This is where our spirituality comes in.

We are very religious people, but for the most part we are unchurched. Most of us do not understand the concept of church. Our model is the colonial model of church where the hierarchy is considered the church and the laity is a passive recipient of the faith, however interpreted. We need to change this concept so that we can all fully participate in the body of Christ and apply our religion to our daily lives. This necessitates breaking old patterns, establishing new paradigms, experiencing new models.

As new immigrants, we live in a survival mode. Most of our Hispanic communities try to survive in poor areas of large cities, alienated from nature which has been the environment in their countries of origin, alienated from people of other cultural backgrounds and alienated from each other as they struggle to get through their difficult daily routines. Many go to church on Sundays, where they expect to receive spiritual comfort and where the priest is supposed to supply whatever it is that will provide that support. When a community is physically and emotionally drained from daily living, how is it going to learn to be that new model of church which requires of its members time, commitment, responsibility, and more hard work? How can those members of the community form a group that interacts in mutuality, if mutuality is not practiced at home, in the family? How can that community trust one another when the double standard between men and women is prevalent in their lives? There is much work to be done and it will be a long process of change.

Part of the process of change has to do with coping with the pressures felt from that part of the society which insists that we are not good enough until we can completely assimilate. There is a large number of people in the United States who would like us to assimilate and lose our language and cultural heritage, become part of the old melting pot. Some of them are people who have had to do that after their own immigration, after suffering their own put-down and oppression. They are people who have lost their historical memory and do not remember anymore who they are, where they came from, or what their ancestry can teach them and their children. Others are those who consider themselves the true "Americans," the dominant group, of European descent, after whom the whole society needs to be molded. We Hispanics in the United States need to know ourselves for who we are, honoring and remembering our varied ancestry, claiming our life-giving cultural values and traditions, keeping the richness of our language and music, becoming a new spiritual community on a journey to make this society a better one for everyone.

Insisting on our own identity has the curious effect of rending us invisible. We are not seen by the people who do not like our difference. We are often ignored, shunned, or rejected.

Since we have left our countries of origin, we are also invisible to those we have left behind. I am sad to say that in my own experience, most of the people in our countries of origin do not think of us unless we have and keep very close family and friendship ties, travel back and forth, and maintain ongoing financial ties with them. They soon forget us otherwise, and believe that we have lost our traditional values, feel superior, and have settled here to an affluent way of life that radically separates us from them. We are often forgotten or misjudged.

So, what is our hope for the future?

In order to renew ourselves, I believe that we have to invest our energies in small communities which gather to address identifiable and common needs. These communities can emerge almost anywhere. They can be culturally homogeneous or diverse, depending on the circumstances, time, and place. Their work is not easy because personal issues need to be addressed, as well as community issues which can be controversial. Their work is political as well as religious. Quality of life must be a priority, and life itself needs to be constantly celebrated in its various aspects.

I now live in a small community of faith where our work is to live simply in mutual support and love, sharing our deepest selves with each other and offering the same to those who come to us for rest and renewal. We believe that in our own way we are reconstructing the church. We are five women, Episcopal priests, who run a retreat center for women. The quality of life for women is our priority at this time. In order to address other women's life issues we must first address our own. This is no easy task. It takes time, patience, trust, and love. Ritual is very helpful.

I believe that to reconstruct the church we need to have small projects. We need to gather in small groups, in mutuality, forming small communities of faith who can look at our own lives and see where the Holy dwells among us. Our small communities can have a ripple effect on the larger society.

These communities can be the places where we can experience our strength, where all are participants, where new language and new symbols are born, where we can be transformed. Out of these communities can come the new theologies which will allow us to understand our experience from a new perspective. In these communities the Bible can be read in a new way, with new eyes to find the word of God for us today in this place and in this time.

I wish for the Hispanic community in the United States a new vision:

the vision of a great nation in dialogue within circles of mutual respect and care; people teaching and learning from one another; men and women, children and adults sharing their inward and outward journeys; people living their lives daily in the light of the gospel message; the vision that the Holy is revealed in relationship.

Faith, Belief, Humbleness, and the Hermeneutics of Transformation

Joseph C. Nyce

EVERYWHERE I GO I have the sense that things aren't really as they ought to be. Sitting in church, conducting everyday business transactions, participating in local township boards, watching local and world news, or walking down the streets of our cities, I am never far from that feeling. When verbalizing this feeling I realize that I am not the only one who feels this way; I just get the impression that this is a subject that is not to be discussed. When mentioning these feelings in a white American context I seldom get a denial, just a response of resignation: "well that's just the way things are," "you're not going to be able to do anything about it," "yeah, but what do you expect?" "is it better anywhere else?" Well, I expect something better.

Everywhere I look things aren't right. There is unfairness and injustice; intimidation and manipulation; deception and untruthfulness; arrogance and aggressiveness, even violence.

We hear of a corporation's top executive receiving a multi-million-dollar bonus in the same year that corporation lays off twenty thousand workers. Is there no connection between these two, no link of responsibility, no sense of community? How can one corporation be so callous on one hand and so generous on the other? Under what line of reasoning do these two coexist?

We sit next to each other in church on Sunday to celebrate the nearness of the Reign of God where we are to live by love and mutual concern, work hand in hand for the welfare of the underprivileged, and seek justice for the oppressed. Then we go to our homes and jobs and make decisions that have tremendous negative impact on the welfare of our neighbors, the

46

poor, and the oppressed. Is there any connection? Does the Reign of God expounded on in church have any impact on our economic decisions in our work and our daily dealings? Or have we shielded ourselves from any direct responsibility by our beliefs? Have we carved out a safe place for our religion by claiming that the church is somehow different from the world? Can we really separate the church from the state or from any other part of our lives and activity? We are the world. We are the church. Who are we fooling?

When we try to combine the two we fail miserably. One of the primary functions of our government is to provide for the welfare of the disenfranchised. We have elaborate programs to provide for those with limited resources and opportunity. Well-meaning people go to work each day to develop and administrate these programs, thinking they are serving their fellow citizens. But, the programs they produce are so cumbersome and so expensive that these burdens consistently add numbers to the welfare rolls. We create our own clientele. Rather than make it easier for people to become self-sufficient, we force more and more persons into dependency.

Am I out of step? Am I just a dreamer and an idealist? Is there no real connection between our understanding of the call of the Reign of God and the reality of daily living? Drugs, crime, poverty, greed, war, and even governments are readily admitted as blights on our humanity. What is disheartening is that our collective public will does not seem capable of doing anything that can be claimed as a big step toward correcting any of these injustices. Everyone is doing something but nothing really changes much. Good people with good intentions are working on all these problems through all the opportunities available to them, but the situation remains constant. Churches, governments, social groups, concerned societies of all sorts all work at the problem. Why is the effect so minimal?

Is it simply the fact that there are more greedy and bad people than caring persons? Are the crooks and deceivers in the majority? Or is it a case of a few bad apples spoiling the whole basket? I don't think so; and I also don't think we can excuse it because we were all created sinners.

I believe it is time we ask ourselves another question. Is it possible that things aren't right, not because there are too many bad people in the world, but because there are too many good people doing the wrong things? Have we deceived ourselves into believing that our efforts at goodness are taking us to the promised land when they are actually churning the cauldron of evil?

We have constructed a social environment in which we have not only fooled ourselves about our efforts at establishing what is good and right but have built our own prisons. I am referring to our propensity to order our existence through the establishment of systems and institutions and the way we have misused this process.

Institutions and systems are formed out of the needs of the people. They are a product of our creative natures and are intended to move us along in the task of fulfilling the purpose of creation. We create them to help us relate to each other and our world.

The misuse happens along the way and is a result of these creations assuming an importance much greater than their original function. They develop a life of their own. Whether it is because they have the capacity to outlive each individual, or because they provide a mechanism through which we can ignore our individual ignorance, they achieve an importance greater than the individuals who created them or those who keep them going. This becomes our prison.

How does this come about? Religious, philosophical, or scientific beliefs are used to justify a specific set of laws or rules which affirm a particular order to our daily lives. These laws and rules become the skeleton of an institution or system. The power behind these structures is seen to be somehow exemplified by, embodied in, and entrusted to these institutions and systems. The creative freedom exercised by the individuals or groups who established them is somehow mysteriously relinquished. Furthermore, the system or institution is seen as operating within certain boundaries of responsibility which are intended to limit or focus its effect, but really function to free it from responsibility to any other rules or laws. Individual freedom gets buried somewhere in or beyond the system. Each particular institution or system is only answerable to its own rules and laws and is therefore free from all others while the individual seems subject to the rules and laws of all the systems and institutions she or he comes in contact with. The freedom exercised in establishing the structure gets swallowed up in subjectivity to the rules and laws of each system or institution. Responsibility becomes the task of the institution, but since it is now compartmentalized it really becomes diluted. Individuals are expected to perform for the institution and within the system. Individuals are no longer seen as its creators but as its subjects. Freedom becomes expressed in the values and principles of the institution and system. The result is a powerlessness on the part of the individual whose main task is to carry out the mandate of the institution and work for its propagation. In so doing, it is believed, each individual is somehow living out the values and basic beliefs affirmed by the creation of that system or institution. The fact that these may conflict with or contradict some other value or law does not have to be addressed as long as a system remains true to its particular premises. The individual is left alone to deal with the discrepancies. There is no mechanism for integration. The resulting feeling of powerlessness adds to our sense of the deterioration of our values and systems. We feel trapped by our own creations. This imprisonment leads to marginalization because the only other alternative seems to be to close our eyes and fight harder to preserve the specific values championed by that institution.

One of the primary characteristics of this condition is that the position or office of the institution is where the power and responsibility resides and not with the individual holding that position. Thus you can have a president whose personal life and behavior are anything but exemplary as long as she or he can handle the duties of the office. You can have a minister whose personal life is a disaster, and you can have a born again Christian head up a business concern whose economic policies are ruthless and aggressive.

Examples of the misuse and distortion of this process are endless. In the Free Enterprise System everyone accepts the law of "buyer beware" without anyone having to be responsible for the values of this law, the inhuman way it forces us to relate to each other, or the distinct advantage it gives to the rich and powerful to control the poor and marginalized. A government "of the people, by the people, and for the people" can be held hostage by large and powerful special interest groups. And local governments can run on the principle of the preservation of property values without ever being called into question. I could bore you with examples.

This is why I continue to feel that things aren't as they ought to be. This is why I continue to search for new avenues of hope. This is why I am less and less drawn to the conventional sources of hope — church, education, politics — for the answers.

Yet I constantly feel compelled to search, to reach out sharing my experiences in the hope of finding allies who are alert to the call of creation; to seek liberation from bondage without violence, to execute justice without arrogance, to pursue creativity without destruction, to continue to move toward the goal of creation.

Certainly something innate to our natures wants to resist evil. We feel compelled to pursue right and correct wrongs. Why do we look so foolish when we respond to these innate callings?

We all know evil when we encounter it. Do we know goodness when we see it? Certainly! Can we be absolutely sure? Probably not! Do we have to decide again and again between these two? You bet! Are our decisions necessarily right? No! What then?

This grave uncertainty is the reality of our situation and the foundation of this inquiry. The important thing is not whether we are absolutely right or absolutely wrong, but how we relate to and deal with our imperfect decisions. That is what most clearly defines the human condition. The keystone of this condition is to be humble. This is the particular distinction I want to focus on because I believe it allows us a way out of our bondage. However, I wish to concentrate on a certain aspect of humbleness which is not normally associated with that phrase. By humble I am not referring to an expression of inferiority, dependence, or unworthiness. I am not interested in emphasizing a condition of lowliness or submission. Rather I am describing a modest, unassuming, unpretentious, unpresuming attitude without arrogance that simply understands our incompleteness as human beings. To limit our understanding of this term to the above meaning I will use the word humbleness rather than humility. Humbleness is not a popular subject, but we need to understand it if we are to discover the full extent of our humanness and be able to respond appropriately to our Creator.

We seem to be unique in all creation in that our actions can be informed and altered by our thinking and reasoning. Our tendency has been to see this uniqueness as somehow placing us at the top of a hierarchical view of creation — indeed as sort of a link between the creator and the rest of creation. Furthermore, we have apparently assumed that this reasoning capacity includes the ability to determine the difference between right and wrong. A fine distinction needs to be made here. While it is evident we have the capacity to distinguish between right and wrong, and probably have the responsibility to do the same, we must see that as distinctly different from knowing the difference between the two. The latter, unless I am misinterpreting, is what is described in Genesis as the original sin. We have the capacity of rationalizing the responsibility for sin and evil to the Creator, but where does that get us? Why not accept our full humanness, which means accepting the uncertainty of our existence and the responsibility for our actions and behaviors in the face of that uncertainty? Why not try humbleness?

We do just the opposite. We assume we can know God and God's will to the point where we are certain of the difference between right and wrong. We then draw a line between good and evil and begin the job of playing God. In the secular world this takes on the form of perfectionism and professionalism and becomes canonized in our systems and institutions. In the religious sphere it emerges in various schemes of eternal salvation. But in all cases the fundamental premise is that somehow what is good and right has been determined absolutely. There is no room for humbleness. There is no allowance for the truth of the human condition that we really don't know for certain. Thus there is no room for faith, because faith is really nothing more than consciously living out the truth of this uncertainty. Instead we collapse faith into beliefs which become the standards for good and right. There is no room for faith and the power and grace of God, the one who created this whole miracle we can't quite figure out.

My journey through this struggle between faith and beliefs focuses primarily on the institution of the church. That is where my strongest beliefs are grounded, indeed, that is where I first learned about faith.

In religious institutions goodness is the real agenda. Religion claims to be the conscience of society. It is through religious beliefs that we spell out what we mean by goodness and what we believe to be the will or command of the Creator. Certainly our churches and religious institutions embody our understanding of goodness!

When we take off the wrapping what do we find? O.K. I guess we have to cut some slack for the two Jimmys — Swaggart and Bakker. After all, we are all sinners. And maybe it just seems that there are a lot of incidents where members of the cloth are found in various situations of impropriety. Maybe we shouldn't expect our church and its leaders to somehow live out the goodness we claim to affirm. Certainly if we do expect this we will be disappointed.

Sadly, the incoherence and hypocrisy we experience in other institutions and systems pervades the church. Most of the decision-making positions in our churches are held by persons who have distinguished themselves in the secular world. As an institution, the church suffers from all that I described earlier; it imprisons us just as surely as our educational, economic, legal, and cultural systems do.

For the religious, the assumption that we know the difference between good and evil does not show itself in perfectionism, but rather in the belief that we can know the plan and will of God. The result is one of a number of salvation schemes. Here goodness is tainted by sin. Sin becomes the birthmark of the human condition, and salvation comes from God. Goodness does not manifest itself necessarily in action but in obedience and knowledge — to know what is right. We can and do know the plan of salvation. We are sinners and what we need to do is recognize our sinfulness, repent of our transgressions, and prepare ourselves for an eternal existence with God that forever answers our anxiety over death and meaninglessness.

This is the doctrine I have been brought up on. I have been raised in the particular tradition of the Protestant Christian religion known as the Anabaptists. I have been and am a believer. I am also a sinner. I have hurt people — even those I love.

As I mature I have to admit that I am becoming more and more aware that the anxiety I struggle with most is not the one my religion and society seem to have willed me. I'm not overwrought with concern for where I'm going to end up or from whence I came. I don't insist that God lay out the blueprint of creation for me to know. I do not fear God, nor do I agonize over whether I am saved and will be accepted by a God who cannot accept my sinfulness. I do want to know that I have lived in such a way that I have helped to move this miracle of creation toward its fulfillment.

In pursuing this latter concern I find less and less help from my religious training. Living by faith in God appears to be as out of step with both religion and society as it was when Jesus tried it. Where do I go from here?

When I strip my mind clear of everything but the bare essentials (or think I have), I am left with three fundamental assertions. My hope is that these basics might be an agreeable starting point for our dialogue. First, the only thing I am absolutely certain of is that I do not really know how this fantastic creation, and I in particular, got here and what is going to happen to me when I die. Second, I am in awe of the mystery and miracle of existence and its Creator. Third, there seems to be a flow that I will call the God force, which means for me that there is a will or intention to creation that I can serve but never fully know.

I have just described faith. Finding ourselves in a condition of un-certainty, sensing a flow or direction that pulls us toward its fulfillment, and a power much greater than ourselves responsible for it all, we feel the compulsion to move on. That is living by faith. Faith is the conscious desire to walk to the drumbeat of creation, not knowing for certain the will or purpose of creation, but feeling the presence of God whose love is only understood through the movement of that creation toward its fulfillment. Faith is not the stating of beliefs about the purpose of creation but asking questions that lead to new questions and a perpetual openness.

Do we live by faith? We certainly exist by faith, but we have a difficult time living by faith. Most, if not all, of the evil in our world is the result of our failure to live by faith. Living by faith is to celebrate our uncertainty. Living by faith says we must admit that the will and aim of creation is in God's hands (if she has hands). Living by faith means we must fully and completely recognize our humanness, which is nothing more than having humility be the hallmark of our existence.

Our efforts to resolve the anxiety of uncertainty have consistently prevented us from living by faith and resulted in tarnishing the flow of creation. These efforts are the source of evil. Failure to live by faith is the source of sin in the world, and insisting on knowledge of the will of God is the root of all evil.

Living by faith means we take each step into the future in the face of uncertainty. Most of us, if we take time to reflect, realize that along with this uncertainty comes an anxiety that produces a compelling need to understand and determine a purpose to life. From the most eccentric mystic to the most down-to-earth scientist, we endlessly pursue the need to unlock the key to existence: "How did it all happen and what is the order of things?" Our condition of having to live by faith conjures up a basic need to believe in something. The anxiety that goes with living by faith makes us vulnerable to the need to believe.

Individuals, groups, and cultures have all responded to this anxiety. Whenever we are controlled by that anxiety we collapse faith into beliefs. When asked for a statement of faith we generally emit nothing more than a delineation of a system of beliefs. Indeed this has been so pervasive that most of us don't even recognize or experience our condition of existing by faith until after our specific beliefs break down.

Faith and belief are not one and the same. One of the major sources of violence and evil in the world is the result of believing people failing to recognize this difference. We are called by the nature of our existence to live by faith, but the anxiety accompanying this fact leads us to construct beliefs as a way of ordering and directing our existence. This understanding of our existence provides answers to our anxieties, but at the same time runs the risk of creating a false sense of security which dulls us to the real nature of our condition. This false security results when our beliefs become certainty and begin to inform us of the "true" nature of things. Under this false security we become a people of purpose who know the difference between right and wrong and in fact know the will of God. Once we buy into this certainty we have lost the distinction between ourselves and God. We have eliminated the need for God. We know the plan and the pathway and now all we need is to execute. Our knowledge has replaced God. This is the beginning of sin, the root of all evil.

Two apparent assumptions of our Western Christian thinking seem to lie at the heart of our dilemma. The human mind has a rational capacity that does not appear anywhere else in nature. The human mind is unique in creation. Throughout the development of civilization we have celebrated this uniqueness. We have assumed this attribute to be that which gives humans a special connection with the Creator; and in many situations we have attributed this same rational capacity to the Creator.

But, what if the Creator genius formed us with a rational capacity simply as our defense mechanism, as our way of self-preservation in much the same way the lion has claws and the snake poisonous venom? Maybe our rational capacity is not to be sanctified but simply utilized within creation to preserve the species. If we hold it as the apex of creation we become monsters in the same way a lion would be who is all claws or a snake who is all venom.

The other assumption is that the nature of humankind is the source of sin. Growing up I was taught that my natural urges were to be resisted because the body was sinful. Only by a conscious effort, which in fact was an exercise of the mind, could I overcome my sinful tendencies. The implication here is that sin is somehow inherent in the created body and salvation is available only through the intervention of the mind or will, through a rational process we support by beliefs.

I contend this is just backwards. First, it is quite precocious of us to assume that sin is somehow part of the created universe, an assumption which in fact assigns the source of sin to the Creator. Furthermore, sin can only be sin if it is of our own doing, in other words the misuse of our created natures. I am suggesting that sin is the manipulation of our created natures by the rational process. The source of sin is not our bodies but in the way we use our minds. When we act out this reasoning in a way that dominates and controls rather than cooperates with creation and nature, we sin.

At first blush this appears to place a negative value on our rational capabilities. This is not the case. Our rational capacity has neither a negative nor positive value inherent in it; rather it has the potential for either or both. What I want to disclaim vigorously is the notion that the more advanced our mental and rational capacities become, the closer we approach the essential truths of existence and the nearer we get to understanding God.

Our thinking, theorizing, and postulating are really efforts to control our environment and to protect our existence. They are defensive actions aimed at self-preservation and control.

So, what does this mean for us? We need to place a qualifier on each and every one of our rational exercises, a statement that goes something like: "we have established behaviors and ordered our environment the way we have, based on our observations and best judgments and understandings of what is right and good. We admit, however, that we know only in part and that our best understanding is only our perception of the way things are and ought to be. Therefore, we realize they are subject to error, even gross error." Such a qualifier to our rational exercises can guard against the rages of sin. It can temper our ambitions and curb our desire to control and dominate. It preserves the absolute demarcation, whether we want to admit it or not, between us as humans and the blasphemy of playing God. It checks us from opposing the will of the Creator. All that our thinking needs for us to be truly human and remain open to the movement of creation is humbleness.

What does it mean to be humble? Does it mean to be reserved, withdrawn, or submissive? Certainly not! Should we be self-debasing, self-deferring, or apologetic? No! Being humble has nothing to do with subduing or minimizing our human characteristics. It takes only one word to describe humbleness: openness. To be humble is to be always open to the limits of our understanding. To be humble is to recognize that we are incomplete, that we know only in part, and that our understanding is incomplete and may even be misguided.

How can this work for us? First and foremost it means that destructive behavior is not in step with the flow of creation. Wars and violence of all sort are contrary to the God force. We can no longer recognize or justify an activity as a Holy War.

But wars may be too easy an example. No one likes a war. Yet, aren't wars just a projection of who we are as human beings? Isn't the collective made up of the sum of its parts? If that is so, then in order for our civilizations and cultures to function more in step with the flow of creation we as humans must be enhancing creation, not fighting it. The answer lies in us as individuals discovering our humanity. If we are to help create a better world we need to be open to the creative forces around and within us. We need to be humble. And to repeat, the way to humbleness is openness.

What is the nature of this openness? It means to be attuned to the forces which come from within and outside that take us beyond our limited experience and knowledge. Some have called it conversion and some transformation. In either case it entails a willingness to move beyond the truths, facts, and beliefs that have informed our existence and accept new possibilities and parameters that lead from destructiveness toward creation, away from rigidity toward flexibility, away from domination toward cooperation, and away from defensiveness toward inclusion.

We must be willing to say, "the way I understand things and have put things together is not THE way; there may be another or a better way." We need to be able to recognize when these constructions are not working. That is being humble. It does not denounce the past and the present in favor of the future, but recognizes the incompleteness of human experience and understanding. It does not discount our present knowledge and wisdom but admits to its particular prejudices. It is a willingness to be wrong and a deep desire to move constantly toward the goal of creation. Being humble is an exercise of our faith.

Can this hermeneutic work on a personal basis? I was forced to try it. My daughter asked me to perform a second marriage for her. Her first marriage, at which I performed the ceremony, ended in divorce. My problems were with my "beliefs" concerning marriage and divorce.

I grew up under the teaching that divorce was wrong and that marriage was forever, until death separated the partners. I was also taught to believe that when you married you promised God to stay together until death. These beliefs encouraged other beliefs, such as, since divorce was wrong it was unnecessary; thus, the reasons for divorce were always selfish and could be worked out if both persons try. Also I believed that the institution of marriage was instituted by God and, therefore, was a sacred trust that made it larger and more important than either of the partners within the marriage. Reinforced by these beliefs, my daughter's request presented me with a real dilemma. Could I and should I perform the second marriage?

On the other hand, my daughter wants me to perform her ceremony again. It is just as important to her as the first time, and maybe even more so. My heart was pulling at the bindings of my beliefs. What was I to do?

I started by questioning my basic belief that marriage is an institution ordained by God. Is this institution somehow above and beyond our need to be humble? Is this institution somehow free from the qualifier we need to apply to all our beliefs, or does it fall into the same category as all our other institutions, systems, and social customs, and thus become a victim of our limits of understanding?

It is not difficult for me to conclude that the will or thrust of creation says that man and woman are essentially made for one another. They need each other to procreate the species. But is there anything in the way man and woman are created that says a particular man must take a particular woman and stay with her and her alone the rest of their living days? No! Other forms of life have varied patterns. Some mate for life, others don't. In some cases a male may service many females. What makes the human being different? Our ability to reason about ourselves and our situation; our ability to determine the importance of the nuclear family; our capacity to work out what seems best both for our survival and our well-being.

The key word in the last sentence is "seems." Our institution of marriage is only the best way we know to create an atmosphere that appears conducive to enhancing physical, psychological, and spiritual growth. It seems to us that love is most fully celebrated through a relationship of commitment between one man and one woman. We have determined the nuclear family to be the best way to raise a healthy family. But, in all these statements the same admission applies: these are our best judgments within the limits of our understanding.

We can try to sanctify these judgments and attribute them to God, but real openness knows that this is really a process of reverse justification. In fact, the frequency of failures in marriage confirms that it is not a perfect solution. The humble test — openness — will not allow us to endow marriage with God-given authority.

On the other hand, the fact that we keep trying it over and over again seems to confirm that this kind of union and relationship is both desirable and in step with our created natures. Our task is to make it work for us. Can we use marriage to enhance our openness? Can we discover through this kind of relationship experiences that take us beyond ourselves? Can this union be creative and life-enhancing? We seem to answer "yes" over and over to these questions. Marriage is vital for us because of its potential to produce life and expand us beyond ourselves.

Marriage is an institution we have created because we think it best enhances the relationship between a man and a woman. We believe it to be an excellent way to express love between the sexes and to participate in the creative forces of the universe. We believe it is an appropriate response to God's mandate for life. Thus, we ask God to bless it. God does not impose it on us.

Then what about divorce? We certainly cannot be blind to its existence as I was taught. It doesn't even seem to help to say that divorce is wrong. Divorce is nothing more than an indicator of our failed efforts to relate in a way we intended. It is simply an admission of a failed attempt. We must live with it and be responsible for it. It is neither right or wrong, but simply our best solution within our limited perspective to allow persons to be free from a life-choking situation. Divorce is a tragedy, but it is not a curse.

Yes, I will perform the marriage ceremony for my daughter for the second time. I will ask God to bless this marriage just as I asked it for the first marriage. Only this time I will not be blinded by my beliefs. I will admit that marriage is our idea and our attempt at fulfilling relationships to the maximum. Marriage might fail; that is up to us. We continue to place our hope in it because we believe it is an excellent way for us to help each other get closer to God.

This is liberation! — to be freed to live in the flow of the creative process. One thing this exercise has taught me: whenever you feel a tension between your heart and your head, lean toward your heart.

As I was working through this problem I was reminded of the way my "beliefs" about marriage influenced the way I understand relationships. The fact that these beliefs bound me in my relationship to my daughter and her particular request makes me realize that they also have had a strong influence on my relationship with my wife. I guess there is no stopping humbleness once you let it get started!

If this hermeneutic can help us personally, it can also work on a social level. How can humbleness begin to move us away from a situation where things always seem to be something different than they ought to be? To get at this question I would like to interact with two experiences I had simultaneously. While I was reading a book titled *Suffering and Hope* by my friend Chris Beker, I also witnessed in horror the terrible bombing of the Federal Office Building in Oklahoma City.

The popular and official response to this hideous act is that it was done by a few fanatics who are nut cases. True, this does not seem to be the kind of thing that could or would be done by a regular John Doe citizen. But, the dialogue, accusations, and implications that flew from all corners after this tragic event suggest something more is going on. President Clinton pointed a finger at the extreme right. The vocal right pointed to the paranoia of the President and the failed programs of the liberals. Everyone was looking for a cause and a reason while friends and neighbors were digging through the rubble looking and hoping to find a breathing body.

What was really going on? We apprehended a suspect who was known to be part of, or had connections with, a militia group. Immediately the militia groups across the country were put on the defensive, justifying themselves by claiming that they were in existence to preserve the true values this country was built on. They claim to be the true Americans who are defending the basic principles of our land. When one militia member who called into a popular radio talk show in New York City was asked if he could imagine a situation wherein a militia member could ever do anything as drastic as what happened in Oklahoma City, he replied, "I don't really think so, but if we ever felt we were called to do anything that fell outside the limits of the laws of this land, the very first thing we would do is get down on our knees and make sure we were doing the will of God."

Now we are getting to the heart of things. Oklahoma City was bombed, not because the far right is fanatic or demonic, not because the liberals are bleeding-heart tree huggers who are robbing us of our fundamental rights and forcing big government down our throats, but because someone felt the need to "do the will of God."

Tell me please, from the point of view of what is enhancing for human life and God's creation, what is the difference between:

The bombing in Oklahoma City
The bombing of a bus in Tel Aviv
The bombing of Hiroshima
The Holocaust
The Crusades

The Inquisition
The violence in Northern Ireland
The killing in Bosnia
The U.S. Civil War
Slavery
The claiming of America by the Europeans
The slaughter in Cambodia
Joshua at the battle of Jericho
Etc., etc., etc. . . . ?

All these events are characterized by extreme violence against humanity. All were carried out by persons who were either doing the will of God or were convinced they were carrying out the cause of "truth" or "rightness." It appears that frequently the result of an activity conducted on the basis of knowing absolutely what is the ultimate good is violence against humanity.

This brings me back to the difference between faith and belief. Faith is the willingness to act based on trust in God's abiding presence and inherent goodness. It is the capacity to act without knowing fully the consequences of that act, but also being willing to be responsible for the outcome of that activity. Faith means being willing to act without first having the justification for that action.

This is different from the way we commonly use beliefs. A belief is a rational understanding or explanation of a phenomenon. Beliefs are often explanations of universal or cosmic conditions or situations. They are rational structures by which we attempt to order our lives and our world. The problem comes in the fact that they can also be mechanisms through which we justify our behaviors and actions. When beliefs inform our actions and behaviors there is room for faith to function, but when beliefs justify our actions and behaviors they become deific.

Returning to the violence against our fellow human beings listed above, I contend that violence is the result of persons (usually men) acting on the basis that beliefs justify behavior. If I believe I am doing the will of God or serving the realm of "right," I have become God. I have assumed the authority of God and have overrun the boundaries of justice. Violence has no check once actions are carried out under the authority of God.

This way of appropriating beliefs into behaviors has moved us away from our humanness. We have chosen to assume the realm of God and are no longer acting as humans. We no longer realize that we do not know everything — we have forgotten our humbleness. We have become arrogant and are armed for violence. We are no longer persons of faith.

There is one more aspect of the Oklahoma bombing that I want to focus on. A great number of people have been claiming that hopelessness is really the mood of our current times. The prevalence of evil and the meaningless suffering it generates has brought us to the point of "numbed silence."[1] However, when I recall the human response to the Oklahoma bombing, especially by those who were most directly affected, I get a very different picture. These people did not put on sackcloth and sprinkle themselves with ashes. They did not regress into a cocoon of self-pity or hopeless wailing. No, they banded together and pitched in to help the suffering and comfort the grieving. I can't remember a clearer demonstration of faith in life and in the ongoing purpose of creation. This suggests to me that inside all of us is a faith that is just waiting to be expressed. This untapped faith is inside all of us, but our current beliefs, ideologies, systems, and institutions do nothing to elicit it. They are concerned with the wrong thing. They think they must supply the truth of the meaning of existence rather than provide the vehicle through which we can show that we are a vital part of the creativity of God's world. We live, relate, propagate, and create in spite of ourselves. Regardless how much of a brake we place on our creative urges by our rational need to know, we create. Faith is the vehicle of our creativity and unless our beliefs inform our faith, we find ourselves falling outside of God's creative stream. When our beliefs are used to justify our actions, authenticate our existence, or solidify our power, we have lost faith, assumed arrogance, and become violators of God's creation.

Chris Beker, in his book *Suffering and Hope,* gives me great help here. Beker suggests that all suffering in the world that results from human injustice (and that includes everything on my prior list) can be reduced to an ultimate source — idolatry. Beker states, "Idol worship is the source of human injustice and of its attendant suffering in God's creation: and idol worship is not readily open to rational analysis and discussion because it has an irrational base. The 'worshiper' of an idol donates confessional status to it, which is exactly the idol's hidden power. Contrary to what we may think, an idol is not recognized as such by its adherents, but rather is for them an object of 'ultimate concern.' "[2]

Beker goes on to claim that the "absolute subject — the object of our pride since the enlightenment — is passionately engaged in dominating the world." According to Beker "the idolatrous glorification of the ego's power and 'lordship' causes immense suffering in our world. The 'exchange of the truth of God for a lie' . . . produces the illusion of omnipotence, a

---

1. See, for example, Chris Beker, *Suffering and Hope* (Grand Rapids: Eerdmans, 1994), particularly chapter 6.
2. Beker, *Suffering and Hope,* 80-81.

'boasting' which Paul applies especially to the pride of the 'religious person' who elevates himself or herself in the name of God."[3]

Here Beker is very close to the claim I am making. Beker builds on the apostle Paul's claim that idolatry is the "exchange of the truth of God for a lie." I wish to push both the apostle Paul and Chris Beker a little further and claim that idolatry rests in the claim that we can *know* the "truth of God." Idolatry is not based on a particular truth we claim but on the arrogant claim that we can know the truth.

The human being has been endowed by the Creator with the insatiable need to know. This is the root of our creative potential, but it is also the potential for evil. Along with the gift of creativity comes the responsibility to guard against arrogance. Once we are sure we know, we have closed off creativity and put on the mantel of knowledge. Once we have forgotten or ignored the uncertainty in faith we become vulnerable to the error of idolatry. This is the avenue to idolatry and to sin. Sin, which is characteristic of the human condition alone, is the result of the arrogance of knowing. Sin is converting the urge or need to know into a permanent structure. It is building a concrete monument under an idea, placing a figure on it we call a truth, thus forming an idol. It is substituting the creative *need* to know with the arrogant *claim* to know, thus initiating a dominating process through which we make what we know the reality against which we measure all of creation. What better label for such arrogance than idolatry!

The simple truth is that we really don't know for sure, we only make informed guesses. As long as we remember that what we believe are guesses and that we act on faith, we remain human and creative. Once we think we know and act on the basis of the truth of that knowledge we become transgressors of creation. Such arrogance will absolutely cause violence against creation.

We are the perpetrators of all violence. God's creation suffers because we believe we know. This is not to say that we will not cause pain or that all suffering is the result of our sin. We will be the initiators of suffering and pain precisely because we don't fully know. However, by being aware of our capacity to cause pain and remembering our humbleness we retain the compassion to minimize that suffering whenever it occurs and to constantly reduce its effect on all creation. Pain is not the fruit of sin, violence is. We sin by acting on the belief that we know God's will, thus causing violence.

Does this mean that only the religious sin? No, it means that anyone who arrogantly acts as if what they think or who they are is the only thing

3. Beker, *Suffering and Hope*, 81, 82.

that matters, is sinning. It also means that any one of us who performs functions, which in her or his heart knows is out of step with God's purpose but are justified within institutional or systemic standards, is sinning.

Earlier I referred to the misuse of our systems and institutions. Now we can understand this abuse as a form of idolatry. Can you think of a better label for a system or structure that has developed to the point where it has robbed us of our freedom — indeed eliminated the need for faith and calls only for obedience — and enslaved us within its rules and laws? To be humble in this situation means we must exercise our openness by transforming those systems and institutions that enslave us or create new ones. To defend or to work to preserve mechanisms that enslave or cause violence is to deny our humanness and to perpetrate evil.

This means that we as individuals must once again take charge of our institutions and systems, because without us in control they have no heart. Each system and institution, if it is to remain the tool it was created to be, must be transformed by each generation. We are the life of the institution and the system. We must take hold of it once more. For instance, we must get over the idea that the government of the United States is great because of the genius of Jefferson and realize that our government has the potential to serve us because Jefferson had the nerve to be humble. He was brave enough to display and pursue his openness. We are called, not to praise or worship his work and accomplishments, but to follow his example. Our country and form of government can only be great if we all are Jeffersons. Only if we are open to our world, have faith enough to step into the unknown, can we claim to be the rightful heirs of Jefferson. We are not called to defend or preserve what he created, but to continue the creative process he started. This is how we can be freed from our systems and institutions.

I am not unaware of the implications these thoughts have for the professed doctrines of our particular religions. Do these comments suggest that I am not a professor of the Christian message? I can claim absolutely that Jesus of Nazareth is my savior. Having said that, however, I must add that I claim this not because somehow his blood has satiated a bloodthirsty God who can only associate with souls who have been washed clean of sin. No, that is too demeaning a notion of God for me. Jesus of Nazareth is my personal savior because his death has exposed my sins to me in a way that cannot be avoided. His death has shown what my beliefs, when encased in certainty, can do to the flow of Creation. Those beliefs destroy just as surely as did the beliefs of the Jews and the Romans. Jesus has saved me from that if I am willing to understand and live by faith and love. If I do not exhibit such faith through humility I am simply one of the mob screaming "crucify."

Jesus of Nazareth is my savior because he showed me how to live. He demonstrated what can happen when you live by what you believe but are humble enough to recognize the presence of God in the world. Jesus' humility, yes his humanness, was operative because of his acute awareness of the reign of God. Something beyond his beliefs, something so real he could sense it in every situation, gave him the power to love and transform the world around him. Jesus is my savior because he showed me the real potential in humanness — that through humility we can get in touch with the reign of God and be more in step with the flow of God's creation.

But what about the resurrection and the fulfillment of the Promise? Does Jesus live? You bet! There is nothing more alive and operative in my experience than the life and death of Jesus of Nazareth. How then can I even think of denying the resurrection? Furthermore, when I compare what I know to what God demonstrates every moment of my existence, who am I to doubt that Jesus walked out of the tomb on the third day? I will not limit God's power and activity to what I know.

The same goes for the fulfillment of the reign of God, life after death, or heaven, or whatever else you want to call it. Every description of heaven I have ever heard leaves me with the desire to stay six feet under. Heaven doesn't excite me; but when I look at creation and see the way nature constantly brings forth new life, I have faith there is life after death. The question I need to ask myself constantly is "can I have faith enough to stay open to the flow of God's creation and be humble enough not to get in its way"? Can I be firm enough in my beliefs to be able to contribute to the God force but free enough from them to see when what I believe is getting in the way of where God's creation is going.

What does all this have to say to the work of the Gospel of Jesus Christ? I'm not sure there is any salvation of value except the salvation of creation. Are we called to existence only to save ourselves? When we examine the life and message of Jesus, do we see anywhere a concern over personal salvation? Isn't it rather a life of concern for the poor and suffering of this world and a message of relief from such suffering? Isn't it a message of liberation from bondage through the good news that God's reign is present and available to all those who have faith to live in the reality of God's love? Aren't we called to openness? Aren't we called to discover our true humanness — our humility?

Isn't it also fairly clear that the life and message of Jesus had a rocky relationship with the religious and political knowers of his day? Isn't it time we accept the judgment of Jesus that as long as we continue to try to save ourselves we are lost and that only in losing ourselves in faith will we be found? Doesn't it seem clear that Jesus was constantly battling against the beliefs, systems, and institutions of his day? Can we ever hope to be a part of God's creative force unless we recognize the priority of faith over our beliefs?

I firmly believe that we will never get a handle on the violence that infects our existence until we deal with our arrogance. We will not be able to walk with Jesus of Nazareth until we recognize the relationship of our claims to truth and violence. We will never be able to exercise our faith until we discover our humbleness and recognize that only God knows, and that we are created to seek.

From Snake Handlers to Stones Crying Out: Wellsprings of Hope in the American Academy

NANCY A. DE VRIES

UNEXPECTEDLY, IN THE BLEAK Princeton midwinter of 1975, Dick Shaull began his "Christian Faith and Social Transformation" course with an article on snake handling as a religious phenomenon. In rural, isolated, Appalachian congregations, unworldly, disregarded white poor were calling upon the power of the Holy Spirit in order to handle poisonous snakes with no physical damage to themselves whatsoever. This outbreak was reported in a number of places; it was widespread and growing. Shaull wanted us to think about this within the context of the theme of the course: the social and political transformation of individual lives and human communities through the power and vision of Christian faith.

At that time, snake handling in the Cumberland struck me as a kind of American Protestant Shroud of Turin. My immediate reaction was not dissimilar to the undertones of uneasy Vatican spokespersons when reports start rolling in of new sightings of the weeping Virgin Mary. I had signed up for "Christian Faith and Social Transformation" looking forward to Frantz Fanon's "Myth of the Veil"[1] and The Wretched of the Earth,[2] with Sartre's introduction. I was anticipating immersion in theoretical and theological reflection with the struggles of my African American and non-Western brothers and sisters in faith. The examination of a bizarre religious phenomenon among impoverished, uneducated, white American southerners did not meet my expectations for dramatic action and involvement,

---

1. Frantz Fanon, "Myth of the Veil," in Toward the African Revolution: Political Essays (New York: Grove Press, 1988).
2. Frantz Fanon, The Wretched of the Earth (New York: Grove Press, 1991).

both emotional and intellectual, in the revolutions and reformations of communities and nations which were taking place around the globe and in the lives of the persons sitting next to me in the gray Speer library classroom.

The relevance of the snake handlers to a course dealing with social transformation was initially difficult for me to see. The reason I failed to see this was because there exists in us a tendency to ignore or dismiss the situation of some because particular people or types of experience do not fit certain categories of marginalization and oppression. The educational significance of the snake handlers lies in the recognition that preconceived notions exist about who might legitimately be considered oppressed or marginalized, and, more to the point, who might not. An examination of such, only some of which may be consciously held, reveals categories of understanding which erroneously exclude definitive patterns and occasions of marginalization and oppression.

The lessons of the gospel according to Shaull continued to unpack themselves across the decades. When I moved East to one of *U.S. News and World Report*'s best colleges as university chaplain and lecturer in religion eight years ago, the pedagogical intent of Shaull's snake handlers gained clarity. What I have learned serving as chaplain at formerly Protestant academies, within the collegiate context of institutional power, economic privilege, and intellectual elitism, is that the Protestant Christian community, which I deeply love and serve as pastor, is substantially marginalized. It is within this context of institutional marginalization that Protestant Christians have found their identity, and therefore their voice. Their newly emergent voice is a sign of vitality which the secular culture has little or no imagination to perceive, in the same way my class failed to perceive the significance of snake handling among Appalachian whites. Within the collegiate ecumenical Protestant community which I serve, the fresh appearance of that voice is a sign of the power of God, and the power of God is a basis for hope.

The History of the American Academy

Christian faith and practice are marginalized in the mainstream American academy today.[3] The marginalization is initially difficult to perceive for a

___

3. It is my intention to give primary focus to the story of American colleges and universities which were founded by European American Protestants in the East and South in the early days of the emerging nation. These institutions became the definitive models for

variety of reasons. Foremost among these factors is that for many years most major American universities were in fact the progenitors, proponents, and trustees of the theology, spirituality, and the culture of Euro-American Protestantism in the United States. Protestant perspectives did indeed provide the ideological underpinning and *modus vivendi* of the prestigious early academies of the East and South. Although the Protestant position of power and privilege in the academy has been steadily eroded since the mid-nineteenth century, critics continue to suppose that White Anglo-Saxon Protestants and their interests administer these institutions, control their boards of trustees, dominate their cultural life, and produce graduates who will perpetuate the tradition. Thus the presupposition exists of continued Euro-American Protestant hegemony in the academy. However, in the academy's official and informal relationships with Christianity and to campus religious life in general, Protestant hegemony has been gone for many years. Moreover, the administrative and programmatic structures which enshrined it have been deliberately taken apart for the past quarter century. Curricular decisions have eroded Protestant hegemony for much longer. To grasp the reality of the marginalization of Protestant Christianity in the life and study of the modern university, it is helpful to have a sense of the history of the American academy.

The academy as we know it, and the liberal arts tradition in particular, derives its heritage from European cathedral schools. These schools served to transmit knowledge and religious truth, but also to perpetuate culture. Both religious truth and the culture of the university were Christian. The Protestant Reformers of the sixteenth century embraced and continued this relationship with the university. Their offspring, American Protestants, founded and supported academies and built the spirit and forms of their Protestant vision right into the bone marrow of the institutions of the emerging nation. American Protestants sought to create the kingdom of God in America. Crucial to this enterprise were the colleges they planted for the training of Protestant clergy and Protestant Christian citizens. These academies proliferated steadily as the frontier unfolded and America moved westward in Massachusetts, to New York, then Ohio, Illinois, Iowa, and

---

higher education in the United States. Interesting evidence exists of similarities to the dynamics at historically black colleges and universities. Other examples of the American academy, including women's colleges, Catholic colleges, denominational colleges, overtly evangelical colleges, and institutions with Jewish roots are also part of the story of American higher education. However, colleges considered for this chapter were founded as Protestant academies. These schools are analogous to the institutions which I have served as college or university chaplain. The reflection in this essay has been developed around my own experience of ministry in these contexts.

beyond. George Marsden, chronicler and historian of the Protestant academy in America, says this about the relationship between early American liberal learning and Protestant Christianity:

> The Reformation began at a university with a scholar's insight, and educational institutions long played a major role in Protestant success. Educated clergy, trained in interpreting authoritative texts, were essential to challenge Catholic authority and to forestall spiritual anarchy. For centuries in Protestant countries, including the Protestant colonies in America, the clergy typically were the best-educated persons in a town or village. In this country, until well into the nineteenth century, higher education remained primarily a function of the church, as it always had been in Western civilization.[4]

Most educators were clergy, trained in theology at least as well as they were trained in other disciplines. Presidents of colleges founded by Protestants were invariably clergy, and often taught senior courses in Moral Christianity, which applied Christian teaching to a variety of contemporary and historical issues. The worship of God was part of the daily schedule, often occurring twice or more: morning and evening prayers, with a full daily worship service. Students and professors alike worshiped on Sundays with the congregation whose local and denominational leaders had founded the academy.

The tenor of much of early American higher education was not only Christian, it was openly evangelical. Church-related colleges were unapologetically evangelical, but even state colleges and universities founded after the American Revolution were also evangelical Christian, although nonsectarian.[5] Most American colleges founded before the Civil War were founded by churches and were supported by state and local taxes. Even with separation of church and state, an assumption existed that church and state should work hand in hand, because these institutions served both public and ecclesiastical interest simultaneously.

The need for more advanced, technological education in order for the American academy and the United States itself to compete in world markets began the process of disestablishment of the classicist education offered

4. George Marsden, "The Soul of the American University: A Historical Overview," in *The Secularization of the Academy, ed. George Marsden and Bradley J. Longfield* (New York: Oxford University Press, 1992), 10.

5. Bradley J. Longfield, "From Evangelicalism to Liberalism: Public Midwestern Universities in Nineteenth-Century America," in *The Secularization of the Academy,* 47.

with evangelical Christianity as its core. More specialized training was needed, and both federal and private interest funding was forthcoming. The Morrill Land Grant Act of 1862 provided funding for the development of technological, scientific, and agricultural studies in state schools, and thus became the first major cairn along the road to the secularization of the American academy. This road became an expressway.

Protestant leaders were faced with very real problems which the demand for technological expertise occasioned, with its accompanying professionalization of faculties, whose members, unlike their scholarly forebears, did not know Protestant Christian theology as well as or better than their given fields. Protestant leaders sought to bring ideological and institutional change which would save the academy and its Protestant Christian influence. It is particularly within this context that the religion of the academy shifted from evangelical Christianity to the ideological dominance of liberal Christianity.

The liberal Christianity of the Progressive Era reasoned that all the earth was God's, therefore nothing could be studied that was not within God's domain. The great welding together of "God and Truth," enshrined in the mottos of academic institutions, such as Colgate University's *"Deo ac Veritati,"* was now exegeted with new emphasis: all truth has to do with God, indeed truth *is* God; there is little need to distinguish between the two. Although this way of thinking unknowingly set a course for the removal of the academy from the sphere of influence of Christianity, it still had its own elements of supersessionism. Frederic Henry Hedge, in an 1866 address to Harvard alumni said, "The secularization of the College is no violation of its motto, *'Christo et Ecclesiae.'* For, as I interpret those sacred ideas, the cause of Christ and the Church is advanced by whatever liberalizes and enriches and enlarges the mind."[6]

The Social Gospel additionally provided the rationale for increased emphasis on technological training because of the demand for highly trained professionals to serve a world in need. The former concept of service to God was gradually translated into service to country on the lips of Protestants widely tolerant of substantial diversity. Such Protestants became increasingly careful not to speak the name of God in the public sector.

During this period, many colleges formally separated from their divinity schools, and established undergraduate departments of philosophy and religion, the curricula of which were nonsectarian in nature, and frequently leaning toward the universalist. Institutional change as radically invasive as this, even when undertaken by respected leaders and supported

6. George M. Marsden, *The Soul of the American University,* 9.

by many in the rank and file, does not come easily, and soon Christians were fighting for the heart and mind of the American academy. The quintessence of that battle occurred around the issue of how the creation of the world was to be taught in the academy. Liberal Protestants favored Darwinism, while fundamentalists and a conservative hard line of Christians, fearful of all that was being rapidly lost, insisted on biblical literalism. Liberal Protestants forged an alliance with progressive secular proponents of the scientific method. Together they embraced Darwinism. Fundamentalists and many traditional Protestants, whose spokesperson became the silver-tongued William Jennings Bryan, rejected it. Both sides still regarded the education afforded the youth of America at colleges and universities a crucial public trust. Fundamentalist and conservative Christians in the larger society attempted to press curricular and tenure demands for orthodoxy in colleges and universities. They sunk the teeth of wealth and power into those demands, and many liberal Protestant professors were dismissed.

Thus, in the early years of this century, there emerged the first major national argument about the desirable but only marginally attainable goal of "academic freedom." The threat Christian fundamentalists made to academic freedom was real. That threat fueled an alliance between liberal Protestants and secular, increasingly antireligious, progressive thinkers, that would continue well past the middle of the twentieth century. Although its use in the American academy is a twentieth-century phenomenon, the notion of academic freedom has an ideological root in the nineteenth-century German university, with its concepts of *Lehrfreiheit* and *Wissenschaft,* freedom for professors and the "sanctified righteous ideal of a scientific search for truth,"[7] respectively. The American Association of University Professors (AAUP) was founded in large part to protect the public speech and political activities of (1) professors who taught the scientific method, (2) progressive thinkers, and (3) political liberals. Progressive philosopher, advocate of the scientific method, and liberal Protestant, John Dewey, helped found the AAUP between 1913 and 1915. He became its first president.[8]

Although the AAUP began with the noble intention of protecting free speech for progressive thinkers and those who employed the scientific method for pursuit of truth, nonetheless the AAUP's ideology ironically, but overtly, carried within it the seeds of repression for those who were

7. Marsden, *The Soul of the American University,* 297.
8. Steven C. Rockefeller, *John Dewey: Religious Faith and Democratic Humanism* (New York: Columbia University Press, 1991), 286.

already marginalized in the mainstream academy. Deemed to have no merit were the grievances of conservative and traditional Protestants because they were judged to lack the scholarly superiority of the scientific inquiry into truth. Nicholas Murray Butler, the President of Columbia University, who, in 1904, brought John Dewey to the Columbia faculty from the University of Chicago, said that academic freedom was limited by "common morality, common sense, common loyalty, and a decent respect for the opinion of mankind." He felt that all would be well if persons in the university followed the principle: "behave like a gentleman."[9] One wonders if assumptions and prejudices underlying this way of thinking contributed to the reason that claims of violation of academic freedom made by Catholics, Jews, and Marxists were also dismissed.[10] AAUP guidelines stipulated that no professor should speak dogmatically without possessing the superior knowledge of scientific truth in the professor's field of study. However, the existence of God, a God who relates to us personally, cannot be demonstrated, legitimated, or domesticated by empirical ways of knowing. Thus, in this context, the presumption that traditional Protestant Christians could not be intellectuals of the first order was established, ideologically vested, and freely articulated.

James Leuba, a professor of psychology at Bryn Mawr College, published in 1916, *The Belief in God and Immortality: A Psychological, Anthropological, and Statistical Study.*[11] Leuba believed, as did many of his professorial counterparts, that the more scientific inquiry was employed as a means to pursue truth, the certain result would be that educated Christians would forsake their faith. Scientific education, Leuba thought, would, at minimum, prompt a confessional Christian to at least refashion belief and to abandon a personal concept of God in favor of strong ideals. Such a revision is certainly a departure from traditional Protestant Christianity. The questions in Leuba's surveys of professors and students, and the analysis in his published results were regarded as "scientific." Leuba clearly regarded the Christian belief in a God with whom personal relationship is both possible and desirable as the backwater of unenlightened, uneducated, traditional Christian thinking.

9. Walter P. Metzger, ed., *The American Concept of Academic Freedom: A Collection of Essays and Reports* (New York: Arno Press, 1977); Nicholas Murray Butler, "Academic Freedom," *Educational Review* 47 (March 1914): 291-94, as cited in *The Soul of the American University,* 299-300.

10. Marsden, *The Soul of the American University,* 296-97.

11. James Leuba, "The Belief in God and Immortality: A Psychological, Anthropological, and Statistical Study" (Chicago, 1921 [1916]), cited in Marsden, *The Soul of the American University,* 312, 292-96.

John Dewey's unfolding perspectives about traditional Protestant Christianity may be detected in an excerpt drawn from Dewey's 1902 piece "Academic Freedom." Dewey delineated two types of academic institutions.

An ecclesiastical, political, or even economic corporation holding certain tenets . . . certainly has the right to support an institution to maintain and propagate its creed. [These] teaching bodies, called by whatever name [were not to be confused with] the university proper.

Marsden interprets Dewey: "While professors at partisan institutions might deplore the narrowness of such schools and work to speed their transformation into true universities, in the meantime, they would have to accept that schools had a right to limit free inquiry, so long as their standards were clearly stated."

In contrast to these "partisan institutions," Dewey writes, "To investigate truth; critically to verify facts; to reach conclusions by the means of the best methods at hand . . . that is precisely the aim and object of the university."[12] The idea that confessional Protestant Christian faith is by nature anti-intellectual, partisan, and tainting the scholarly enterprise was firmly planted. In addition, while forward-thinking and humane ideas about race, religious diversity, sexuality, the role of women, and immigration did not *a priori* stem from the "scientific" epistemology of the progressives, any more than these new and essentially overdue ways of thinking violated the ideological roots of traditional Protestant Christians, it was assumed by many that they did. The demarcation of this entire political and social agenda provided the "modern university" with a moral justification, even a mandate, for disestablishing Protestant Christianity. The academy's ideological and structural changes began as accommodation to technological demands, then attempted the legitimate reordering of the academy for a more egalitarian and inclusive system, but moved unwittingly, and with virtually no self-recognition, from the dismantling of Protestant privilege to the extreme marginalization of Protestant Christianity itself.

12. Marsden, *The Soul of the American University,* 298. Marsden's comments are interlaced with his quotation of John Dewey in Dewey's "Academic Freedom" *Educational Review* 23 (1902), 1, 3, reproduced in *The American Concepts of Academic Freedom: A Collection of Essays and Reports,* ed. Walter P. Metzger (New York: Arno Press, 1977).

The Marginalization of Christianity in the Academy

The resulting dimensions of marginalization for practicing Protestant Christians in the academy have been legion. Single examples do not catch one's attention, but to those who value the tradition, and who love and pray for Christians on campuses, the accumulation is overwhelming. The dismantling continues as the academy moves towards the millennium.

By the mid-twentieth century, colleges and universities ceased hiring clergy presidents. To placate alumni and board members who were unhappy with this development, institutions created the role of the chaplain, and hired Protestant clergy to fill this role. At the same time, required chapel services began to have substantial secular content mixed in with Protestant liturgy. A humorous example of the confusion wrought by this transition in the content of required chapel services is evident in an anecdote of a philosophy professor, who, from the context of his Judaism, assumed that the doxology, sung in daily required chapel services he attended as an undergraduate, was simply part of Amherst College ritual. A few years later, as he began his career as an academic, this professor delivered a lecture in the setting of a required chapel service/assembly of another university. The assembly began with the doxology. The philosophy professor rose and thanked his host campus for welcoming him with the Amherst college hymn! As the century progressed, required chapel content became largely secular and later required chapel was abandoned altogether.

The creation of chaplaincies was one of the academy's concessions to the displaced and discredited Protestant establishment. Protestant chaplains were placed under the supervision of university presidents because of the insistence of boards of trustees. Chaplains were taking over a role which had previously been filled by presidents: namely, the religious nurture of the entire collegiate community. Chaplains were to relate to all constituencies of the academy: its scholarly life, its student life, its alumni and boards, its great celebrative and solemn institutional moments. As the prominent role of student personnel offices increased, chaplaincies were often taken out of the president's office and placed under deans of students, who frequently had neither scholarly knowledge of the Protestant tradition, nor suitable comprehension of what ministry in any environment entails, much less the college campus. Chaplaincy roles in student life offices are often reduced to nonacademic student activities, a type of youth pastor for the academy.

When chaplaincies were first established in universities, there was an effort to hire seasoned, capable, clergy-academicians into these positions. In recent years, particularly following the campus unrest of the late

1960s, which was often aided and abetted by chaplains, mostly entry-level clergy have been hired as chaplains in American colleges and universities. Entry-level clergy are not well-equipped for the successful accomplishment of college chaplaincy, which requires deep faith, grace under fire, enormous political savvy, moral courage, scholarly expertise, an articulate public voice, profound human wisdom, compelling personality, and great compassion. In addition, chaplaincies were initially tenurable positions with faculty status, whether or not they included teaching responsibilities. It is more common now to place chaplaincies within administrations where they are subject to the typical administrator's arrangement of the one-year renewable contract. Chaplaincies frequently have a cap, a limit on the number of years a person may stay in the position. It also appears to be the unconscious practice of many academic administrations to balance their affirmative action ledgers within the realm of religious ministry. Administrators whose hiring tendencies demonstrate little regard for the objectives of affirmative action frequently hire women and minorities for chaplaincies. Staff selection for religious life may reflect a distressing disregard for affirmative action.

In the 1960s, campus Christians no longer worshiped with their founding congregations, even on a voluntary basis, and ecumenical campus churches were established. As the disestablishment of Christianity progresses, such student congregations struggle against great odds to survive. In recent years, religious life funding has been cut back during times of economic crunch, and religious life goals are not considered for major fundraising campaigns.

The worship needs of Protestant Christians are often overlooked, and sometimes flouted. University events are not infrequently scheduled on Sunday mornings, and various holy days may be eclipsed by the university calendar, as well. Minimal, ineffectual concern is periodically evidenced for noninterference with non-Christian religious observance, but it is beyond the realm of comprehension of the university that scheduling exams or course registration on Sunday morning is more than inconvenient to Protestant Christians. Campus congregations and chaplaincies have been forced to share chapel space with music and performing arts programs, and chapels have been renovated to remove chancels and create stages for performers, because of the desire to utilize the extensive seating capacity in most chapel sanctuaries. Christians may be expected to subordinate their regularly scheduled use of chapel space, even for Sunday worship, to the rehearsal and performance needs of music and theater groups, or visiting performers.

Many college and university chapel buildings, often originally financed by the family of the university's founders, have had all overt religious symbolism removed, including nonsectarian religious symbols. Chaplains and Christian groups occupying such chapels are expected to refrain from placing crosses on chapel walls, both in the sanctuary and out, because of the offense they are said to bring by their very presence to the nonreligious and to non-Christians. Some universities have even attempted to de-Christianize the art and architecture of chapels legally designated as historic landmarks. As almost an eerie echo of liberal Protestants unknowingly signing away their birthright at the beginning of the century, some of the more recent disestablishment of Protestant Christianity has been initiated and even championed by chaplains themselves. It is not terribly surprising that in this context the majority of alumni who offer financial support to Christian students on campus do so outside of university channels, through parareligious groups. Nonetheless this is a tragedy. Lack of alumni funding in chaplaincy programs encourages university administrations in their assumption that the educated alumni do not care deeply about the religious life of Christian students on the campus. This is unfortunate because alliances between Christian alumni, college chaplains, and Christian students are very beneficial, and can literally help campus Christian practice survive.

It is essential to understand that the core life of the university is its teaching and learning. The devaluing of the Christian tradition within the scholarly life of the university has far-reaching implications. The attack in some classroom settings on Christianity as anti-intellectual, immoral, and superstitious has continued essentially unabated, while professor-chaplains are watched carefully to make sure they do not engage in unscholarly work or "proselytizing."

Issues of religious repression in teaching and learning reassert themselves in the context of curricular reform, which challenges the assumptions of established religion in general, and Protestant Christianity in particular. Non-Western and non-Christian religions may be seen as being more appropriate for scholarly examination than Christianity, precisely because there are fewer adherents, and the adherents that live on campus may be people of color, whose intellectual life is more easily disregarded because of racism. In this way, the curriculum of religion departments may unwittingly take on a paternalistic and anthropological flavor.

Theologians and seminary-trained scholars are increasingly held in lower esteem than their professorial counterparts graduated from secular universities. Confessional Christianity on the part of faculty members in some quarters has come to be viewed as undesirable at best, and a veritable block to clear thinking and scholarly research at worst.

This pattern of marginalization of Protestant Christians and the academic study of their religious tradition has not diminished with time — it has increased. Even as the century draws to a close, and the winds of religious revival filter through peoples and nations across the globe, religion faculties still feel the need to establish the object of their academic discipline as worthy of serious scholarship. It is not unusual for serious scholars to be tenured, promoted, and given leadership only if they take careful pains to separate their Christian perspectives from their scholarly work, institutional service, and for the most part, from their public lives.

It is especially important to consider the double marginalization this lays upon committed Christian scholars who are from Africa, Asia, and Latin America, as well as that of African Americans. Acceptance of their work, if such acceptance is forthcoming, or even of their presence in the midst of an academic world which is still overwhelmingly Caucasian and American, may have the flavor of patronizing condescension. Moreover, if European American scholars of the Christian tradition have difficulty getting their colleagues to take their work seriously, how much more difficult is it to genuinely engage the interest of the academy, with depth and commitment for the scholarly consideration of Christianity on other continents?

An insidious, though often unintentional, manifestation of marginalization of black Christians is the assumption that courses in African American or African religiousness are for black students alone. Obviously, students of color deserve the chance to study their traditions and cultures in the academy, but should these not also be of interest to European Americans and others? An additional irony is that the curricular and non-curricular marginalization of Protestant Christians serves to further distance Asian, African, and Latin American Protestant Christians, as well as those who are perceived the beneficiaries of white Protestant hegemony.

Another unexamined assumption about the content of religion courses is that the curriculum must be constructed in such a way that Christian students will learn what is wrong with their tradition. There can be a disturbing presumption of moral superiority behind this way of thinking. Examples of this include: Womanist theology should be taught so that African American women will break the cycle of oppression by black men. Protestant Christianity courses should spend significant amounts of time on the burning of Servetus in Calvin's Geneva, the misogyny of John Knox, and the anti-Semitism of Martin Luther. Catholic tradition courses must emphasize the Inquisition and the marginalization of women. It is absolutely the case that those who teach courses in the Christian tradition cannot afford to ignore important moral accountability, or to romanticize their tradition's past, but does not the Christian tradition have genuine moments of glory, beauty, and undiminished moral integrity as well? Do we wish to ignore the empowerment of its many peoples across the centuries, or their contributions to our common life? Is it not important to give students visions to live by as well as challenging the shortcomings and offenses of a tradition they sense to be their own? If we in the academy are to be honest and consistent, we would do well to ask what traditions we exempt from the moral judgments upon their sins and shortcomings that we require of Christians. Why do we judge some and exempt other traditions? What pedagogical assumptions are utilized in such decisions?

Reservoirs of Hope

The extreme marginalization of Protestant Christians on the university campus unleashes the spiritual experience of being driven into the wilderness. As our biblical and American forbears were led by God out of Egypt, into the wilderness, so we also begin to find and clarify our identity in the wilderness. Our identity as Protestants is as a people of God "who belong, in life and in death, to Jesus Christ." In the words of the Heidelberg Catechism, "this is our comfort and this is our hope."[13]

St. Paul's words take on new meaning in this context.

> Therefore, since it is by God's mercy that we are engaged in this ministry, we do not lose heart. We have renounced the shameful things that one hides; we refuse to practice cunning or falsify God's word; but by the open statement of truth we commend ourselves to the conscience of everyone in the sight of God. . . . *We are afflicted in every way, but not crushed; perplexed, but not driven to despair; persecuted, but not forsaken; struck down, but not destroyed . . . so we do not lose heart. . . .* Our inner nature is being renewed day by day.[14]

Perceiving and embracing our identity in the midst of the wilderness is the beginning of empowerment. The discernment of identity and its attendant empowerment is a gift God gives particularly to the marginalized. It is a wonderful irony, because the process of disestablishment of a people or

13. *The Book of Confessions,* "The Heidelberg Catechism," (New York: Office of the General Assembly of the United Presbyterian Church in the United States of America, 1970), 4.001.

14. II Corinthians 4:1-16.

tradition works to break down identity. Finding identity in the midst of the wilderness is difficult, because of the manifold and erroneous messages given us about who we are. At worst, Christians on campus are encouraged by some to think of themselves as a throwback, as inadequate and biased scholars (in a world assumed to be objective) and as emotional as opposed to intellectual, therefore subject to irrationality. It is taken for granted by some of our academic detractors that traditional Christians are Caucasian, racist, hierarchical, supersessionist, and domineering. It is not easy to get through that set of signals to find out who we are, and to remember Whose we are.

It is wonderfully ironic and redemptive that the continual assault of the memory of the sins of Christendom provides the impetus for acknowledgment, confession, repentance, and vigilance for Christian communities on campus. Aware of our sins, we may be freer and more able to reform ourselves *and the very institutions which marginalize us!* There is tremendous power for honest self-assessment, reform, and new creation in the legacy of the Protestant principle *Semper Reformanda,* "reformed and always reforming." This heritage is a gift of grace which we must use. Protestant Christian capacity to be reformed and to reform is a sign of empowerment.

There are signs, rare and precious pinholes of light, of the emergent voice of committed Christians on campus. One is the renewed investment Christian students are making in Christian community, in being the body of Christ for each other. Another sign of the power of God is that Christian communities are becoming not only ecumenical, but more genuinely inclusive than in the past. Campus Christian groups are in the fragile beginning of bridging racial and class lines, because they have been given the capacity to sense the presence of God in those genuinely different from themselves. Many Protestant campus congregations are more likely to be genuinely inclusive than most of their counterparts off-campus. Conservative and liberal Protestants are reasserting their commonality as Christians. Catholics and Protestants are finding ways to build meaningful bridges to each other, not just in dialogue, but in common worship. This genuine and voluntary diversity of Christian community is not only biblically mandated, it is also a gift of the Holy Spirit.

Another sign of empowerment for the community of faith is the increasing realization that it is within the context of Christian *community* that we are empowered. As the excesses of individualism in American society become more evident to us, we become more and more the body of Christ, and sense "the one hope that belongs to our call."[15] Our ability

---

15. Ephesians 4:4.

to be community with and for each other increases in the midst of the decimated social world of the American academy is a sign with vitality and power. Protestant Christians may be able to model this for the academy in a manner not possible for many other groupings of people on campus.

The single most striking sign of hope given to the academic Christian community may be the gradually increasing trickle of secular persons who are attracted into our midst, and who move quickly forward to attain Christian maturity. They are attracted by the power of God through the reemerging voice of Christians. The voices of student Christians, and their faculty and administration counterparts who have struggled against marginalization, found their identity, and embraced their calling, is indeed a song in the wilderness. I believe that if their voices are silenced, the very stones upon which the academies are built "will cry out."[16]

In many ways, professing Protestant Christians are the snake handlers of the academy. As the snake handling of marginalized southerners is bizarre in the larger society, so the academic who prays to a trusted deity is bizarre in the world of twentieth-century North American scholarship. Professing, confessional Christians are an embarrassment to the academy and assumed by many to be ignorant and uneducated. Some of us are regarded as an anthropological curiosity. We have been given signs of empowerment which are no more discernable to the academy around us than the phenomenon of snake handling by Appalachian Christians is discernable to American society.

Appalachian Pentecostal Protestants have been denied many blessings and opportunities of American life by poverty, prejudice, and institutionally structured injustice. But the snake handlers have not been stripped of their faith and its resources. They have not been denied the power of God to transform their lives. With the gospel's indication of snake handling as a sign of divine presence[17] in their memory banks and the Apostle Paul on Malta in their cloud of witnesses,[18] Appalachian Christians call upon the name of the Lord in the midst of their disempowerment, and they are given a sign. The sign given them, snake handling, is a stumbling block and foolishness itself to those outside their community. But like the crucifixion, it is the essence of power to those for whom it is an effective sign. It is a basis for hope.

What is there to say about hope in the context of marginalization? It is always a mistake to underestimate the transformational power of hope.

16. Luke 19:40.
17. Mark 16:18
18. Acts 28.

Hope is the single most radical of human responses to oppression, because it simply will not accept defeat. Hope envisions the kingdom of God as reality, and it refuses to accept the status quo of marginalization as definitive and unalterable. Biblical hope does not pray the so-called serenity prayer, "Help me to change the things I can change. Help me to accept the things I cannot change and give me the wisdom to know the difference between the two." Hope does not acquiesce to the things it cannot change, but hope knows how to survive, even thrive in the wilderness, assured of the promises of God, even without those promises fleshed out and in hand.

Hope rooted in the promises of God for the kingdom of God and its blessings for all the people of the world creates a radical commitment. Such hope characterizes the inner orientation of persons and communities towards the enormous problems they must face, and it is evident in their praxis. People of hope know that although the powers of oppression seem insurmountable, ultimately evil, no matter how overwhelming, no matter how subtle, sophisticated, or culturally acceptable, does not have the last word. Jürgen Moltmann writes:

> The Christian hope is directed to a *novum ultimum,* towards a new creation of all things by the God of the resurrection in Jesus Christ . . . [Christian hope] is itself summoned and empowered to creative transformation of reality, for it has hope for the whole of reality. Finally, the believing hope will itself provide inexhaustible resources for the creative, inventive imagination of love. In the medium of hope, our theological concepts become not judgements which nail reality down to what it is, but anticipations which show reality its prospects and its future possibilities.[19]

Radical hope takes a view both broader and longer than many secular persons in contemporary American society are able to embrace. Biblical hope overcomes the andocentric egocentricities of individualism. Hope assumes that God is the final arbiter. One may move into the future, with uncertainties and anxieties, perhaps, but with confidence that the justice and mercy of God will prevail, for the community, if not for our individual selves. Love and justice will triumph, if not in our time, in the time that is to come. Hope never loses confidence in the trustworthiness of God. Hope is future-visioned. Hope "looks forward to the city which has foundations, whose builder and maker is God."[20]

19. Moltmann, Jürgen, *Theology of Hope* (New York: Harper & Row, 1965), 33-36.
20. Hebrews 11:10.

Of Faith and Politics:
Father Francisco González Lobos and the
Carrera Regime in Guatemala, 1839-1865

Douglass Sullivan-González

As a young seminarian, I'll never forget Richard Shaull's 1981 chapel speech memorializing the death of Archbishop Oscar Romero of El Salvador. Professor Shaull challenged the unquestioned principle in our society that a "well-functioning" capitalism required a "healthy" six percent unemployment. Shaull concluded that such a requisite must be challenged, systematically transformed. Shaull demanded the seminarians incarnate our faith in the life of those "six percent" who had been marginalized by the world, and call others to a similar faith commitment in Christ.[1]

I had been raised within a highly individualistic understanding of the faith, regarding "politics" and "economics" as beyond my reach, but peculiar circumstances had sensitized my eyes and ears to the struggles in Latin America. I had stumbled across liberation theology at my Baptist University after two summers of intense missionary work along the Rio Grande. Untimely death and poverty of the region created in me an openness to the biblically centered liberation theology advocated by many prominent Catholics and Protestants. Then, Romero's assassination in March 1980 and the religious sisters' brutal murders in the following December, all within the small Central American country of El Salvador, demanded a fundamental rethinking of my faith commitment. Shaull's timely words and his personal engagement created the possibility of my future work.

To summarize an already long introduction, my doctoral work focused on religion and nation-formation in nineteenth-century Guatemala.[2]

---

1. Richard Shaull, Princeton Theological Seminary, March 1981.
2. Some of this material will also appear in my book, *Piety, Power, and Politics:*

I discovered within the archives of Guatemala's Catholic church a remarkable struggle of one regular cleric, Father Francisco González Lobos, who labored to incarnate the faith in very difficult political circumstances. Both his actions and his reflections serve as a historical marker to the formative theological and ethical dilemmas facing leaders of the Catholic church with the fall of the Spanish monarchy and the rise of the nation-state. Religious leaders now had to redefine their relationship to the emerging community, known as the "Republic," and constantly reevaluate their role with each new power block that assumed leadership of the nation. Consequently, relations *within* the Catholic church suffered cross-examination. As the political world changed, so too did the theological reflections of Catholic clerics in Guatemala. The question became: how could theological convictions of committed Catholics shape the emerging political economy of Guatemala?

The Catholic church's former basis of authority, cultivated in the *patronato* of the Hapsburg Crown, had already been challenged with the rise of the Bourbon throne in the mid-eighteenth century. The Enlightenment's adoration of "reason" over "revelation," the political and economic freedom of the individual, and the social contract between ruler and ruled spread quickly among the literate and illiterate. The Catholic church was no longer seen as crucial to the maintenance of the Crown's colonies under the Bourbon throne. Notably, the Absolutist leaders in both Portugal and Spain expelled the Jesuits in 1759 and 1767 respectively, and then the Spanish Bourbons forced the church to exchange its endowments for public bonds in the early nineteenth century. All these state-initiated actions led to a "conceptual" distancing between the church and the state. As Richard Graham stated, "these measures unwittingly undermined the belief that the state was God's surrogate on earth."[3]

With Independence, the liberal state ruled the church without inhibition! Independence in Central America came by administrative default when the liberal-controlled court in Spain engendered a conservative revolt in Mexico. Faced with the prospect of annexation to the Mexican Empire, white Creoles declared Guatemala independent in September 1821 and maintained Guatemala's primacy with dependent, provincial leadership in the future independent states of El Salvador, Honduras, Nicaragua, and Costa Rica. By 1829, a dominant group surfaced, and pursued classic

---

Religion and Nation-Formation in Guatemala, 1821-1871, to be published by the University of Pittsburgh Press.

3. Richard Graham, *Independence in Latin America: A Comparative Approach,* 2nd ed. (New York: McGraw-Hill, 1994), 27.

"liberal" trade and political policies. Led by the Honduran, Francisco Morazán, the Central American nations remained united under a federal agreement, and severely restricted the institutional Catholic church. Morazán closed down the regular orders, expelled the Archbishop, suspended the state-mandated tithe, and secularized marriages and burials.[4]

Such governmental measures both severely curtailed the Catholic church and inadvertently created the conditions for the demise of the liberal state. With the suspension of most regular orders, the Catholic church struggled to fill parishes as the number of clergy declined, and church buildings fell into disrepair throughout the countryside. Regular clergy who chose to remain in Guatemala pursued "secularization," rescinded religious vows to the Order, and committed themselves to the authority of the local diocesan bishop. The Franciscan González Lobos was forced to secularize, to stop being "Franciscan," in order to preach as a diocesan parish priest during the tumultuous 1830s. Morazán quickly assumed the rights of the colonial *patronato,* much to the protest of local religious leaders, and appointed sympathetic priests to churches located in crucial political areas.

By the middle 1830s, Father Francisco González Lobos had been assigned to work in the remote eastern highlands of Guatemala, and came into contact with the emerging mestizo population, descendants of unions between European and Native Americans, long ostracized by European elites and their native-born children, Creoles. This population sector of the old captaincy-general known as Guatemala would become the critical political force in the late 1830s and bring to power a mestizo known as Rafael Carrera. When the political leaders of the State of Guatemala deeded over half the national territory to a fly-by-night British colonization project, mestizos in eastern Guatemala, already aggravated by other governmental measures, revolted.[5]

In a remarkable way, a multiclass and multiethnic alliance of Indians and mestizos successfully challenged the Central American liberal, Morazán, and white Creole control over the emerging national government through the charismatic leadership of Rafael Carrera. With victory through insurrection in 1839, Carrera challenged, and reversed in some ways, and slowed in others, the forces advocating social and economic integration, a

4. J. Lloyd Mecham's unsurpassed analysis of nineteenth-century church-state relations in Latin America highlights how this classic drama between nascent state leaders, such as Morazán, moved quickly against the Catholic church once their power base was consolidated. See J. Lloyd Mecham, *Church and State in Latin America: A History of Politico-Ecclesiastical Relations* (Chapel Hill: The University of North Carolina Press, 1934).

5. William J. Griffith, *Empires in the Wilderness: Foreign Colonization and Development in Guatemala, 1834-1844* (Chapel Hill: University of North Carolina Press, 1965).

Europeanization, of Guatemala. Excluding the Caribbean, Carrera was Latin America's first non-white to come to power and rule on the basis of popular insurrection.

Always central to the list of grievances voiced by Carrera in particular, and by those who followed him in arms, was their "religion." The liberal state had threatened those living in eastern Guatemala with a loss of property and with an "invasion" of Protestant foreigners. Throughout Guatemala, people saw pulpits go empty and numbers of ministers diminish. When Carrera revolted, people demanded a restoration of "their" religion. Far from the tool used by the elite to manipulate the masses, religious convictions generated an insurrectionary fury to bring back their priests, their church, their "religion."

The traveling diplomat, John Lloyd Stephens, published a vivid account of his journey through Central America during the late 1830s and early 1840s. Though he craved to unravel the mysteries of the pre-conquest world of the Maya, Stephens could not escape the insurrection led by Carrera in Guatemala. Recently arrived in the capital for the first time, Stephens witnessed the insurrectionary triumph of the military caudillo, Rafael Carrera, and his "tumultuous mass of half-naked savages, men, women, and children, estimated at ten or twelve thousand."[6] Stephens described how Carrera's indigenous followers, upon entering the abandoned plaza and within earshot of the terrified white elite shouted "Long live religion and death to strangers!"[7] A political uprising incited by religious concerns had laid siege to the entire pyramid of inherited power.

Prominent to Carrera's success was Father González Lobos. Known as the "guerrilla priest," González Lobos allied with Carrera in the early years, and then equivocated his support under duress from the Catholic hierarchy. His actions, born of mixed motives, highlights the ever-present relationship between theology and politics, between a faith in Christ, a commitment to one's people, and the politics of the Catholic hierarchy. The life of Father González Lobos, an intriguing mixture of charisma, hubris, and dedication, illumines the difficult decisions and classic ethnic and class conflicts confronting lay workers, pastors, and priests who sought to live their faith out in the midst of dying colonial institutions and emerging nation-states.

As the Latin American historian, Enrique Dussel, noted in his magnum opus work on the church in Latin America, current liberation theolo-

---

6. John Lloyd Stephens, *Incidents of Travel in Central America*, vol. 1 (New York: Harper and Brothers, 1841), 230.

7. Stephens, *Incidents of Travel in Central America*, 232.

gians mistakenly examine only the last three decades of strife in their countries to uncover the God of history at work in the lives of their people. The continuous strife to incarnate the faith in difficult political circumstances did not commence with Medellín in 1968. The God of both the Exodus and the Christ event has been at work even before peoples from the European world came into contact with the Americas. Dussel called on church historians to recover a lost history of liberation by reexamining our people's history. If any century lies hidden from the meticulous pens of thoughtful analysts, Latin America's nineteenth century holds a treasure of accounts of remarkable attempts to live the faith in the midst of very difficult political and economic transitions.[8]

We who live in the late twentieth century have much to learn from those who survived the tumultuous years of Independence and nation-formation. Tensions within the colonial world surfaced with rage in St. Dominique (Haiti), New Spain (Mexico), and Venezuela, while in other parts, Independence was achieved by default. In all these regions, elite and popular groups struggled "to reimagine" a community without formal ties to the colonial power. Native peoples who resisted colonial dominance took advantage of the shifting locus of power to reassert their autonomy in western Guatemala while mestizos and Indians blocked the path of white elites who pretended and assumed hegemony in central and eastern Guatemala. And native-born elites looked to identify and lead these divergent popular forces to greater personal gain.[9]

Such reimagination required reflection at all levels of society. Pulpits and the palace balcony became the locus of official discourse, and the printed broadside posted on street lamps engendered popular debate. Local gazettes attempted to create an arena of public discourse, but the colonial weight of centralized power inherited from the Spanish thrones quickly crushed any semblance of "free" debate. Censorship was the rule, not the exception. Thus, historians are forced to look for conflict situations in order to read "society's text." What appear to be petty elite struggles in "banana" republics to the untrained eye are real attempts to redefine the community. The blood of the folk mixed with the economic interests of the elite made the mortar and brick of nineteenth-century Latin America. In all of the struggles, ordinary and unordinary Christians attempted to understand how

8. Enrique Dussel, ed., *Historia de la Iglesia en América Latina,* 6 vols. (Salamanca, España: CEHILA, Ediciones Sígueme, 1983).

9. I am indebted to Benedict Anderson for his understanding of "nationalism." See Benedict Anderson, *Imagined Communities: Reflections on the Origin and Spread of Nationalism* (London: Thetford Press, 1983), 15.

the Divine worked with their lives. The struggle to understand the "ought-ness" of the faith emerges with the story of one cleric, Father Francisco González Lobos, who found himself allied with his parishioners from eastern Guatemala in the midst of a political upheaval. Once in power, though, the rebellious priest found himself at odds with the Catholic hierarchy and with a vital part of his parishioners.

The Guerrilla Priest

No other priest inspires the imagination and creativity of this period like the ex-Franciscan, Francisco González Lobos. Surprisingly little biographic information is known about him. Though he has not been the subject of a systematic investigation, he is publicly remembered as the feared guerrilla priest, "Padre Lobos," who once commanded a significant portion of Carrera's troops.[10] From the initial insurrectionary years through the tumultuous 1840s, González Lobos was drawn almost naturally into conflict situations, never fearing professional or personal consequences. His actions, though, were not guided by a clear ideological vision or well-articulated theological commitment. Rather his deeds sprang from a complicated mix of values and principles that were neither completely altruistic nor egotistical.[11]

The few records that exist indicate that González Lobos entered the

10. [Frederick Crowe], *The Gospel in Central America; Containing a Sketch of the Country, Physical and Geographical — Historical and Political — Moral and Religious: A History of the Baptist Mission in British Honduras and of the Introduction of the Bible into the Spanish American Republic of Guatemala* (London: Gilpin, 1850), 162, and Stephens, *Incidents of Travel in Central America,* 226.

11. Three ecclesiastical trials against González Lobos provide the basis of our interpretation of the guerrilla priest. The first judgment involved his participation in Carrera's insurrection, while the second church trial focused on González Lobos' role in the death of an indigenous community leader in San Pedro Pinula in 1844. The final judgment grew out of González Lobos' equivocal role in Guatemala's Civil War in the late 1840s. Though not comprehensive, these records provide a glimpse into the personality and philosophy of a priest who identified with the insurrectionary masses and challenged the authority of the Catholic church. Archives researched for this article include the Benson Latin American Collection at the University of Texas at Austin, the Latin American Collection at the University of Tulane, the Kenneth Spencer Research Library at the University of Kansas, and in the following Guatemalan archives: El Archivo Histórico Arquidiocesano "Francisco de Paula García Peláez" (AHAG); la Biblioteca de la Universidad de San Carlos "César Brañas"; and el Archivo General de Center América (AGE). In addition, funding by the Tinker Foundation and the Fulbright-Hays Dissertation Grant provided essential support for research.

Franciscan order in 1822 and was ordained to the sacred diaconate on June 14, 1828. He briefly accompanied Guatemala's Archbishop Casaus y Torres to Havana during the Archbishop's forced exile in 1829 but returned to Guatemala in 1831 to initiate measures leading to his secularization and to serve as a parish priest.[12] In 1835, González Lobos left Guatemala for Tabasco, Mexico, due to his impoverished condition and "to soothe an unhappy mother." He worked for fifteen months in Mexico before returning to Guatemala, "his country," a half year prior to the Carrera insurrection.[13]

González Lobos served as a parish priest in the zone of insurrectionary activity, Guatemala's eastern highlands. He was licensed to minister in Santa Rosa, on February 3, 1838, and later in Jalapa, in August 1838.[14] One month after his assignment, González Lobos was accused of performing religious services outside of his assigned parish area and working with the insurgency. Antonio Larrazábal, at that time the Vicar General of the Catholic church, when notified of González Lobos' conduct, initiated a legal procedure against the priest within the church. Five government soldiers were brought to testify against González Lobos.

The first soldier, Lino Morales, a twenty-year-old, unmarried Nicaraguan who had accompanied Morazán's troops, was captured by Carrera's guerrillas on August 15, 1838. Morales declared that while in captivity he heard González Lobos saying mass in the principal doorway of the church in Jutiapa on August 19, 1838, and also said that González Lobos performed mass and baptized children in Santa Rosa. Morales was later transferred to Mataquescuintla, and there saw González Lobos baptize a child. Margarito Martínez, a sixteen-year-old Guatemalan and Federal soldier, confirmed Morales' version of events. He had also witnessed González Lobos performing mass in Santa Rosa. Sebastian Hernandez, a twenty-five-year-old Guatemalan, was also captured in Jalapa and was a

12. Carlos Alfonso Alvarez-Lobos Villatoro, "Doctor Francisco González Lobos," in *Revista de la academia guatemalteca de estudios genealógicos, heraldicos e históricos* no. 8 (1983), 193-94. A copy of Francisco González Lobos' ordination paper to the sacred diaconate of the Franciscan order is located in AHAG 1828.180, Box T1 100.

13. Francisco González Lobos to Provisor General, January 1837, Guatemala, AHAG 1837.9.1, Box T1 81. This particular correspondence enables us to deduce that González Lobos was originally from Tabasco, Mexico, since he went to be with his ailing mother. How and why he went to Guatemala in 1822 to begin his ministry with the Franciscans is unclear. After fifteen months in Mexico, he felt more at home in Guatemala, and returned toward the end of 1836.

14. Promotor Fiscal, "Francisco González Lobos," Guatemala, September 1838, AHAG 1838.108.4, Box T1 83. See also the clerical listing of 1849 and 1862. The record is not clear on González Lobos' pilgrimage from January 1837, when he was assigned to Patulul, until August 1838, when he was assigned to Jalapa.

personal acquaintance of the guerrilla priest. Hernandez confirmed, along with two additional soldiers, that González Lobos had performed mass in Jutiapa.[15]

Additional evidence implicated González Lobos. A printed circular written by González Lobos directly tied him to Carrera's insurgency. The circular, written to the inhabitants of Antigua, was from the "Army of Liberation and Protector of Order and of Religion Commanded by General Rafael Carrera," and signed by González Lobos. In this particular pamphlet, González Lobos tried to assuage the fears of Antigua's residents who found themselves under siege, asserting that Carrera's troops were not barbarians, thieves, and rapists, but honored men who cherished public morality.[16] In the battle of Villa Nueva, September 9, 1838, where Carrera's troops were forced to retreat, Federal forces captured a logged book of military orders that had thirteen pages signed by the priest. Portions of the book were copied into the trial record and showed that González Lobos, who signed as Major General, had given general orders and rules of combat.[17]

In a passionate and intimate letter to Francisco González Lobos, Antonio Larrazábal, the Vicar General, confronted the guerrilla priest "as a companion who cherished him immensely and was concerned for his spiritual and worldly welfare." Offering González Lobos a way out of his legal difficulties, Larrazábal told González Lobos that he understood that "unfortunately, the enemy took over territory in your parish and you were pressured to turn your services over to the caudillo Carrera against your wishes and to abandon your parish." Larrazábal expressed dismay at the difficulties facing González Lobos since he had embraced this political party. "God has given you more than adequate instructions to understand."

Larrazábal assured González Lobos of absolution if he were to abandon Carrera. Larrazábal called on him to repent and to distance himself publicly from the caudillo, particularly for the benefit of the state of Guatemala. As Larrazábal affirmed, the state of Guatemala "looks at you as one of the principal agents of its terrible sufferings. The government does not doubt that the priestly influence encourages and sustains and pushes forward the most perverse plans within a class of people who are not sufficiently capable of discerning just from unjust, truth from lies."

15. Promotor Fiscal, "Francisco González Lobos," September 7, 1838, AHAG 1838.108.1, Box T1 83.

16. Francisco González Lobos, *Antigueños* (Guatemala: September 2, 1838), AHAG 1838.108.5, Box T1 83.

17. Antonio Letona [Promotor Fiscal], "Francisco González Lobos," Guatemala, September 1838, AHAG 1838.108.9-12, Box T1 83.

Pushing his point further, Larrazábal confronted González Lobos' involvement in the insurrection.

> You know, my companion, that our Divine founder of our Holy Religion would never allow his ministers to take part in the sedition of the people. Our inheritance, given to us before he ascended to the heavens was the conservation of the peace. And our Lord reprimanded [Peter] the head of the church who attempted to defend the Christ with the sword. Suffering, humility, and patience of the faithful were the only powerful weapons that shined forth in the most flourishing age of Christianity, and the most fertile seed in propagating Christianity was the practice of these virtues.[18]

Adding his voice to a historic theological debate within Christianity, Larrazábal attempted to persuade the minister to use peaceful means to further the goals of the church's missions and to dissuade those prone to violence. Larrazábal's choice to condemn Padre Lobos' involvement in the rebellion rather than provisionally to accept the rebellion as a just struggle suggested the Vicar's elitist protection of the status quo.

In a strange turn of events, a possible peace accord, to be established through a negotiated settlement in December 1838, pushed the Federalist president and military leader, Francisco Morazán, to write and ask for González Lobos' assistance. Morazán wrote Catholic authorities requesting them to issue González Lobos the necessary license for the priest to aid in the pacification of the people of Guatemala. Larrazábal conditioned his permission on a face-to-face talk with González Lobos.[19] But then the renegade leader of Los Altos, Agustín Gúzman, wrote Larrazábal, attempting to pressure the Vicar to drop his demand that González Lobos go to the capital. Rather, Gúzman asked Larrazábal to allow González Lobos to minister to Carrera's troops so that peace could be established in the Mita district. Gúzman commented that it was necessary to have someone at Carrera's side who was dedicated to peace.[20]

In his own correspondence to Larrazábal, González Lobos assured the Vicar that he had always been true to the Catholic faith. If his actions had detoured from canonical law, "it was due to human nature." He had

18. Antonio Larrazábal to Francisco González Lobos, Guatemala, 1838, AHAG 1838.108.7-8, Box T1 83.

19. Francisco Morazán to Antonio Larrazábal, [1838], AHAG 1838.108.13A, Box T1 83; and Antonio Larrazábal to Francisco Morazán, Guatemala, [1838], AHAG 1838.108.13B, Box T1 83.

20. Agustín Gúzman to Antonio Larrazábal, [1838], AHAG 1838.108.18, Box T1 83.

joined Carrera's forces in order "to aid the unhappy and the disgraced."[21] In partial fulfillment of Larrazábal's demands, González Lobos published a letter to Carrera's soldiers clarifying his role in the insurrection on November 6, 1838. Acknowledging that they had fought for the well-being of the people, he said it was now time to pursue these goals by peaceful means. In an amazing clarification, González Lobos admitted that "God had never wanted his dogmas and precepts to be understood or to be supported with the noise of a cannon or with the edge of a sword. Religion is pure and loathes all violent means. If you believe that religion and our country are motives to impel us to a blood battle, be aware: religion rebukes bloodshed and enjoys peace."[22]

González Lobos additionally called on the insurgents to pressure General Carrera to achieve peace through a mutually benefiting treaty. González Lobos' diplomacy evidently succeeded since the Treaty of Rinconcito was signed a month later on December 8, 1838. In this treaty, Carrera tactically surrendered, returned to Mita, and became the area's recognized district chief in return for peace. González Lobos was formally given permission to accompany Carrera to the Mita district to ensure Carrera's fulfillment of the peace treaty.[23]

In his formal petition for absolution, González Lobos confessed that he had joined Carrera's troops but explained that he did so because of a series of events that he could recount only orally to the Vicar. González Lobos evidently told Larrazábal that he had been pressured to serve the caudillo for fear of losing his life to Carrera's hordes. He admitted, however, that though his intentions were always just, he could not guarantee that he had not committed some "irregularity" in his participation with the insurrectionary forces.[24]

To what extent had González Lobos truly distanced himself from Rafael Carrera in the final and uncertain year of the insurrection? Had the famed guerrilla priest denied, even lied about, his involvement with Carrera and his role as major general? Or had he tactically distanced himself from Carrera in response to pressure from the Vicar? All evidence points to two conclusions. First, González Lobos had not severed his relations with the

21. Francisco González Lobos to Antonio Larrazábal, Santa Rosa, 28 January 1839, AHAG 1838.108.21-2, Box T1 83.

22. Francisco González Lobos, *A los gefes oficiales y soldados del General Rafael Carrera,* Mataquescuintla, November 6, 1838, AHAG 1838.108.20, Box T1 83.

23. Promotor Fiscal to Francisco González Lobos, February 10, 1839, Guatemala, AHAG 1838.108.25, Box T1 83.

24. Francisco González Lobos to Antonio Larrazábal, Guatemala, 1838, AHAG 1838.108.24, Box T1 83.

caudillo, Carrera. Carrera followed through on González Lobos' advice to negotiate a key treaty in December 1838. In all likelihood, Carrera would have been crushed or his forces reduced to insignificant bands if he had not had time to retreat and recuperate. Carrera was quick to call on González Lobos again. The priest was offered the position of Major General in June 1841 but declined because of his obligations to the church.[25] And second, González Lobos surely misinformed church authorities as to his real involvement with Carrera. His equivocal stance guaranteed him a certain, immediate measure of professional security but, in the long run, undermined the famed priest's integrity in future conflicts with the church hierarchy.

The Price of Power

A second trial against Father González Lobos reflected not just the continuity of a strong relationship between the caudillo and the priest but pointed to some of the social and economic problems brewing among Carrera's supporters that led to political rancor in 1844 and eventually to civil war in 1847. A land dispute resulted in the murder of an indigenous leader from San Pedro Pinula, located on the eastern fringes of the capital city, in 1842. The leadership of San Pedro Pinula wrote the Vicar of the Catholic church accusing padre Francisco González Lobos of murder. Their *jefe político,* Juan Ventura Vicente, they claimed, had died at the hands of the famed guerrilla priest.

The indigenous community's version of the incidents which led to Vicente's untimely death told how Francisco González Lobos arrived at San Pedro Pinula in response to a denouncement made by the town officials concerning the Indian principal, Juan Ventura Vicente. According to the leaders of San Pedro Pinula's indigenous *común,* on February 5th, Francisco González Lobos arrived to celebrate the patron saint, and in a drunken state, called Juan Ventura Vicente and other indigenous leaders together and denounced Ventura Vicente. González Lobos, therefore, removed forcibly the jefe político's staff and hit Vicente three times in the head and broke the staff in the process. In the melee, Francisco González Lobos then ordered Juan Valdes to stab Vicente. González Lobos then ordered Juan Ventura Vicente, now almost dead, taken to the plaza and executed. The *común* of San Pedro Pinula said that González Lobos subsequently ordered

---

25. Santos Carrera to Senior Minister of Supreme Government, Guatemala, June 14, 1841, AHAG no. 23, box T4 62.

the town's Indians, including women, to be put to death. So the entire indigenous community took to the mountains to escape death.[26]

Antonio Larrazábal ordered an immediate investigation into the charges and through the testimony of some people closely related to the events, was able to uncover a few more details of the murder. In Larrazábal's eyes, these witnesses were "honorable, accredited, and did not pertain to the plaintiffs or were not involved with the parish priest, Francisco González Lobos." The first witness was Vicente Cerna, the future military leader of Chiquimula, and Carrera's successor to the Presidency in 1865. Cerna informed Larrazábal that Juan Ventura Vicente, who held the community's staff, had been threatening order with his large groups of Indians. After discussing the particulars with Carrera, Francisco González Lobos was ordered on February 2, 1842 to "repress and make an example" of Juan Ventura Vicente and the rest of the mountaineers. Cerna explained that González Lobos sat on the order and did not act.

Two days later, on February 4th, Juan Ventura Vicente went to the convent with twelve Indians and González Lobos asked him "by what authority do you carry that staff? Why did you say that no one has authority over you? And why did you say that the town officials were a bunch of thieves?" Cerna said that Ventura Vicente denied the accusations. González Lobos continued: "Why do you go around saying to the people that they shouldn't obey their priest, but only you?" Ventura Vicente defended himself, saying that he had been appointed to oversee their land.

At this point, Cerna recalled how González Lobos lunged toward Ventura Vicente and grabbed his staff, and a riot broke out between the soldiers and the Indians. Ventura Vicente was subdued after being hurt in the head, and was taken to the plaza. A shot was soon heard, and when the witnesses arrived at the scene, found Ventura Vicente shot dead, allegedly trying to escape. Cerna concluded his testimony that González Lobos was not drunk; he never gave an order to shoot Ventura Vicente, nor did González Lobos hit him in the head. The troops, affirmed Cerna, were very worked up by the Indian, Juan Ventura Vicente.[27]

Francisco Aragan confirmed Cerna's testimony with a revealing perspective. Aragan claimed that Ventura Vicente was stirring up the people (andaba revolucionando) and encouraging the people to only obey him.

---

26. Común y principales to Provisor Vicario Capitular, San Pedro Pinula, February 1842, AHAG 1842.13.1, Box T2 83; and Antonio Larrazábal, "Oficio," Guatemala, February 11, 1842, AHAG 1842.13.7, Box T2 83.

27. Antonio Larrazábal, "Oficio," Guatemala, February 1842, AHAG 1842.13.1, T2 83.

After the fight over the staff, Aragan said that Vicente Cerna took the Indian leader to the jail where he was shot while trying to escape.

Ygnacio Argueta recalled González Lobos asking Ventura Vicente why he promoted war against the Indians and Ladinos of Jalapa. Ventura Vicente responded that "he was empowered by an authority: he was commissioned in the name of the *común* of the people to be in charge of land disputes and land survey." When González Lobos tried to take the staff away from him, Juan Ventura Vicente resisted and was hurt in the scuffle, and later shot while trying to escape.

The tragic scuffle which led to the murder of the indigenous leader, Ventura Vicente, pointed to the extent to which the padre, González Lobos, complied with Carrera's desires in making an example of the rebellious leader, and reflected the degree to which Carrera was slowly isolating himself from his eastern supporters who had brought him to power on the wings of insurrectionary fury. The record also indicates that the ethnic conflict between mestizo and Indian fed part of the anger between the two parties. As Carrera and González Lobos proved, their combined authority was more than enough to deal with the popular challenge. The apparently popular interpretation among the indigenous people of San Pedro Pinula encouraged many to seek shelter in the mountains for fear of community-wide reprisals. Interestingly, the indigenous community appealed to the Vicar, Antonio Larrazábal, for divine justice against the perpetrators, but church officials supported the version of events put forward by the witnesses sympathetic to González Lobos.[28]

Yet the internal conflict between mestizos and indigenous peoples did not overshadow the external threat challenging the Carrera government from neighboring El Salvador. Barely five years had elapsed since the famed military caudillo from the eastern highlands of Guatemala, Rafael Carrera, had triumphed over his liberal enemies in 1839 and set in motion a series of events which led to the establishment and consolidation of an independent republic of Guatemala. Now, neighboring El Salvador threatened to reintegrate Guatemala into the Central American Federation through military intervention. During the events surrounding this 1844 military contest of wills, the Salvadoran president tried to entice the famed guerrilla priest, Francisco González Lobos, to join his forces in their goal to oust Carrera. González Lobos had served since June 1841 the Catholic parish in Jalapa, in eastern Guatemala — a potential battle line as Salvadoran troops entered on Guatemalan soil. In his response to the Salvadoran's invitation, González Lobos refused the entreaty, simultaneously

28. Larrazábal, "Oficio," February 1842.

reaffirming his loyalty to Carrera and his willingness to die for *la patria*. A priest accompanying the Salvadoran president, who identified himself as the "Vicar of the Army," tried again to convince González Lobos to join up with the Salvadoran forces to liberate the Guatemalan people from its oppressor. González Lobos curtly responded, "I am Guatemalan, I love my country and for her I will risk my life, especially when her rights are threatened."[29] González Lobos gave vent to his "irritation," caused, he said, by the enemies of his *patria* who committed wrongs in its sacred territory, and concluded that he hoped to see the invaders receive their just punishment. He had clearly taken "Guatemala" as the focus of his loyalty.[30]

Less than two decades later, the influential Guatemalan bishop, Juan José Aycinena, would cultivate a theology incorporating views not dissimilar to these popular sentiments expressed by González Lobos and other rural clerics in Guatemala. Aycinena reflected on Guatemala's covenant with God in an 1861 sermon commemorating Independence from Spain. Unscathed by the fires of Independence while firmly defending the faith of the Catholic church, he claimed Guatemala had been divinely chosen and protected like the biblical Israel, so long as it defended God's laws. Aycinena asked rhetorically,

> What more could a nation desire than what this magnificent promise offers? . . . Behold the reason why our Republic, being a Catholic congregation, has the right to appropriate the divine promise, and if we fulfill the divine condition — and time will tell — God will not change the rules: He will reward the good and punish the evildoers.[31]

Religious discourse during the Carrera years explicitly evolved an understanding of nation. Priests like Father González Lobos and Bishop Aycinena worked with both popular and elite discourse to ensure the nation as an ideological, theological, and political reality.

29. Francisco González Lobos, *Contestación* (Jutiapa: May 29, 1844), AHAG, Box T2 56.

30. Francisco Malespin, *Carta que dirige al Sr. General Presidente del Estado del Salvador, al Sr. Presbitero Francisco González Lobos* (Guatemala: May 24, 1844) AHAG Box T2 56; Antonio Letono to Francisco González Lobos, Guatemala, 1846, AHAG 1846.5.3 Box T2 91; Francisco González Lobos, *Contestación* (Jutiapa: May 29, 1844), AHAG Box T2 56; Manuel Serrano, *Carta del Sr. Vicario del Exército Salvadoreño al Sr. Cura de Jalapa Francisco González Lobos* (Jutiapa: May 24, 1844), AHAG Box T2 56.

31. Juan José Aycinena y Piñol, *Aniversario XL de la Independencia de Guatemala: Discurso religioso pronunciado en la Santa Iglesia Catedral el 16 de septiembre de 1861* (Guatemala: Imprenta de la Paz, 1861), 9-10.

Though the guerrilla priest survived the second trial brought against him, his penchant for military prowess pushed his rapport with church officials to the brink. Archbishop García Peláez was notified that González Lobos' name had appeared on Carrera's Army battalion list in charge of military operations. Soon thereafter, the Archbishop received a letter, May 1844, from González Lobos requesting that he be nominated as the Vicar of the Military *(Vicario Castrense)*. García Peláez chided him, saying that it was ridiculous to those who understood the meaning of the title originally given to the King of Cordestra, Spain: he subsequently denied the request.[32] During that fateful year of 1844, when many clergy distanced themselves from the caudillo, only González Lobos accepted the nomination as Chaplain of the Army. But as the year came to a close, even Father González Lobos admitted that the job was overwhelming for just one chaplain. Citing his deteriorating health, González Lobos resigned as Carrera's chaplain. Church pressures had taken their toll on the priest from eastern Guatemala.[33]

The Civil War (1847-1851)

By 1847, Carrera's charisma could not sustain his popularity. Though the caudillo had assumed control of the presidency by 1844, his regime tottered as disparate groups from eastern Guatemala demanded an end to the caudillo's arbitrary and opportunistic rule. Similar incidents to the death of the indigenous leader, Juan Ventura Vicente, had undermined Carrera's authority. When a prominent leader was executed for attacking Carrera's grain farm, eastern Guatemala exploded into revolt. The mestizo leader chose self-exile in Mexico while the political territory of Guatemala appeared to fracture into three separate states. Not until Carrera's return a year later and after prolonged war did Carrera reestablish control over Guatemala. His success in battle came through his appeal to large groups of indigenous peoples from the western highlands of Guatemala and from loyal mestizo supporters in eastern Guatemala.

To those unfamiliar with Guatemalan history, this civil war paints a

32. Francisco González Lobos, *Boletin Oficial del Exercito,* Guatemala, June 12, 1844, AHAG 1844.58.6, Box T2 86; Francisco González Lobos, Guatemala, 1844, AHAG 1844.58.3, Box T2 86; Francisco García Peláez to Francisco González Lobos, Guatemala, May 27, 1844, AHAG 1844.58.4, Box T2 86.

33. Francisco García Peláez to Francisco González Lobos, Guatemala, July 5, 1844, AHAG 1844.48.2, Box T2 86; and Francisco González Lobos to Francisco García Peláez, Guatemala, [1844], AHAG 1844.58.18, Box T2 86.

confusing picture. Ideological labels and political affiliations hardly capture the distinct fissures of conflict surfacing in the countryside. Infighting within the white Creole and nascent mestizo leadership led to the formation of multiple guerrilla bands. Indians, themselves divided by language, took advantage of the confusion within Ladino leadership to vindicate their local grievances against the Spanish-speakers and razed Ladino towns. And the church leadership mourned the apparently cyclical death and brutality that seemed endemic to the novel experiment of Independence.

Once again the famed guerrilla priest and ex-regular was causing problems for the Archbishop's besieged church. Now the famed priest was accused of fighting in battle on the side of the insurgents against Carrera's forces! Though testimony would clear González Lobos of this charge, his priestly ministry had become the source of conflict once again. Word had spread to the capital that González Lobos had participated in the battle of Patzum in July 1848 where Carrera's weakened forces fought victoriously over the insurgents led by Serapio Cruz. Prisoners brought to testify before church authorities presented conflicting and vague testimony, often hearsay, about González Lobos. One prisoner swore he saw González Lobos enter the fight and encourage other soldiers to enter into battle, while another saw the priest minister to the wounded only. Another witness saw González Lobos join Cruz's troops, remembered him carrying a gun, but also recalled the priest trying to head towards Carrera's troops, and officers detaining the priest. One prisoner heard the priest trying to lead troops but knew that the troops suspected him, and another witness recalled seeing González Lobos with a small gun, but remembered the priest trying to leave on horseback before he was captured by insurgent soldiers.[34]

González Lobos presented a well-thought-out defense which not only proved his case but humiliated (and thus angered!) church authorities. While pastoring in Panajachel (located on the western slopes of Guatemala City, González Lobos had to leave for fear of his life since Carrera had called on the Indian villages to attack the Ladinos. During this departure, Cruz's forces captured and detained him until the battle of Patzum. González Lobos claimed that he worked with the wounded during the action and had carried no weapons. He never was present in the actual fighting but removed to a neighboring village. He only held weapons while soldiers lit their cigarettes. González Lobos did admit, though, that Cruz offered

    34. Francisco García Peláez, "Para esclarecer," Guatemala, January 10, 1849, AHAG 1849.12.23, Box T2 98; Francisco García Peláez, "Mediante," Guatemala, February 19, 1849, AHAG 1849.12.18, Box T2 98.

him the head of a division, but he turned it down. To support his testimony, González Lobos presented his own witnesses who confirmed his defense; presented a letter from Cruz (the insurgent leader) who reiterated that González Lobos had only been detained because of his past connection to Carrera; and turned in an acknowledgment from the current Guatemalan president that no documents had been found linking the priest to Cruz.[35]

Church authorities concluded that most of the witnesses' testimony was hearsay yet the priest's confession that he did bear arms went against clerical law and precedent. Also, church authorities chastised González Lobos for the "disrespectful language" he used in his defense. He was sentenced to nine days of spiritual exercises in a convent.[36]

Indeed, the ex-regular was not known for his deference! The Archbishop and church authorities had no case against González Lobos. But their frustration with the priest was exhibited in their lengthening the judicial process against him. They were able to censor him by not providing him with the essential license to say mass and hear confession. González Lobos' penchant for conflict fundamentally challenged the hierarchy's understanding of the role of the priest in society. Born out of his pastoral ministry, González Lobos had ended up in the heart of battle. From the point of view of church authorities, he had sought out conflict and compromised the institution.[37]

35. José Maria Barrutia, Guatemala, September 24, 1849, AHAG 1849.12.36, Box T2 98; Serapio Cruz to Francisco González Lobos, Palencia, February 9, 1849, AHAG 1849.12.14, Box T2 98; M. Paredes, "Certifico," Guatemala, [1849], AHAG 1849.12.11, Box T2 98; Francisco González Lobos to Francisco García Peláez, Tuxtla, Mexico, July 21, 1848, AHAG 1849.12.5, Box T2 98. Francisco González Lobos to Francisco García Peláez, Guatemala, October 13, 1849, AHAG 1849.12.42, Box T2 98; and Francisco González Lobos to Francisco García Peláez, Guatemala, October 18, 1849, AHAG 1849.12.44, Box T2 98. In this correspondence, González Lobos made it known to the Archbishop that Carrera's brother, Santos, was partly responsible for the difficulty. González Lobos charged that Santos Carrera, in order to save his son, who had fought with the insurgents, persuaded Rafael Carrera that González Lobos had encouraged the people of Jalapa to fight Carrera's government. Evidently, as the letterhead indicates, González Lobos joined Rafael Carrera for a brief time in Mexico, and evidently patched up his questioned relationship with the caudillo.

36. José M. Barrutia, Guatemala, November 12, 1849, AHAG 1849.12.48, Box T2 98; and Friar Juan Zepada, Franciscan convent, November 25, 1849, AHAG 1849.12.50, Box T2 98.

37. Francisco González Lobos to Francisco García Peláez, Guatemala, September 21, 1849, AHAG 1849.12.37, Box T2 98.

Whither Faith and Politics?

There are few heroes of the faith in nineteenth-century Guatemala. Yet theologians and historians that work from a faith commitment in Christ know the weight and power of sin. To dream of breaking the shackles of economic and political domination became a part of the fiery vision of so many Latin American Christians during the latter half of the twentieth century. History does instruct us that the weight of past historical decisions does influence the present. The victory of Carrera heralded a new chapter in Central America: a non-white charismatic man rose to power on the back of a popular insurrection designed to counter the elitist drive toward a Europeanization of Guatemala. As Carrera's army grew in force, witnesses pointed to key allies in his brigade. Crucial to Carrera's success was Father Francisco González Lobos. The former Franciscan defied ecclesiastical law to be with his parishioners in the heat of battle, and to even work towards a just settlement of the conflict. González Lobos' commitment mirrored the commitment of so many other prominent Latin American priests whose authority grew out of his ministry with a marginalized people.

Historically, the "Republic" of Guatemala emerged in contradistinction to the United Provinces of Central America. This conservative regime, autocratically ruled, favored the institutional Catholic church. Yet the political autonomy experienced by these once marginalized peoples — both mestizos and Indians — even challenged the integrity of the organization of the Catholic church. Carrera, who evidently sought to protect clerics, like González Lobos, from the capital hierarchy, even demanded that "Guatemalans" elect their own bishop!

In December 1840, Rafael Carrera published an open letter attacking the church hierarchy's inability or unwillingness to fill the unserved parishes. Carrera was angered that church officials had suppressed a number of fiesta days. A part of Carrera's platform had been to protect the people's traditions, and now the institutional church was subverting his restorationist platform. Carrera proposed a nationalist, almost Protestant-like, church council in which the people could express their frustrations and where authorities could respond to their demands.[38] Though no formal action was taken in response to Carrera's letter, his dissatisfaction with the church politics intimidated the Creole leadership.

While the capital elite feared the eastern caudillo, priests like Gon-

---

38. Rafael Carrera, *Religion* (Guatemala: Imprenta del Exercito, December 1840), AHAG no. 12, Box T4 58. See also Antonio Larrazábal, *Edicto, con el breve pontificio relativo la disminución del número de dias festivos* (Guatemala: Imprenta del Exercito, 1840).

zález Lobos made Carrera's victory possible. Various clergy supported Carrera and his insurrection, and at least two died in the ensuing conflict. Father Aqueche, parish priest of Mataquescuintla, died after a prison confinement and Father Duran, who had previously served in Esquipulas, was executed by Morazán's troops.[39] A revolt inspired by the religious convictions of eastern mestizos radically challenged a centralist government run by the descendants of the Spanish Empire. The political and theological consequences of the revolt evolved over the next three decades.

Priests like González Lobos integrated themselves into a popular insurrection born out of their pastoral commitment to these eastern parishes. Most likely, these priests identified with the people who revolted, sensing the threat of loss of land and religion among their parishioners. Their local villages had been negatively impacted by the politics and economics of the last decade, and thus priests joined the mobilization without authorization from their religious authorities. Consequently, a new theology emerged in Guatemala. Strangely, a Protestant-styled covenant theology became popular within the next two decades with many in Guatemala City and in eastern Guatemala. Printed sermons indicated that "God had chosen Guatemala" and would protect it so long as its people guarded its religion. When El Salvador and Honduras threatened invasion in 1851 and 1863, historical evidence indicates that parish priests rallied the people to the defense of their "country" and volunteer armies quickly mobilized for the encounters. According to some of the Guatemalan clergy, history itself gave witness to Guatemala's favored status in the eyes of the Divine when Carrera's troops triumphed in these military actions.[40]

Such conclusions may be difficult to accept given the general focus on the majority indigenous population of Guatemala and the perennial conflicts between state authorities and Indian communities. Yet historical research shows that the emerging mestizo population in the eastern portion of Guatemala became the critical political force with Independence. Thus priests like González Lobos played critical roles in the creation of the understanding of the "Republic of Guatemala." As already discussed, this

39. "Necrologia," in *El Tiempo,* Guatemala, September 11, 1839, AGCA; and Rafael Carrera, *Memorias del General Carrera, 1837 a 1840,* edited by Ignacio Solis (Guatemala: Tipografia Sánchez y de Guise, 1906), 83. Lee Woodward, in his monumental *Rafael Carrera and the Emergence of the Republic of Guatemala, 1821-1871* (Athens: University of Georgia Press, 1993), cites six priests killed by Morazán's troops, four of whom were confirmed in this research.

40. For further information about sermons during the Carrera period, see Douglass Sullivan-González, "Religious Discourse and Nation Formation in Guatemala, 1839-1871," *The Americas* (July 1997).

notion of Guatemala necessarily challenged the integrity of the disappearing indigenous communities in eastern Guatemala. And like his Creole predecessors, González Lobos acted out of a similar ethnocentrism with regards to the indigenous peoples. To this day, Guatemala remains trapped by this bipolar world between Spanish speakers and indigenous peoples.

Inexplicably, González Lobos was pastoring among indigenous communities by the end of the 1840s when Civil War erupted. Since Carrera had unleashed the fury of his indigenous admirers against all Spanish-speakers, González Lobos had to flee his parish. Yet the famed guerrilla priest moved adeptly among all the groups in arms. He had built a strong reputation to be recognized and admired for his courage and his pastoral skills. Church authorities regularly recoiled against his lack of deference, but clearly, González Lobos had discovered the basis of a new spiritual authority among Guatemala's Spanish-speaking population. By the 1850s, scanty records exist concerning the whereabouts of Father González Lobos. Other than his broadsides printed during the Carrera insurrection and his correspondence with ecclesiastic authorities, Father González Lobos left only one theological tract published in the year of his death, a collection of prayers dedicated to the "Immaculate Virgin Mary, Our Lady of the Poor." Drawing on his Franciscan heritage for his final contribution to the faithful, González Lobos petitioned the blessed Mother of Jesus "to maintain the purity of faith within the Guatemalan Church, ensure the fear of God among the temporal authorities, bless her faithful people, pour out her riches over the poor, and give rest to the souls in purgatory." He evidently sought retirement in the cool climate of an Indian parish in the western highlands of Guatemala where he died in 1861.[41] His lived experiences serve as a historical marker for Latin American church historians and for social ethicists.

Politically, we learn that the Catholic church adjusted to new political circumstances with the fall of the Spanish empire and established a strategic alliance with the conservative government of Carrera. Clerics like González Lobos mediated the new relationship with the government and enabled the

41. Francisco González Lobos. *Novena a la Inmaculada Virgen Maria que bajo la invocación de Nuestra Señora de los pobres se venera en la Iglesia de N.S.P.S. Francisco de Guatemala* (Guatemala: Imprenta por L. Luna, 1861), 13; Carlos Alfonso Alvarez-Lobos Villatoro, "Doctor Francisco González Lobos" in *Revista de la Academia Guatemalteca de Estudios Genealógicos, Heraldicos e Historicos* no. 8 (1983), 193-94. In one last record in the Guatemalan Catholic archive, President Rafael Carrera allotted a monthly pension of 50 pesos to Father Francisco González Lobos due to his poor health. See Manuel Echeverria to Francisco García Peláez, Guatemala, March 28, 1856, AHAG 1856.101, Box T2 117.

church to articulate a vision of the nation, the new community that emerged in contrast to the liberal (and anti-Catholic!) federation of Central American states. Conservative Catholics achieved what liberal elite ideologues had dreamed: a popular and comprehensible vision of the nation distinct from the Spanish empire. Born of peculiar historical circumstances, the notion of the "Republic of Guatemala" became formalized during Carrera's rule. Theological convictions helped shape political realities.

Yet theological affirmations did not mediate the centuries-old conflict between Native Americans and the descendants of Europe. Nor did the Spanish-speaking mestizos bridge the ethnic divide in Guatemala. The death of the indigenous leader under the leadership of Father González Lobos proved that this new political force would repress when necessary any Indian who did not defer to mestizo leadership. The sins of the past could not be overcome and to this day fragment the nation. Though a theology emerged through the praxis of defense of the "patria," it could not bind the many into one. For the indigenous peoples of Guatemala, the elite — both Creole and mestizo — "invented" Guatemala, an alien community capable of harsh measures when not obeyed.[42]

42. Eric Hobsbawm and Terence Ranger, eds., *The Invention of Tradition* (Cambridge: Cambridge University Press, 1983), 1; and Eric Hobsbawm, *Nations and Nationalism Since 1780: Programme, Myth, and Reality* (Cambridge: Cambridge University Press, 1990). Hobsbawm wanted to uncover how dominant groups create a link with the past in order to legitimize the present through rules and rituals. "Historical novelty implies innovation" and the historian's task is to delve into the dynamics of this social invention (Hobsbawm, *Invention of Traditions,* 13). Ernest Gellner concluded that such innovation may imply the destruction of other communities. "Nations," added Gellner, "as a natural, God-given way of classifying men, as an inherent political destiny, are a myth; nationalism sometimes takes pre-existing cultures and turns them into nations, sometimes invents them, and often obliterates pre-existing cultures; *that* is a reality" (Hobsbawm, *Nations and Nationalism,* 10).

PART TWO

New Theological Questions in New Historical Situations

Neoliberalism and Christian Freedom:
A Reflection on the Letter to the Galatians

Elsa Tamez

RICHARD SHAULL has been prominent in Latin America for having shown us the liberating message of the Protestant Reformation. In this article, written in honor of his seventy-fifth birthday, my intention is to retake the fundamental themes of the Reformation found in Galatians and reread them in light of today's economic reality. Thank you, Dick, for all that we have learned from you.

Today the words *free* and *freedom* are in vogue, being applied more to things than to people: free market, pricing freedom, free trade, freedom to compete and to consume the preferred products. But as more freedom is given to the movement of objects, there is less freedom for human beings. There are those who are not free to buy because they do not have the means to do so, and there are others who believe they are free but are not because they buy what the market dictates. The more freedom there is for the market, the less freedom there is for human beings, more reification, less human identity. That Latin Americans are freer today to vote in elections does not change in any way the growing dehumanization, because the globalization that benefits some has a negative effect on most.

Today's situation leads us to restudy Paul's critique of the law, beginning with grace, and to ask ourselves how we can be free and live with freedom in our society, which is oriented toward economic, political, and cultural globalization. By deepening the sense of being free and the sense of freedom, we can better discern those processes of social, political, and economic freedom to which we are called as sons and daughters of God.

In Latin America during the last two decades we concentrated on doing theology in relation to the struggle for transformation from oppres-

105

sive economic and sociopolitical structures. We spoke about the historic practice of Jesus and the importance of following him in the building of God's reign. We did not pay a lot of attention to the specific women's, indigenous and black movements that also, from their perspectives, contributed to the analysis of society. Nor did we take seriously other categories, such as the body and day-by-day existence. Nevertheless this theology was in tune with economic and political processes in Latin America at that time and responded to those challenges. With today's recomposition of the world, we need to rethink our theological foundations.

Today the economic, social, political, and cultural situation is so bad that it is difficult to do theology with the same language that we used a few years ago. We would not be credible even if we included the support of specific groups. That theology is an advanced theology. The exclusion, dehumanization, fragmentation, and lack of global alternatives is so great that it leads me to think of the necessity of returning to basic elements of traditional Christian theology: the salvation of the human being given by Christ through the will of God. It is clear that this does not mean returning to the dualism between personal and social salvation or giving priority to one or the other. It means rereading the primitive kerygma in light of the message of today's situation, which is, "Every man for himself, every woman for herself." This is not an evangelical message, but "another gospel," a "different gospel." The soteriology proclaimed by the market does not save because there is no room for grace.

In this article we want to reflect on the meaning of Christian freedom in a society that proclaims itself free. We will take up only two points from Paul's letter to the Galatians: freedom from the present evil age and freedom from the law.

Christ has set us free from the present evil age (Gal. 1:4)

In the greeting of his letter to the Galatians, Paul includes one of the oldest christological formulas from the primitive tradition. Speaking of Jesus Christ, he writes: "Who gave himself for our sins to set us free from the present evil age, according to the will of our God and Father." In this brief christology we have freedom from the present evil age, God's design for freedom, and the mediation of freedom. The fundamental fact is the liberation of human beings from the present evil age. Many have understood this text in an individualistic, private, and dualistic way. God removes me from the material-world because it is evil. That kind of affirmation leads to irrelevant theologies and the rejection of political practice. What needs to be reread is the meaning of freedom and the present evil age, or the perverse world from which Christ frees us. If we speak of freedom, it is because some kind of oppression is being experienced. And that is evil. Paul contrasts two powers: Christ and the world, not the creation created by God but the perverse world that oppresses and enslaves. That is why he speaks of freedom. The affirmation that Christ frees us from the present evil age is foundational and universal, valid for the time of the Galatians and valid for our time.

For this message to be pertinent we must discern the evil of this age, this eon, for the times in which we live. Only then will the central soteriological message be more than a dogmatic formula that is adopted in a rational and private manner. The gospel of Jesus Christ is good news only when it becomes pertinent and generates a true metanoia: a change in life, attitude, and practice.

When there is more freedom for things and less for persons, we find ourselves in an evil age. If it is true that society, under neoliberal economics, prioritizes the freedom of the market for higher profits at the cost of actual lives of human beings, then the present evil age is today's free market society. It is not the market in itself, for all societies need the market. But today's market economy is guided by neoliberal policies which are not oriented by the criterion of life for all people. It enslaves and/or excludes members of society.

In Galatians 1:4 Paul uses the Greek word *exeletai,* "to free," "to liberate." He does not use here the Greek word commonly used for redemption. In Galatians he uses the figures of slave and free, so he could have used the term *apolyo,* "to rescue," "to redeem" used in other christological formulations (Rom. 3:24). *Apolyo* is a term that is used secularly for the buying of a slave's freedom. Thanks to the *peculium,* the rescue payment, the slave could take on the status of freeman. The use of *exeletai* strictly contrasts the status of free and the status of slave. Here in Galatians Paul speaks of liberation without the slightest stigma for former slaves. In fact, it echoes the liberation from Egypt when God pulled them from Pharaoh's grasp. The liberation which is alluded to in this christology is radical; it deals with human emancipation that goes beyond the social or the political. It is the realization of the right to be human, free from any kind of slavery or structure that diminishes human dignity or worth. It does not exclude politics and economy, but it includes a fundamental awakening of the consciousness of being a free person in a free community. This encompasses everything, including racism, sexism, despotism, even one's own self. The only thing that is excluded from this freedom is the freedom to enslave, to kill, or to diminish the dignity of others.

We Christians quickly avoid receiving the gift of being free subjects, masters of our own destiny. There is distrust of human frailty and fear of the power of sin to lead us in ways that are contrary to God's design. For this reason, we very quickly emphasize that we are free from sin and slaves for Christ. This is a legitimate concern. We humans are fragile and many times we do not know how to use freedom. However, if Christ frees us from the evil age to be his slaves, we cannot speak of the grace of God. For that reason, before we can come to such an affirmation, we must affirm the complete liberation of which Paul speaks in Galatians. To be free from the present evil age, is to discern this age, to distance ourselves from it, to critique it, and of course, not to allow ourselves to be carried away by unjust economic laws that are racist, patriarchal, excluding, and antihuman.

According to this very brief christology, the mediation of liberation occurs because Christ gave himself for our sins. This christology is among the oldest. Other letters use the formula that Christ "was handed over" (Rom. 4:25) or "God gave him up" (Rom. 8:32). "Christ, who gave himself for our sins" makes reference to his act of atonement. There is a clear Jewish influence in this formula because in Jewish thought the martyrdom of the righteous atoned for the sins of others. The phrase "for our sins" appears in plural, which is not a Pauline expression. Paul understands sin to be a power that enslaves (Romans). He, therefore, uses the word sin in its singular form.

We can ask ourselves then, how is it that when Christ gave himself for our sins, we were freed from the present evil age? It is a difficult question. We are accustomed to repeating dogmas blindly without any reflection about the possible profound significance they might have for the present. I think that the self-giving of Jesus Christ makes freedom possible because with his act of self-giving he intervenes with a different logic than the logic of the evil age. It is the logic of grace.

In a society of "every man for himself, every woman for herself," nobody is saved. There is no grace, no solidarity, no consciousness of being free. All who seek in this way to save their life, lose it. Since all feel condemned to seek their own good in order to save themselves, they condemn whoever gets in their way. Dominated by the logic of seeking for one's own salvation in a world of competition, we enter the world of sin, sinning constantly against our neighbor. In a society of each one for himself or herself, we all transform ourselves into sinners, even against our own will. To end this fatal logic, Jesus Christ, the human face of God, dramatically calls attention to a new logic unknown by the present evil age. A logic of grace, a logic of infinite love. This logic does not ask for more sacrifices because Christ took them on himself once and for all for everyone. We do not have to ask for the sacrifice of anyone, nor do we call for the sacrifice of those who sacrifice others. The sacrifice of atonement ended on the cross of Golgotha. The crucified body of Jesus on the cross shows what a society is capable of doing. The resurrection of that body demonstrates God's design for the crucified. In Galatians 1:1, Paul begins his greeting with the event of the resurrection of Jesus Christ by God. It is God's will that all of God's creatures and habitat be freed in the same way as the resurrection of the One whom society assassinated, because he gave himself for the sins of all men and women. Paul deliberately includes this christology in Galatians because he sees the danger that with the Judaizers' preaching in favor of the law, they forget they have already received freedom. For Paul, the Galatians have been freed from the present evil age and those local customs that enslaved them. Following the law could be a threat to the freedom that they already enjoy in Christ.

Christ freed us from the law; we establish justice by faith

What we have just reread above is in fact a christological formula that Paul includes in his greeting, and is closely connected to the central thesis of his letter: justification by faith and not by the law.

The problem within the Galatian community is that some are at the point of submitting to the requirements of the Mosaic law and circumcision to achieve God's justice: to be just and to be considered just by God and therefore saved. Motivated by this controversy, Paul rethinks the concept of salvation. For him it was fundamental that the law not be the essential criterion of salvation, but faith and God's grace. The interconfessional disputes over this point generally center on the marked difference between God and human beings (all of the initiative has to come from God because nothing good can come from the human being) or on the counterposing of faith and works. But Paul goes much deeper. He starts with a radical critique of the law in his society, showing that its very mechanisms tend to dehumanize persons and do not produce life (Gal. 3:21) or justice (Gal. 2:21).

Being Jewish, Paul criticizes the law. How was this radical change of interpretation possible, even to the point of placing antithetically faith and law? In the Hebrew Bible, texts are not found that contrast faith and law. To the contrary, they appear to be intimately related.

Maybe the life experience of Paul, as he lived on the periphery of the Jewish religious world, led him to consider the negative side of the law. As a Pharisee he zealously followed the law. To comply with the law he violently persecuted and arrested those who thought differently. He even approved the death of Stephen according to Luke in Acts. When God reveals to him that the Crucified One has been resurrected, he realizes that God was identified with the Crucified One, whereas Roman and Jewish law had condemned him. Justice had not come from the law (Gal. 3:21). The Roman law condemned an innocent man, Jesus Christ, to a cross. Jewish law cursed him who hung on the tree, and to Paul, Jesus is nothing less than the Son of God. Moreover, the law marginalized and excluded many of those who were not under that law.

The fulfillment of the law according to the letter, independent of the conscience, cannot be required for salvation. When the law is not written in the heart and the conscience together, it is easily manipulated. It becomes hardened into the letter of the law, institutions, and traditions, often turning against human beings. In Romans, Paul remarks that when the law joins with sin the consequences are lethal (Rom. 7:11).

When Paul recognizes the limitations of the law, he seeks to diminish the importance of the law and prioritizes another logic capable of seeing reality from the perspective of grace. He calls it faith, grace, or Spirit. This is stated categorically when he affirms, in Galatians 2:16, "yet we know that a person is justified not by the works of the law but through the faith of Jesus Christ. And we have come to believe in Christ Jesus, so that we might be justified by faith in Christ, and not by doing the works of the law, because no one will be justified by the works of the law."

In this text, Paul explains to the Galatians that they have already believed in the event of Jesus, therefore they have been justified. They have been freed from the law and for that reason do not need to submit themselves to the law. If they do so, they may lose the freedom they have.

The term "to justify" is not used much today. It is easier to understand its sense when it is related to the terms *justice, just, injustice.* To be justified by faith means that justice can be established independently of the law. Paul's theological explanation is that God, through the liberating life of Jesus Christ, makes them just by God's grace and transforms them into subjects who are capable of practicing justice. They can practice justice guided by their own consciences that have been renewed in Christ and not by the dictates of the law. This happens because of the gift of the Spirit (Gal. 3:5).

Now, if to the brief christological formula we have seen above we add the Pauline thought on justification, faith, and law, we have more theological elements in order to critically analyze our position towards "the present evil age."

The logic of the market reigns in our society as "each man for himself, each woman for herself." We are all trying to save ourselves following the rules of the law imposed by the neoliberal market society. We think that if we do not follow the rules, we are lost. And, in fact, when the market laws are fulfilled perfectly, without any kind of interference, many are left outside, including small- and even medium-sized producers. The rules imposed by the IMF and the World Bank seriously harm those sectors that need health care, education, housing, and price controls by the state.

From the beginning the law of supply and demand, for example, excludes the great majority who cannot meet its demands. The demands of consumerism are becoming greater and more frequent all the time, and the level of alienation for those who cannot consume deepens. Society becomes a dead-end street in which those who are excluded from the market seem to be abandoned by God.

To hear that we have been freed from the law in the sense of its enslaving, external logic is good news, not just for those in Paul's time, but also for those of us today who are living hectic, demanding, and self-destructive lives.

The gospel announces today that persons do not receive their dignity and freedom by fulfilling the law, but by God's grace and God's mercy for all humanity. Whoever submits to the law is a slave. There is no need of the merits that the logic of mercantile society demands in order to be considered a person. What is needed is to believe the truth that in Christ God became human, a free person, to show us the logic of faith by his own faith.

The faith of Jesus is the key for understanding the gift of justification. Traditionally it has been translated as faith in Jesus Christ. However, the phrase can also be translated as the faith of Jesus Christ. That is to say that the life of faith that Jesus lived is what made possible his own justification and justification for all. In the Gospels, Jesus followed the law when it was in favor of human life. He removed himself from the law and transgressed it when it became an enemy of human beings.

In Galatians 4:6 Paul uses the figure of the child of God. Just before this verse he has repeated again the christological event, "But when the fullness of time had come, God sent his Son, born of a woman, so that we might receive adoption as children" (4:4-5).

To be called a child of God is to be considered a person with dignity. The Roman emperors were to be called sons of God and were considered divine. The Jews also considered themselves children of God because of God's covenant with the people of Israel. But Paul makes it very clear that divine filiation comes by faith. In the christological event we see again the maximum solidarity of God, who takes on history in all its human dimensions: "born of a woman and under the law." Jesus unmasks the logic of the law by his faith. As can be seen, the liberation occurs from below and means the abolishment of slavery to the law and makes the slaves into free sons and daughters. Those freed from the law have their own voice. Before, the law took possession of persons and ruled over their lives. Now, they have become subjects, persons with a voice that cries "Abba, Father." God has infused them with the Spirit of Christ and has made them heirs by the grace of God.

We obtain the freedom that Paul speaks of in Galatians by consciously and decidedly receiving the gift of freedom from the present evil age and from the law that enslaves. The message is directed to all; there is no exception. The debate between Paul and his opponents was precisely that the non-Jews did not have a place within the people of God if they did not become circumcised. By declaring freedom from the law, the message is universalized and reaches all persons who want to walk according to the logic of faith or the Spirit. This logic, says Paul in Romans, is that which moves toward life, justice, and peace. For this reason we must insist that freedom is more than just freedom from the alienation of the law. In order to live together in freedom, human beings need a guide that always challenges them toward the constant renewal of consciousness and of practice. That is why Paul is clear that what is ultimately important is "faith working through love," the "new creation." Life lived in faith is not easy. The law is easier to follow than faith. That is why Paul has to talk about the necessity of being clothed with Christ, of living in Christ and as Christ. Taking on the faith of Christ will be the guarantee that we live the freedom of free sons and daughters and not return to being slaves of the present evil age or of the law.

The Christian freedom of which Paul speaks in his letter to the Galatians is totally opposed to the freedom offered today by our society. To evangelize today in our society means to make the call to be free and at the same time to repudiate "the other gospel" proclaimed by the neo-liberal market economy.

"For freedom Christ has set us free. Stand firm, therefore, and do not submit again to a yoke of slavery" (Gal. 5:1).

Development and Inculturation:
A Christian Reflection on Modernization

PHILIP L. WICKERI

IT HAS NEVER BEEN EASY to determine where Richard Shaull belonged theologically. Where he was was not as important as where he was going. When I first met him the spring of 1968, a critical time for those of us involved in the student movement on college campuses, he spoke about the need to recognize the end of the road and the possibility of envisioning a new beginning in what we had thought was already a revolution in thought and action. The word "possibility" figured prominently in his speech. Although I did not realize it at the time, Dick's power to think anew came from his reappropriation of Christian faith, continually reinterpreted in a pilgrimage in mission which took him from North America to Latin America and back again.

In the course of this pilgrimage, he has been particularly interested in the communities and movements of hope which have emerged among the young, the poor, and the marginalized. In these social movements, Dick has borne witness to the vision of Christ, the power of the Spirit, and God's continuing call to conversion and transformation. His interest was never academic. And so, as he helped us to understand and define what he termed "the new ecumenical" situation, he would never allow us to think in the abstract or in isolation. Instead, we were pushed to consider what our reflection might mean for our own struggles, and for the concrete situations of those around us. Only in this way could our life, in some imperfect and incomplete way, indicate the possibility of God's redemptive purpose.

Over the last twenty-five years, this perspective has continued to challenge and inform my own pilgrimage in mission. For most of this time,

113

I have been living and working in and around China, following the tremendous changes which have been taking place in the society of this nation, working with the church as it has reemerged from a time of isolation and repression, and in the process, trying to discover how Christian life and mission in one particular part of our world relate to the broader ecumenical situation for our time. For the past twelve years, I have been on the staff of the Amity Foundation, where a good part of my work has been trying to discover what a Christian perspective on modernization means for issues associated with social development in China, and for the current ecumenical situation. It is out of this situation that I am called to address the issue of modernization.

The Question of Modernization

In Europe and North America, "modernization" has become something of an old-fashioned concern, displaced by more fashionable questions associated with "postmodern" capitalist societies. I have no objection to the "postmodern" quest, providing it is understood as the context for a certain sector of liberal intellectuals. Indeed, this may prove to be a creative area of exploration for a contextualized European or North American theology.[1] But this is not an area of theological inquiry which can or should be universalized. As the recently concluded World Food Summit has again shown, the issues of modernization and development are more relevant to the needs of most of the world's population. Modernization, therefore, is a far more important concern for a theology which can respond to the aspirations of the poor and the marginalized.

Questions associated with "modernization" and "modernity" have posed problems for Christianity, on both practical and theoretical levels, since the time of the Enlightenment. Within both ecumenical and Catholic Christian communities, modernization is most directly concerned with two related sets of issues: those associated with mission and development on the one hand; and those related to contextualization and inculturation, on the other. These two sets of issues are not often treated together, but it is important for both that they should be, for their interaction can be mutually enriching and theologically suggestive.

1. This is the argument of the Indian Catholic theologian Felis Wilfred in "The Postmodern with Teeth: Opportunity for a Creative Western Theology" (unpublished manuscript, 1994). This paper was kindly referred to me by Georg Evers of Missio, the German Catholic Mission Institute.

The first set of issues is more concerned with *society*[2] and social ethics, with the ways in which Christianity is experienced and lived out in the economic, political, ethnic, and gender structures of a given context. Development is most directly related to the socioeconomic aspects of modernization, but, as we shall see, a Christian perspective on development goes deeper than that. The second set of issues is concerned with *culture*[3] and theology, with the way in which Christianity is articulated and expressed, in theology, liturgy, and ecclesiology. Inculturation is more concerned with the "nontangible" aspects of modernization, but it must also address the basic socioeconomic realities. Of course, culture and society cannot be divided so neatly, and that is precisely the point of departure for this paper. Our examination of the way in which the issues of development and inculturation are related to each other around the question of modernization seeks to contribute to a better understanding of the relationship between Christianity and modernization in the world today.

Questions about development and inculturation emerged in the encounter between Christianity and the developing world of Asia, Africa, and Latin America. Ecumenical discussion of development issues began in the 1960s and 1970s in the context of the debate over mission and development,[4] but this was in turn based on a discussion which started in the nineteenth century about the relationship between mission and evangelism, on the one hand, and education, medical work, and social service on the other. Should education and social service work be an independent aspect of Christian mission in its own right? Or should such activities be seen as an indirect form of evangelism? The discussion of inculturation grew out of the encounter between Christianity and culture in the missionary and ecumenical movements.[5] This encounter is as old as Christianity itself, but questions of indigenization and contextualization were given new urgency

2. *Society,* for our purposes, will be defined as the aggregate of economic, political, ethnic, and gender relations among people in a given stage of historical development. This definition owes much to Marx and Weber, but it is supplemented by insights from contemporary social criticism.

3. I accept Clifford Geertz's definition of *culture* as "a system of inherited conceptions expressed in symbolic forms by means of which men communicate, perpetuate and develop their knowledge about and attitudes towards life." See his *The Interpretation of Cultures* (New York: Basic Books, 1973), 89.

4. A good summary is found in Richard N. Dickerson, "Development," in *Dictionary of the Ecumenical Movement,* ed. Nicholas Lossky et al. (Geneva: WCC Publications and Grand Rapids: William B. Eerdmans, 1991), 268-74.

5. The most comprehensive treatment of inculturation is from a Roman Catholic perspective. See Aylward Shorter, *Toward a Theology of Inculturation* (Maryknoll, N.Y.: Orbis Books, 1988), especially Parts III and IV.

as Christianity moved beyond the Eurocentric world of Christendom into the non-Christian worlds of Asia, Africa, and Latin America. The appearance of indigenous, contextual, or inculturated theologies, especially since the 1960s, reveals the wealth of theological and cultural resources which have become available for recasting the theological enterprise.

Development and inculturation issues do not presuppose a common understanding among all participants who are involved in the debate, but they do presuppose an interpretation of Christianity which does not begin and end with the question of salvation. However important the question "Am I saved?" may be to individual Christians and evangelists, this is not necessarily the primary question for Christians, nor is it the focus of Old and New Testament teachings. Developmentalists and contextual theologians agree that concerns about creation and redemption must be kept together, for theology is not so narrow as to be only concerned with the Christian community, especially in those parts of Asia where Christians are a tiny minority.[6]

This means that the issues of development and inculturation are associated with what Chinese researchers term "Christian culture," that is, Christianity as an aspect of culture and an object of scientific investigation and academic discussion. Symposiums such as the one organized in Beijing by the Amity Foundation and the Chinese Academy of Social Sciences in 1994 have tried to emphasize the common ground in academic discussions of modernization and development, regardless of the participants' religious or ideological viewpoints.[7] This helps to open up the question of modernization to a wider audience.

As a social and cultural phenomenon, Christianity has never been very consistent. Even a casual survey of Christian history reveals an inconsistent array of ideas, beliefs, and practices, all under the name of Christianity. In the present discussion, the point is not to talk about what is true and false in Christianity, but to speak about religion as a cultural system for which ideas about development and culture have a more general interest. Clifford Geertz's definition of religion as a culture system is relevant here:

> Religion is a system of symbols which acts to establish powerful, pervasive and long lasting moods and motivations in men (and women) by

6. This has been a concern for many Chinese theologians. See, for example, K. H. Ting, "Creation and Redemption," *The Chinese Theological Review* 8: 153-59.

7. The conference report is entitled *Christianity and Modernization: A Chinese Debate* (Hong Kong: DAGA Press, 1995).

formulating conceptions of a general order of existence and clothing these conceptions with such an aura of factuality that the moods and motivations seem uniquely realistic.[8]

Christianity, like all world religions, is part of the complex whole of human life. It supplements our view of the world, even as it tries to open us up to a vision of a different world. The theologian Paul Tillich once said that "religion is the substance of culture, and culture the form of religion." He may have overstated the case on the religious side, but he is suggesting an idea which is not very different from that of Chinese social scientists over the last fifteen years,[9] and it is also related to Geertz's more comprehensive definition.

Modernization and Development

Development may be briefly defined as the promotion of human well-being through social change.[10] As such, development is central to modernization, and one's approach to development has direct economic, political, and socioethical implications.

Since the 1950s, there has been a wide-ranging debate over the best ways of achieving development in Asia, Africa, and Latin America, with alternative approaches derived from capitalist and socialist theories, and alternative visions promoted by institutions as diverse as the World Bank and the variety of community-based nongovernmental organizations (NGOs) in the Third World. Although there has been general agreement on the need for capital formation, the enhancement of human technical skills, industrialization, and infrastructure in development, there has been wide disagreement on the strategies and priorities which are most conducive to general well-being and the promotion of a just development for all sectors of society.

Among Western and Third World NGOs concerned with poverty and development — and this would include most ecumenical Christian agencies — there has been the consensus that the impact of the world economic system in developing countries has been the single most negative factor

8. Clifford Geertz, "Religion as a Cultural System," in *The Interpretation of Cultures,* 90.

9. Essays on social scientific views of religion and culture may be found in publications of the Chinese Academy of Social Sciences, Institute of World Religions; Nanjing University's Institute of Religious Studies; and in a variety of other publications. Many of these have been translated in the *China Study Journal,* edited by Edmund Tang.

10. Richard N. Dickerson, "Development," 268.

on development in the Third World. This has become a kind of "progressive NGO neo-orthodoxy," and it has often resulted in a rejection of efforts which make use of development projects, social reform, and market-oriented strategies to foster social change, in favor of vaguely defined alternatives based on "conscientization," "solidarity," and "people's power." Here, I wish to dissent from this position, risking the gasps and snorts from my more conscienticized colleagues in Christian and development circles. I believe, quite simply, that they have put political consideration above the real concerns of the poor.

The arguments for what I have termed the "progressive NGO neo-orthodoxy" has been well summarized by my friend John Sayer, now director of Oxfam Hong Kong:

> (Many NGOs) hold the position that the single biggest cause of poverty, or impediment to development, is the global economic structure and its agents: the transnational corporations exploiting workers and natural resources; the World Bank and the IMF making the poor poorer with structural adjustment policies; the banks creating a debt problem with their loans; the bilateral and multilateral aid agencies creating dependency with their conditional aid; and the international trading conglomerates extracting wealth through unfair trade. The present global economic system, the argument runs, creates and sustains unequal relationships between nations.[11]

Sayer goes on to argue that this analysis — derived from the dependency theory popularized in the 1970s — needs to be challenged, especially in light of economic developments in East and Southeast Asia over the last decade. I agree. And so we may ask: Are the primary causes of poverty to be found in the internal conditions of developing countries rather than in the relationship between developed and developing countries? Do the newly industrializing countries (of East and Southeast Asia) offer the most convincing examples of widespread eradication of poverty following an export-oriented, capitalist model? Is it an inevitable pattern, for which there is no shortcut, that developing countries pass through a period of authoritarian government, and that the path to civil, political, and human rights lies in the attainment of a certain level of economic development? Does the legacy of "ultra-leftism" and the strategies of market-oriented reform in China have any lessons for other parts of the world? Should we accept

11. John Sayer, "Pursuing Change: The World of Development Agencies in the 1990s" (unublished manuscript, April 1994), 1.

that the overwhelming amount of human productivity, leading to improved economic situation of the poor, is achieved by those millions who find some niche in the existing, competitive, chaotic, market-oriented economic system? Is it time to end our ambiguous attitude towards capitalist growth and the world economic system and make it clear that we see our job as critical engagement with economic forces as they exist?

This line of questioning suggests that the unique achievements of capitalism cannot be overlooked, particularly the fact that capitalism releases individual creativity and organized cooperation in development. For many Western and Third World NGOs, what is needed is a critique of "anti-capitalist romanticism"[12] which overlooks the need for building up a society's material base. More than fifteen years ago, Bill Warren argued that

> Contrary to widespread populist-liberal opinion, the Third World has not been marked by stagnation, relative or absolute, in the postwar period. On the contrary, significant progress in material welfare and the development of the productive forces has been made, in an acceleration of prewar trends. The fact also runs counter to current Marxist views, which have stressed the alleged impossibility of vigorous national development in the Third World within a capitalist framework.[13]

It is very easy for progressive NGOs to jump to a wide-ranging critique of the world economic order rather than focus on the prosaic day-to-day work of helping people improve their socioeconomic standing in *real existing* society through the successful completion of concrete projects. It may seem more relevant and "progressive" to be involved in development issues in terms of social critique rather than working on particular projects or building up social structures. Critique is, of course, essential, but the purpose of social criticism should be to suggest alternative strategies and new ways forward. In development work, the focus should be on results more than process, and on action and reflection more than the issuing of prophetic statements. Development means a great deal more than socioeconomic modernization, but modernization remains the basis of what most of us do most of the time in development work, and it has an important bearing on relationships between development agencies in the North and the South.

12. The term is from Bill Warren, *Imperialism: Pioneer of Capitalism*, ed. John Sender (London: Verso, 1988), 7.
13. Warren, *Imperialism*, 252.

This means that we will always be dealing with compromises and proximate solutions. As Michael Walzer has written in another context: "The promised land is not utopia; it is just a better place to live than Egypt." To say that the achievements and continuing importance of capitalism cannot be rejected, is not to deny the need for reform and restructuring. The market is not a panacea for all social problems, and capitalism need not be endorsed as the best form of political and economic organization. Moreover, although it may be most important for development agencies to concentrate on a given society's internal problems, basic contradictions in the present world economic order remain. Capitalism has a role to play, but questions of social planning and resource allocation associated with socialism are also important. And it is precisely at this point that the experience of China over the last fifteen years needs to be studied for its broader significance on issues associated with modernization and development.

China is attempting to use market mechanisms within an overall socialist framework. This has been a central premise in Deng Xiaoping's "socialism with Chinese characteristics." Although many questions remain as to what this will mean for Chinese society over the long term, and particularly what will happen to the public sector of the economy, there have been widely recognized achievements in social development in China since 1979. The reforms have improved living standards for all sectors of the society, even though new questions have emerged (about internal migration and the ecology, for example) in the course of the reforms.

It has been our experience in the Amity Foundation that concrete development projects, with specific but limited development goals, have a far greater effect on poverty alleviation than do outside programs aimed at changing the ways in which people think about poverty and development. For small NGOs like Amity, building up a society's productive base should take precedence over the "postmodern" critiques of development and modernization which focus too exclusively on consciousness raising, "fundamental change," and nontangible aspects of social transformation. It is for this reason that Amity concentrates on projects in integrated development, involving well-digging, irrigation, medical training for rural doctors, supporting education at provincial teachers' colleges, all of which address poverty alleviation in a specific and concrete way. The nongovernmental sector has an important role to play in this regard, as the society moves away from a centralized approach to economic and social policy.

By focusing on China's poorer areas, Amity efforts have also helped to address some of the new problems which have arisen with China's modernization, for example, the gap between rich coastal areas and the poorer hinterland; the ecological impact of development; and the need to encourage popular efforts to deal with social needs that used to be handled by the government. On a broader level, studies such as *Poverty and Development: A Study of China's Poor Areas* by Yan Ruizhen and Wang Yuan[14] indicate the positive effect that government policies of reform and openness have had on China's poorer areas. The approach to development and modernization in this volume is similar to the one which has been suggested here.

In a short essay, the most we can do is suggest an approach to development and modernization which is relevant for this context. The discussion which I have introduced here raises a variety of questions which need to be pursued elsewhere. The point is to indicate a general approach to development as a basis for further discussion of our theme.

Development in Christian Perspective

Development issues became a special focus of ecumenical Christianity beginning with the 1966 Conference on Church and Society in Geneva. The development question was further highlighted at the Uppsala Assembly of the World Council of Churches (WCC) in 1968, and the formation of the Commission on the Churches' Participation in Development (CCPD) in 1970.

Beginning in the 1970s, there was a growing recognition that earlier ecumenical conceptions of development were inadequate. The new perspective combined perspectives on economic growth, self reliance, and social justice. Although there was no unified ecumenical perspective on development, this new perspective argued that:

(1) The traditional understanding of development was too narrowly focused;
(2) There was a need to emphasize what happens to *people* in the development process. The focus could not be entirely on structures;
(3) There is not necessarily a harmony of interests between rich and poor;
(4) Typical measurement of development (emphasizing GNP and per capita income) is inadequate because the poor receive a disproportionately modest share;
(5) Many national and international structures reinforce injustice (partic-

14. Yan Ruizhen and Wang Yuan, *Poverty and Development: A Study of China's Poor Areas* (Beijing: New World Press, 1992).

ularly affecting the poor, women, and minorities). This meant, for many Christians, that liberation was a better term than development;
(6) Development puts an enormous strain on the environment. Thus, environmental side effects of development projects need to be more seriously considered;
(7) Top-down (or trickle-down) development is inadequate. There should instead be an emphasis on "people's participation" in developments, and on the creation of "justice, participation and the integrity of creation" (JPIC).[15]

This ecumenical perspective had a positive impact on the churches' response to development in the 1980s, by calling them to a greater sense of responsibility for the whole world *(oikumene)* in which we live; by criticizing the existing social systems with which most churches in the West and the Third World were inextricably linked; and by emphasizing the priority of *human* concerns in any Christian approach to development. These concerns are important not only for Christians, but for all people who are interested in issues of development and modernization.

However, there will also be a particular Christian perspective on development which will overlap with, but not be identical to, the broader agenda of society. Just as there is a "common ground" between Christians and other people of good will within a given society, so there are "reserved differences" which are essential to any Christian understanding of development. These differences have to do with questions of motivation, community relationships, and the interpretation of development and Christian participation.

1. Christian Motivation

In Geertz's definition of religion cited above, religious symbols are said to "establish powerful, pervasive and long lasting moods and motivations in men (and women)" which cause them to believe and act in certain ways. On one level, Christianity is about what moves people, what enables people to hold fast to ideals, what empowers people to transcend their own individual interests to act in ways that enhance the general good. This is what makes Christian motivation significant for development work.

There is a Chinese saying to the effect that religion motivates people to do good. Similarly, the Christian motivation for participation in development is based on an ethical apologetic which is derived from the Bible and inspired by the teachings of Jesus Christ. This has been interpreted in

15. Dickerson, "Development," 270-71.

a variety of ways, depending on theological orientation, context, and historical situation. Space does not permit us to spell out all that this means in Christian understanding, but there is a wealth of literature to identify the key elements of a Christian social ethic which motivate churches and individual Christians to participate in social development.

The reason that Chinese theologians have emphasized love as God's primary attribute is also relevant for our understanding the Christian motivation in development work. In his foreword to the recently published *Theological Writings from Nanjing Seminary,* K. H. Ting writes of the importance of Jesus Christ as the revealer of God's love:

> The reason we say that Christ is the revealer of God's love is that in reading the four Gospels we are so deeply moved by his kind of love to the end for men and women that no lesser description can be sufficient. In him humankind received an insight into the way the highest reality in the universe exists by loving. The first attribute of this existence is not so much his coercive power and might . . . but this love to the end. Love is the first factor in the universe, the mover in the work of creation. A universe of love is in the process of being formed. We are still uncompleted products of the process but at the same time co-creators with God.[16]

Love is both the key to reality and to the human experience of God, and human beings are called to become co-creators with God in the process of creation. God's work of creation, redemption, and sanctification cannot be separated, and God's love becomes the link which holds them all together. The emphasis on God's love in the ongoing process of creation, redemption, and sanctification constitutes a very powerful religious motivation for Christian participation in society. It calls upon Christians to respond in kind to the needs of their fellow human beings, whether or not they are believers (cf. Matt. 25:31-46), and this becomes one way of expressing what it is to be a Christian. Love has always been an important motive for the Christian mission,[17] and as for Christian involvement in development work, it may be the most important motivation.

16. K. H. Ting, "Foreword" to *Theological Writings from Nanjing Seminary,* translated in *The Chinese Theological Review* 8: 4-5.

17. See for example J. van den Berg, *Constrained by Jesus' Love: An Enquiry into the Motives of the Missionary Awakening in Great Britain in the Period Between 1698 and 1815* (Kampen: Kok, 1956). Also David Bosch, *Transforming Mission: Paradigm Shifts in Theology of Mission* (Maryknoll, N.Y.: Orbis, 1991), 286-91.

2. Christian Relationships

Christian communities are built on relationships of faith, hope, and love. Faith commits, love unifies, and hope inspires. In terms of Christian participation in development work, Christian communities are first and foremost communities of historical and this-worldly hope.

The "system of symbols" which Geertz speaks of in his definition of religion is authorized and structured by a given community of faith. The second aspect of the Christian approach to development is concerned with the Christian community, the church, and the relationships it established between men and women in a given context and within the wider world. The church can be both an agent of development on its own terms, and part of a broader international ecumenical network of churches the world over. The church is a social organization and part of the society in which it stands, but it also has its particular religious dimension and international dimension, making it a complex social and cultural entity.

In almost every country of the world, the church has served an important function in promoting and sponsoring development work. Churches have pioneered in educational, medical, social service, and welfare work since the nineteenth century, especially through mission work in Asia, Africa, and Latin America. The political implications of church involvement in these areas has been justly criticized, especially in those areas where colonial expansion went hand in hand with the Christian missionary endeavor. However, the contribution of the churches in such diverse areas as higher education, publishing, the promotion of women's rights, and medical care for all have been recognized around the globe.

Since the 1950s, it has been increasingly recognized that the Christians of a given country are the best interpreters of the mission of the church in their own particular situation and context. The Three-Self principle of Chinese Christians was pioneering in this respect, but there are now similar understandings among ecumenical Christian communities all over the Third World. This movement has been associated with theological understandings of indigenization, contextualization, and inculturation. Structurally, this has been termed a church-based approach to mission, and it means that Christians from overseas should not set up mission boards or Christian institutions in areas where the church is already present without consultation with the local church. This has become axiomatic in the ecumenical movement.

It was also in the 1950s that churches in many parts of the world became interested in development work, and it was natural that churches and church agencies became both the sponsors and initiators of development projects. Today, churches are involved in development work in almost every Asian country, and their work is supported by substantial contributions from ecumenical development partners in Europe and North America. European development agencies have been especially important in this regard, channeling government development funds to NGOs in the Third World. Although there may be a declining pool of resources for church-supported NGO development work in the 1990s, the network of relationships which have been established for this purpose will continue to be important for ecumenical Christian communities.[18]

All of this suggests that relationships within the Christian community are central to the churches' involvement in development work, both nationally and internationally. The local church is an agent for development, not only as one social organization among others, but as a community of hope which is founded on faith in Jesus Christ. Moreover, as part of a broader informal international network, the church is involved in programs shared with the global Christian community. And as a social organization within its own country and society, it is in the best position to judge and evaluate the participation of international Christian organizations engaged in development in its own context.

3. Christian Interpretation

Religion is not only concerned with motivations and relationships, but also with interpretation, in Geertz's words, with "formulating conceptions of a general order of existence and clothing these conceptions with an aura of factuality." These conceptions are interpreted by men and women within the believing community, and they become authoritative for the believers' understanding of reality.

There will be a variety of Christian interpretations of development, but there are also common elements within the ecumenical Christian perspective, as indicated in the seven points outlined at the beginning of this section. In a recent essay on the subject, an Indian theologian placed holistic human development at the center of the theological concern:

> Theology, the *logos* about God . . . has to do with the whole of creation, because Christians believe that the God who created order out of disorder

18. See Jenny Borden, "Government Funding and the Ecumenical Sharing of Resources," *The Ecumenical Review* 46 (July 1994): 311-15.

had a purpose, and this purpose has to do with the welfare of human beings.[19]

He goes on to argue that just relations among people is the focus of development (Amos 5:24; Isaiah 1:17; Micah 6:8; and *passim*), and self-reliance the goal of development. Justice and self-reliance are interpreted in opposition to unjust relations and dependency.

One could cite other essays written on theology and development with very different interpretations of what development means. Some church organizations see development primarily as a *praeparatium evangelicum,* a prelude to preaching the gospel, planting the church, and conversion. Other church organizations have particular theological interpretations, for example, opposition to contraception and abortion, which limit the ways in which they are prepared to take part in development programs. And, as was noted above, some Christian groups are so preoccupied with the question of individual salvation that they ignore the question of development altogether.

It should be obvious that certain Christian interpretations of development are more conducive to cooperation with those outside the Christian community than others. In the example cited above, there should be no religious or ideological reason why progressive non-Christian Indians should not accept the author's conclusions about the focus and goals of development, even if they disagree about the ways in which he interprets these goals and arrives at his conclusions. Indian Christians are a tiny minority on the subcontinent, but they are still an integral part of the society. As with religious believers in any society, they need a certain sense of autonomy and independence, both structural and ideological, in order to formulate their interpretation of development.

This autonomy and independence will be beneficial to society, for it will encourage the participation of Christians in the broader social process and it will allow them to make their own unique contribution to social development. There will, of course, need to be dialogue between Christians and non-Christians over the focus and goals of development, but the participation of Christians in this discussion will be enriching, not constricting. As society develops and modernizes, there will be a richer pool of people to participate in the development process.

A Christian perspective on development — which has here been described in terms of Christian motivation, relationships, and interpretation —

---

19. Gnana Robinson, "Christian Theology and Development," *The Ecumenical Review* 46 (July 1994): 316.

can only emerge from a church which is prepared to identify with the needs and aspirations of the broader society, and at the same time, maintain its distinct identity as a people who believe in Jesus Christ. It is at this point that society and culture interact, and that Christian participation in development becomes a question of inculturation.

Development and Inculturation

One of the reasons that development and inculturation have been artificially separated in academic discussions, is that the two have often been cast as antithetical to each other. Socioeconomic development, in this line of thinking, is concerned with modernization, which is conceived in an overly centralized top-down approach. Socioeconomic development, therefore, is best left to governments, corporations, banks, and the United Nations. In contrast, questions associated with culture concern not the future but the past. Theologians and the churches should content themselves with issues of cultural preservation, and leave the questions of development to the professionals.

Such an approach is entirely at odds with a perspective on development which emphasizes the promotion of human well-being through social change. Culture has a direct bearing on human well-being and social change, and it is therefore an important part of any discussion of development. It may be the proximate purpose of development organizations to contribute to socioeconomic modernization, but they will also have an understanding of what kind of modernization is implied, and what modernization will mean for the men and women involved in the development process.

Religious culture, including Christian culture, is not to be destroyed in the development process, for it is part of the fabric of human society. Moreover, culture can become a positive factor in shaping a development perspective and promoting socioeconomic development. According to Aylward Shorter,

> What is required in integral development is integral human development. It is not sufficient simply to improve material conditions or standards of living through development aid. What is required is to change people's hearts, to give them a confidence and a pride in themselves and an openness to one another.[20]

20. Shorter, *Toward a Theology of Inculturation,* 243.

Shorter continues to say that culture may help people to adapt to social changes, and confront the dehumanizing effects of some aspects of development and modernization. Culture can also help people to adapt to new circumstances and to learn more about what is needed for development. Culture, moreover, can help people cooperate with one another in order to improve their situation and contribute to human betterment.

This is why inculturation is so important for Christianity, not only for societies where Christians represent a minority, but also for the societies of European and North American Christendom. Inculturation means more than the *accommodation* of Christianity to a particular social and political milieu. It is different from *indigenization,* which has a view of culture which is too static and backward-looking. Inculturation goes deeper than *contextualization,* with its emphasis on historical particularity and social change, and its preoccupation with present realities.[21] Inculturation means the incarnation of the gospel in a particular culture, in a way which gives new direction to the culture, "so that it becomes a force that inspires culture, gives direction and effects renewal, thus giving rise to a new reality not only in a particular culture but enriching the universal church."[22] It is a term which applies to all levels of human development, and one which has become especially important for theological thinking in recent years.

One way of approaching inculturation is by drawing on the distinction which Clifford Geertz makes between the *force* and the *scope* of a cultural pattern. This distinction applies not only to religion, but to any symbolic system which orders human experience. By "force" he means the thoroughness with which a symbolic pattern is internalized in individual personalities:

> We all know that such force differs between individuals. For one man, his religious commitments are the axis of his whole existence . . . he is god-intoxicated, and the demands flowing into everyday life from religious belief take clear precedence over those flowing from any other source. . . . For another man, not necessarily less honestly believing, his faith is worn more lightly, engages his personality less totalistically; more worldly, he subordinates other forms of understanding to religious ones less automatically and less completely.

21. For a comparison of inculturation and other similar terms, see Peter Schineller, *A Handbook on Inculturation* (New York: Paulist Press, 1990), 14-24.

22. From Nicholas Standaert, "The Fascinating God: A Challenge for Modern Theology Raised by a Text on the Name of God Written by a Seventeenth Century Chinese Student of Theology." Licentiate in Sacred Theology Dissertation, Fujen University, 1994, 1-2.

In the latter case, *force* is less prominent than *scope*. *Scope* refers to "the range of social contexts within which religious considerations are regarded as having more or less direct relevance." Scope is concerned with the breadth of religious understanding, the areas of life in which religious meaning can be applied. Although force and scope are related in every religious believer, they are not the same thing. In religious situations where "force" is dominant, beliefs may be very fervent, but also narrowly conceived. Geertz's example here is Islam in Morocco. In contrast, where scope is dominant, religion is seen to affect every area of life, though in a more worldly way, and the example he cites is Islam in Indonesia.[23] More generally, "force" predominates in all expressions of religious fundamentalism, while "scope" is more emphasized in religious liberalism.

For the Church, inculturation means the transformation of both the force and the scope of Christian faith, and it initiates a movement beyond fundamentalism and liberalism. Force is redirected insofar as faith is opened up in new directions, and broadened by questions facing the society and culture as a whole. The scope of inculturation is expanded in the process. Enlarging the scope of religious belief may mean decreasing its force, narrowly conceived, but it also means drawing on that life-giving force in the movement of individual and social change. Such change is impossible without the force and fervency of belief, and it is this force which moves people. Inculturation helps the church take its place as an authentic expression of culture, in all its force and scope, thereby influencing all other cultural constructs — inspiring, giving direction, and promoting renewal.

Inculturation is already suggested by the term "Christian Culture" which has been popularized in China in recent years, a term which, as we noted above, reflects an understanding of religion as an expression of culture. In this respect, Christianity is not a set of dogmas and beliefs, but a living and breathing reality, with an identifiable social base, a cultural reality which has important international implications, not only for the Christian community, but for the society as a whole. The term "Christian Culture" came into the Chinese lexicon in the 1980s as a positive reevaluation of Christianity, in contrast to the negative interpretation of all religion as construed by Chinese Marxist-Leninist orthodoxy. In conclusion, I want to suggest one way in which the *force* and *scope* of "Christian Culture" helps to bridge the gap between inculturation and development in the Chinese context.

---

23. Clifford Geertz, *Islam Observed: Religious Development in Morocco and Indonesia* (Chicago and London: University of Chicago Press, 1968), 111-13 and passim.

Christianity has grown very rapidly in China in over the last two decades, and it has become a movement which represents a significant social force in many rural areas. And yet, similar to Christian movements in other developing countries, the basic educational level among rural Chinese believers has remained quite low. As Christians, we may say that the rapid growth of Christianity in China shows that the Spirit is moving to reshape individual lives and particular communities, so that they embody the hope which comes from a new life in Christ. This is a positive movement of inculturation. But as Christians we may also admit that the growth of Christianity in its present form reflects the underdevelopment of rural China, and this suggests the need for greater attention to the issues of development which we have been discussing here.

Chinese social scientists have correctly observed that rural Christians have at best a rudimentary grasp of the basic tenets of Christianity, and a weak cultural and intellectual foundation. Chinese Christian leaders tend to agree with this analysis and they have therefore identified *"raising the 'cultural level' of rural Christians"* as an important area of concern for the Church. This expression may sound odd or even patronizing to Western ears, for it seems to suggest an implicit elitism in the relationship between well-educated urban Christians and their poorer counterparts from rural China. In some respects, it does indeed indicate the differences which exist between urban and rural Christians in China, and we shall return to this point shortly. But there should be no romanticizing of the experience of Christians from rural China because their lives, their beliefs, and their worldview also reflect their situation of poverty and underdevelopment. There is, therefore, the need to relate rural churches to the broader issues of church and society, and in this sense, raising the "cultural level" of rural Christians means deepening their grounding in basic Christian belief, encouraging them to work for social development, and increasing the *scope* of their involvement in church and society.

Raising the cultural level of rural Christians is first and foremost an educational concern, and the church is in an ideal position to carry out the task. In some parts of China, Christian converts are often illiterate. In Shenyang, for example, up to sixty percent of the Christians in some areas are formerly illiterate women. Churches organized literacy classes to teach the women to read the Bible, and now many of them can read, not only the Bible, but also other things as well. There are similar examples from churches in many other parts of China, and indeed, the world over. Raising the cultural level of illiterate Christians helps to make them both better Christians and better citizens.

The development of inculturated liturgies may be another way of raising the cultural level of the Christian community, and it also serves an educational function. Liturgy no less than the sermon has been a teaching device in the church for at least two thousand years, and it encourages Christians to learn by heart large sections of the Bible and basic Christian doctrines which are used again and again in weekly worship. Moreover, an inculturated liturgy can help protect the local church against heterodox tendencies and what has been termed outside "infiltration" aimed at undermining the local Christian community. If a church has its own liturgy and form of worship, Christians will be less susceptible to the manipulations of poorly educated itinerant evangelists and those who might wish to use Christianity for their own purposes. Liturgy helps to provide for worship done "decently and in good order" and it teaches the importance of structure, response, and cooperation. In this sense, an inculturated liturgy may have an indirect impact on the structure and attitudes required for the broader development needs of a society.

Rural churches in which most of the congregation are new believers may place undue emphasis on the question of individual salvation, to the exclusion of other dimensions of Christian existence. There may be a great deal of *force* in this interpretation of Christianity, but inadequate *scope* for a more complete Christian witness. As a result, local churches may not understand the social dimension of their faith, nor will they see themselves as potential partners in social development. Raising the cultural level of rural Christians helps to introduce the broader implications of Christian faith and promotes a more active development role. This has been encouraged through programs of education and Bible study, and serves as an important dimension of Christian outreach. In encouraging church-sponsored social service projects, the Amity Foundation is also helping to develop a Christian concern for development.

But the *force* of the experience of rural Christians also needs to be taken seriously, and this is something which is often overlooked by well-educated urban Christians. The fact that Christianity has established itself as an authentic religious movement in the Chinese countryside has important implications for inculturation and development in the Chinese context. For example, experiences of physical and spiritual healing, similar to those of Christians in other parts of Asia, Africa, and Latin America, have been well-documented by Chinese and foreign researchers.[24] Although this has often led to exaggerated claims and heterodox tendencies within the rural Christian community, these experiences cannot simply be dismissed.

---

24. See, for example, Alan Hunter and Kim-kwong Chan, *Protestantism in Contemporary China* (Cambridge: Cambridge University Press, 1993), 145-52.

Indeed, they have been formative for many churches, and provide an introduction to the faith for many Christians.

It is important to listen to what rural Christians are saying about themselves, and to learn how they interpret the ways in which Christianity has changed their lives and enriched their communities. For it is the *force* of the Chinese Christian experience which provides the motivation, the sense of community, and the interpretation of the world which are basic to Christian existence. Without this *force,* they would not be Christians in the first place. Before moving to a critique, it is first necessary to discern what is authentic about the experience of Christians from rural areas and to discover how this may represent a genuine movement of spiritual renewal which is of value for the Church as a whole.

Scope without *force* can become sterile and enervating, just as *force* without *scope* can be narrowing and irrational. The challenge for the Chinese Church is to recognize the spiritual force of rural Christianity as it tries to enlarge its scope of understanding. The Spirit always creates communities of hope in unlikely places, among the young, the poor, and the marginalized. The scope of the Spirit's activity is universal, but the gifts of the Spirit have a force all their own. It is the task of the church to discover ways of using these gifts which will be conducive to inculturation and social development.

Church and Society —
Or Society and Church?

WALDO CESAR

Introduction

Two extraordinary moments, in the second half of the twentieth century, one hundred years after the definitive establishment of Protestantism in Brazil, stand out in the history of the church. The first begins in the middle of the decade of the fifties, and extends until the military coup of 1964. The second has fully developed in the nineties and gives every sign of a vitality that could cross over into the next millenium and be a part of it for many decades. The early stages of both of these movements, as well as their later development, are not restricted to rigid periods of time, defined by the generations who lived through the contradictions out of which these movements grew. In the forties, some efforts of church renewal, originating principally in youth movements, contributed to the development of a daring ecumenical project during the decade of the fifties, generally known as *Igreja e Sociedade* (Church and Society). And the systematic and astonishing growth of neo-Pentecostalism that is taking place in the nineties must be traced back to its origin in the arrival of Pentecostalism in Brazil at the beginning of the century.

There are marked differences between these two movements. There are also some similarities, if we take seriously the social and cultural — and religious — context which in many ways favored, or opposed, both a greater commitment of the church with Brazilian society and the emergence of popular religiosity of a charismatic type. Old labels are often applied to these manifestations. To the first, progressive and ecumenical; to the second, alienating and separatist. Reason vs. emotion, secularity vs. religious

133

fanaticism. These and other classifications, however, do not even apply exclusively to any distinction between these two forms of religious experience and of confrontation with the world. Nor is it a matter necessarily of opposition, which distinguishes a theological vision of society, with history and tradition, from an ecclesiology directed toward the day-to-day struggle of the masses of disinherited. This being the case, I will attempt here to indicate the circumstances which contributed to the appearance of these remarkable moments in Brazilian ecclesiastical history and the relations between them as well as their importance for providing another perspective for the analysis of Brazilian reality. By this I mean, how have the Protestant churches, including the Pentecostal churches, predominantly turned in upon themselves, situated themselves in the context of Brazilian reality? And vice versa: how to evaluate movements of renewal in these churches starting out from a *secular* perspective, that of the church as a sociological entity which is attempting to break with its limitations or traditions and respond to the reality around it, whether this be through a structural vision of the social process or through actions directed toward the day-to-day struggle of the poor for survival?

Thus the questions being raised refer both to the movement during the fifties, called "Church and Society," and to the expansion of neo-Pentecostalism during this last decade of the century, which we will call "Society and Church." It is a matter, essentially, of indicating the contrasts and the similarities, in many ways *produced* by the society in which both moments are situated, the one centered more on a theological vision of reality and the other oriented toward creating an intense religious experience which aims at changing the life of the individual and, as a consequence, society itself.

Many sociological and theological implications follow from events of this nature. The research, theses, articles, and books produced over the last few years, both inside and outside of ecclesiastical circles, in Brazil and abroad, demonstrate the historical, social, cultural, and religious importance of these movements — the first marked by the military intervention in national life, and the second by the reconquest of democracy and the freedom of expression and of meeting.

These are factors that must also be weighed in this attempt at an evaluation on our part, along with the parallelism between situations generally seen as more or less isolated phenomena but which in reality are permeated by the ecclesial context, with all the contrasts and divisions which characterize Brazilian Protestantism.

I. Church and Society

Early in 1955, on the initiative of Richard Shaull, then a professor at the Seminary of the Presbyterian Church of Brazil, and myself, a "Commission on Church and Society" was created in Rio de Janeiro. The ecumenical composition of this group was quite representative of the theological and ideological differences that characterized the diverse branches of Brazilian Protestantism. In the Commission that was organized, there was, however, a general agreement that the churches should establish criteria for, as well as forms of, action in face of Brazilian reality, although there was no unanimity as regards the scope and the nature of the work to be developed. Autonomous when first organized, this Commission, during its first year of existence, became a part of the Evangelical Confederation of Brazil (CEB), an organ of interdenominational cooperation made up of the six principal historical evangelical churches in the country, and was given the name, "Sector of Social Responsibility of the Church."

It was my task, as executive secretary of this new organism, to promote the program mapped out by the Sector. In a short time, the evangelical currents that supported this new project (which gave a new lease on life to the CEB, an organism that was more or less stagnant at that time) extended beyond the number of churches associated with the Confederation. Even representatives of Baptist and Pentecostal churches, while maintaining an informal relation with the Sector, supported the idea of assuming a greater commitment in relation to Brazilian society. In a short time, however, the first difficulties, ideological and institutional, arose. We were exploring paths until then unknown or rarely trodden by the evangelical currents in the country. This dialectic between values and structures (in the words of Roger Bastide) oscillated between the commitment with important sections of Brazilian society and the reactions of the more conservative wing of the churches officially associated with the CEB.

We can better assess the dimensions of these internal conflicts if we recall the themes chosen for the four national consultations sponsored by the Sector between 1955 and 1962. The thematic evolution expresses a process of commitment which grew as the national crisis grew, hesitating between profound "basic reforms" and the return to the old oligarchies. If the first consultation (1955) dealt in general terms with "The Social Responsibility of the Church" as a program of study and action, the second (1957) was more specific, speaking of "The Church and the Rapid Social Changes in Brazil."

One of the most daring manifestations of this period of change was the construction of the new capital of the country — Brasilia — a city that arose where before there was nothing, in the geographical center of the national territory, built by the hands of more than thirty thousand workers. When signing, in the open air, the first official act on the spot chosen for the location of the future capital, the president, Juscelino Kubitschek, made a declaration that seemed more than anything else like a promise of a religious nature: "From this central plain, from this solitude which will very soon be transformed into the 'brain' of the most important national decisions, I cast my eyes into the tomorrow of my country and I foresee this dawn with unbreakable faith and a confidence in its great destiny that knows no limits."

In 1960, when the new metropolis was inaugurated and some social reforms were introduced, with many of the leaders of the Left occupying key positions, the Sector of Social Responsibility of the Church held its third consultation. The theme explored "The Presence of the Church in the Evolution of Nationality." Alongside of representatives of the Brazilian evangelical churches and leaders of the World Council of Churches, who gave financial support to the project, this meeting counted on the participation of sociologists and educators who were not Christian. This novelty, which on the one hand provided new arguments for those opposing the Sector, on the other hand opened new paths for a more comprehensive analysis of Brazilian reality.

Christ and the Brazilian Revolutionary Process

The last consultation took a leap forward not only thematically but also geographically, which gave it great importance. The previous meetings had taken place in the Rio–São Paulo axis, until that time the political and cultural center of greatest influence in the country. But this meeting occurred in 1962, a time of growing tension in the face of the advance of social reforms and popular movements, among which the Peasant Leagues (Ligas Camponesas) stood out. The Northeast of the country, with one third of the population of Brazil, was the symbol as well as the reality of the struggle between the past and a possible future in which the ownership of the land would not be in the hands of a few landlords. The popular slogan of the time was *reform,* for the more moderate, and *revolution* for those who believed in the radical idea of a single movement of "evolution of Brazilian nationality."

Thus the city of Recife, capital of Pernambuco, in the heart of the Northeast, was chosen to be the site of the fourth national consultation. Present were 167 delegates from seventeen states, representing sixteen denominations. The theme made the headlines of the newspapers of the city and had repercussions in Rio and São Paulo: "Christ and the Brazilian Revolutionary Process." It also echoed, even more strongly, in those evangelical circles not in conformity with this type of Christian witness, above all because it focused on a region in which all the contradictions in Brazilian reality appeared to be present. Recife, with a population at that time of 800,000 inhabitants, had 200,000 unemployed and 70,000 prostitutes, including children as young as thirteen years of age. The daily struggle of people for survival was most evident both in the speeches and the debates, with interaction between social scientists and theologians. Among the distinguished sociologists and economists present were Gilberto Freyre, Celso Furtado, Paulo Singer, and Juarez Brandão Lopes. Joao Goulart, the president of the country who would be deposed two years later, sent a telegram of congratulations. The Governor of the State of Pernambuco was present at the opening session of the conference and listened to the sermon of the president of the Sector, the Reverend Almir dos Santos, who interpreted the meaning, for that moment, the words of Luke 4:18: "The spirit of the Lord is upon me because he has sent me to preach good news to the poor, that is, to the economically disinherited." Other authorities in both the church and the state were present, including a representative of the commanding officer of that Military Region, responsible for "national security" in the Northeast. For the first time, a consultation organized by Protestants in Brazil was dealing with the controversial diversity of confrontations that were becoming more and more radical between popular movements, social institutions, the church, and the armed forces.

The "Conference of the Northeast," as it came to be known, marked the beginning of the end of the Church and Society program. Later we learned that the organs of security of the state accompanied daily all that was said and done in the conference. For the military authorities, the headlines of the newspapers confirmed their suspicions about the subversive character of the meeting: "Christ present in the Brazilian crisis"; "Protestants propose a Christian revolution"; or the words of a Protestant bishop: "The church cannot live in conformity with exploitation."

Curiously enough, it was not at the Conference of the Northeast but rather at a meeting in 1960 in São Paulo, on a day when the meeting was in full session, that a man sought me out who identified himself only when we were alone, as he insisted on a private conversation. He was an agent of the feared DOPS — Department of Political and Social Order. He wanted to know what we were discussing and what we meant by this business of "the presence of the Church in the evolution of nationality." I asked him if he had much time at his disposal. "Why do you ask that?" And after a few moments, he added: "Of course I have time. But why?" To explain the meaning of the theme and the meeting I would have to begin with the prophet Amos, more than 700 years before Christ. "Why?" he asked again. Soon thereafter he interrupted me, saying that he was satisfied. He only wanted to attend the afternoon meeting but he warned me not to introduce him or mention our meeting. This showed that those responsible for the repression that would come with full force in 1964, were already investigating what was happening in a program that claimed to be engaged in studying Brazilian reality and giving a new meaning to the commitment of the church with Brazilian society.

Following the Recife conference, objections to the project Church and Society grew within the Confederation. Even before the Conference of the Northeast, the board of directors of the CEB had manifested their dissatisfaction with the theme and the poster and brochures promoting the meeting. In them, the phrase "Christ and the Brazilian Revolutionary Process" was superimposed over a diffused image of agricultural tools, on top of which a cross was hanging at one side. The vivid red background frightened the apologists for a message that would sound more tolerant, and made them get red in the face.

This attitude, coherent with the anticommunism that was used as a label for any attempt to bring about change, in the church or outside of it, uncovered a paradox: in none of the preparatory consultations of the Sector of Social Responsibility of the Church — and much less in the four national meetings — had the CEB permitted the presence of Roman Catholics. Marxists, yes; Catholics, no, although the former were not named explicitly. The fact is that renowned Marxist intellectuals participated actively in the debates of the social themes that constituted the programs of the conferences, in some of which they were present. How explain this type of tolerance? Did the polemical rancor against the Catholic Church, because of the persecutions of the past, have more weight than the fear of a possible victory of the Left? Something like this was perhaps hidden or made manifest — in the observation of one of the members of the board of directors of the CEB, pastor of one of the member churches, during a break in one of its official meetings in which I participated. He said, in my presence, and in a personal reference that was somewhere between naive and ironical, that the Confederation should not limit too much the activities of the Church and Society program: "After all, if the Left should win in the next elections, we will have Waldo there to defend us."

As the opposite happened, the persecution by the ecclesiastical authorities was ruthless. It began even before the coup. In the months immediately preceding the overthrow of the President of the Republic, Joao Goulart, toward the end of March 1964, when the victory of the repressive forces appeared more than likely, a purge began in the CEB, in the seminaries, in Protestant schools, and even in some local churches. My expulsion, alongside of three other executive secretaries, happened in this time of anticipation of the defeat of the Left by the military forces. Several years earlier, Richard Shaull had been asked to give up his chair at the Presbyterian Seminary. After all, his initiatives and activities in theological education, in preaching, in the student movement, in contacts with the Dominicans, in the ecumenical movement, in books and articles he published — all this was seen as "subversion" of theology and of the established order. And many of his students, and others who worked with him, would have to pay for their complicity in and support of the idea of a church closer to the poor and disinherited in the society in which we were living.

An Ecumenism Beyond the Churches

The ecumenical experience lived during the ten years of the Church and Society project had opened — or expanded — the circle of relations and activities among the branches of Protestantism in Brazil, churches that previously had hardly known each other or were limited to more or less superficial forms of cooperation. This experience also strengthened the international ecumenical dimension through the World Council of Churches and opened perspectives for nonofficial work with sectors of the Catholic Church. In addition, we were now more "free" to enter into contact with non-Christian people and institutions dedicated to what was then called the humanization of life through the participation of the people in the shaping of their destiny as Nation.

At the same time, the persecution was intensified and we were scattered. Many were imprisoned or went into exile abroad. This created a great vacuum of leadership, among people disposed to take on a new role in Brazilian reality but not totally prepared for it. The *popularization* of the church and of other social movements, which before the military coup appeared to be moving toward the attainment of power, suffered its greatest blow along what had appeared to be a most optimistic trajectory.

Little by little, however, attempts to struggle against a dictatorial regime were rearticulated. When the political-military restrictions were at their height, nongovernmental organizations began to make their appearance — the NGOs. All of them, though somewhat isolated, were engaged in social projects of support for deprived people. Almost all of these new expressions of struggle were inspired by the winds of renewal that were blowing in the ecumenical movement and the Catholic Church. The ecumenical proposal of John XXIII brought together, at the Second Vatican

Council, representatives of twenty-eight non-Catholic churches, with the objective of promoting "the union of Christians and the adaptation of the Church to modern times." In Medellín (1968), the Church declared its option for the poor (which was reaffirmed in Puebla in 1979) and prepared the ground for a more explicit formulation of the theology of liberation and the Base Christian Communities. These communities grew rapidly in the Catholic Church (it is calculated that the number of organized groups reached 80,000 in the country), and they enjoyed relative autonomy.

Thus the decade of the seventies, in spite of all the persecution, stands out as a time of alternative movements, in Brazil as well as in Latin America, which was also dominated by totalitarian regimes. The response to the North American missions, political-military and economic, with the support of multinational corporations and the new industrial class (at times favored by the rise of populist movements), took two different expressions: the organization of guerrilla movements, hoping to conquer imperialism by force of arms, and the NGOs — nongovernmental organizations as forms of mediation between foreign aid and the popular classes. With international support, the NGOs were able to survive thanks to their structure, which is flexible, open to change, at times somewhat ambiguous, and not always juridically established.

Through them also arose a new expression of ecumenism which, although somewhat *divided* internally, brought together indistinctly, persons from various churches, or from no church. Through this new experience, we gained a different dimension from that which confined us in confessional circles, leading us to cross, at times with astonishment, these "non-ecclesiastical roadblocks," in the words of Gustavo Gutiérrez.

This ecumenism beyond the churches, which was at the same time a manifestation of the struggle against the repression, had its most significant expression, if we might make this claim, in the establishment of the Editora Paz e Terra in 1966, on the initiative of Protestant and Catholic lay persons. Although watched closely by the dictatorship, this publishing house was able to publish works of theologians as well as Christian and non-Christian thinkers never before published in Brazil — Paul Tillich, Dietrich Bonhoeffer, Harvey Cox, Oscar Cullman, Roger Garaudy, among others. In this way, a new space was opened in which intellectuals and political leaders (I refer here to specific sectors) were able to discover allies in the world of the church and of Christian faith.

The review, *Paz e Terra,* was the motor that moved the publishing house. With almost 300 pages, the ten numbers that were published bimonthly with a printing of 10,000 copies contained articles from Brazil and other countries which emphasized the importance of "the dialogue and the humanism which make it possible for human beings to make the universe their home." The editorial in the first number reminded the readers that ecumenism, in its original meaning, spoke of the "inhabited world, which means home, land, city, family, the economy, politics." Among those who wrote articles for it were distinguished intellectuals of that time, those in other countries being contacted through correspondents. In the United States, this function was carried out by Richard Shaull.

At the beginning of 1967, I was arrested because of my work as Director of the review *Paz e Terra* and representative of ISAL (Church and Society in Latin America) in Brazil, along with other accusations of subversion. I was imprisoned and held in isolation for one week in a unit of the Army Police. That was followed by a process against me in the Military Justice system and a new attempt to imprison me in December of 1968, when I had already sought refuge outside of Rio. The situation became even more difficult for the survival of the review, which was forced to suspend publication in December of 1969. But the great new reality, in spite of all the ups and downs in a time of uncertainty, was this experience of fraternity based on justice and love as the fundamental elements of unity and commitment. And in this, the Christian community both distinguishes itself from and identifies itself with the world and those who struggle for a better society.

An Interlude

What would have happened if the coup of '64 had not taken place or if the Left had taken power? How would the conservative wing of the church have behaved in the face of the continuity of a movement that was leading a new process, both ecumenically and in relation to social and political reality? Everything indicates that the coup would have come, sooner or later. Or if not, probably the CEB and other ecclesiastical and para-ecclesiastical institutions would have decided, in anticipation of repression by the police and the military, to close down officially the Sector of Social Responsibility of the Church. This, however, would probably have meant its survival apart from the CEB, similar in character to the alternative nongovernmental organizations that were spreading across the country at that time.

In a certain sense, this is what happened. A group that was representative of various Protestant branches, alongside of Catholic brothers, founded the CEI — Ecumenical Center of Information — responsible for the monthly publication of a small bulletin providing national and international news that could encourage the network of persons and institutions dissatisfied with the authoritarianism in church and society. The CEI had substantial support of a committee organized in the United States, which began as a temporary *Ad Hoc Committee* but ended up continuing in existence for a number of years, during which time it promoted meetings of Latin Americans and North Americans in different cities of the continent. Here also we counted on the initiative and participation of Richard Shaull, then based in the United States as a professor at Princeton Theological Seminary.

We might say that the repression, by closing the public spaces of our action, opened new horizons of solidarity, put to the test because of their clandestine or semiclandestine character. The geographical spread of authoritarian regimes, occupying the Latin American continent, had as its counterpart an ample and courageous circle of people opposed to them who became more and more committed to the people and their suffering. The ecumenical horizon expanded into the *secular* realm, which at that time appeared to us more open and more courageous than the little world of the Protestant leadership. The relational sense of Brazilian culture (suggested by the anthropologist Roberto da Matta) was experienced as a newness of spirit and a new *praxis*. The critical reflection of Ernst Troelsche on the abandonment of cultural values by the Protestantism of his time (which also comes through in the theology of Paul Tillich) became much clearer at that time as the result of this immersion in a terrain which formerly divided our thought and action in society. But it is important to remember that this experience of new social relations and of companions who were not Christian, which also uncovered in the churches something that was unknown to them, was nourished by the expectation that the military coups, with all that they represented that was antipopular and antidemocratic, would be of short duration. But that was not the case. In Brazil, power in the hands of the military, passed along to four generals in succession, lasted more than twenty years.

This long and seemingly endless interlude marked profoundly my generation and the generation that followed, born under the sign of authoritarianism, of censorship, of official lies, of fear, of exile, of tortures, of death. We lost many companions, in Brazil and in other countries of Latin America. We spoke to each other in a low voice. We looked behind us to be sure that no one was following us. Culture, the arts, education, and public health suffered a setback that in many aspects cannot be made up for. Peasants, with a limited capacity for organization, were abandoned to their fate. The churches added to their historical divisions a more radical ideological component. Moreover, we began to ask ourselves what had been the meaning of a whole decade of hope for a better world, and if the type of option represented by the Church and Society project had really established paradigms capable of transforming, if not society at large, at least the churches from which it emerged and in which it developed.

Here we should come to grips with a complex problem. Now, more than thirty years after the Conference of the Northeast, the theses, articles, and debates indicating the historical interest in this period of study and action, have not yet dealt with an important question: whether the institutional structures and the form of the historical currents of Protestantism had — or have — real possibilities of incorporating a vision and a type of action directed toward a world of "rapid social change." This expression, current during the time of Church and Society, was out of line with the slow perception of the accelerated developments taking place around us, social as well as technological, nationally and internationally. It was not just the day-to-day happenings in our cities that surprised us with their arbitrary character and their violence. The news of the making of the first hydrogen bomb; the beginning of the space race with the first artificial Russian satellite, followed a year later by the Americans; the consolidation of North American hegemony over Latin America through the large amount of aid provided by the Alliance for Progress — all this weighed down on our heads as an inexorable destiny which appeared to call into question all our utopias of a free, independent, and democratic continent.

II. Society and Church

With the political opening, the restructuring of institutions and of life occurred as circumstances permitted. It was not an easy process, nor a rapid one. The vices of the dictatorship hung on for a long time and may not yet be totally eradicated. Nevertheless, twenty-nine years later, direct elections are once again being held; human rights are reaffirmed; political exiles are returning; and the spirit of citizenship is manifesting itself everywhere. However, Brazilian reality continues to be full of contradictions: one foot in modernity and the other stuck in the past. We have a new currency, on a par with the dollar, inflation is under control, but unemployment is growing and the distribution of income is one of the most unjust in the world. Poverty, hunger, and disease affect a quarter of the population of 150 million. Nearly twelve million Brazilians, those called the "without land," continue to be systematic victims of violence and segregation. These few indications of the great misery of a people who live in one of the richest regions of the planet highlight the daily weight of incalculable suffering.

A simple analysis of this list of inequalities — or a simple reading of the newspapers — carry us back frequently to the question of the fifties: And what about the church? How does the church relate today to society? Today, if we wish to take up again the historical picture of that decade, when we no longer have a project capable of bringing together the Protestant denominations, we should humbly recognize that the proposition *Church and Society* may express an inversion of terms and perspective. This is not a matter of playing with words but of how we look at our mission. We must start from reality to propose actions — as well as structures and forms — capable of giving some response to church and society. In the not-too-distant past, as we said, we started out from the church as it was, with the expectation of changing the world. Today we should speak of *Society and Church*.

Is there any indication that this perspective can be a viable one? As a matter of fact, the NGOs, with the extraordinary variety of issues they deal with and of social agents working in them, have, in many instances, an institutional and ecumenical structure that goes beyond the capacity of a program directly subject to ecclesiastical politics. But the issue is not just that of starting out from the churches. Efforts being made at present toward a united witness of the historical churches in Brazil, such as CONIC, the National Council of Christian Churches, which has been in existence for only a few years, do not have the social dimensions of the old project, Church and Society, and much less can it be compared, either institutionally or financially, with what is being accomplished by some NGOs. There exist still other organizations and churches, which are part of the extensive world of alternative experiences. One example is the AEVR, Brazilian Evangelical Association, a rather pluralistic combination of national and local churches, evangelical institutions, and individuals, of a more or less charismatic tendency. This and many other para-ecclesial entities have social objectives or support small projects responding to human situations the solution to which should come from governmental organs. It is this failure of government agencies that creates conditions for the nongovernmental world to prosper. But in this final decade of the century, these organizations also face a crisis, given the present economic and political situation, both national and international, in addition to the enormity of the problems which are growing with the increase of population and with the ideology of globalization.

I want to turn again to the great experiences of faith within ecclesiastical circles, some of them born in the whirlwind of the struggle against repression. The theology of liberation, today the victim of theoretical critiques in certain theological circles and restrictions by the Vatican itself, played an insuperable practical role in the decade of the seventies. The CEBs — Base Ecclesial Communities — constituted beyond doubt the most expressive representation of a theological formulation oriented toward the social reality of the people, their suffering and their hope. This experience not only opened paths for greater social participation on the part of thousands of members of the Catholic Church, but also awakened new leadership, self-confidence, and creativity. The richness of popular religiosity found in Afro-Brazilian religions also gained new expressions *inside* the Catholic Church, including, in some parishes, the combination of Afro rhythms and dances with the ritual of the mass.

On the other hand, the well-known process of growth of popular Protestantism through the Pentecostal movement has accelerated, but *outside of* the historic denominational structures, although its charismatic expression has penetrated into the historical churches and even the Catholic Church. Thus there is emerging, with renewed force, the base for a new form of church. In spite of its proselytism and its extreme divisiveness, the charismatic experience of this new Pentecostalism — neo-Pentecostalism — and its penetration in the poorest strata of the population of the country, would seem to indicate the possibility of a *transdenominational and social* dimension that transcends institutional structures and *unites* in spirit wherever that may happen, without the limitations that traditionally mark off the theological, geographical, and historical territories — or even those of class — of the historical churches. The style of known ecclesial forms — and here perhaps should be included the institutional limitations of the ecumenical movement — gives the appearance of aging in the face of a dynamism that invokes the Holy Spirit and lives a new experience of faith and spirituality.

The Pentecostal Response

It was this exceptional transformation in the Brazilian ecclesiastical and religious scene that brought Richard Shaull back to Brazil, twenty-five years after his forced return to the United States, during which time he was not allowed to enter the country in which he had worked for ten years as a missionary. His surprise with this radical change in the Protestant picture was already a cause of astonishment in other religious sectors, both the historical churches, including Catholicism, and social scientists from Brazil and other countries. As had been discovered by ISER — The Institute for Studies of Religion — through its research project, New Birth, the Pentecostal movement in recent years had organized five new churches each week in the geographical area of Metropolitan Rio, the fruit of the conversion of 300,000 people in a period of three years. Today, the Pentecostals represent about fifteen percent of the population of the state, or 1,500,000 active members.

Shaull had been following the increasing number of studies, research, and theses that were appearing in the country. And on his recent trips, beginning in 1993, he suggested a new approach to the analysis of the Pentecostal phenomenon, in which an interdisciplinary perspective would be predominant. That is, the sociological dimension of a movement of a religious nature would be more *comprehensive,* not only as a methodology for the study of human behavior (M. Weber) but also as an instrument to cover all dimensions involved in a given situation — which, in this case, includes the perspective of a theologian.

The proposal interested me from the beginning. I had worked on this theme with the sociologist Christian Lalive Depinay, in 1967, starting from his research in Chile, with its extension to Brazil, as well as with ISER in the years that followed. And in 1989 and 1991 I participated in seminars sponsored by the WCC, in Costa Rica and in Chile, in which the central question was that of the meaning of the Pentecostal expansion in Latin America for the ecumenical movement. In the meeting in Santiago, Chile, I presented a paper, the title of which — *Survival and Transcendence* — in a certain way attempted to indicate theological lines which related ideas with religious behavior and other aspects of human conduct in society (M. Weber), in the light of a perspective that might offer new issues for sociological analysis.

It was thus that I began to work again with Richard Shaull, now in a different historical context from that of the decade dedicated to the project Church and Society, but also similar with reference to what concerned us earlier, that is, the relation between faith and social reality. But now this new reality has not only taken on dimensions that are much more complex, but the church has grown in such a way that it has today a regular place in the news media, in addition to having its own instruments for mass communication. Here I refer especially to the Universal Church of the Reign of God (IURD), which did not even have a central place in the research we undertook, but which demanded our attention because of its numerical growth and the radical nature of its message and behavior. In most instances, the press or television refers to the IURD in extremely negative terms, and to its leaders as exploiters of popular faith through its demand of a tithe and sacrifices which can only add to the difficulties daily experienced by the most disinherited population of the country. Our visits to temples, almost always filled, with their four services daily, and the interviews we made of a score of members of the Universal Church (and

of other Pentecostal branches) indicate how much the Pentecostal movement contributes to the survival of thousands — millions — of people dissatisfied with their situation and with their previous religious experience.
This contribution has a spiritual dimension based on the power of the Holy
Spirit as well as a material effect in the sense that all of life is seen as
either subject to the power of the Spirit or it will be dominated by Satan.

We cannot here give more details about the nature of charismatic
worship and the radicality of what they emphasize as it is expressed in
lives transformed by the Spirit. It is important, however, to point out the
relation of neo-Pentecostalism with daily life, opening spaces that the
historical churches reserve for Sundays and special holy days. It is the
quotidian, the social reality of the day-to-day, that nourishes a new spirituality and gives meaning to lives formerly abandoned to their fate or to
the contingencies of collective misery. The new believers, as they pass
through a *new birth,* become spontaneously missionaries among their families, friends, and colleagues at work. The IURD, like other Pentecostal
branches, is also involved in the political realm, promoting the election of
its pastors and members to municipal councils and state and national
legislatures. Although they appear to lack a political vision that is more
global and less *parochial,* this fact has a symbolic dimension that is both
numerical (to demonstrate the growth of the church to the world beyond
it) and social (participation in the making of political decisions). Whether
it be in this context beyond the boundaries of the church, or, more importantly, in attendance at church services, on which strong emphasis is placed,
everything — poverty, sickness, unemployment — is placed in the hands
of God with the certainty that the difficulties of life will be resolved in *this*
world, as the immediate fulfillment of promises which were formerly
reserved for the future life. The church of the day-to-day is the church that
starts out from social reality — Society and Church.

This research offered us a fascinating academic and spiritual experience, which cannot be explored within the limits of a chapter. The interdisciplinary research, which had the title of "Pentecostal Response in Brazil
to the Suffering of the Poor," sponsored by the Research Enablement
Program of the Overseas Ministries Study Center (New Haven, Conn.) will
provide the material for a book to be published in 1997. Among the
questions raised by this study is that about the future of this movement,
on the eve of a new millenium, as well as that of what will happen to the
historical churches which have become stagnant in time and in their
temples. And in addition to this: What is the significance of all these new
ecclesial developments for the ecumenical movement and for the traditional
theology that presides over the old institutions of the church? In other

words, as Richard Shaull has pointed out, everything indicates that we may be in the process of articulating a new paradigm of salvation, with the need for a reinterpretation of the history of redemption as a whole, related to the new signs by which the Spirit challenges the churches to a new commitment to the life of and in solidarity with the disinherited of society.

The Roman Catholic Church
in Latin America: A Protestant Perspective
on the "New Evangelization"

ALAN NEELY

ON OCTOBER 8, 1992, Pope John Paul II arrived in Santo Domingo, the capital of the Dominican Republic, to commemorate the five hundredth anniversary of the arrival of Columbus and to open the Fourth General Assembly of the Latin American Conference of Bishops. The Conference, known as CELAM, had met only three times previously, in Puebla in 1970, Medellín in 1968, and in Rio de Janeiro in 1955. Santo Domingo was reported to have been chosen because it was the first seat of the Spanish colonial government, and because it was the Roman Catholic diocese where the initial evangelization of Indo-America began.

The choice of Santo Domingo was, of course, calculated, but — according to Pope John Paul II — not to celebrate the conquest and coloni- zation, but to commemorate the evangelization of Latin America.[1] One could wish that Santo Domingo had also been chosen because it was there, on the Sunday before Christmas 1511, that an incredibly courageous Dom- inican priest, Father Antonio de Montesinos, lifted his voice against the atrocities being committed by the Spanish colonists against the native American population.

Although for many in Latin America and elsewhere the quincenten- nial of the arrival of the Europeans was not something to laud or roman- ticize, from one perspective, the Church did have something to celebrate. No other area in the world has been so widely affected by Roman Catholic Christianity as has Latin America, nor is there any other continent where

---

1. Howard W. French, "Pope's Mass at Dominican Monument to Columbus," *The New York Times,* October 12, 1992, sec. B.

Roman Catholicism is more deeply rooted and interwoven with the culture. From an impartial perspective, Latin America today is overwhelmingly Roman Catholic. It is the *most* Roman Catholic of the world's six continents. According to Church statistics, 88.25% of the people are Roman Catholics. Recognizing that this figure may be inflated, it is nonetheless indicative of the strength and extent of the Church's influence in the lives of the people. Despite apparent inroads made by Protestantism since the 1950s, most people in Latin America still consider themselves Roman Catholics, and even those who leave the Church for a Protestant "sect" retain the lasting imprint of their Catholic formation and their Catholic culture.

Assuming the Church's statistics are at least indicative, what is the meaning and significance of Pope John Paul's call for a "new evangelization" of the continent? It should be noted that it was in 1983 in Port-au-Prince, Haiti, that the Pope first urged Latin American bishops and all the faithful to begin a "new evangelization" of the continent. Pointing to the approaching 1992 quincentennial, the Pope said:

> The celebration of the half-millennium of evangelization will have full meaning if it represents your commitment as bishops, along with your priests and the faithful, . . . not to evangelization, but to *a new evangelization.* It is new in its ardor, in its methods, and in its expression.[2]

Several facets of what the Pope proposed deserve comment. First, the evangelization he said was to be *new,* that is, unlike the first evangelization in the sixteenth and seventeenth centuries. It was to be different in *ardor,* in *methods,* and in *presentation* — all of these words suggesting an awareness of and a desire to avoid the questionable aspects of the first evangelization, namely, the mixed motives, the forced baptisms, and the often superficial presentations of the gospel by the sixteenth- and seventeenth-century missionaries. To be equitable, we should note that the Pope did acknowledge what he referred to as the "excesses" in the way in which the indigenous people were treated. Likewise, in his homily given during a mass celebrated in the provincial town of Higüey on October 12, 1992, John Paul said the quincentennial was an appropriate time to ask "for

---

2. John Paul II, "Pour Une Nouvelle Evangelisation de L'Amérique Latine," *La Documentation Catholique* (Paris) 80 (April 17, 1983): 435. See also Robert Niklaus, "Global Report," *Evangelical Missions Quarterly* 19 (July 1983): 258-60, and Marlise Simons, "Pope in Haiti," *The New York Times,* March 10, 1983, sec. A. Emphasis is mine.

pardon for offenses and create the conditions for the just development of all, especially those most abandoned."[3]

The new evangelization proposed by the Pope, however, is not totally new, for like the first it is clearly an undertaking sponsored by those in power, the Vatican and the Latin American hierarchy, not a movement bubbling up from the grass roots. There are other similarities between the two evangelizations as well, but these became evident only when the Pope began to flesh out the details of the enterprise and one could assess what was, before, little more than ecclesiastical generalities.

Historical Reflections on the "New Evangelization"

Several Roman Catholic theologians have remarked that the idea for a "new evangelization" began not with Pope John Paul II, but rather with Pope John XXIII, who explicitly spelled out his goal in the Second Vatican Council. The immediate goal, he said, was to "let some fresh air into the Church" through an *aggiornamento,* that is, an updating of Roman Catholicism, moving the Church into the twentieth century. Pope John XXIII's long-term goal, however, was Christian unity and ending "the age-old divisions of Christendom."[4] In his opening address to the Council, Pope John declared that modernity did not signal the end of Christian faith, and it did not undermine the mission of the Church. Rather, modernity, the Pope said, represented a sign of the times that could guide the Church in her pilgrimage. He challenged the prelates "to make a leap forward in doctrinal insight and the education of consciences . . . in light of the research methods and the literary forms of modern thought."[5] Then in one of the most celebrated challenges in Christian history, the Pope called on Roman Catholics to show "mercy and goodness toward the brethren who are separated" from the Church and to manifest "everywhere the fullness of Christian charity." "[N]othing," he said, would be "more effective in eradicating the seeds of discord, nothing more efficacious in promoting concord, just peace, and the brotherly unity of all" than mercy and goodness.[6]

3. French, "Pope's Mass."

4. Christopher Butler, *The Theology of Vatican II* (London: Darton, Longman & Todd, 1967), 6.

5. Peter Hebblethwaite, "John XXIII," in *Modern Catholicism: Vatican II and After,* ed. Adrian Hastings (New York: Oxford University Press, 1991), 31.

6. See Walter M. Abbott, ed., *The Documents of Vatican II* (New York: Guild Press, 1966), 717.

Unfortunately, Pope John XXIII died of cancer in June 1963, and the Council continued under the new pope, Paul VI, who, while manifesting more caution, nevertheless appeared to be nudging Roman Catholicism forward into the modern age. If the Church was to be truly contemporary, up-to-date, and Catholic — according to many attending Vatican II — she had to give herself in service to humanity *(le service de l'homme)* and be more democratic, more open to decentralization, diversity, pluralism, and ecumenism.[7] It was on this note and with unrestrained optimism that the Second Vatican Council closed in 1965.[8]

The impact of this historic event on Latin America can hardly be overemphasized. The bishops had recognized and underscored the fact that the Church was "the body of Christ," not necessarily equated with the Roman Catholic institution[9] or with its mission. Furthermore, they insisted, the Church was an "extension of Jesus Christ's ministry in this world, a ministry that was threefold: pastoral, the care of believers;[10] ecumenical, efforts to heal the divisions among Christians;[11] and missionary, taking the gospel to those areas and peoples who had not heard and where the church had not been planted.[12]

Latin American bishops heard all of this gladly, and they took Vatican II seriously, if not literally. Consequently, when CELAM convened for the second general conference in Medellín in August and September of 1968, the basic question was: how should we interpret and apply the positions delineated by Vatican II in a continent where Christianity has prevailed for more than four centuries, where the vast majority of people are professing Roman Catholics, but where injustice, poverty, hunger, malnutrition, oppression, social and economic exploitation, marginalization,

---

7. See the multiple references to the struggle over the question of collegiality in Adrian Hastings, ed., *Modern Catholicism: Vatican II and After* (New York: Oxford University Press, 1991), 53-54, 85-87, 91, 223.

8. "Many theologians believed that in the process of reception the new — that is, the concept of the *collegium* — would play an explosive role. . . . The normative element (they hoped) would prove to be not the compromise finally written into the document but that which was new in comparison with the existing tradition. . . . The view was not accurate." Quoted by F. J. Laishley, "Unfinished Business," in Hastings, *Modern Catholicism,* 223.

9. "Lumen Gentium" or the "Dogmatic Constitution on the Church," in Abbott, *Documents,* 7.

10. "Apostolicam Actuositatem" or the "Decree on the Apostolate of Lay People," in Abbott, *Documents,* 489.

11. "Unitatis Reintegratio" or the "Decree on Ecumenism," in Abbott, *Documents,* 341.

12. "Ad Gentes" or the "Decree on the Missionary Activity of the Church," in Abbott, *Documents,* 584, 660.

and premature death are endemic?[13] It was out of this Medellín conference that liberation theology with its strengths and limitations publicly emerged.

Opening the meeting, Pope Paul VI depicted the Church not as an institution to be served, but as a "servant church" or serving community whose mission included social transformation, not simply personal or collective conversion. Salvation, he declared, was not limited to the personal dimension of life, nor only to life after death. Rather, there was, he insisted — citing "Lumen Gentium" (8.) and "Gaudium et Spes" (39.) — a "direct relationship between salvation and this world." Moreover, "the Church, like Christ," he said, "is sent 'to' the world and 'for' the world" as "a 'Servant' Church whose option is clearly for the poor, the weak, and the dispossessed."[14]

The emphasis given by Vatican II to the "doctrine of collegiality" — which to Protestants sounds fairly benign — was anything but benign. To progressives, it suggested a dramatic and radical shift from the ultramontanism[15] of Vatican I (1869-70) to a decentralization of authority, that is, a transfer of power or control from the Vatican to the various national and regional conferences of bishops scattered across the world.[16] The issue of collegiality, however, became a principal arena of intra-ecclesial contention.

It is difficult to grasp or explain developments in the Roman Catholic Church during the last thirty years unless one is aware of the struggle that has gone on between Rome and the various regional and national bishoprics, religious orders, base Christian communities, and individual priests and laypersons. The struggle has not been principally doctrinal, that is, about orthodoxy or correct theology, so much as it has been a struggle over the government of the Church. And though many Latin American bishops rejoiced to see the papacy divesting itself of its traditional claims of absolute primacy (certified by Vatican I), unfortunately, the celebration of a new era

13. The theme of the conference was "The Church in the Present-Day Transformation of Latin America in the Light of the Council."

14. Louis J. Luzbetak, *The Church and Cultures* (Maryknoll, N.Y.: Orbis, 1988), 123.

15. The position favoring supremacy of papal over national or diocesan authority.

16. Article 22 of "Lumen Gentium" stated: "Just as, by the Lord's will, St. Peter and the other apostles constituted one apostolic college, so in a similar way the Roman Pontiff as the successor of Peter, and the bishops as the successors of the apostles are joined together . . . in conciliar assemblies which made common judgement about more profound matters in decisions reflecting the views of many. The ecumenical councils held through the centuries clearly attest to this collegial aspect." Hebblethwaite contends that the struggle over collegiality began in Vatican I, which emphasized the pope's "primacy," i.e., claimed that the pope like Peter was preeminent among the apostles in ruling over the Church, 31.

of collegiality was short-lived.[17] For hardly had Pope John XXIII been buried and Paul VI assumed the Chair than the Vatican functionaries who make up the *curia* began a scramble to counteract what they saw as decentralization gone amuck. It was too late to affect noticeably the Medellín meeting, which now nearly thirty years removed appears to have been something of an anomaly. But it is still too early, I believe, to predict the long-term effects of Medellín 1968. Many Latin American theologians insist that Medellín marked the turning point between the first and second evangelizations of Latin America because for more than four centuries, they contend, the Church assiduously cultivated ties with governments and ruling elites. Medellín, they insist, set her free to "start a new journey."[18] The first evangelization, according to Leonardo Boff, was under the banner of invasion and colonization. A truly new evangelization, Boff continues, will be "under the banner of liberation."[19] Perhaps so, but it is now clear that the Vatican had other ideas.

To appreciate the full range of what has happened, one must go back to 1970, less than two years after Medellín, when the statutes of CELAM were changed to allow presidents of national episcopal conferences in addition to the regularly named delegates to participate in CELAM deliberations. Immediately this increased the number of prelates loyal to Rome who could influence the decisions of the body. Two years later, 1972, these churchmen, with voice and vote, began to effect a radical change in CELAM. The initial signal of change came when the arch-conservative Bishop Alfonso López Trujillo of Colombia was elected CELAM'S General

17. Monsignor Manuel Larrain, Bishop of Talca, Chile, and first president of CELAM, said that the Medellín meeting of CELAM was the "first case in the whole of church history where the concept of episcopal collegiality had been realized." Enrique Dussel, "Latin America," *Modern Catholicism: Vatican II and After* (Oxford University Press, 1991), 320.

18. Cited by Jose Oscar Beozzo, "Medellín: Vinte Anos Depois (1968-1988)," *Revista Eclesiastica Brasileira* 192 (December 1988): 790.

19. "The first evangelization of Latin America took place under the sign of subjection, because it took shape as part of the project of invasion and colonization. It gave rise to a colonized Christianity, which reproduced the religious models of the Iberian centres. From its very beginnings it was contradictory, because alongside the political and religious domination there were always prophetic spirits who denounced and resisted the perverse nature of the colonization in the name of the humanitarian spirit and liberating content of the Christian message, defending the Indians and condemning the evil of slavery.

"The new evangelization puts down roots in this prophetic and pastoral tradition. It is taking place under the sign of liberation. It is giving rise to a unique Christianity, bearing the stamp of ordinary people, brown, white, Latin, indigenous and black, pointing the way to new forms of church structure and also one of the forces for social change on the continent." Leonardo Boff, "The New Evangelization: New Life Bursts In," *1492-1992: The Voice of the Victims,* ed. Leonardo Boff and Virgil Elizondo (London: SCM Press, 1990), 130.

Secretary. The principal departments of the organization were then moved to the Bogotá headquarters so that Bishop Trujillo could exercise closer control over them. Criticism of liberation theology, sporadic and somewhat muted before, became strident and more frequent.

When the General Assembly of CELAM convened for its third meeting in the city of Puebla, Mexico, in 1979 — delayed a year because of the sudden death of Pope Paul VI, and even more sudden death of Pope John Paul I — CELAM was under the control of the reactionaries and elements loyal to Rome. The new pontiff, John Paul II, moved with adroitness to take charge of the Puebla conference, but the messages coming out of the meeting were, nonetheless, mixed. As for the pronouncements of Vatican II and Medellín, there was a kind of "tipping of the hat" or polite acknowledgment, and optimistic observers put their own positive interpretations on the Pope's words.[20] We now know the rest of the story. John Paul's messages did appear to call for a needed balance in evangelization. He said, for example:

> "We mutilate radically the importance of liberation if we fail to include liberation from sin and all its seductions and idolatries . . . if we neglect the side of evangelization which liberates and transforms man, making him the instrument of his own development as an individual and as part of the community . . . or if we forget that dependence and slavery are contrary to fundamental rights, rights not granted by governments and institutions — however powerful they may be — but rather established by the Creator and Father of us all."[21]

But less confident and more cynical onlookers noted with growing apprehension the direction in which things appeared to them to be moving. Following Puebla, López Trujillo was reelected president of CELAM and then elevated to the rank of Cardinal. The attack against liberation theology intensified,[22] obviously with the approval of the Vatican. Cardinal Joseph

20. I remember reading the Pope's addresses given in Mexico in 1979 and feeling that he was sending intentionally a double message. On the one hand he reaffirmed Medellín's "preferential option for the poor," but at the same time issued pointed warnings against all forms of Marxism which were thinly veiled attacks on liberation theology and its proponents.

21. *Puebla Document,* 485.

22. The attack was led by Cardinal Joseph Ratzinger, who issued two successive documents critical of liberation theology: "Instructions on Certain Aspects of the 'Theology of Liberation" (1984), and "Instruction on Christian Freedom and Liberation" (1986). See the *National Catholic Reporter* (September 1984): 11-14, and *Origins* 15 (April 17, 1986): 713-28.

Ratzinger, named as prefect or head of the Congregation for the Doctrine of the Faith on November 21, 1981, began singling out the leading liberation theologians for investigation and for what many regarded as Vatican intimidation and harassment.[23] Also, prominent progressive bishops were steadily forced into retirement and replaced by churchmen loyal to John Paul. Then came the sudden and unexpected collapse of European and Soviet Communism which appeared to justify the Vatican's hardline position on Marxism. Quickly, predictions were freely and frequently made that liberation theology was now *passé*. And though a few pockets of resistance remained, such as the National Council of Brazilian Bishops, their messages and calls for remaining faithful to Vatican II and Medellín lacked the impact they had made before. Individual theologians out of sync with the Vatican were for the most part silenced or they appeared guarded in what they said and wrote. Some, such as Leonardo Boff, apparently gave up the struggle from within the ranks of the clergy and asked to be laicized.

By 1990, the centralization of power under Pope John Paul II was virtually complete, and final preparations for 1992 and the fourth General Assembly of CELAM began. In 1968, the bishops at Medellín, echoing the spirit of Vatican II, called for the "evangelization" of baptized Roman Catholics in Latin America, and when in Haiti in 1983 Pope John Paul II spoke of the need for a continental "new evangelization," it appeared to some that he was simply renewing the call of Medellín. One cannot say what was in the Pope's mind at that time, but what ensued appears to represent not a continuity between Vatican II, Medellín, and Santo Domingo, but rather a contrast. John Paul II insists that "the constant reference point" of all his pastoral actions — including, one would suppose, his version of a "new" evangelization project — is the Second Vatican Council. But, as Peter Hebblethwaite put it, John Paul "is no longer talking about a future program, but claiming to have realized one. Pope John Paul *thinks* his pontificate is the fulfillment of Vatican II."[24] The question is, Is it?

23. According to Joseph Gremillion, "Brazil became the focus of contention over liberation theology when Cardinal Joseph Ratzinger, head of the Congregation for the Doctrine of the Faith, issued in 1984 a formal Instruction severely criticizing this ecclesiology which had begun animating much of the regional church of Latin America since its 1968 Medellín Assembly. A few months after Ratzinger's critique, he summoned to Rome Brazil's best-known liberation theologian, Leonardo Boff, to be examined and placed under a formal ban of silence on theological subjects." "Justice and Peace" in Hastings, *Modern Catholicism,* 191.

24. Hebblethwaite, "John Paul II," in Hastings, *Modern Catholicism,* 448.

How New Is the "New Evangelization" of Latin America?

Apart from the institutional changes that have occurred among Latin American bishops (CELAM), the interventions of Cardinal Ratzinger, the silencing of and attempts to domesticate many theologians, what do we know about John Paul's ambitious plan of evangelization?

First of all, the Santo Domingo documents are not reassuring, but only time will tell what the long-term effects will be. Despite this explicit limitation, there are, it seems, some strong indicators concerning the direction in which the Pope wants the Church to move.

The "new evangelization," the Pope says, is to be christocentric. Unless one is familiar with the thought underlying the theology of liberation, John Paul II's description of his proposed evangelization's being "christocentric" appears reasonable. Liberation theologians — following the lead of Vatican II — however, said that the point of beginning for doing theology and for evangelization was the human condition. John Paul's choice of terms, therefore, appears to be a veiled attempt to distinguish the new approach from the evangelization encouraged by Medellín.

Granting the fact that this may not have been the Pope's intention at all, one needs only to read carefully John Paul's first encyclical, *Redemptoris Hominis* (1979), "The Redeemer of Men," and his latest encyclical, *Redemptoris Missio* (1990), "On the Permanent Validity of the Church's Missionary Mandate," to appreciate the significant shift in perspective. Most observers read *Redemptoris Missio* and are impressed by its depth and theological balance. It is not a polemic, but rather a carefully worded and tightly reasoned challenge to the Church to see and implement the missionary mandate. Though there are passages here and there with which one could take issue, I choose to regard the encyclical as an example of solid Roman Catholic missiological thinking. My misgivings about what the Pope has said arise partially from his encyclicals, but more from his less formal statements.

Announcing the approaching General Assembly of CELAM in Santo Domingo, the Pope said, for example, that christology would be the basis of every discussion, "Jesus Christ, Yesterday, Today and Forever."[25] The question is, however, what kind of Christ is he offering as the centerpiece of this "new" evangelization? Is he to be the Christ of the gospels who preached good news to the poor, proclaimed release to the captives, opened the eyes of the blind, set at liberty those who were oppressed, and proclaimed the year of Jubilee (Luke 4:18-19)? Or

25. "Discurso del Santo Padre Alla II Assemblea Plenaria de la Pontifica Commissione per L'America Latina," *CELAM* 242 (August/September 1991): 3.

is he to be a "dogmatically interpreted" Christ, a domesticated, gentle, otherworldly Christ who threatens none of the power centers or structures of injustice and oppression? Is John Paul's the Christ who cleansed the Temple or — as one critic put it — is he to be little more than an international papal nuncio?[26]

It is impossible for many who know the suffering of the poor in Latin America to imagine the Christ of the gospels not representing a constant threat to those who ignore or want to put a positive spin on the deepening economic, social, political, and religious crisis that characterizes life in this part of the world today. It is no less disturbing to ponder the impact of a Pope who seems far more concerned with a loss of church members than with the loss of lives.

The "new evangelization," according to John Paul II, is to be in perfect harmony with the Magisterium. John Paul II's own words need to be considered. The "new evangelization," he said, is to be:

> a reflection on the past, present and future of Latin America: a reflection which will give new impulse to the Evangelization of the continent on all levels and in all sectors of society . . . [which require] doctrinal precision, in perfect syntony with the Magisterium and Tradition of the Church, and determine its objectives and pastoral lines, according to the demands of our time, under the perspective of the third millennium of Christianity. . . . It requires drawing a new evangelizing strategy, a global plan for the evangelization of the Latin American peoples and that constitutes an answer to the courses of the present time, among which the major ones are the growing secularization, *the grave problem of the advance of sects* and defense of life in a continent which allows one to feel the destructive presence of a culture of death.[27]

Nestled between otherwise perfectly legitimate concerns are two troubling phrases. One appears addressed to the proliferation of Christian base communities which, if Leonardo Boff was correct in his *Ecclesiogenesis,* represent a much greater threat to the centralization of authority than does the doctrine of collegiality. The "new evangelization" is to be, according to the Pope, in "perfect syntony with the Magistery and Tradition of the Church."[28] Is he saying that there will be no place for a "people's

26. J. B. Libanio, "Puebla — Evangelização da America Latina: Um Desafio," *Tempo e Presenca* 21 (July 1978): 23 (14-28).

27. "Discurso del Santo Padre," 4. Emphasis is mine.

28. In his encyclical *Redemptoris Missio,* John Paul refers to the "Ecclesial Base

church," no room for spontaneity, and no toleration of dissent? Is he reasserting the Church of the bishops, archbishops, and Pope as the only mother and teacher of the faithful? If he is, then there will be no priesthood of believers, only the priesthood of the hierarchy.

The second disconcerting phrase suggests *the "new evangelization" will serve as a counterforce to the proselytizing activities of the Protestant sects.* This second allusion is troubling because it could mean the clear reversal of the spirit of Vatican II regarding non-Roman Catholics. Have John XXIII's "separated brethren" become, at least to John Paul, "ravenous wolves." This appears to be the case if we compare his reference to "the grave problem of the advance of sects" in Latin America with other things he has said. For he has warned Latin American bishops repeatedly about the steady loss of the faithful to the fast-growing non-Roman Catholic groups that appear to be exploding throughout Latin America.

During his 1992 visit to Brazil, John Paul II, speaking to the Brazilian bishops, said:

> "I am well aware that the spread of these cults and groups can count on strong economic support and that their preaching tempts people with fake miracles, misleading them with distorted simplification and sowing confusion, especially among the simple people and those most lacking in religious instruction. Therefore, it is important that your pastoral work, with profound missionary awareness, be able to take over those very areas where such groups are active, awakening in the people the joy and holy pride of belonging to the one Church of Christ, which subsists in our Holy Catholic Church."[29]

It seems, at least if one takes these words at face value, that the ecumenical Pope John XXIII has been replaced by an angry and combative John Paul II, who, according to one news report, blasted in scorching terms the "evangelical Protestant 'sects.'" Not only did he accuse them of financing their nefarious activities with money from outside — presumably from the United States — but he also characterized their evangelistic activities as the seduction of the naive and uninformed with counterfeit miracles and confusing them with misleading "simplifications." The

---

Communities," but he says that they "must live in union with the particular and the universal Church, in heartfelt communion with the Church's pastors and the magisterium" (51).

29. "Pastoral Challenges," *Catholic International* 21 (December 1991): 1003.

Brazilian bishops, therefore, were exhorted by the Pope to initiate "a counter-campaign of Catholic evangelization."[30]

It is not surprising that leaders in the Roman Catholic Church are preoccupied with what has become a veritable hemorrhage of their members to non-Roman Catholic churches, 600,000 annually by some estimates in Brazil alone. But a "counter-campaign" sounds like something out of the nineteenth century or earlier than a missionary strategy designed for the next millennium, nor even for the last decade of the twentieth century. Neither was it the kind of approach one would have hoped would be the climax of the commemoration of the quincentennial of the first evangelization. Yet Pope John Paul II's words were: "Let's celebrate the Fifth Centennial by pursuing throughout the American continent . . . a 'new evangelization,' in the fashion of the first apostles to the Americas." Then followed one of the more puzzling papal comments about this whole situation, a comment which appeared to idealize the first evangelization and ignore the mistakes, excesses, and injustices.

> "Aware of the word of Christ (Mk 16:16), the first missionaries, moved by their faith in the words of Christ and by their love for souls, have accomplished an admirable work by presenting Christ to the peoples they discovered. At the same time, they developed an enormous work of social and cultural promotion which today makes up the proud patrimony of the whole continent and is part of the national being of this country. The artistic and literary monuments, the grammar books and catechisms in the major Indian languages, the regulations and laws are some of the fruits of *the work of a civilizing civilization.* The good news had been deeply proclaimed even before the European population settled permanently here and the good news had always been a factor of harmony and defense of the rights of the weaker."[31]

It is difficult to believe that even John Paul II would use the phrase "civilizing civilization." To link the first evangelization of Latin America with the imposed Europeanization of the people and cultures as something to be revered displays an incredible insensitivity to the historical reality, not the least of which is the fact that several of the indigenous civilizations had flourished in the Americas for centuries long before the Europeans

---

30. "Pope Warns of Protestant 'Sects,' " *The Times* (Trenton, N.J.), October 14, 1991, sec. D.

31. "La 'Nouvelle Evangelisation' Fera Germer la Justice," *La Documentation Catholique* 85 (June 1988): 546-49. Emphasis is mine.

arrived and, in some respects at least, were morally equal if not superior. The Pope's words therefore sound more like a promotional piece written in a previous age than a missiology fashioned for the coming millennium.

Implications of the New Evangelization

The implications of Pope John Paul II's words need to be considered. Vast numbers of people in the world, even in Christianized Latin America, need to hear the gospel. The question is, are any of the unevangelized hearing the gospel from those whom the Pope considers as "sects" and "cults"? If history is an indicator, then one must feel that wholesale condemnation of all non-Roman Catholic evangelization going on in Latin America is unfortunate and misguided. One does not have to approve of every attempt to proselytize as being wholesome evangelism. But the fact is, the Protestant presence in Latin America during the last century and a half has not only benefited the populace as a whole, it has also contributed to a measure of reform and revitalization in the Roman Catholic Church as well.

The "missionary era" continues in Latin America, not simply because hundreds of missionary agencies send their representatives to Central and South America as well as the Caribbean, but because foreigners can still enter, live, and work under the auspices of a church or mission group in most Latin American countries. Also, many national Christian churches welcome the missionary presence for a number of reasons. But unless those who are sent go with a different attitude from those missionaries of the past, that is, unless they have a knowledge of Latin American history and go with an openness and an appreciation for the culture that they encounter, and unless they are deeply committed to the suffering millions of the continent, then neither they nor those who send them will have learned much from history. More seriously, they will repeat many of the same mistakes the European conquerors and missionaries made five centuries ago.

. . . And What About Liberation Theology?

This brings us to a final question, what does the "new evangelization" portend for the theology of liberation?

Following the astonishing and unexpected dismantling of the Berlin Wall, the collapse of the Soviet Union, and the electoral defeat of the Sandinistas in Nicaragua, an inordinate amount of self-congratulating occurred in the United States as well as talk about the bankruptcy of socialism and the triumph of capitalism. Almost immediately, several self-anointed authorities stepped forward and solemnly declared the inevitable demise of the theology of liberation, tied as it was, they said, to Marxism. For a number of reasons, some of which may be attributed to the failures of the Soviet system, the mounting problems in Cuba, and the political changes in Central America, liberation theology did lose much of its popular appeal in the United States and western Europe. Before pronouncing it dead, however, a number of questions need to be asked.

How dependent was liberation theology on Marxism? Is the future of the theology of liberation truly linked to that of Marxism? Though in the minds of most opponents, the womb of liberation theology is found in *Das Kapital,* the real roots can be traced to the Bible: to the Pentateuch, the Old Testament prophets, the teachings of Jesus, and the life of the early church. Liberation theologians did employ a Marxist critique of capitalism, but at the same time they rejected the atheism, dialectical materialism, and economic determinism of Marxist orthodoxy. Also, some were openly critical of the so-called dictatorship of the proletariat which resulted in authoritarian states and bloated and repressive bureaucracies. Admittedly, criticism of communist regimes was not a major emphasis in liberation theology, but it was there for anyone who studied it seriously. As Philip Berryman noted, analysts who accuse liberation theologians of being negative only in regard to the United States are either unaware of these facts or they choose to ignore them.[32]

It is simply incorrect to assume that liberation theology is somehow dependent on and indissolubly joined with Marxism.

Has capitalism triumphed? Even if liberation theology were inseparable from Marxism, it may be premature to conclude that the latter is dead. What in Eastern Europe appears to be a wholesale rejection of communism may in fact turn out to be just that. Closer examination, however, indicates that what occurred was the internal collapse of centrally planned economies aided and abetted by widespread disgust with their corrupt and grossly mismanaged regimes. It is clear that many Eastern European leaders, if not most of them, were totalitarian, not committed to justice or to economic and social egalitarianism, but rather committed to protecting their own positions of privileges. Consequently they employed whatever tactics, including brutality, they deemed necessary.

Some observers are now certain that the collapse of these regimes proves that centrally managed economies will not work, and that the wave

---

32. See Giulio Giardi, *Faith and Revolution* (Maryknoll, N.Y.: Orbis, 1989), 22.

of the future for Eastern Europe — indeed for the whole world — is free enterprise. Economies do appear to be moving away from public to private ownership of industry, and there is evidence that the only dependable motive for increasing production is the desire for profit. Assuming these to be incontestable, what is needed, it is argued, is an economic environment where entrepreneurs can operate completely free of government control. For capitalism is an economic system that functions best unencumbered by political restraints. Those with a knowledge of economic history can be excused for being dubious.

Furthermore, it remains to be seen which economic model the Eastern European countries will ultimately choose to follow. Will it be that of the United States, Great Britain, Germany, Scandinavia, Singapore, or Japan? It is possible, if not likely, that rather than putting industries in private hands, these newly emerging "democracies" will opt for mixed economies such as the "welfare capitalism" or modified socialism of Scandinavia. Sweden is an example where the vast majority of production is in private hands, but corporate profits as well as personal incomes are taxed at exceedingly high rates by U.S. standards in order to finance their comprehensive system of social security, health, and welfare.

Curiously, in Great Britain and the United States, there appears to be a growing disenchantment with the results of privatization and deregulation. Set free from previous government regulations, Wall Street and the savings and loan institutions were ready-made for unscrupulous manipulators. The amount of white-collar crime that occurred during the 1980s, according to the General Accounting Office, cost the citizens of the U.S. between $325 and $500 billion dollars, almost double what was initially estimated.[33]

Those who are inclined to hold up the U.S. economic and political system as a model for the rest of the world would do well to stop long enough to reflect on what really is happening here in our vaunted democracy: the blatant selling of the government to those with wealth, unrestrained and often unpunished greed and dishonesty, increased hunger, homelessness, use of illegal drugs, crime, and despair. The sense of disillusionment and alienation is so profound that virtually half the electorate do not even bother to vote. Unless we are about to witness a universal transformation of human nature, it is premature to assume that the present economic system is the last.

Does liberation theology have anything to say? A careful reading of liberation theology will reveal one central postulate to account for the greed, injustice, oppression, suffering, and poverty in the world. Fundamentally,

33. *The New York Times,* April 12, 1990.

it is not the result of economic and/or political systems. It is the result of sin, sin that infects all individual and social projects. Gutiérrez wrote in his first work:

> Sin — a breach of friendship with God and others — is according to the Bible the ultimate cause of poverty, injustice, and the oppression in which people live. In describing sin as the ultimate cause we do not in any way negate the structural reasons and the objective determinants leading to these situations. It does, however, emphasize the fact that things do not happen by chance and that behind an unjust structure there is a personal and collective will responsible — a willingness to reject God and neighbor. It suggests, likewise, that a social transformation, no matter how radical it may be, does not automatically achieve the suppression of all evils.[34]

No proponent of liberation theology has claimed for it the last word. Liberation theology is not the last word, it is *a* word. There have been other words: Augustinianism, Scholasticism, Thomism, Reformation theology, Evangelical theology, the Social Gospel, Fundamentalism, Crisis Theology, Neo-Thomism, Neo-Evangelicalism, Pentecostalism, Process Theology, the World Theology of W. Cantwell Smith, and the Theocentric Theology of John Hick, Raymond Panikkar, Stanley Samartha, and Paul Knitter. Borrowing from the wisdom writer we can say, "Of the making of theologies there is no end."[35]

Liberation theology is not, however, just another in the long series of theologies. In contrast to other theologies, in its most dynamic form it is a theology not of the specialist but of the grass-roots believer. It is a theology of praxis, that is, action-reflection on biblical revelation and history by the poor and the oppressed and from their perspective.

Liberation theology begins not with an answer but with a question: Does the gospel of Jesus Christ have any word of hope for the hundreds of millions of oppressed and poor in the world? Does it have a word for the rich? The response to both questions comes in the form of denunciation and annunciation. Liberation theology calls for the church to stand with the poor and oppressed, for only they are in a position to hear and understand the biblical message for them.

Liberation theology is not a closed system. It is a process in which to be engaged. The theology which emerged out of the Solentiname com-

---

34. *A Theology of Liberation* (Maryknoll, N.Y.: Orbis, 1973), 35.
35. Ecclesiastes 12:12.

munity in Nicaragua is prima facie evidence that theology often is best done not by the initiated but by the common people. Theory has its place, but praxis precedes theory and praxis corrects theory. Theology therefore is not so much something to be studied (as in the academy) as it is something to be done.

What then does the future hold? It now appears that much of the progress made toward economic justice in Central America has been slowed to a trickle and possibly reversed. Furthermore, liberation theologians continue to experience pressure from the Vatican, pressure exerted not only by Cardinal Ratzinger, but also by the Pope through the archbishops and bishops. Bishops sympathetic to liberation theology have been replaced, several prominent theologians and many more priests who have called for social and economic justice in Latin America have been isolated and coerced into silence. Less obvious but equally pressured are Protestant theologians and those who continue to speak in behalf of the poor and oppressed. In a word, it is no longer popular, and it has never been safe, to be an advocate of justice and liberation in Latin America.

At first glance, therefore, it appears that the future does not bode well for liberation theology or theologians. If the prophetic witness can be silenced, if the churches can be at ease with the gross inequities of class, race, and gender, if the coming of the kingdom of God is outside of history, and if the destiny of theology is bound to any single human project, then the future of liberation theology is problematic. But this is not the whole story. *Basismo* is still a force to be reckoned with by the Church.[36] In addition, serious Latin American theologians must continue to write in an *ambiente* of liberation theology's powerful and persistent influence.[37] Without fanfare, doing and reflecting on theology continues, much of it around the theme of liberation. In July of 1995, for instance, the Comunidad de Educación Teológica de Latino América (CETELA) met in Medellín,

36. See David Lehmann, *Struggle for the Spirit: Religious Transformation and Popular Culture in Brazil and Latin America* (Cambridge, U.K.: Polity Press, 1996), 25-36. Also, John Burdick, *Looking for God in Brazil: The Progressive Catholic Church in Urban Brazil's Religious Arena* (Berkeley: University of California Press, 1993).

37. This is true whether they are Protestant or Roman Catholic and whether they approve or disapprove of the theology of liberation, e.g., José Míguez Bonino, *Faces of Latin American Protestantism,* trans. Eugene L. Stockwell (Grand Rapids: Eerdmans, 1997); Jon Sobrino, *The Principle of Mercy: Taking the Crucified People from the Cross* (Maryknoll, N.Y.: Orbis, 1994); Carlos R. Piar, *Jesus and Liberation* (New York: Peter Lang, 1994); and Lehmann, *Struggle for the Spirit* (1996). Moreover, liberation theology is a part of the theological scene in Africa and Asia. See, for example, Michael Amaladoss, *Life in Freedom: Liberation Theologies from Asia* (Maryknoll, N.Y.: Orbis, 1997).

Colombia. The topic was the future of Latin American theology. Richard Shaull was there as one of the "padres" of liberation theology as were other representative Protestants, evangelicals, Pentecostals, and Roman Catholics. Some of the participants were individuals internationally known, though not all. Shaull described the meeting as follows:

> Everybody present seemed to take for granted the more common criticism of TL [the theology of liberation] in terms of its too close identification with one particular ideological option and political struggle. And it was generally recognized that the situation now in Latin America, as the result of the dominance of the global market economy, is a desperate one for vast numbers of people and calls for a very different pastoral approach. Many spoke of the need to have an approach that was not limited to the economic factor, but took into account the fuller human reality. And some recognized the need to take the religious world of poor people much more seriously.
>
> One of the best indications of the way things are moving is this: In this meeting, women, indigenous, blacks and pentecostals were each given a chance to present their perspectives.
>
> One final comment. I was quite impressed by the spirit and the intellectual abilities of many of the younger generation, especially. And I was also encouraged to find that, while the social concern at the heart of TL is as strong as ever, there is a growing interest in spirituality, and especially in exploring further the cultivation of the life of the Spirit and the development of theology and reflection on social responsibility in that context. All this leads me to look hopefully toward the future in the evolution of LA theologies and what they may contribute to the life of the church.[38]

The future is still open. If you were told that in the mid-1970s a major news magazine in the United States published a 7,000-word essay arguing that capitalism would not likely survive, would you be shocked? If so, go to a library and find the July 14, 1975, issue of *Time* and note the cover story: "Can Capitalism Survive?" The opening paragraph states, "As Capitalism approaches its bicentennial, it is beset by crisis. Increasingly, its supporters as well as its critics ask: 'Can capitalism survive?' "

Now, more than twenty years later, the same question is being asked about alternative economic systems, especially socialism and communism. The question would be legitimate, were capitalism able to produce, as Adam

---

38. Letter to Alan Neely from M. Richard Shaull, July 17, 1995.

Smith promised, universal wealth that would raise from poverty to plenty "the lowest ranks of the people." But only the most doctrinaire champion of free enterprise would dare make such a promise today. Capitalism is now recognized as a means to create wealth for some, but certainly not for all. And though Germany, Japan, Korea, and the United States have generated unprecedented wealth, few would claim that poverty and injustice have been eradicated even in these lands.

Liberation theology will inevitably change. Likely it will not continue to attract the amount of attention nor the number of adherents evident during the past two decades. It may become a historical curiosity. But unless history ends, the struggle for justice will go on, and where the church is faithful to the gospel and sides with the poor and the oppressed, "theology from the underside" will emerge. It may not be called "liberation theology," but when people become subjects rather than objects of evangelization; when Christians refuse to absolutize human systems; when praxis precedes theory and love is the guiding principle of behavior — given the kind of world we have — "theology from the underside" will bubble up. Also, wherever the enslaved, who too image God, claim their right to freedom; wherever Christ is murdered with the consent or "at the behest of ministers of worship,"[39] "theology from the underside" will, like leaven, ferment and spread.

39. Girardi, *Faith and Revolution,* 121.

PART THREE

The Challenge of New Paradigms in Ecumenical Theology

Conversion, Incarnation, and Creation: The New Context in African Theology[1]

Timothy M. Njoya

Introduction: The Relationship Between Conversion and Incarnation

My theology arises where western Christianity ends and where African conversion experience begins. This conversion experience is the birth of a new postcolonial and even postindependence consciousness which understands that there is a basic difference between missionary Christianity and indigenous African Christianity.

Missionary Christianity belonged to a mixed family of theistic, apologetic, mechanistic, scholastic, classical, evangelical, and dualistic traditions that had no sense of accountability to African history. Africans were forced to submit to the great, infallible, and far-off God of Abraham, Moses, Augustine, Aquinas, and Luther. The God of Calvin, Schleiermacher, Barth, John Wesley, and Billy Graham was delivered to them wrapped in sanitary towels; God too nonpartisan, not vulnerable. African experiential theology begins with a radically new understanding of the dynamic interaction of conversion, incarnation, and creation.

I begin with conversion. Salvation is an endogenous life born by conversion experience, and owing nothing to any prior salvation or lack of it, not mediated by any religion to another. Conversion gives birth to its own messianic vision, didache, or pedagogy. It is not a flight from one

---

1. The editor is indebted to the Rev. Roderic P. Frohman, D.Min. (Prin.) for his theological insights and editorial expertise in preparing this manuscript. This article is a condensation and re-formation of a more lengthy Njoya essay, "God — Being and Existence."

religion, community, or condition to another, but is an event that generates and continues its own life.

The conversion experience articulates its own original story, didache, containing its own political, theological, and economic agenda. The conversion experience, formed by the process of creative change, becomes its own pedagogy or witness. This pedagogy communicates the gospel not as a reconstitution or reconstruction of any past religious experience but as the consequence of Christ's incarnation in real historical situations. The Holy Spirit empowers conversion experience to become a transforming witness through diaconia and koinonia as in the first postresurrection conversion experience, Acts 4:32-37.

The emergence of conversion experience with this kind of vision called for the transparency and accountability of all political and civil institutions. This theology has sparked a powerful sense of responsibility that is now transforming the Kenyan sociopolitical landscape. People are empowered by their conversion experience to transform their own existence into new political forces that the Kenya government tries to curb by pitting right-wing missionary religion against the call for accountable and transparent governance. The use of missionary Christianity as a spiritual inhibitor against a more messianic vision of conversion experience has not halted the offensive against authoritarianism.

Without this revolution of conversion experience Africans would never have noticed the disintegration of independence into an oppressor's gift, ex gratia, to the oppressed. It is ironic that independence has turned into a gift of imperialism to nationalism. Unlike God's creation, which complements the Creator by procreating itself, independence complements imperialism by degenerating into debt burdens, sectionalism, factionalism, and tribalism. Our churches took too long to realize that independence had deviated from God's creative process, the conversion experience, and had become nothing but a cornerstone for the reconstruction of colonial injustice and the rebuilding of a slave society. This became deadly hostile to the transforming effect of conversion as a catalyst for mutual repentance, forgiveness, reconciliation, and a better society. The oppressor hijacked independence from its messianic goals by teaching the oppressed the oppressor's pedagogy.

Therefore, conversion experience is a historical process with an eschatological mission. It is aware of the fact that, despite Africa being the most religious and potentially wealthy continent, it remains historically the most misgoverned, most violent, poorest, most indebted, and most exploited. Africa is inundated by refugees fleeing their rulers, who crave for droughts, famines, epidemics, and natural calamities as they crave tear gas, guns, poisons, and foreign aid in order to perpetuate themselves in power. By the World Bank's record of 1996, Africa is poorer than at independence and is exporting more capital to the west than it did during the colonial times and the slave trade. This is because, having eaten the fruits of others' struggle for independence, the dominant elite turned to eating the tree, ate the roots, and are now eating the soil.

Ten years after Kenyan independence I could foresee independence hijacking the struggle for freedom when I read in Galatians where Paul condemned Christians for taking conversion as a reconstruction and revision of Judaism. Now western churches and governments are imposing strict donor conditions on their puppet African regimes to ensure success in the contextualization of imperialism. The catastrophe of donor-imposed liberalization and structural adjustment programs bear testimony to this. Conversion must recapture the original messianic goal of the struggle for independence, namely justice, by wrestling with inequalities which the so-called new world order has popularized and globalized to transcend the need for local accountability. Conversion experience does not need donor conditions.

The donor Structural Adjustment Programs are at best nothing but mechanisms of helping the poor to identify themselves with their opposite pole, the rich, and forget about identifying themselves with God. They are neocolonial tools of exploitation. The current western strategy of globalizing its culture and power at the expense of tribalizing and localizing others is not different from the old missionary strategy of universalizing Christianity at the expense of other religious experiences. The monist pride of the "Great Commission," which had its pinnacle during the slave trade and colonialism, did not decline because of lack of support from western churches, but because it lacked accountability to any conversion experience. Universalism is the liberal game of elusivity and brushing unrepented history under the carpet, to mystify imperialism. By its very nature a monocentric system cannot become liberal, dual, plural, inclusive, and universal except by pretense. Monism feigns itself to be an angel of charity, a great commission, the white man's burden, manifest destiny, and donors' cartel, treating underdeveloped nations like beggars in proportion to their distances from God and from their nature.

Conversion experience encapsulates history and eschatology. It is messianic. It understands that God's Spirit is incarnate within the struggle of natural systems of science and logic. Hence it can be affirmed that God is subject to these struggles.

Conversion experience is like clay on a potter's wheel, where God and existence check, balance, and remold each other. The Creator and creation covenant themselves to be governed by the same rules. God and existence share a common inception, baptism, life, death, and resurrection without either party losing its free and intrinsic uniqueness or dominating the other.

Therefore, secondly, conversion experience is informed by God's incarnation in Jesus Christ. It involves the people and their environment. It liberates and synthesizes the energies engulfed by fear and paralysis into fulfilled existence.

Incarnation converts people of different historical and ecological backgrounds to become God's equal counterparts in the mission of reshaping the future of the universe. This frees African conversion experience from any obligation to a theology of reconstruction of neocolonialism. God's incarnation empowers creation to re-create and transcreate itself into a new creation (II Cor. 5:17). It helps creation to overcome its imprisonment to nature, culture, and environment.

Incarnation takes care of God's responsibility for what goes right or wrong with creation. God assumes responsibility for creating things that are free to enjoy God and themselves without God's interference. This makes creation something that turns out right or wrong in the hands of a sovereign Creator (Jer. 18:1-6). God permits creation the possibility of working according to God's intention in order for the relationship between God and existence to be dependent on grace, freedom, and reciprocal enjoyment. When something goes haywire with existence, there is automatic mutual estrangement between God and existence. The cross is the most vivid evidence that when existence sins, God shares its penalty.

What God creates, God governs, with the logic of vicarious liability whereby the principal is liable for the crimes committed by the agent. On this premise God vacates God's immutable attributes, becomes subject to fallible existence and gets incarnate in our finite nature. Incarnation changes God's attributes from being infallible, omnipotent, omniscient, almighty, and perfect into being available, accessible, responsible, answerable, and liable. There are no circumstances under which evil can force God to abdicate God's responsibility for any part of existence.

This accountability of God for both good and evil is the underlying principle of God's incarnation, grace, and good governance. By participating in existence, the Maker of all things becomes liable for the wrongs taking place in God's creation and shares the penalty of sin on the cross. The cross stands for God's redemptive humility. God does not wash God's hands of responsibility for creating a perfect existence with such freedom that it can be used to remain perfect or deviate from perfection.

Under the western theological administration God was not considered accountable to creation. Africans had no chance of survival on the basis of western theology. They could not rely upon missionary doctrine in their struggle to make slave masters, colonizers, and dictators accountable to creation or to God. Missionary faith gave corporations and governments license to become absolute masters over the destinies of people to whom they were not accountable. Africans had to turn to their conversion experience as the only hope for survival. God's incarnation was at work in, and accountable to, their conversion experience. It was not in the interest of missionary Christianity to teach slaves that God was a responsible Creator who, by directing history from within, becomes accountable to actual reality. This left slave masters, dictators, and colonizers to do with creation as they wished without a theology to hold them accountable to their victims.

The fact that God subjected Godself to the things God created frees all things from being subject to any state authority that is not accountable to them. God drinks the same cup that creation drinks. There is no theological basis for any creature to make itself absolute or subject itself to another with which it has no mutual accountability. God's incarnation takes place in the world by making accountable even those political, economic, and social conditions that are abusive and offensive to God's image. This was not part of missionary theology.

Missionary theology conceives a neutral God who directs history from outside. This is as repugnant to incarnation as Freud's and Marx's idea of history directing itself by selfish desires and interests. Freud and Marx aggravated the situation by developing their own internal determinism in which existence fulfills itself by psychoanalysis and materialism. Certainly, consciousness is a subtle form of matter and everything in the universe experiences a certain degree of change. But this consciousness finds fulfillment in being conscious of something outside the substance that produces it. It is through conversion that matter experiences being made, remade, and transmade into a new and free form of consciousness. Western Christianity blundered by denying the presence of God's incarnation in the material relationships. It feared being accused of harboring Marxism. Freudianism and Marxism stumbled by denying existence's accountability to the Creator. To them creation remained doomed, fixed, and imprisoned in its own prior existence, predetermined by its past, without a future. If creation is always in the present, without past or future, with no chance for re-creation and transcreation, existentialists would not have evolved.

In western traditions God is credited with only positive creativity. God is worthy of praise and thanks for what goes right under God's authority but is not worthy of blame and complaint for whatever goes wrong. This part-time God, who absconds God's obligation when things turn negative but takes credit when they turn positive, becomes the role model for companies that refuse their accountability to the poverty and environmental degradations caused by their profits. A perfectionist God is responsible for the instincts by which leaders can escape their commitment to taxpayers, marital obligations, parental duties, and social responsibilities with impunity.

A vacuum is left in western theology as to whom belongs ultimate accountability for the harm and disrespect inflicted on creation by dictatorship, slave trade, and colonialism. This is the infallible God in whose likeness African dictators are made. The Lutheran and Calvinist Reformation blundered by attacking papal infallibility rather than attacking God's infallibility from which the pope derived his. Reformers could not believe in the infallibility of God as a heavenly Ruler without this being the model, modus operandi, for God's earthly rulers.

Our African God does not govern mortal existence with an outside infallible omnipotence but only by mutual respect that opens God to petition, intercession, bargaining, negotiation, and change. God is an amazing Creator who puts Godself under the scrutiny of public inquiry in which God is available for attacks and questions by what God creates. The western idea of a monolithic God destroys the link in all religions, namely, "that every created thing reflects some of the attributes of its creator."[2] God becomes incarnate in all religions by being known to finite and fallible existence. An omnipotent and omniscient God who cannot be entangled with the carnality of civic responsibilities is too remote to understand the reproof of Jesus, "My God, my God! Why hast thou forsaken me?"

Incarnation affirms God's freedom from the prison of omniscience, omnipotence, and infallibility and accounts for God's humility and accountability to creation. Thus, God's incarnation and creatures' conversion act in a complementary manner to procreate the world. At the cross God and creation travel together on an equal, reciprocal, and relational orbit, on the basis of mutual respect. Incarnation and conversion are where God and creature are bound together by mutual life and common death.

So, conversion is analogous to the repetition of God's original act of creation, but not its recurrence or reconstruction. New existence is the result of creation, re-creation, and transcreation. Incarnation assists everything that God makes to pursue, with its own existence, the image of God the Creator, the Recreator, and the Transcreator. For its own fulfillment it pursues freedom of participation in God's work of relaunching creation anew.

    2. "Report of the Patmos 1995 International Symposium on Religion and Environment," *Daily Nation* (October 1995), 3.

The western idea of chopping off the soul from political and economic salvation, hardly biblical, works havoc in Africa. It enabled missionaries to build Christianity on the basis of European mechanistic experience without any sense of accountability to the messianic struggle of the local conversion experience. The Great Commission technically colonized the fallible believer with infallible dogmas. This dogmatization of Africa by western Christianity contradicted the incarnation of God in fallible, available, and accessible situations where prayers, censure, and crucifixion can touch God.

The soul-extracting missionary Christianity works like the poaching of rhino horns and elephant tusks. The sole interest of poaching Christianity is hacking off the precious horns from rhinos and tusks from elephants without any accountability to the remains. They do not care that tusks and horns cost the animals their lives. By using the gospel as a soul-hunting technology Christianity helped colonialism to exploit people like objects. The type of Christianity produced by soul-poaching methods is the fastest growing in the world. In Africa, it lacks intellectual, moral, and political accountability for exerting the least influence on human relationships and public life. In Rwanda and Kenya it flourishes oblivious to political massacres. It gives the dictators false assurance that they are mirror images of an infallible God, above-the-law, beyond the crown of thorns.

Incarnation As Suffering Restraint in God's Self-Accountability

Incarnation as realized through conversion experience is the African's only hope for survival. It makes God involved, available, accessible, and accountable to the process of transforming the world into a new and better creation. God participates in existence's joy and suffering and affirms God's accountability to creation, which God called into existence ex nihilo. God's accountability is attested by integrating God's love and freedom into the substance of fallible existence as in Christ's suffering on the cross. In the divine provision, an infallible God becomes fallible, or vulnerable.

God's incarnation helps all creatures to participate in God's action of determining their own final shape, whether that shape manifests the Creator's glory or deviates from it. Christ sent the Holy Spirit not to interfere with the freedom of existence but to participate in its struggle to perfect its likeness with God. The groaning of the Holy Spirit comes from sharing with existence its defects, which like medicine, animates existence to heal itself without being colonized by God in the healing process.

Incarnation, therefore, takes care of three cardinal principles. First, incarnation is a likeness of the original time and space that God called into existence out of nothing. Second, incarnation affirms that existence has a God-like creative mind, love, and freedom with which it can respond to God's acts of creation on the basis of mutual respect and participation. Christ the new Adam is not a reconstruction of the old Adam, but a re-creation and transcreation. Third, God becomes part of existence so that when existence goes haywire, as is most likely to happen, God the Holy Spirit helps existence to repent and recover. God suffers with existence.

The cross is the answer to the question of whether God can have God's cake and eat it too. God is not an African dictator who welcomes only the creation's praise and thanksgiving but not its sin and ingratitude. Salvation, by God's provision of Christ and as effected by the Holy Spirit, does not happen inevitably, like falling in love or caring for our families, but bids us partake in God's love for our enemies and seeking their best good, and forgives "our debtors."

God partakes in existence's continuous freedom of creativity, in which existence reproduces itself into more complex forms of experience, from elements to compounds, inorganic to organic, and unconscious to conscious mind. Evolutionary history has reduced the diversity of living species to less than one percent of the original species.[3] The greatest threat to the survival of all species is this strange newcomer, the human creature, if it continues to avoid responsibility for the damage its profits inflict on the environment. "For more than a half a billion years, evolutionary processes have constantly generated variations on themes established in the Cambrian explosion . . . *Homo sapiens* is able to understand the shape, extent, and value of earth's diversity. Indeed, we have a responsibility, as well as a self-interest, to value it."[4]

Human creativity is not limited to the social and material realm. It is not even confined by mechanistic forms of metaphysical and spiritual projections. It populates such realms with fantasies, demons and angels. Scientists claim to have noticed creative characteristics similar to our planet's in half a billion other planets in the universe, with material energies like the ones from which our minds evolved.[5] Marx hinted at the same creativity when he said, "People are made of what they eat." In Genesis we read, "God formed humanity from the dust of the earth." This affirms that out of existence can evolve complex life.

3. Richard Leakey, interview with T. M. Njoya on 24 May 1996 in Nairobi, Kenya.
4. Richard Leakey and Roger Lewin, *The Sixth Extinction* (New York: Doubleday, 1995), 75.
5. *Mid Stream* 19, no. 1 (Jan. 1980): 11.

Despite the power and complexity of creation, God is restrained by God's self-accountability and contract with existence not to meddle with existence's freedom of creativity so that creation can serve, glorify, praise, and enjoy God willingly, freely, and in love. God's self-restricting covenant with creation is attested by the crucifixion as seen in Noah's rainbow. Noah's rainbow stands as the cross before the cross to protect the freedom of creation from the Creator and the rights of the governed from violation by the governments.

God has made existence a free "manifestation of God's creative activity. Romans 8 indicates that it is not yet complete but that it is yearning for fulfillment. It is in process. It is going somewhere. It is moving from void to completion or fulfillment. It is moving from disarray to integration."[6] The gist of the Christian catechism is that creation takes part in God's joy of creating it. The Holy Spirit, acting as divine suffering in existence's bodily system, converts existence from captivity in its imperfections to enjoy its freedom in a new form.

The missionaries did not understand this. They baptized Africans by replacing their old names with new ones to affirm and seal conversion experience as a fact of life's newness — except that the new names were older European names. Instead of perceiving conversion as re-creation, the missionaries perceived it as identity switch, a trade-off of African individuality for a European one, a form of religious debasement. They misunderstood conversion as the sale of the heavenly half of creation to the earthly half, and vice versa. However, true African baptism integrates conversion with incarnation and estranged people are reconciled and given the right to take part in God's creativity.

Therefore God does not universalize God's reign and freedom but participates in the people's struggle to create their own governance and freedom according to their own needs. God's incarnation in our struggle for freedom avails grace, justice, and love to the struggle. This inaugurates the birth of a new creation, a new earth, and a new heaven, where the converted oppressors and oppressed become united. A new South Africa is able to emerge only from the converted oppressors and oppressed, united to forge a new common future. This reconciliation of formerly opposed forces through God's incarnation and human conversion, cannot be confused with the unproductive ability of the conquered to Africanize, indigenize, or emulate the conqueror's religion, government, and thinking habits.

Conversion is an act and process of receiving God's life in our lives,

6. "Report of the Patmos 1995 Intl. Symposium," 16.

politics, and other activities. The Bible clearly shows that in conversion experience various and diverse creatures become incorporated in the image of the invisible God, the firstborn of all creation; for in him all things in heaven and on earth were created, things invisible and visible, whether thrones or dominions or rulers or powers — all things have been created through him and from him (Col. 1:15-16).

As co-creators with God, all things in existence are stakeholders in each other's creative and governing power. Power belongs to all participating in creating and not to a few who hold high positions. This was the purpose of God's incarnation, that all creatures may participate in God's work of creating them and each have a share in the results.

Africa cannot be free without ridding itself of the donor idea that the gospel is a finished product which African Christianity receives from the west. The African conversion experience resolves the problem of Hendrick Kraemer's missiology in which Christianity and African religions are considered "mutually exclusive and discontinuous of each other."[7] I have never read western missiology in which God's incarnation takes place anywhere else other than in the western churches, philosophies, and culture, making them universal and others provincial. The Holy Spirit has the power to effect God's incarnation in any part of the world without the need for van Leeuwen's idea that "if one thing is crystal clear, however, it is that the end of western domination does not in the least mean the end of expansion so far as western civilization is concerned; on the contrary, that would appear to be the point of achieving conquests greater than any it has made hitherto."[8]

Nobody becomes the object of the gospel, grace, or salvation, but an active subject. The gospel is not what Jesus does but the impact in the life that incarnates what Christ does. The kerygma is mere verbiage unless it frees those who hear it from the bonds of tired faith, sterile confessions, petrified liturgy, and lifeless religiosity. It is quite ludicrous for the few who enjoy preaching, eating, sleeping, politics, and sex to subject others to being nothing but the objects and means of their own actions.

During the Cold War, the missionary-minded westerners feared the African's conversion as another Mao's great march, Castro's Bay of Pigs, and Kierkegaard's "Attack upon Christendom." But conversion experience does not methodologically develop qualitatively different from the theology of *ecclesia reformata semper reformanda*.

7. Hendrick Kraemer, *The Christian Message in a Non-Christian World* (Grand Rapids: Praeger, 1961).

8. A. T. van Leeuwen, *Christianity in World History* (New York: Scribner's, 1964), 13.

The Relationship of Creation, Conversion, and Incarnation

Conversion experience is possible because creation is not a finished product or fixed event. In the act of conversion God makes what God is creating to take part in determining its own final shape. God makes Godself party to this temporal experience and brings into it creative powers by which God originally created existence, ex nihilo. Conversion is the human response to creation and incarnation. By incarnation God infuses existence with God-like life. In creation the Creator shares with existence the sovereign freedom of self-determination.

This divine permission in creation, to work with God or to do things without reference to God, flows from God's own freedom. It ties God's hands from interfering with the freedom of existence unless invited by faith. This creates mutual respect and accountability between God and existence. It makes God and existence equally and mutually accountable for what happens in this world. This divine accountability to creation is what made Christ pay on the cross the penalty accruing from God's permission given to creation to enjoy freedom without God's interference.

The freedom, which various components of existence God allows to enjoy, enables them to propagate themselves into prolific natural, cultural, political, or social beings. God's share, God's freedom and creativity with creation, is attested by God telling the animals to reproduce themselves (Gen. 1:24-25), vegetation to have seeds (Gen. 1:12), and human beings to "multiply" (Gen. 1:28). The western mind did not comprehend that all forms of existence have capacities and rights to participate in their own creation, and that these physical elements evolved into living organisms four billion years ago. To think of converting Africans as passive objects without their participation was therefore a criminal offense against God and nature. There is no possible way of understanding the place of incarnation in creation without seeing creation as a joint Creator-creature venture. Every form of matter has a minimum consciousness which responds to God's call to evolve into more conscious stuff. Jesus confirmed this fact by saying "I tell you that God can take these stones and make descendants for Abraham" (Matt. 3:9) and when he said "I tell you, if you keep quiet the stones themselves will start shouting" (Luke 19:40). Balaam's donkey talked.

The incarnation of Christ attests to the fact that conversion recapitulates the primordial chaos and recreates it into differentiated entities with various degrees of perfection. When God becomes natural, natural activities like accidents, spontaneity, and deviations become fun and exciting despite being accompanied by pain. Quantum physics has the possibility of taking us beyond western determinism, paternalism, and rationalism, which cast doubt on the idea of creation ex nihilo. The processes scientists discredited as magic are no longer magic but scientific prospects.

In *God, Cosmos, Nature and Creativity,*[9] Paul Davies applied quantum physics in cosmological order, saying, "For it is no surprise to quantum physics that the universe pops into existence from nothing at all. It may bother other scientists, but quantum physicists are happy with the idea of cosmic spontaneity." This frees creation from confinement to deterministic and authoritarian views of law and order. While conversion occurs independently of the forces, feelings, recollection, and minds participating in it, it enlists their contribution into its process.

As long as existence is in a process of transition, reality is neither absolute nor neutral. Things can undergo wear and tear and the creativity to replace the wear and tear without conversion experience. Conversion is a basic improvement, a metamorphosis from worse to better beyond the repair of wear and tear. Conversion carries an experience like conception, birth, growth, death, or resurrection. One may be aware of some event of conversion in one's life but as it grows, it becomes a complex process, vocation, and discipleship, bigger than the disciple or personality. Remember the conversions of Paul, Constantine, and Luther. They became structural adjustments to the existing institutions. When conversion conforms to the existing traditions it fails to transform them. Now Africans are regretting that their independence conformed to the structures of colonialism. Independence is continuing to undergo structural adjustment under the duress of the World Bank.

So, since incarnation is God's self-limitation, or finitization into a form of existence, this gives allowance for creation to participate in divine activities with freedom and joy. The prophet Jeremiah (18:1-12), supported by Matthew 25:31-36 and Revelation 21:1-8, speaks about the freedom of a reciprocal relationship of God and existence. The three passages show God as a Being distinct and free from existence but granting existence equal and full distinction and freedom apart from God. God and existence are mutually exclusive, discontinuous of each other. The eternal distinction and discontinuity comes into existence without losing God's divine identity. By God's own gracious incarnation God comes to the human realm, inviting people to "Come let us argue it out" (Isa 1:18).

God plays dice with creative freedom by setting out to make a perfect pot and then exercises the freedom to shape it to be something other than what God originally intended (Jer. 18:4). It would take a mechanical and Calvinist Creator, different from our African God, to take away risk and fun from anything before it goes haywire.

9. *God, Cosmos, Nature and Creativity,* ed. Jill Gready (Univ. of Sydney, 1991-1994), 15.

The truth discovered by Jeremiah that "the vessel the potter [God] was making of the clay was imperfect in God's hands, so the potter reworked it into another vessel [not the reconstruction of the broken one] as it seemed good to God." This liberates the world from the false understanding of God as a cowardly, unilateral, and irresponsible quitter who resigns from divine responsibility when the going gets tough and who plays it safe by predetermining things to act according to how they were created. It was the same perfect clay that was spoiled which God used again for making a perfect pot.

"God gives creation freedom to become all that it wills to become. . . . Consequently God was responsible for the holocaust, slavery, wars of genocide, AIDS and cancer. God is responsible for the crash of the TWA flight 800."[10] Only in dual thinking can God have a double nature, one nature responsible for good and the other exempting itself from responsibility for bad. There is nothing that evolved, whether the HIV virus or smallpox, that evolved without God's attention and with unfettered freedom to do its will. Without this complete freedom nothing, not even dictators who inflict worse genocide and holocaust than epidemics, would be held accountable.

God puts up with a lot of hell where things, visible and invisible, cause the Holy Spirit to suffer the consequences of their ill-fitted selfishness. God permitted the "Accuser" to visit all manner of calamities upon Job and Jesus, and accompanied Lucifer's fall to the hell (Isa. 14:12) where Jesus went to deliver the captives.

Through incarnation the Creator shares with creatures the blame for evil and the task of rehabilitation. Earthly systems of governance must reflect this availability, accessibility, correctability of God in their governance.

God's Responsibility for Evil

Imagine that God, who is perfect, omniscient, omnipotent, watches sin taking place, right in God's own hands and instead of rudely interrupting it, or dropping creation like Moses dropped the tablets, God waits to suffer the consequences. Grace! Excellence! Greatness! When evil diminishes the creature's self-worth, polarizing creation with the threat of becoming its own opposite, nonexistence, God arrests and reverses the threat by being at the receiving end.

This is nothing like the western authoritarian consideration of sin as rebellion against God or as going astray from God's law. If sin is rebellion or going astray, it would mean that God feels God's power threatened by

10. A sermon by Rev. Robert Little, Burke (Va.) Presbyterian Church, July 21, 1996.

creatures. Sin from an autocratic feudal perspective is insubordination, revolt, insolence, insurrection, revolution, or coup against God. It is absolutely impossible for finite existence to revolt against an infinite God. Only Christ, Father, or Holy Spirit could revolt against God's eternal unity.

Creation sinned by failing to enjoy God, according to the 1765 Church of Scotland Shorter Catechism, "Man's chief end is to glorify God, and to enjoy him for ever." God's punishment is not experienced by existence as revenge or reprisal but as loss of joy. Good governance cannot happen without accepting responsibility for evil and restoring people's rights to enjoy being "God's children" (John 1:12).

This first sin turned into a hierarchy of domination when Adam, the man, refused accountability for his action, blamed Adamah, the woman, for his fall. Then Adamah blamed the reptile. Instead of trying to regain self-worth, a perfect likeness, Adam tried to look superior by making Adamah look inferior. The consequences polarized the world into various conflicting elements whose disequilibrium forced the Apostle Paul to agonize "For I do not do the good I want, but the evil I do not want is what I do" (Romans 7:19).

Conversion experience attests to the fact that God created things with some inherent possibility for deviation and that this possibility precedes double predestination. If predestination were to come prior to conversion and incarnation, it would make the diversity of species and liberation of captives impossible. God's act of creation was like whistling (starting) things into a march of existence and at the same time God whistling God's self into the same march. The late starters in this creation, race, planet earth, Abel, Enoch, Noah, Abraham, Moses, Rahab, Ruth, David, Cyrus, Esther, and others, joined the marathon of existence "looking at Jesus the pioneer and perfecter" (Hebrews 11 and 12:2) and the "Alpha and Omega" (Rev. 1:8, 26:1, 22:13) of existence. Early starters and later comers are guaranteed equal earnings (Matt. 20:1-16) and blessings.

This aspect of God as the one who partakes in the race for existence, and sins when God's creation sins, has not been accounted for in the western scholastic, classical, feminist, missionary, and liberation theologies. They still think of God as a clean white guy who shirks responsibility for sins happening in "God's kingdom." The view of the Synoptic Gospels is that "The reign of God is within you" (John 17:21) and not an external determinism orchestrated by an omniscient, transcendent, Augustinian, Almighty, Barthian, and Calvinist Outsider. God is not an outsider who escapes from history to avoid penalty for tortures, gas chambers, disappearances of relatives and violation of human rights. On the cross Christ paid the penalty of children neglected, wives battered, and police brutality. Christ does not enjoy historical amnesia. He remembers the memory of slave ships.

Since Job and Jesus knew that it was God who allowed all manner of evil to inflict them they did not beat around the bush looking for scapegoats; they directed their anger for what befell them against God. They did not blame Satan, Pilate, the Sanhedrin, or the crowd for predicaments but asked God, "Why hast thou forsaken me?" God's responsibility for evil is what grace, Immanuel, availability, or accountability means. God delayed God's intervention, abandoning Jesus to suffer the most horrible evil imaginable, the murder of God. Job ignored Satan's role in his misery and went straight for God's throat, charging, "God has handed me over to evil men" (Job 16:11ff).

The responsible incarnate God differs from Calvin's perfectionist God, who predetermines who shall be God's praisers and thankers and who shall be hell's ungrateful complainers. The human likeness with God is downgraded by Calvin's belief that "we cannot think of ourselves as we ought to think without utterly despising everything that may be supposed an excellence in us."[11] Calvin further said, "We call predestination God's eternal decree, by which he determined with himself what he willed to become of each man. For all are not created in equal condition; rather, eternal life is foreordained for some, eternal damnation for others.[12] According to Calvinism, existence goes through motions of inevitable life and death without any right to alter its destiny. This is what B. F. Skinner calls "operant behavior." Fortunately for conversion experience, God foresees imperfection coming, witnesses it happening, allows it to happen, and provides the means of escape. According to the gospel of Christ, God puts predestination in the hands of creatures so that they can determine for themselves whether to praise or not, whether to go to hell or to heaven.

Richard Shaull's analysis of the Lutheran Reformation[13] is historically but not theologically correct. Luther's revolution betrayed itself by not holding God accountable for all historical evils. If Luther and Calvin were the ones who discovered Mary pregnant before marriage, they would have offered abortion services and sought for condoms to ensure that Mary did not have another unauthorized aberration. After knowing the baby Jesus to be the Son of God, they would have put the mother on a special vegetarian diet, bottled water, and natural herbs to save Jesus from being born contaminated with mercury and radiation. Jeremiah was more radical than the Reformers. He took all ecological, religious, and political aberrations to be God's responsibility. The Babylonian captivity was God's "wheel" (Jer. 18:3) of correcting social

11. *Institutes of the Christian Religion* (Philadelphia: Presbyterian Board of Religious Education, 1928), 641.

12. T. F. Torrance, *A Calvin Treasury* (London: SCM Press, 1963), 101.

13. *The Reformation and Liberation Theology* (Louisville: Westminster/John Knox, 1991), 25-50.

and moral abnormalities. When God said, "Can I not do with you, O house of Israel, just as the potter has done? Just like the clay in the potter's hand, so are you in my hand, O house of Israel" (Jer. 18:6), what did God mean? God meant, "See here! For three years I have come looking for fruit on this tree, and still I find none. Cut it down! Why should it be wasting the soil? The gardener replied, 'Sir, let it alone for one more year, until I dig around it. If it bears fruit next year, well and good; but if not cut it down' " (Luke 13:6-9).

Summary: Human Involvement in God's Incarnation

We began by saying that our God is an accountable God who pays the penalty, suffers, and dies for the sins for the things God has created. To be like God is to be accountable for one's being, deeds, and possessions. Loss of pain is to leprosy what loss of accountability is to sin. Conversion restores our ability to feel accountable. Conversion responds to God's accountability. The holy God suffers and dies with the inhuman and the dehumanized so that they can recover their likeness with God. Christ is God's incarnate power which transforms the inhuman to human, dehumanized to dignity, imperfection into perfection, impunity to accountability. The entry of Christ in evil transactions transforms them into their opposite, makes them creative.

This new theological understanding is crucial for the continuity of generative creation in the third and subsequent millennia. It differs from existing mechanistic theologies because they excuse God, and by extension, the Church, from accountability to the consequences of exploitation and injustice. If God did not want to suffer for the evils done by God's creation, God would have suspended creation's freedom, discarded the defective creation, and started another creation, out of nothing, all over again.

Such is the creative emanation of God that makes a community responsible to God and itself, without which there is no police, military, or constitutional force to make people respect each other's dignity. Where people are not accountable to each other in their unconscious they cannot be one in the conscious. In theological terms, "If the Lord does not build a house the work of the builders is useless" (Psalm 127:1).

Without the accountability of the Creator to creation, conscious to the unconscious and governors to the governed we cannot have mutual, just, and humane relationships in existence, society, family, and politics. Religion, economics, and politics will be at the mercy of the whimsical interests of the benefactors. Christ is God's accountability and the Holy Spirit the suffering guarantor of that accountability to existence. Existence responds to God by faith affirming itself through conversion experience.

Public Liturgy — A People's Theology in Aotearoa, New Zealand

GEORGE ARMSTRONG

THE LAST FIFTY YEARS of this century and millennium are the theme of this chapter. The focus is upon particular intersections of the Christian faith and Church with the prevailing political and economic conditions.

The early part of this fifty years, particularly with the Vietnam War and the attempt to open up New Zealand ports to U.S. nuclear submarines, involved prominent issues of militarism and nuclear weapons systems. There was substantial church opposition to the involvement of the New Zealand Armed Forces in the Vietnam War and this was symbolized in the Good Friday "Procession of Witness" in Auckland in 1968. The church involvement was, of course, but part of a much larger opposition. The attempt to bring nuclear warships into New Zealand ports began in the mid-seventies. A "Peace Squadron" of small boats was initiated from St. John's Theological College in Auckland in 1975. It was from St. John's also that the Good Friday incident of 1968 had originated.

By the latter part of the fifty-year period, the peace squadrons that had been formed throughout New Zealand had actually accomplished what they had attempted. New Zealand, and also the South Pacific, had been legislatively designated nuclear-free or nuclear weapon-free zones.

But by this time, the major issue for church and society was different. Economics had moved center stage. Here again, church and state were at odds. The opposition of the church to the state's ambitious neoliberal monetarist policies was more substantial and official than had been its opposition to the Vietnam War or to nuclear weapons systems impinging on New Zealand. Official ceremonial church opposition was expressed in the Wellington Anglican diocese by the "Cathedral marching on the Parliament," a procession in 1991 of the diocese's formal leadership from a vigil in the Cathedral to the Prime Minister at Parliament next door.

The beginning and end of this fifty-year period were thus marked by a church protest. In 1968 and 1975, the twin gestures were against militarization and nuclearization. The end of the period saw the Cathedral officially "up in arms" against the Parliament over New Right economics.

This essay characterizes these two protest gestures, the first consisting of two distinct episodes, as occasions of "public liturgy." They were media-intensive events which made a substantial impact. Yet they were intended as primarily acts of worship and witness and mission, seeking and conveying a divine interpretation of the meaning of the public directions of the nation.

This essay is a welcoming of its readers into the essence of Aotearoa, New Zealand. It is a sharing with you some of its deepest realities.

More than all of this, it is an invitation to communion with us, itself a call to worship.

Public Liturgy

Liturgy or worship is a larger enterprise than is usually understood within conventional Christian theology. Liturgy as used in this chapter refers to the expression of a primal and deeply rooted corporate human instinct. Human groups and societies have an urge within them to express in language or symbolic action their fundamental societal and religious concerns. In New Zealand — as elsewhere on the planet — public liturgy often takes the form of public demonstrations or protests. The "antinuclear" and "antimonetarist" public liturgies of this chapter aspired to be both protest liturgies and more than protest liturgies.

Liturgy and worship are both orchestrated and unpredictable. The choreography is designed by leaders or liturgists with a sense of the wide range of symbols and aspirations and commitments of the potential participants or "worshipers." Often, however, the most memorable and apt symbols leap from unscripted acts and gestures evoked in the spirit of the liturgical event itself. When Stephen Sherie stretched out his hand across the broiling water separating his motor boat from the submarine *Haddo,* his intent was to hoist to safety a canoeist trapped atop its nuclear hull. A few moments before, Sherie's boat had liberally daubed the bow of the black nuclear monster with radiation-warning yellow paint. But in that later split second, poised in eternity, Sherie, a mild-mannered bespectacled steel worker, was inspired not only to haul the canoeist to safety but to himself leap and change places. Sherie was captured in the subsequent front page newspaper photograph dancing a quasi-religious jig on the hull before the conning tower and gesticulating to the submarine commander to "turn this bloody thing around." The banner headline over this unforgettable image read "Hot Welcome for Yellow Submarine." So often in those months and years did that sort of miraculous image arise that we began to trust and expect it. Not once were we disappointed.

Liturgy achieves more than a cool mirroring of what the worshipers think and feel. The mirror held up by liturgy actually functions to transmit and transfer exhilaration and apprehension to those who behold the liturgy from afar in amphitheater and temple. The drama is interactive in this wider sense amongst the beholders as amongst the true believers.

As well as transmission and interaction, there is a strong concentration of emotion and meaning. As when a mirror focuses the sun's rays into an incendiary beam, so public liturgy can effectually multiply the energies initially present. Worshipers end up "energized"; spectators born again; those who came to scoff remain to pray; those hostile or threatened are disconcerted or disarmed by the humanity and good humor of their opponent.

Ritualized drama is too pale a construction to put upon liturgy's communion with the sacred and transcendent. Liturgy touches tenderly the ultimate mysteries of existence and of potentiality both personal and societal. It is an invoking and a making present of whatever forces of history and heritage, whatever mysteries and gods and saints ever were. The power and beauty, the creative and redemptive love of the universe convene in liturgy to purge imperfection, to raise the liturgists far beyond any egotistic exhibitionism, to fulfill heaven and earth's noblest intentions.

A dominant motif of this liturgical yearning for the "not-yet" is that of inclusiveness and reconciliation. This is not a question of friends and enemies, of winners or losers. This is a struggle amongst ourselves over the meaning of our common culture, the direction of our common future. Certainly, protest liturgy is bound up with preventing, defending, defusing, and dismantling. But this apparent antagonism is in essence an affirmation of the whole of life. The liturgy defends our whole selves against the threat to our whole selves that has arisen within one part of ourselves. As the Vietnamese Buddhists urged at the height of their agonies, seeking a better way: "they are our brothers [and sisters] whom we kill."

Compare these notions of liturgy and worship, not unfamiliar to Christian liturgical scholars, with the routine recitals of public worship in churches! While not entirely dissimilar, the absence from church services of worldly connections and deep human emotion gives rise to creative questions about the faithfulness of church liturgies to the gospel of Jesus, their professed liberative savior of the world. There are good reasons for the low appeal and low estate of the churches in skeptical and secularized New Zealand. But for the Christians involved in initiating (with others) this chapter's rituals, their public liturgy aspired — with some success — to marry Christian with "natural" symbols and energies. It seemed just possible to them that a liberative Christianity might be able to be reappropriated by a whole People in process of institutional renewal throughout its political economic and cultural forms.

Grand Narrative: Two Contexts and Two Texts

Ahead and astern are the two contexts in which the narrative of this essay is "anchored."

The anchorage astern, in the 1960s and 1970s, is militarism, nuclear weapons, and "cold" war. Ahead in the 1980s and 1990s lies the born-again global economy of triumphal capitalism, where corporations rule the world, where the gospel of GATT dictates the unquestioned assumptions of all media discourse.

The New Zealand ship of state is immobilized in the contradiction between the anchorages. Public liturgies have "celebrated" each context, seeking to match the contexts with appropriate sacred "texts," to unfurl as it were protest flags above the stalled vessel, to interpret and influence the situation and — above all — to get the ship of state under way again, its course reset in more adequate, human, and agreed directions.

Nuclear Free Liturgy

The two protest liturgies, the Good Friday Procession of 1968 and the 1975 founding of the waterborne Peace Squadron, are twin sisters of the same impulse, arising from two parts of the same context: war and nuclear war.

So remote from killing fields and nuclear silos, New Zealand was a surprising location for spectacular antiwar and antinuclear engagement. But nowhere else perhaps in the world have the antinuclear energies of indigenous and settler, of women and men and children, engaged more visibly, inclusively, and institutionally against bombs and The Bomb than in these southernmost islands. Early in these last fifty years New Zealand declared a kind of war-against-War. It appears — at least for a moment and at least symbolically — to have prevailed. Doubtless there are countless peace candles lit at far greater cost and with far less visibility. New Zealand's role may well be a liturgical one, to be a peculiarly manifest spectacle to the world.

Maori theologian Rob Cooper ponders — not without a touch of humor — how it is that indigenous Maori vocation, a costly vocation indeed, resurges in Aotearoa at a time of multiple nuclear apocalypse:

> . . . have you ever wondered why it is that we have been introduced so late into Western human history, at least in terms of its military development?
>
> How is it that we've arrived on the scene just as the curtain seems to be coming down, not to the roar of thunderous and approving applause, but to huge blasts of apocalyptic dimensions?
>
> What is our part in all this? . . .
>
> We, Tangata Whenua, Have Learned Much
> We have learned, to our cost, of the power of politics and its military methods of achieving objectives. . . .
>
> We have learned that there is a "price" to every use or misuse of ourselves, our lands, waters and seas, and this world. We have learned, precisely because we retain those essential values which make us sensitive to the very world we live in. We have learned that Human Development is only authentic when it is complete; when it promotes the good of every person and of the whole person.
>
> For me, this is the contribution we have, which can be brought into this world, seemingly gone mad.
>
> We are Tangata Whenua — not only people of the land, but people out of and from within the land.
>
> We are the upright walking earth, possessing everything that God intended for the common good. . . .
>
> We have grasped Christianity with an unshakeable Grip because it makes sense to everything that is noble and good in being Maori.[1]

Maori and indigenous perception, like that of women, needs no additional logic to be persuaded of the monstrous violation of the human cosmos implicit in nuclear weaponry.

Saint Paul experienced and expressed his ministry as bittersweet. The Apostle felt himself set forth as a theatrical spectacle to the world. And he

1. Rob Cooper, *Peace and Human Development — a Maori Perspective.* 1985. Unpublished discussion paper for Te Runanga Whakawhanaunga i nga Hahi o Aotearoa.

was the last into the arena. Rob Cooper's piquant questions are similarly
spiced. Those of us at the center of the closing of New Zealand harbors to
nuclear warships heard with amazement the mighty *Time* magazine asking
was there something wrong with the water down there in New Zealand
that had rendered its inhabitants so irrational. Did the New Zealanders not
realize that they were undermining their own ultimate security: the ANZUS
military alliance binding Australia, New Zealand, and the U.S.A. and sealed
with the bloody partnerships of World War Two? *Time*'s irony may have
been clumsy, its humor labored. But New Zealand's pariah status was
assured: just when we had made one of our most conspicuous contributions
to world peace! The text of St. Paul and the experiential context from which
it arose, the concept of being, at his finest moment, a spectacle of foolishness and disgrace, aptly fitted New Zealand's situation as a nation. The
experience of Jesus is of course the experience of Paul — and of all the
Hebrew prophets — writ large.

Thus does text arise from context, sacred text from sacred context.
Revelatory experiences find utterance in revelatory symbol and effectual
action. Sacred text calls across history to sacred text because a congruence
of contexts and discoveries renders them mutually illuminating to one
another. The communication which electrifies such an encounter signals a
communion of saints as well as a communication between saints. St. Paul's
and Rob Cooper's and the Peace Squadron's contexts and texts are mutually
illuminating.

These are some of the labyrinthine ways through which appropriate
exegesis and hermeneutics must pass. The above conclusions about Paul
and Jesus and the prophets seem simple and obvious enough. Yet the logic
of sacred texts and contexts are not accessible to those whose actual lived
experiences are not significantly congruent. Gospel wisdom is hidden from
the wise and revealed unto babes. Only "the things that are not" can, in
the wisdom of God, "bring to nought the things that are."

Good Friday Public Liturgy 1968

For all of us at St. John's Theological College, the evening of Good Friday
1968 developed as usual. As usual, fifteen hundred or so Anglicans and
other church people assembled at the foot of Auckland's Main Street. The
procession through Queen Street, following the processional cross and the
bishop, was designed as a "quiet contemplation of the crucified" (as the
bishop later argued). It was also a "procession of witness," intended to
display to any bystanders the nature of the Christ who was being honored

and remembered by his worshipers. When several of us from St. John's College, myself as a lecturer and a dozen or so students arrived on the scene with placards, we realized for the first time that we might not be welcome. Asked to leave our placards behind by the bishop — who was under heavy pressure from some of the lay faithful, we compromised by saying we'd follow behind the main procession and not as part of it. For all of us placard carriers, it was our first experience of "public liturgy." We children of the theological 1960s were destined to learn fast.

Bemused, the media scented some significance in the subsequent scene of a bishop sending a posse of police to remove us from his procession, contaminated when we had later joined ourselves too close to the main body to be distinguishable from it. Television cameras, famished from thin ecclesiastic procession fare, fell upon us gratefully. The print media put us on their front page but focused on the issue of domestic authority within a normally monolithic church.

Newspaper photos pictured the slogans on the placards:

> *Christ died for the Vietcong;*
> *Christ died for ANZACS* [NZ and Australian armed forces];
> *Christ died for All;*
> *Make Love not War;*
> *You?*

Underneath the headlines *Church Procession Placard Bearers told to Move Off* and *Bishop 'Expels' Demonstrators, No Reprimand for Eight with Banners,* the story pieced itself together:

> Eight people who carried slogans on banners behind a procession of witness up Queen St. last night were asked by the Bishop of Auckland, through the police, to leave the procession: . . . a spokesperson for the group of placard carriers said: 'We were really trying to show that Christ is really involved on every side of things'. . . ."

This event was a "liturgy within a liturgy," with some structural resemblance — as it transpired — to Jesus taking his gospel amongst the scribes and Pharisees at the temple in Jerusalem. Had the scribal and pharisaic mind of Jesus' era not been on other things, they might have recognized in Jesus a recall to ancient Hebrew standards and spirit common to all of them. One young scribe of the 1968 era, a priest who was not amongst the protesters, discerned the ironic revelation within the contemporary events. It was quintessential "public liturgy" in which the spirit of the "scribal" response to the thing witnessed to by the liturgy-within-a-liturgy reduplicated the essentials of the original scribal response to Jesus. A very complex and powerful constellation of feelings was being conjured up, as if by incantation, to conjoin this 1968 event with that original two-thousand-year-old Good Friday crucifixion which was its alleged inspiration.

Don Battley, the young priest, coined the phrase *placarding Christ* in his closely argued letter to the editor of the national Anglican newspaper *Church and People:*

> The declared purpose of the Procession was to witness to the Crucifixion, to 'contemplate Christ crucified' and to forward the renewal of the Church in the Diocese. The placards did no more than proclaim the meaning of the Crucifixion in contemporary terms. But it was alleged against the placard-bearers that they were gatecrashing and were trying to use a religious procession for political purposes. One is reminded that the witness of Christ himself was distorted and given a political twist: 'we found this man perverting our nation, and forbidding us to give tribute to Caesar!' Apparently we are as capable as the religious people of A.D. 29 of misreading and misrepresenting those who would use unorthodox and risky methods of proclaiming today the universality of God's love towards people. . . .

Battley's letter concluded on a painful note:

> The fault of the placard-bearers was that they violated our pietistic view of Good Friday A.D. 29 and confronted us with the conflicts of Good Friday, 1968. Their rejection by the majority of us was ominously true to form. I wonder if I am alone in remembering, with some shame, that at the moment of crisis when the authorities moved against 'the troubler of Israel,' 'they all forsook him and fled.'

In this Good Friday experience, we neophytes had stumbled upon truths too deep for liberal philosophy or theology. Indeed we had long had the 1960s rhetoric of "total immersion," the "holy in the common," "holy worldliness," the Pentecostal point being in the engagement. Now in the living of this rhetoric came a very different caliber of revelation. For all our impulsiveness and diverse egoism, we experienced in our own personal and corporate bodies something of Jesus' incarnate Way which I myself had not had from books or prayers. It had an earth taste to it which both confirmed and tested religious faith to the uttermost. We had stumbled into a historical configuring of ourselves which left us in a dynamic posturing uncomfortably similar to that of Jesus face to face with his adversaries. To be excommunicated from our own church for our attempt to be loyal to the deep tradition of that church, this was to ultimately locate us experientially within the essence of the whole prophetic tradition.

This first Vietnam War context and text had its origins in the period immediately following the second world war. The postcolonial struggles for self-determination surged on in parallel with the rising drive between the superpowers for containment. The heavens and earth were colonized by nuclear weapons systems of East and West. Confrontation had come to a head in South Vietnam and in the revolt of Western youth against the logic of their militarized patriarchies. The Good Friday Liturgy in New Zealand had been part of this revolt. Even at this early stage of the fifty-year period, the economic fundamentals of Third World "development" fueled by Great Power — controlled capital and ideology were also revealing themselves. The economic, technical, and political development initially hailed as the new name for Peace was beginning to be exposed as but one more mechanism for competing and domineering world powers. Third World ecumenical analysis dwelt upon these factors in regional and world assemblies and consultations without end. Nuclear weaponry and to some extent nuclear power came to be a symbol of the oppressive totalities which had hijacked the broadly democratic aspirations for people-centered and people-controlled development. The possible use of nuclear weapons had always been a feature of the Indochina instabilities of the late 1950s and 60s. This lurking apocalypse leapt to center stage for New Zealand by the middle seventies even as the hot war-fires were dampened down in Vietnam.

The 1968 Good Friday protesters had spent the sacred noon to three o'clock three-hour period of Jesus' hanging on the Cross to listen to and discuss Albert van den Heuvel's tape-recorded addresses. Van den Heuvel headed the Youth Department of the World Council of Churches, which had in 1967 published a Risk series paperback "The Development Apocalypse — Will International Injustice Kill the Ecumenical Movement?" Van den Heuvel and ecumenical youth reflected concerns that had surfaced also at the 1966 Geneva World Conference on Church and Society. High on its agenda had been the Vietnam War.

The struggle against war and the nuclear threat had thus never been single issues for the ecumenical church. Together with the economic and soon the gender and race questions, they were increasingly woven in a single tapestry of understanding requiring a profound and wide-ranging response.

The Anti-Nuclear Peace Squadron

It was nuclear issues that were preoccupying the minds of the more progressive students at St. John's College when I returned there in 1973 from
doctoral study with Richard Shaull in Princeton. The struggle to outlaw
French atmospheric nuclear bomb testing from the Pacific region was
reaching full strength and was to have Labor Government official support
in the sending of a naval frigate to join the protest fleet. The theological
students carried me off with them down to the wharfside where they handed
over safety harnesses purchased by funds collected at the College.

By 1975 and the formation of the Auckland Peace Squadron from St.
John's College, it was the U.S.A. and its mammoth Trident submarine
program that was in the limelight. Each Trident was a virtual battery of
ballistic missile launchers, engineered into a battleship capable of heroically
prolonged deep-ocean undetectable submersion. A massive volley of independently targeted multiple Hiroshima's could streak to their targets from
any one of these vessels at the touch of a button. *The New Zealand Herald*
asked whether nuclear ship visits were the "Thin End of the Trident." The
article quoted extensively from a letter from Nils Peter Gleditsch, executive
director of the Oslo-based International Peace Research Institute:

> The United States may be considering operating nuclear-armed Trident
> submarines in the South Pacific . . . this may be the aim of the upsurge
> in American naval activity in the South Pacific over the past eighteen
> months or so. 'The long term goal of this activity seems to be directed
> towards retaining Australia and New Zealand as military allies,' Mr.
> Gleditsch says. . . . More particularly, the increased naval activity may
> be directed towards 'ensuring favorable attitudes in the future towards
> deployment of Trident submarines in the Pacific. 'The Trident system
> may well require some sort of shore installation in the South Pacific,'
> Mr. Gleditsch says. This might be either command or control facilities,
> or perhaps for access to ports for nuclear vessels supporting the Trident
> submarines. The range of the Trident missile, he says, is such that a
> submarine could cruise almost as far south as New Zealand and still be
> capable of landing its missiles on Soviet targets.

Pressure was on the New Zealand government to accept again visits
from nuclear-powered U.S. warships. But by this time also, the general
environmental movement was growing apace, mobilized and resolute from
a successful campaign to overcome any attempt to lay groundwork for
future nuclear power stations in New Zealand.

One of the most powerful images to etch itself in my memory from Princeton was the televized spectacle of a waterborne Quaker public liturgy at Port Covington (Baltimore) in 1971. Richard K. Taylor's *Blockade! A Guide to Non-Violent Intervention* (Maryknoll, N.Y.: Orbis, 1977) describes this "non-violent intervention" in considerable detail. The dominant image was of a tiny kayak with a lightly clad crew of two dwarfed under the towering bows of the arms-laden Pakistani freighter "Al-Ahmadi," preventing its onward deadly voyage to fuel the U.S. government-supported dictatorship's massacre of the people of East Bengal.

This image stirred within me, infant in the womb, as I watched the bruising figure of Robert Muldoon wrest the helm of state in 1975 from the incumbent Labor Prime Minister. First amongst Muldoon's actions was an invitation to the U.S. nuclear navy.

The 1968 Good Friday Event had earlier moved us from innocence to guile. Though still harmless as doves, we would now by 1975 be wise as serpents. From the Peace Squadron's first prayerfully calculated announcement we moved with great ethical and spiritual care, sensing that this might become a major and lengthy enterprise, played out in direct contravention of central government policy. We were not wrong. Those of us who had inched our way through the mid-1960s towards a public ministry of action, had together stumbled upon new but dangerous broad tunnels into truth.

We had accurately anticipated the hostility of a national Conservative Government. We had, however, no notion of the breadth and depth of the inheritance into which we were now entering. As the day drew closer for the entry of the nuclear cruiser *Long Beach,* on the first day of October 1976, public interest rose spectacularly. We could not have guessed that what was imaged on that day, in the teeth of the government's armed forces and police resources, would in a very short time become itself the official policy of all parties in government.

The Peace Squadron deliberately chose to invent for public liturgy language, logic images, and strategies which, though in full harmony with Christian spirit, was capable of evoking and articulating the thoughts and visions of a broader societal constituency. We certainly abandoned such esoteric if evangelically powerful Good Friday images as Jesus "dying for" all. In the event, the curious twinning of a biblical "David and Goliath" with a Peter Sellars' "the mouse that roared" image was typical of the many happy coincidences that made possible a very strange mix of publics, from atheist to born-again Christian. What the Peace Squadron essentially sought were forms of action and spirit eloquent in themselves — without need of words (though there were to be plenty of those) — expressions of truth fundamental for both religious and secular imaginations. Further, in the action, as with the Quaker canoeists at Baltimore, the symbolic image and the pragmatic tactic were one and the same thing. Pragmatically we sought the physical and permanent absence of nuclear armed and powered warships from the port of Auckland. Likewise the Baltimore Quakers were out to stop the concrete dispatch of those weapons. Symbolically, frail tiny craft threatened by a towering knife-edge of steel or a submarine making a reckless bolt for its berth through a mass of small pleasure craft, mirrored concretely in the local situation the distant and global form of the same menace, our own backyard become a Tiananmen Square or a South Vietnamese village.

It became eventually my responsibility to be spokesperson for this unlikely and delightful armada. Its varied membership taught me how it might be possible to be priest to and prophet for a far larger and more diverse congregation than anything within the church as formally constituted.

For myself the Vietnam Good Friday Event had confirmed my determination to go against convention if need be, whatever the consequences. The Peace Squadron confirmed this change of life direction, turning me actively outward from the temple and towards the streets. The first discovery, brand new in the earlier antiwar context, of the Truth that lay only most fully in congruent action and profoundly present in Christian faith, was proving true in the fully secular arena also. Apart from a few warlike individuals, the support from the churches and from the Anglican church was this time astonishing and followed us out into streets and harbor.

The first engagement of the Peace Squadron with a nuclear warship came after an elaborate build-up. Journalist Geoff Chapple reported on the entry of the *Long Beach*:

> The Auckland peace squadron took to the water in earnest for the first time as the 17,000 ton nuclear cruiser the USS *Long Beach* neared the Harbor Limit threshold of the Port of Auckland. The resulting engagement had the air of Gentleman's chess game. Two men were arrested on the water. Both were skippers of large stylish sail boats. One was Phil Amos, the Minister of Education in the Labor Government which had lost the election the previous year to Mr. Robert Muldoon's National Party. The other was Mr. Pat Taylor, company director of a boatbuilding firm and of a bullion and precious stones business. The *Long Beach* commander, captain H. C. Schrader, came ashore complimenting the peace skippers on their seamanship and offering them places in his ship's company.

A letter from the squadron sought to reach out in common humanity to Captain Schrader. The letter hoped to reach through to and beyond the personal to the political.

> Our protest is not directed against you personally, nor your men, nor against the people of your great country whose hospitality and generosity many of us have enjoyed. Many of our most determined members have never been protesters before. Many of us do not like confrontations, especially against an old friend and ally to whom we feel real gratitude on account of its role in the last World War. Many of our boats carried both husbands and wives: a sign of total dedication which a family man like yourself will appreciate. Our protest is a positive one. It is an affirmation of Peace and Life over against Death.

With the next warship visit, the façade of pleasant gallantry was to fall away. On January 16, 1978, the five-thousand-ton hunter killer submarine *Pintado,* tucked in behind the New Zealand navy frigate *Waikato,* powered into the midst of the protest fleet of small craft cruising quietly just outside the limits of the choice Waitemata Harbour. According to Geoff Chapple, the navy's no-nonsense entry plan was to cleave the protest fleet at 10 knots. Navy wasp helicopter pilots were simultaneously to lower their craft just above the mast tips of any protest vessels likely to block the channel. The forty-knot downdraft from helicopter rotors, or grappling hooks swung from above, would disable the small craft. Chapple described the subsequent events:

> Roy May, in a cruising canoe, found himself in the middle of the action.
> 'I hadn't meant to, but with the speed of approach, and the fact that the Waikato had veered, I found myself in the middle of it. A helicopter was just above me, and I couldn't move the paddle. In this type of canoe, you have to keep moving the paddle to keep it upright.'
> May saw three of the six kayaks on the water overturned. He described the helicopter blast as 'like being beaten with ten thousand pillows.' He strove to dig his paddle into the water. 'I got the blade up, and then it was torn from my hands. It was attached by a rope, but I couldn't get it back.' . . . May saw his canoe get within fifteen feet of the submarine's huge propeller, and only the tip of it stayed above water. . . .
> 'I had double flotation inside that canoe and I knew if the screw was pulling it that far down, then if I went into it, I wasn't going to bob up like that.'

The Captain of *Pintado,* Commander J. J. McDonald, had one eye on the unintentional hero struggling at his reversing stern. His other was on a very deliberate sailor on his bow. Thirty-nine-year-old Dave Wray set out from his Waiheke Island home that morning in a twelve-foot wooden dinghy, with a four and a half horsepower Seagull motor on the back. 'I keep out of politics,' says Wray.

'I've been here for twenty years, and I'm proud to say I've never voted. I turn wood, and fish for a living, but when I heard about the sub coming in, I was incensed. This was my personal act of conscience. I've got five kids. I want these waters to be safe for them. The Hauraki Gulf is their backyard. . . . We're always in boats, we know how to handle them. . . . It was for all the kids coming up, that we want these waters to remain safe from the accidents possible with nuclear power, and the nuclear weapons these things carry. It's their playground. . . . I assessed the situation, and it didn't feel dangerous. We went right up on his deck, and slewed off again and sat on the water. We got our opportunity to go in and we took it, and we'll do it again.'

A few moments later, the N.Z. frigate spotted a gap. . . . *Waikato* strained in response to yet one more order (eighty in eight minutes) from the captain on the bridge. She bolted for the gap. The submarine tucked in smartly behind, leaving the peace fleet churning in its boiling wake.

No one had been injured.

The police made no arrests.

Damage totalled one mast broken by helicopter down draught and one severed propeller shaft.

The New Zealand Herald was the country's largest and most conservative daily newspaper. Ted Reynolds of *The Herald* had made it his business to attend the organizational meetings prior to the *Pintado*'s visit. Two days after *Pintado*'s arrival on January 18, 1978, a full-page feature article by him appeared entitled "Anatomy of a Nuclear Protest." Of the helicopters Reynolds wrote:

> Helicopter 'Hurricane' Brings Chaos
> Helicopters appeared to add greatly to the danger. . . .

Two experienced journalists, Chapple and Reynolds, were in agreement.

Chapple's conclusion after Pintado was that a balance had tipped. Aucklanders in their holiday-making thousands crowded the many vantage points which ringed their splendid harbor. New Zealanders generally had the benefit of comprehensive in-depth radio, newspaper, and television coverage. The majority had begun to swing in behind the Peace Squadron.

Geoff Chapple undertook a careful political analysis:

> By contrast with the police handling of the *Long Beach* demonstration, the entry of the *Pintado* seemed like a military operation. The authorities in charge of getting the *Pintado* through the protest fleet are careful to point out that it, too, was a police-controlled operation. (There is, after all, something ominous in spelling out an operation by the New Zealand military against New Zealand citizens). . . . Quite simply, the peace fleet had posed a challenge to the state greater than the state could handle with its police resources. So the military had been used in a way seldom seen in this country. The state had bared its fangs in a way which was both ominous and a measure of Peace Squadron effectiveness. . . . A further question is that the protesters, by making New Zealand ports a trouble spot for nuclear craft, is in a way conversing directly with the United States Navy command, over the head of the New Zealand Government. Commander McDonald rang his operational commander in Japan immediately on berthing at Jellicoe Wharf. The operational commander was told of the dangerous entry. If the United States command decided, therefore, that New Zealand ports were becoming too dangerous for their ships, New Zealand Government policy would have been subverted by a minority group of activists. But, in its favor, the Peace Squadron has the fact that the nuclear ships issue was not put to the people at the last election. The Squadron may even be acting on behalf of a majority. Within days of the *Pintado*'s arrival, the letter column to The New Zealand Herald — a conservative sounding board — was running nine-seven against nuclear ships. With parliamentary Opposition leader Bill Rowling coming out against the *Pintado* visit in a telegram to President Carter, the nuclear ships visits will be a live one for the next election.

The Auckland peace squadron had had ludicrous expectations. It believed it could successfully and safely and responsibly "blockade" the Waitemata Harbor by filling it to overflowing with pleasure craft and people at play. Between a tight undergrowth of sail boats, "fiz" boats, canoes, rafts, surfboards, swimmers, fishing lines there would be no way a nuclear warship would or could pass. The peace squadron expected and celebrated a miracle about to happen. And it did! There were no casualties through those years. The miracle took a little time to arrive. The worshipers could never have predicted the path by which it did eventually arrive, nor the magnitude of it.

But the ludicrous objectives of that handful of boaties were turned by faith into a key part of the massive public pressure which eventually barred nuclear warship and weapon systems by the full force of national and international criminal legislation. This process and its achievement, for those who gave themselves to it, had a miraculous intoxication far beyond things calculable and explicable. This was indeed public liturgy and worship.

Second Context and Text:
The Cathedral That Marched on Parliament

The second context, which emerged in the 1980s and 1990s, is that of "economic restructuring," our own New Zealand version of the "structural adjustment programs" infamous throughout the Third World and now remaking the First World also. Foreshadowed by the ruminations of the New Zealand Planning Council in the late 1970s, the full force of the neoliberal concepts was not to sweep the country until the era of Finance Minister Roger Douglas and his "Rogernomics." Announcing themselves and their policies in apostolic and messianic terms, they hijacked with astonishing ease and rapidity the mobility and hopefulness of the same liberal New Zealand spirit which had rallied to the nuclear-free flag. Thus the liberal Labor Party politicians who had spearheaded the nuclear-free legislation and championed the anti-apartheid cause became the crusaders of the monetarist New Right. The tactics and rhetoric and ideology of this all-triumphant impulse has been analyzed to death by shrewd scholarly and popular commentators. The full cultural spirituality of this development awaits still a commentary which will do it full justice.

The significance of the New Zealand experience should not be underestimated. Become casualties of the electoral process and internal power struggles, the hardest-line ideologues of the reform — architect Roger Douglas himself and his National Party successor as Minister of Finance Ruth Richardson — have, since their rejection by their own electorate, traveled the world first class with the Good News of economic salvation in the deep South Pacific. New Zealand may represent in very much simplified and transparent even if very advanced form, the destiny or fate of the whole First World.

New Zealand is like a cuckoo clock without a case. Exposed for all to view, its large — almost clumsy — cogs, springs, levers, and weights tell out in simple form the essential dynamics of larger and murkier concatenations elsewhere. The same might be said about our religion and spirituality. It is so very obvious, even to us who are embroiled with it.

If the whole global system is in a crisis induced by those who claim to be remedying it, any protective or redemptive mechanisms developed in this "advanced" New Zealand setting may conversely hold much value for those concerned for the full future of the planet.

The Shift from War to Economics

Economics, say conventional textbook scholars like Daniel Bell or Samuel Huntington in diverse ways, is "war by other means." This conquest of the nuclear and arrival of the economic can be dismissed as merely one more demon cast out — ten more taking its place. But to have left war behind — precarious and preposterous though such a proposition in itself may appear — is that not perhaps in itself a quantum leap? Has not history conspired through the ages to prevent precisely such a shift? asks William Blake:

> Art Degraded, Imagination Denied: War Governed the Nations, Rouse up . . . New Age . . . against Hirelings . . . in the Camp, the Court and the University, who would if they could, for ever depress Mental and prolong Corporeal War.

Warriors hot or cold, patriarchy hotly violent or coldly rational, has been forced to shift from their preferred "corporeal" killing fields to heartlands now (in principle) exposed and open. This is not to identify economic class as the ultimate enemy ahead of militarism, sexism, or racism. It is rather to be required to pursue the demons beyond overt militaristic and police violence into the more truly nether regions.

Both the 1968 Good Friday procession event and the founding in 1975 of the Peace Squadron had generally confined their focus to militarism (with an occasional rap over the knuckles to a sexist paternalistic admiral who urged that women and children should not be aboard protest boats). The Peace Squadron did not address the issues of political economy which we had indeed already come to believe underlay the manifest apocalyptic violence enshrined in nuclear missiles, their delivery systems, and the ideological rhetoric which sought to justify them. Sharp public liturgy focus on economic systems of "killing peoples softly" had to await the 1990s. Economic principalities and powers were yet to have to answer for the fearful consequences of their methods and results, their means and ends.

The Peace Squadron and Peace Movement could be criticized as "single-issue" liturgies or campaigns. But as a shrewdly open-ended "single-issue" event, the Peace Squadron managed exactly to match large public aspirations of the time and, from there, channel its self-multiplying energies towards richer comprehensions and more comprehensive achievement. So it was that the Peace Squadron and the Peace Movement generally were able to nudge people towards the issues of sexism and racism and eventually classism as these issues naturally and turbulently surfaced with the incoming submarines.

On the Way from War to Economics

The seventies yielded to the eighties. As the early part of our fifty-year period closed, nuclear issues were beginning to move into the arena of inexorable national and international antinuclear legislation. The more demonstrative public debate of the issue had done its work. The nuclear began to fall away astern. The New Zealand ship of state was under way once more.

On the far horizon could already be discerned the small fist of an even more comprehensive cloud. Slow in its beginnings, with the downfall of Muldoon and the triumph of a Labor Government it raced forward, lowering from edge to edge across the rim of the New Zealand future.

Substantially slow official discussion was beginning to take place during the Muldoon era about the future of the New Zealand economy. The churches were involved.

The prestigious Government Planning Council Report "Planning Perspectives 1978-1983" was published in 1978. The Chairman of the Planning Council, Sir Frank Holmes, was also chairman of the Economic Task Force which recommended the setting up of the Planning Council. Backroom elites from church and state met for brief and stormy exchanges. The Planning Council was envisaged to be one of the many bodies that would seek through dialogue a national consensus on major societal directions for New Zealand. It was part of the brief of the Planning Council to consult vigorously with a wide variety of groups. They were eager to meet therefore with the Joint Working Committee of the New Zealand churches.

Economic Logic and Liturgy

Through this brief period, two very different summary versions of the Planning Council's proposals appeared in church publications. I was the author of both.

The first, passionless and impeccable, appeared in *New Citizen,* the Methodist national newspaper:

- Economic growth is the only way to maintain our standard of living and finance the public sector's welfare and social services.
- We need an "export-led economic recovery" to correct our balance of payments, repay international debt, and finance export-sector incentives.
- The free market is the best regulator of prices and services. We must respond sensitively to "signals" from the market, especially from overseas markets.
- Industries and services will have to pay for themselves and not run at a loss.
- Healthy competition will weed out weak enterprises. New Zealand has a "mixed" economy involving both private enterprise and government interventions. Such interventions as are unavoidable should be geared to strengthening our ability to respond to markets, thus giving us a "more market" economy.

My second summary, in the form of a satirical liturgy, was published in the 1978 Twentieth Report from the Joint Working Committee of Roman Catholic and National Council of Churches to the Churches. The Planning Council's "poetry" and "liturgy," though an oft-dreary epic, undeniably evoked concerns tattooed on the inside of Pakeha [NZ settlers of European extraction] skins. Hence my more passionate liturgical rubrics and rituals:

- *A Muffled Hymn to Growth* shall set the tone of the liturgy. All the rich ethnic and cultural diversities of New Zealand are to fuel the furnaces of production. Even the currently disadvantaged and alienated are to be co-opted into a national consensus which would exorcise the grievous "national habit of confrontation."
- *Beatitudes and Anathemas of the "More Market":*
  Blessed is the Export sector. She sleeps not day or night. She pores over signals from the international markets. She garners fruits from public agencies. She is adorned and fueled with judicious public incentives. She respondeth and earneth precious overseas dollars with agribusiness, hortibusiness and every imaginable and unimaginable kind of business.
  Blessed be you who will join the mobile relocatable workforce with portable mortgages and pensions, freed from single-shift days and

restrictive shopping hours. Blessed be the Private Sector — from
whom all Blessings flow.

Woe to the all-devouring parasitical public sector. Cursed be this unruly
Leviathan who sprawls across our economy. Let it pay for itself like
everyone else. Replace not its retiring bureaucrats. Put education on
weightwatchers and let's see if it can be effective after all.

* *Repent* of Saturday night for Monday morning is upon us. Our moment of high carnival is done. The canny overseas investment eye is
upon us. We have spent beyond our means and it is their money we
have squandered. Whether in your overheated swimming pool or
huddled over your one-bar heater, switch down the power and tighten
the belt.
* *Now is the accepted time* to become ascetic and harmonious, lean
and mean.
* *These Three abide.*
Blessed be the Private Sector.
Cursed be the Public Sector.
Better unanalyzed abide the innocuous Voluntary Sector.
These three abide and the greatest of these is perfectly obvious.
* *Sing out Amen* you who cry for the poor. For this is their only way
of salvation too. All shall prosper — eventually.

Our uncooperative disbelief as a Joint Working Committee towards
the Planning Council was palpable. The Planning Council found themselves
and their gospel cast with us in short order in the role of children in the
marketplace. Decently and in order they had piped their liturgy to us. We
had not danced.

We could not be dismissed as lightweights. Economist Dr. Donald
Brash, a leading figure on the Planning Council, declared the *New Citizen*
summary "excellent" but studiously ignored the "liturgy." Don was from
a prestigious Presbyterian family. He had returned to New Zealand from a
World Bank posting in 1974 and spearheaded the development of Merchant
Banking in New Zealand. He later became Governor of the Reserve Bank
of New Zealand.

Curiously, in *New Citizen,* after giving my summary of the plan
(benign compared to the eventual savagery of Rogernomics and of Ruth
Richardson's "Mother of all Budgets") full marks, he moved directly into
a defensive posture:

People of goodwill can be excused for being troubled by George Armstrong's summary of the latest Planning Council Report. Does it imply

that the Planning Council favors a less egalitarian society, with a reduced involvement of Government and potentially, a less generous welfare state?

Does it imply a more ruthlessly competitive society?

The short answer must be yes.

But these things are being advocated not as an end in themselves, but rather as a means of protecting the society which we now have.

Don went on to give a woeful description of the perilous economic plight of the nation:

we are under severe threat . . . have been spending vastly more overseas than earning . . . our debt rising rapidly . . . very high inflation . . . has hurt many of the lower income groups but also has made productive investment less profitable . . . serious implications for employment levels, balance of payments . . . growth in productivity very low . . . standard of living no longer rising . . . an incentive for many to seek greener pastures overseas . . . if trends not halted, New Zealand society as we have known it — basically egalitarian, with relatively harmonious racial relations — will not long survive. We have no alternative but to change our ways.

For the Planning Council ends could justify means. Contrariwise, argued Maori commentator Maurice Manawaroa Gray: "Means must justify Ends." How could means which promoted ruthless atomized Darwinian survival-of-the-fittest behavior be expected to have ends that protect and maintain a culture of sharing and compassion? The two things were not only incompatible. They were contradictory.

Planning Council members came twice to meet with the Joint Working Committee. They came first in full force to present their impressively argued ideas. On the departure of these kings and captains, a universal chorus of dissent arose amongst the Joint Working Committee. They rejected the glowing accounts with which they had just been regaled.

They were affronted by the wolfish appearance of proposals which seemed to be jettisoning several decades of a communal and creative political economy in New Zealand which (for all its faults) had (not without reason) attracted international admiration. Notoriously absent was any commitment to full employment — a staple of New Zealand culture for many years. Ominous was their thoroughgoing negativity towards welfare recipients and towards the whole social-welfare achievements of a generation.

We hoary religionists could also recognize a religious rival when we saw one. We smelt salvationist economics. Perhaps a competitor? Our own church institutions and ideologies were languishing while this shiny new economist dogma seemed set to win every motherhood medal and to remake the whole of New Zealand society in its own well-groomed and well-heeled image.

New Zealand, as a member of the Christian Conference of Asia and the Asian Bishops' Conference, had long been privy to Asian Church postwar analyses. Asian theologians had been participants in the development debates which had preoccupied the World Council of Churches in the 1960s. As Third World Churches they experienced firsthand structural economic injustice. For Joint Working Committee members, some of us well-acquainted with Third World discussions, these same miserable dynamics seemed now about to be gleefully imported amongst our own peoples as well as destined to become a prime export from us to unfortunate other foreign publics from leaders in New Zealand itself. With horror we sensed that the economic logic of our own prestigious Western liberal leadership in New Zealand was not only supportive of Third World-type dynamics but was about to extend them unreflectively and pell mell into our own culture. In what way did they differ from the army officer in Vietnam who argued that he had to destroy a town in order to save it?

Under the impact of Third World liberation theologies, Catholic popes and Protestant and Anglican leaders had to sharpen their sense of the God of the Bible as an unsleeping champion of the poor in preference to devout or affluent souls who cry "Lord . . . Lord . . . I thank Thee that I am not as others." The New Zealand Planning Council's apparent carelessness, ruthlessness, or willful irrationality about welfare services in the face of the inevitable increase of hardship resulting directly from their policies made amiable dialogue between churches and the Planning Council a betrayal of the gospel. Of course there had to be interaction between church and state on this fundamental matter. But we had only begun to understand that polite elite dialogue was no substitute for the fully inclusive, tempestuous, and prolonged interchange which was to engross the whole of New Zealand society as the century later drew to its close.

Anchored in Economics

Church Castigates Government Economic Policy — so wrote a journalist of the Wellington Dominion newspaper on October 9, 1991, telling of the delayed outcome of the Wellington Synod's annual deliberations:

Government policies were favoring the rich few and penalizing the poor, Prime Minister Jim Bolger was told by the Anglican Church yesterday.

The message was delivered by Archbishop Brian Davis during a special service at Wellington Cathedral, attended by Mr. Bolger and other National MPs and a congregation of 650.

The Service had been preceded by twenty-four hours of prayer and fasting.

"We are not a self-righteous church confronting an unrighteous Government. We are conscious of our own faults and failings, but feel compelled to speak what we believe God is calling us to," Archbishop Davis said.

. . . A Statement from the synod of the Wellington diocese, to be read in churches on Sunday, called for the Government to review its policies. . . . There was particular concern about the growth of individualistic, money-oriented values. . . .

This piece of "liturgy," even more than those described earlier, was scrupulously conceived and organically developed according to the exact conditions and atmosphere of the situation. The vigil and "castigation" was held on October 10, 1991 and was decided upon by the full regular Synod of Wellington meeting a month earlier, in Palmerston North, eighty miles north of Wellington, the capital of New Zealand. It was resolved at Palmerston North:

That this Synod ask the Archbishop to call a Special Session of this Synod in the Cathedral, for a Eucharist, followed by a procession to Parliament to present a Statement to the Prime Minister and the Leader of the Opposition. . . .

Such a statement was already in process of being drafted during the Synod.

From the very start of its regular September proceedings in 1991, with the presentation of the social service and charitable agencies reports, the feelings at the September Synod were running extraordinarily high against the economic restructuring policies of two successive governments. Government expenditure and welfare had been slashed. Privatization of state enterprises and assets was proceeding rapidly. The churches' own social welfare resources were under much new pressure as a result. Church analysts and interpreters were methodically and statistically identifying the sources of these deepening levels of distress. The newspeak ideologies and rituals radically refashioned by a business-controlled and enterprise-oriented media had not quite succeeded by 1990 in selling a new conventional wisdom to clothe and legitimate the new ruthless policies.

For all this, the high energy of the Synod's wrath was in danger of dissipating into useless and inauthentic passion were it to find no significant outlet. It may have been an instinctive self-knowledge about this great potential for spiritual and material loss which made the Synod eager to take up the unusual possibility of reassembling a month later and processing between Cathedral and Parliament (which stand cheek by jowl in central pride of place in downtown Wellington). Between the regular September 1991 Synod deliberations and the October special Session of Synod in the Cathedral, much was to happen behind the scenes. The Archbishop, well-aware that he was in a highly formalized official situation, moved very carefully and "transparently" through the required ecclesial procedures. Despite persistent efforts by both Prime Minister and the Archbishop (himself personally much more comfortable with monetarism than with his Synod) to forestall any note of "confrontation," the "castigatory" note in the liturgy could not be eliminated. For all its low-key sunny politeness and friendly chat, the Cathedral Vigil Event was seen for the prophetic outcry that the Synod intended.

Clearly the whole stately panoply of the Wellington diocese at worship in its cathedral could not be dismissed as a marginalized antediluvian Marxist fringe of the church, acting without authority and in violation of the freedom of others, cloaking naive political meddling with a veneer of manipulated theology. This was a whole Anglican diocese (not a notably liberal one at that) pulling out all its liturgical, doctrinal, and ethical stops to trumpet a prophetic and priestly organ blast at directions in the public life of the whole nation.

If repugnance has distorted my critique of neoliberal economics, I must acknowledge that such Western liberal enthusiasms are only too close to me and to my church. How often has our primal inspiration, be it religious or secular, burst out with unbounded and ill-considered exuberance. Were we to steady ourselves, to take heed of significantly different others bound in the same community but often with far less institutional power than ourselves, we might sense that from the same source of our exuberance well forth the most profound contraries. This has happened at many points in the West's long enlightenment. It happened and was over in a flash in the 1960s for the Christian radicals. Was it the same essential and deceptive spirit that informed the radicals from the radical economic Right?

No one expressed this murderous weakness of the Enlightenment better than Friedrich Nietzsche, a century earlier:

> Indeed we philosophers and "free spirits" feel as if a new dawn were shining on us when we receive the tidings that "the old god is dead"; our heart overflows with gratitude, amazement, anticipation, expectation. At last the horizon appears free again to us, even granted that it is not bright; at last our ships may venture out again, venture out to face any danger; all the daring of the lover of knowledge is permitted again; the sea, our sea, lies open again; perhaps there has never yet been such an "open sea."

Nietzsche's delirious delight at the liberations wrought by the death of the old gods — whether of religion or science — was inseparable for him from a deep suspicion about his own delight:

> We firstlings and premature births of the coming century, to whom the shadows that must soon envelop Europe really should have appeared by now — why is it that even we look forward to it without any real compassion for this darkening, and above all without any worry and fear for ourselves?

We have passed this way before, our ancestors and ourselves. With Nietzsche and with Blake, as with Moses, Elijah, Paul, and Jesus, we have a communication channel and a form of communion available to us in public liturgy. Friendly our ancestors — spiritual and cultural — call their warnings to us from the end of their century to the end of ours as we recapitulate their discoveries. Surely these recapitulations have become so historically perceptible as to be capable of embodiment in some transformation of ourselves and of our cultures, religion and economics together, brothers and sisters after all.

The contrast between this event in Wellington in 1991 and the Vietnam War Liturgy in Auckland in 1968 is very illuminating. This was no longer the case of an unwelcome processional tail wagging the dog.

Was this last event with the Wellington Cathedral one of those rare moments when this official church recognized its true nature communally and publicly? Such moments deserve careful scrutiny, not in the hope that they can be routinely ritualized, but in order that the spirit and form of their mysterious confluence may be able to flow more readily as the crisis conditions are resolutely and recklessly embedded throughout our institutions.

It is often observed, with a recognition both grudging and relieved, that the church in New Zealand is one of the few institutions that has stood its ground in the Tiananmen Square of the Radical Right. This cannot be because of the strength of any Radical Left in the churches. Such middle-way liberalism moreover as survives in the church flows in managerial professionalisms of one sort or another oft preoccupied in protecting its own attenuated role. Was the church's authentic passion then capable still of perceiving the rock from which it is hewn, the stump from which once soared (at least in the visionary memory of the Hebrew and Christian prophets), a great tree sheltering threatened and vulnerable peoples? Was there yet hope for this sad relic — drastically pruned now of its pretensions and triumphalisms, but stirring its stump to send forth new growth to rise again for the poor and dispossessed who had been committed to it as its greatest wealth?

It is much easier to protest militarism than money. A massive warship riding over a small rowing boat spells a brutal message legible to the least literate. Relocating factories, making workers redundant, shrinking already thin welfare services are not so easily imaged for the murderous activities that they are.

Nor can the sources and dynamics of monetarist religion be so concretely identified within or between particular nation-state boundaries. These dynamics are the stuff and spirituality of whole economic empires quite outmatching even as they dominate any single state. They form the stuff of both the popular and the intellectual consciousness of a society, from the most populist to the most obtusely intellectual. Their ideology fashions the lenses (a construction of commercial forces and entities) through which all deeper realities are filtered to all sectors in society.

It could be argued that radical deregulation has done us a great favor in New Zealand. It has thrown us back naked or at least barefoot into the whole world jungle of competing forces. Like our brothers and sisters, we are now everywhere and altogether exposed. The Third World is more obviously present in the First. Though this has always been so, it has not been apparent. Now it is being historically experienced by redundant middle sectors of society whom even a million or so of accumulated pension dollars cannot cushion. Bigger barns are more clearly than ever no protection against inexorable economic and physical realities. This is one of the ambiguous fruits of "globalization," a historical process which always remains far larger than all attempts (from Right or Left) to analyze or to master it (whether for private profit or for the supposed social good).

No matter the point to which these profound reflections guide us, we have reached in economics the basics of our life together, from greatest to the least. Old masks inevitably slip and fall, not only under the scalpel of sharp analysis, but reduced to nothing by the basic wisdom of the people inclusively, gathered at the table to eat and to decide together. The wisdom of the new scribe, economic or religious, is long gone, like the gods who sanctified our old inadequate religious and economic half-truths. The news is slow reaching us. But we have the time. We need it to catch up with what has happened to us in our life together.

Conclusion

Many of us religious people felt that we had not begun to understand or even live out our Christian faith until we became actively involved in the political economies of our wider society.

The received notion was that we and the church already possessed the truth and that this truth was largely a truth which was and could be laid out in the form of doctrines and imagery, lived out through genteel liturgy and modest family life. Others beyond our circle of Christianity could and should be brought into our circle of belief and believe more or less the same things as ourselves.

This received truth was fatally wounded by the critiques and upheavals of the 1960s. Mere rejection of conventional orthodoxies, how- ever, or animated and interesting debate about them, were no substitute for their ancient power. Nor could free-ranging mystical enterprises reconnect us. The living truth of faith rose again for us only as a consequence of active engagement from the standpoint of that faith and amidst inclusive community. The active engagement available for many of us was public liturgy. It was action and prayer at the same time.

Most importantly it put us in touch as never before with the sacred texts and contexts of our Hebrew and Christian ancestors who had bequeathed to us the richness of their experience. History and tradition came alive as we found pathways alongside theirs. Were we engaged in concrete liberative achievement of Peace and Justice and Inclusiveness for our day in specific projects? If so and perhaps only if so, Miriam and Moses and their mother, pioneers of the mother-of-all-liberations, would come and commune and communicate with us vividly in the albeit imperfect records of their words and deeds in the ancient Hebrew and Greek texts. Were we at loggerheads, in good faith, with the Prime Ministers and High Priests of our own day over their — and our — conventional wisdoms and standard institutional arrangements? Did they set the police on us for opposing racist apartheid rugby football sport and treat us as criminals for being overridden by nuclear warships?! We discovered the prophets, some of them well-placed themselves amidst their own cultures, in an entirely new way. For even so had they treated these prophets and Jesus before us.

We discovered we were not alone but caught in a congruence of creation which we had not found from our commentaries.

We found ourselves searching for textbooks provided initially only by Third World and First Nations authors and by an occasional unassuming but unerring seer such as Richard Shaull. Now biblical scholars like Norman Gottwald, Ched Myers, Richard Horsley, and William Herzog have arisen. These were scholars who had learnt their truth in their own active experience or as part of a church whose living active communal flesh had nourished them. In today's active contexts they had discovered the power of the ancient texts and applied themselves to them with minute zeal and great descriptive and imaginative powers. A new literature is being born to resource the academies of the coming century.

The sympathy of the mainstream churches for such projects as the Peace Squadron and the total institutional commitment of the Wellington Anglican diocese to the Cathedral Vigil and Declaration of 1991 illustrates the potential of the whole church, in good formation and according to its own venerable and ponderous processes, to catch up with its own origins by a willingness, actively and communally, to place itself in the place where Jesus or the prophets or the matriarchs and patriarchs found themselves located in history.

If we New Zealand Anglicans are willing to keep moving in these directions in relation to economic issues in our country and world, the result could well be an unprecedented flowering and resurgence of a fuller Christianity in our midst.

New Zealand, tight-moored by contradiction at her new monetarist anchorage, is bedridden in a brave new world ruled by the Corporates. Who or what will unparalyze our bedridden patient but our public faith and our public liturgy?

Minjung and Power:
A Biblical and Theological Perspective
on *Doularchy* (Servanthood)

KIM YONG-BOCK

IN HUMAN HISTORY power has been the perennial problem. The reality of power is complex; and the use and misuse of power in all human, social, and political relations and interactions has been the question of utmost importance. In the liberation movements from oppressive powers, the question of power has always been raised not only in terms of use or misuse of power, but also in terms of the very nature of power. The breakdown of the socialist states, the crisis of the modern liberal nation-states, and upheavals in the traditional or semi-traditional despotic and authoritarian states are raising new questions in the newly emerging context of global marketization. The nation-state structures are being radically questioned, for they were the unit structures of the political powers that have been most destructive; and the global market agencies require a restriction of the modern nation-state structures for free interaction and movement of goods and services.

Especially as human history moves towards the twenty-first century, the reality of power is formed in the context of the global market.

The movement of the people of God in the inhabited earth, is in a rapid transition to a radically new world. The peoples are experiencing great trends that change the present world into a radically different world. And yet we do not have a definitive analytical grasp of these trends and changes of the world that determine the life of peoples today. We have to keep trying to discern even the signs of times, as we live and move together in this world.

In the post–Cold War situation and in the manifesting post-modernization, breakdown of modern social philosophies and political ideologies

215

as well as traditional social thoughts exposes a great confusion of social thinking among the peoples in Asia as well as a lack of ecumenical theological direction in the Christian communities; and at the same time it opens a new era of creative and active social thinking in the ecumenical movements as well as social movements in the world. This demands fresh initiatives for theological and social thinking in the ecumenical movement on the question of power.

Signs of the Times:
Fundamental Trends and Changes Among Peoples

1. The world has become one global market. Life on earth, human and natural, is condemned to the global market. There is no realistic option for life outside of the market, whatever the market is and however it operates. When there was an option for socialism, this was not the situation. Practically the market has become an absolute reality, although some think this is not the case, at least in theoretical terms. This global marketization has a profound implication for the peoples in Asia as well as for the whole life on earth. The peoples experience great changes in economic life. The center of *rapid economic growth in the world is being shifted to Asia;* Japan and China becoming an axis of such shift; and Asian dragons and "tigers" play dynamic roles in this process. The global market is very much determined by these developments in Asia.

The peoples in Asia are the most affected by the global marketization and such rapid economic growth in some Asian countries. Yet the powers that play in the market are the corporate entities from in and outside of Asia, and the national states are losing control over the economic life of their own people. These economic corporate entities are the most "creative and efficient" and, therefore, most powerful. They control modern science and technology as well as information and communication in the global market. They seek to knock down any barriers — cultural, national, or political — in order to open highways for their market plays. The market is more determined by the economic corporate powers than by the nation-state governments. This is clearer since the agreement of the Uruguay Round. What is unique in this global marketization is Asian socialist countries, which also embraced the market economy or are in the process of adopting it. They call it a socialist market economy. It is not yet clear what this means for the Asian people. What is clear is that these socialist market economies are also growing very rapidly.

2. The geopolitical change has brought about the fusion of the local,

national, global, and cosmic (natural) horizons by the globalization of the market. The horizon of the market is not one-dimensional; but any subject, individual person, community, or corporate entity in the market must come with this multidimensionally fused horizons of the geopolitics of life. One must think locally, nationally, and globally; and one must simultaneously act in geopolitically fused horizons. This means that a local action will have effects not only on the local level, but also on national, global, and natural (cosmic) levels. This also means issues of life and relations among people, groups, and communities implies the fused horizons in all the levels.

In this process of geopolitical changes the nation-states are adjusting to the global market, and Asian nation states are not exceptions. Indeed, the role of nation-states may be changing and even weakening to protect their own people. What would be the new role of the nation-states in Asia? The people begin to reorganize their life as locality-centered, religious-community-centered, culture-centered, ethnicity-centered, away from the political center of the nation-state.

This means that the people's sovereignty (participation) is being organized locally to respond to the global dynamics of the world market as well as to the national dynamics of powers and principalities. The people seek to participate directly and immediately, for the political mediation of the nation-states is ambiguous.

The symbiotic centers of such power nexus have substantially shifted from nation-state structures to the global corporate entities. The life, the people, and their communities are deeply affected by this shift. Various forms of participatory democracy or direct democracy are sought as a framework in which life, people, and their communities directly participate, and multilaterally and multidimensionally form solidarity linkages to make creative interventions in the global market process.

3. All problems and issues of Asian peoples' life in the globalized market are interconnected. The natural, economic, social, political, cultural, and religious dimensions were analytically distinguished, differentiated, and even fragmented; and they are compartmentalized not only on an analytical level but also on the concrete practical level. Thus the life has been treated in a fragmented way in the past and the present. Or the life has been reduced to one dimension, the material or spiritual, disregarding all other dimensions or subjugating them to one dimension, and organizing them hierarchically with a single dimension on the top, whether it is spiritual or material.

4. The sociopolitical relations in the globalized market are not merely structural but dynamically relational; and, therefore, contradictions and conflicts in the global market are dynamically relational. The struggles,

negotiations, and cooperation, even solidarity among Asian peoples in the global market characterize the power relations across classes, castes, races, genders, and all other conflicting camps among the people, groups, communities, and ecosystems.

5. The electronic information and communication process plays a decisive role in the market, subjugating the subjective agency of life on all levels and dimensions. The high-tech multimedia communication and processing of information is and will be a dominant feature of the global market. It will form a value-added network of communication and information to enforce and accelerate the market dynamics among the life of the people. This is what is new in the postindustrial global market. Particularly human subjectivity is deeply affected as the participatory agency of life in all its dimensions.

6. The religious entities in Asia emerge as countervailing centers of life, giving identity, values, and meaning. Asian religious entities in the global market will feel the third wave of crisis in the global market, and will react to it initially; and yet Asian religions will be great reservoirs of spiritual energy for life and struggle of the Asian people.

The Victims Tell the Reality:
Asian People in the Vortex of the Global Market

1. The life that is victimized as the garden and oasis of life is being turned into a jungle and desert of destroying life. The vitality of life and the power of death are in a bitter contest in the global marketization process.

The fundamental contradiction between society and nature that is implied in the modern industrial culture and society is being intensified in the global market. Natural life and cultural (spiritual) life will be dominated by the vortex of the global market, and their relations will be in dire confrontation in such a way that natural life will be victimized by market-dominated economic and cultural artificiality and arbitrariness. Hitherto the Western industrial culture has dictated the relation between life in nature and life in human society, be it capitalist or socialist. Now the dynamics of the global market will dominate the relation between natural life and life in human society. The culture of the globalized market is not life-preserving or life-enhancing, for the limitless competition engenders the logic of the survival of the fittest and the strongest. The market will allow the winners to dominate the losers. Thus, life will ultimately be the loser, for life will lose the spiritual foundation as well as the natural base due to the arbitrary contradiction between the natural and the spiritual imposed by the global market. This is a negative dimension of the global market-ization; and there seems to be lacking any strong trends to control or balance this trend in the current global situation.

2. The economic victimization of the people — the *minjung,* the communities and consumers — in the global market, will be absolute and limitless; and the mammonism of economic power of the giant corporate entities will dominate life in the global market. The global financial cor-porate powers will be key players in the process. Financial victimization of the people will be noiseless, bloodless, and yet extremely effective. Natural life and human persons and communities will be powerless economic losers in the globally competitive market. The hungry, the poor, and even the not-so-poor middle-class people, together with relatively weak economic agencies, will be victimized in this globalized market.

The national economic security net of self-reliance and protection, whatever there is of it, is being rapidly eroded in the name of open markets. Thus the weak economic agencies in every nation are exposed to the market plays of globally powerful economic agencies. The traditional communities have likewise become vulnerable due to the pressures of the global market forces. This economic victimization process has truly become the global nexus of the economic power that destroys the life everywhere. Hunger, impoverishment, and wasteful consumerism are a few forms of life de-struction and victimization. The irony and paradox is that this process of victimization will take place in the midst of global economic growth and technological advancement.

It is in this global context that the people take initiatives for economic justice, for direct participation and intervention in the market process, and for economic actions for sustainable life.

3. The public or common social security of the peoples' life is being dismantled and subjugated to the jungle of the globalized market; and the people will be exposed to economic, social, political, cultural, and spiritual violence that are fundamentally caused by the global market process. Life will not be secure in this global market; it will be vulnerable to violent conflicts and confrontations in the midst of limitless competi-tions. This violent process is permeating every aspect of relations be-tween and among international and political powers, social classes and cultural groups, national and ethnic groups, caste and religious communi-ties. Peace for life on all levels has lost its foundations, and no way of peaceful resolution of conflicts and disputes among struggling parties is easily found.

There has been a tendency for the peace question to be reduced merely to a question of the reduction or elimination of violent military confrontations among nation-states and political groups; but now it is a question of securing dignity and justice for all living things on earth. The questions of peace and security over against violence are to be understood on economic, cultural, and spiritual levels as well as on social and political levels.

4. Life has politics as its core. It cannot be reduced as a passive object. The global market with "neoliberal" developments has weakened liberal democratic subjecthood for individual persons, powerless groups such as racial and ethnic minorities, and local communities. The people as participating agents in the political process are exposed to the syndrome of apathy, hopelessness, and decapacitation as the global market weakens the national democratic states.

Even the nation-states, as modern political units, democratic or not, have been substantially weakened, if not dismantled. Political victimization has not merely suppressed the political subjecthood of the people, but the participatory process has been weakened by the misuse of power on the global level, weakening any national and community protections of political subjecthood.

5. The global market process is very much dictated by the cultural process of communication and information through high-tech multimedia. The victimization of life is being advanced culturally on levels of spirituality, consciousness, perceptions, and senses. The high-tech multimedia, dictated by the corporate powers and agencies of the global market, subjugate cultural subjecthood, cultural values, style of life, perceptions of beauty, and religious mystery in life, as well as ethnic and national identities of persons and community to the market wasteland of cultural life. The arena of consciousness, perceptions, and senses of life is indeed the battleground between forces of life and forces of victimization of life. This is indeed a "cultural war." The exploitation of postmodernistic sensibilities, especially emerging among the young generations, by the market is a good illustration.

The global market powers will battle against religious communities and spiritual powers of the people, by sapping their spiritual strength. The global market will create spiritual wilderness and wasteland, where the soul and spirit of the people will be broken, and the people will lose the spiritual sources for life. This is indeed a dire spiritual victimization. Religious revivals and the emergence of new religions must be seen in this context of spiritual victimization of the people.

In the *minjung* theology it is a truism that the question of power cannot be separated from the life of the *minjung* in history. The question of power is not merely raised as an objective question of power as such, or even structure or phenomenology of power. But it affirms that the true nature of power can only be properly understood in relation to the lives of the *minjung*. Furthermore, as the victims of the dominant power, it is the *minjung* who are the prime perceiver of the reality of that power. Contrary to the common claim that scientific analyses, both structural and systemic, of society provide a deeper understanding of the reality of power, such analyses in fact have not fully revealed the *minjung* experiences of power realities. The *minjung* experience power as its victims, not as objective scientists.

It is a fundamental principle in *minjung* theology that the social biography (or story) of the *minjung* reveals who they are in their persons and in their corporate body. Suffering and struggle is their prime reality, which is directly related to the reality of power. The reality of power is just as complex as are the experiences of the *minjung*. While it is claimed that power can be analyzed scientifically and objectively, its reality is revealed most clearly in the story of the *minjung*. The experience of the *minjung* and the reality of power must each be understood as a whole.

Today the *minjung* throughout the world face a complex situation of power that is local as well as global. The power complex has a certain socioeconomic base, mingled with political organization and influence, and with religiocultural values and influences, as well as highly developed scientific and technological capacities. Power is never one-dimensional, but is a complex mixture of multidimensional factors. The *minjung* experience the power of transnational corporations as well as the power of local and national economic powers; they live under the domination of the imperial powers, local and national ruling powers, and the combination of all of these. As for the powers of modern and traditional religions and cultures, the *minjung* experience these in the form of technocracy as well as traditional "despotism."

This reality is felt acutely among the *minjung* at the present historical juncture, with its radical global transition and uncertainty about the future. The powers have become conservative and reactive to changes that might jeopardize their interests.

Beginning with the changes in Eastern Europe, the world is in the process of a "reconstellization" which is characterized by the breakdown of the cold-war ideological polar structure, the realignment of the military powers, the reordering of the economic powers, and the rapid globalization of communication and cultural life.

The participation of the *minjung* is being short-circuited in the vortex of these complex global power dynamics; their network is undercut in every direction, so that their struggle is difficult; and the violence of power against them grows more sophisticated day by day, intensifying their unrelieved sufferings.

The *minjung* experience of economic power is not merely poverty, hunger, and exploitation, but is the distortion of the very political economy for life. The modern industrial economy destroys and distorts life on earth. The people cannot participate meaningfully in the planning, production, and distribution of their political economy, whether it is capitalist or socialist. The question of the economic life of the *minjung* goes beyond the issue of class. The question is whether they enjoy a full life or whether their life is distorted. This involves ecological questions as well. The economic life of the *minjung* should be based upon life protection and enhancement.

Social injustice against the *minjung* is based upon social status differentiation, ethnic and racial discrimination, gender discrimination, and other factors — all intertwined with the economic base of the society, although the relation between economic and social realities is not necessarily logical or mechanical. Social bonds by blood, by region, by nationality, and by religion are interrelated in a complex webwork. Social injustice cannot be reduced to the economic base of the society.

The political victimization of the *minjung* is also very complex. Their basic human dignity is violated by the state structures and by the actions and procedures of government. Their rights of participation are curtailed, restricted, and suppressed. The capitalist powers, be they liberal or authoritarian, limit and suppress *minjung* participation in political life. The socialist powers also prevent *minjung* participation in political, cultural, social, and economic life. Secret police operate in both capitalist and socialist states, to suppress *minjung* participation.

The violence against the *minjung* is not only physical but also economic, social, political, and cultural; it is psychological and communal, corporate and spiritual. The victimization of the *minjung* under oppressive powers has intensified as the exercise of power becomes more sophisticated. The rising tide of "people's powers from below" to confront the powers and principalities in all these various arenas has brought new mechanisms of suppression by use of technocratic means.

The *minjung* are deprived of access to science and technology in the industrial society; and they are denied the cultural means to cope with the world information and communication order, now dominated by the global corporate powers. National traditions, religious traditions, and even cultural values are being harnessed and manipulated to suppress the *minjung* as they confront the powers-that-be.

The emerging new constellations of powers and principalities are so complex that it would be illusory to try to analyze them in terms of structures and systems. The dynamics of this power are far too complex for such analytical calculation, though we might still have to rely upon this until we have better means to grasp the new dynamics of power. This power reality is not remote from the life of the *minjung;* rather they experience it immediately in their everyday life.

Here we need to go beyond mere analyses of power contradictions; we have reach out to grasp the interconnectedness of powers in terms of time and history, in terms of space, locus and expanse, and dimension. Social theories have failed in the respect that social contradictions are either too simply interconnected according to logical or structural analyses or left unconnected to fall into fragmentation or reductionism.

The stories of the *minjung* as victims of power truthfully reveal the reality of power: this is a fundamental thesis. If any analysis, scientific or not, does not take into account the story of the victims of the powers, it is not a faithful account of those powers.

Political theories and ideologies are fundamentally justifications of the powers; they are not theories on the sovereignty of the *minjung.* Any theory for social transformation must include the fundamental question of the sovereign *minjung,* including how it is suppressed by the powers. The fundamental failure of Marxism is that it does not have an adequate theory of *minjung* participation; and the failure of liberalism is that it has absolutized the individual self, turning it into the private corporate self, which is the core of its polity. Political liberalism has failed to establish *minjung* sovereignty against the private corporate self, such as the transnational corporations.

Political Biography of the People

The people have suffered under powers and principalities throughout history. Their political experiences reveal the nature of political history and, thus, the nature of political power.

The rise of the political totalitarianism and absolutism as well as the manifestation of colonialism and imperialism have taken place in the West, while ancient despotism and imperialism had risen in the oriental civilizations. Under these political regimes, the people suffered most severely, and they have lost completely their political sovereignty.

For the sake of concreteness, we will take Korean modern political history as an illustration. The *minjung* had suffered under Confucian despotism till the beginning of the twentieth century. The political economy of this regime was that of agriculture, mainly producing rice. The people, commoners, were discriminated against by the ruling Yangban class; they were exploited as tillers of the land and producers of goods, they were forcibly conscribed as corvée, and most of them were subjugated to private and public slavery. They served obligatory military duties, and they were excluded from political participation. Legal institutions were to protect the status and power of the ruling class of the Yangban and therefore functioned punitively. The people became victims of local magistrates, who were administrators, judicial and otherwise. They did not defend the "rights" of the people. In such despotic rule, the people's sovereignty was legally nonexistent. However, the people persistently resisted such despotic power.

Under the Japanese empire and in the divided land under the cold war system of the four imperial powers, the *minjung* also experienced the suffering imposed by modernized totalistic, authoritarian, and military dictatorships. Here we find the stories of the *jungshindae* (the "comfort women"), the war widows, and the workers, peasants, and urban poor, exposing the nature of the political powers in modern Korea.

Biblical Political Order
as the Paradigm of a *Minjung* Politics of Doularchy

Political Biography in the Bible

The stories of the Hebrews under the imperial rule of Pharaoh are told and retold as a paradigmatic expression of the political social biography of the people. The stories of the *minjung* under the Davidic reign are illustrated in the Bible by the story of Naboth and his vineyard. The story of the Suffering Servant under the Babylonian Empire appears in the Servant song of Isaiah 53. The stories of the Crucified One under the Roman Empire and many other crucified ones are also political biographies of the *minjung,* which expose the unjust, despotic, imperial regimes led by the principalities and powers.

The Biblical Paradigm of Dominant Power

The nature of the despotic and imperial powers is described throughout the books of the Bible in the stories of the Egyptian, Babylonian, Assyrian, Greek, and Roman empires and of small kingdoms in the ancient Middle East. The nature of power is very well expressed in Samuel's opposition to the establishment of a kingship for the people of Israel:

> He said, "These will be the ways of the king who will reign over you: he will take your sons and appoint them to his chariots and to be his horsemen,

and to run before his chariots; and he will appoint for himself commanders
of thousands and commanders of fifties, and some to plow his ground and
to reap his harvest, and to make his implements of war and the equipment
of his chariots. He will take your daughters to be perfumers and cooks and
bakers. He will take the best of your fields and vineyards and olive orchards
and give them to his servants. He will take the tenth of your grain and of
your vineyards and give it to his officers and to his servants. He will take
your menservants and maidservants, and the best of your cattle and your
asses, and put them to his work. He will take the tenth of your flocks, and
you shall be his slaves. And in that day you will cry out because of your
king, whom you have chosen for yourselves; but the LORD will not answer
you in that day. (1 Sam. 8:10-18)

The socioeconomic slavery, military regimentation, "official rob-
bery," and negation of the just rule of Yahweh are some of the manifestations of the *arche* of *despotai* (despotic rule). The fundamental character of the despotic rule is that the ruler is the legislator and therefore
above the law. This is extended to the point that the king becomes an
absolute authority, a religious deity. It is very clear that the biblical rulers
used religious trappings to absolutize their authority. Even the Davidic
monarchy, as in the cases of King Solomon and King Ahab, used religious
institutions and trappings to justify their arbitrary actions and rules.

The political power (*exousiai* = authority and force, principalities and
powers) of the pharaohs, emperors, and caesars of the Egyptian, Babylonian, Assyrian, Greek, and Roman empires assumed a divine status to
absolutize their authority. Witfogel calls this "oriental despotism," which
has the distinct political economy of the hydraulic civilization.
T. Van Leewen calls it "ontocracy." The point is that the political authorities of these empires are regarded as divine. Since the laws are the very
expression of their will, they are above the laws and are bound to none.
Their authority is hierarchical, despotic, and authoritarian. Baalism in the
Old Testament is a similar despotic polity; and for this reason the prophets
attacked it fiercely, as it crept into the Davidic monarchy. The monarchs
of the Davidic kingdoms were constantly subjected to pressures and temptations by the desotic rules of the empires and kingdoms surrounding the
people of Israel (see 1 Kings 21:1-15).

The political authority of *arche* in the Bible is expressed in various
forms of hierarchy, patriarchy, monarchy, *basilei* (regime), *despotai*
(despotism), pharaoh, caesar, *kyrios,* baal (lord), and finally *diabolos* (devil
or Satan). *Diabolos* is the Prince of the World, self-appointed ruler of the
world to injure the people and cause their death, directly resisting God and

God's sovereign rule. This is the ultimate denial of God; and when humans obey the *diabolos,* they are resisting God. Biblically and historically, God and *diabolos* cannot coexist in the world.

When the sovereignty of God is not recognized by the earthly authorities, the powers assume sovereign authority, and thus deny the sovereignty of the *minjung,* suppressing and subjugating them.

The Sovereignty of the Minjung under Doularchy

The reign of *doulos* in *oikos tou theou* is the conclusive theme in the Bible.

> If any one would be first, he must be last of all and servant of all. (Mark 9:35)

> And Jesus called them to him and said to them, "You know that those who are supposed to rule over the Gentiles lord it over them, and their great men exercise authority over them. But it shall not be so among you; but whoever would be great among you must be your servant, and whoever would be first among you must be slave of all. For the Son of man also came not to be served but to serve, and to give his life as a ransom for many. (Mark 10:42-45)

> Who has believed what we have heard? And to whom has the arm of the LORD been revealed? For he grew up before him like a young plant, and like a root out of dry ground; he had no form or comeliness that we should look at him, and no beauty that we should desire him. He was despised and rejected by men; a man of sorrows, and acquainted with grief; and as one from whom men hide their faces he was despised, and we esteemed him not. Surely he has borne our grief and carried our sorrows; yet we esteemed him stricken, smitten by God, and afflicted. But he was wounded for our transgressions, he was bruised for our iniquities; upon him was the chastisement that made us whole, and with his stripes we are healed. All we like sheep have gone astray; we have turned every one to his own way; and the LORD has laid on him the iniquity of us all. He was oppressed, and he was afflicted, yet he opened not his mouth; like a lamb that is led to the slaughter, and like a sheep that before its shearers is dumb, so he opened not his mouth. By oppression and judgment he was taken away; and as for his generation, who considered that he was cut off out of the land of the living, stricken for the transgression of my people? And they made his grave with the wicked and with a rich man in his death, although he had done no violence, and there was no deceit in his mouth. Yet it was the will

of the LORD to bruise him; he has put him to grief; when he makes himself an offering for sin, he shall see his offspring, he shall prolong his days; the will of the LORD shall prosper in his hand; he shall see the fruit of the travail of his soul and be satisfied; by his knowledge shall the righteous one, my servant, make many to be accounted righteous; and he shall bear their iniquities. (Isa. 53:1-11)

The is the political economy (*oikos*) of God in which Jesus Christ has fulfilled the Servanthood to serve all, that is, to raise them as subjects of life in the global market.

Phases of Development of *Doularchy* in the Bible

Phase I

The covenant declares the slaves to be the subjects of liberation in the story of the Exodus. The sovereignty of Yahweh is the denial of the sovereignty of pharaoh against Yahweh and over the Hebrews, thus opening a historical space for the sovercignty of the *minjung*. The meaning of the covenant is that God has established a relationship of partnership with the slaves in God's sovereign rule of all creation. Thus, the event of the Exodus is an original paradigm of the political economy of God, in which the servants are lords and subjects.

Phase II

The covenant code in tribal confederacy is a continuation of the Exodus *doularchy* paradigm. In the tribal communities in the Palestine area after the Exodus, slave-based productive relations had continued. In this situation the sovereign rule of God is expressed in the form of the covenant code, especially in the Sabbath laws (Exod. 21:1–33:33).

Now these are the ordinances which you shall set before them.

When you buy a Hebrew slave, he shall serve six years, and in the seventh he shall go out free, for nothing. If he comes in single, he shall go out single; if he comes in married, then his wife shall go out with him. If his master gives him a wife and she bears him sons or daughters, the wife and her children shall be her master's and he shall go out alone. But if the slave plainly says, "I love my master, my wife, and my children; I will not go out free," then his master shall bring him to God, and he shall bring him to the door or the doorpost; and his master shall bore his ear through with an awl; and he shall serve him for life. When a man sells his daughter as a slave, she shall not go out as the male slaves do. If she does not please her master, who has designated her for himself, then he shall let her be redeemed; he shall have no right to sell her to a foreign people, since he has dealt faithlessly with her. If he designates her for his son, he shall deal with her as with a daughter. If he takes another wife to himself, he shall not diminish her food, her clothing, or her marital rights. And if he does not do these three things for her, she shall go out for nothing, without payment of money. (Exod. 21:1-11)

In this covenant code the slave is transformed as someone who has the "rights" over the lords. In fact, in the productive relations of slavery, it is the role of the slaves that undergirds the status of the lord, functionally speaking.

Phase III

In the Davidic monarchy the reign is legitimated on the basis of the covenant code. This means that the rights of the slaves will be protected and the rule of God's justice will be established. The prophetic movement against the powers and principalities is fundamentally toward the order of *doularchy,* in which the powerless, the weak, and the slaves are the partners of God, participating in the reign of God.

The historically existing paradigm of power, such as despotic monarchy, was to subjugate the people and to rule over them. The Davidic covenant demanded that the king be under the covenant code in which slaves were to be liberated and protected. That is, the institution of the king existed to serve the people in covenant with the (elders of the) people (2 Sam. 5:1-3). If the king was established according to the model of the despotic ruler, the people would be turned into slaves (1 Sam. 8:10-18). Here the king becomes the servant of God; and the king is to serve the people, who are God's partner in the covenant. At the same time the king is doubly in covenant with God and with the people of God. The reason for the existence of the king is to implement the covenant code, which is the order of the Exodus.

When this order of reign was disturbed by the "despotic rule," the prophets spoke out against the kings. The first king who was challenged on this ground was King David himself, when he took Bathsheba, killing her husband Uriah (2 Sam. 12:1-15).

Typical of the despotic king was Ahab, against whom the prophet Elijah rose up to defend people like Naboth (1 Kings 21:1-29). The model king was described as one who was faithful to the covenant with God and with the people (2 Kings 23:1-3).

Phase IV

The *Ebed Yahweh* under the imperial rule of Babylon is envisioned as the king of the peoples of God. The prophet speaks of the Suffering Servant, who would reveal the justice (of God) to all nations and who would establish peace. The suppressed nation as the corporate subject of the Suffering Servant provides the form of political identity which would bring about the messianic reign of shalom in which the suffering *minjung* would be vindicated (Isa. 50:4-9). This does not mean that the Suffering Servant will become the despotic ruler. It means that the oppressive rule will end and will be replaced by the rule of the Shepherd, who gives his life for the sheep (Ezek. 34).

Phase V

When Jesus describes himself as the "*doulos* or *diakonos* of all," he is speaking against the worldly political order of the Roman Empire and against the political order of hierarchy, even in the mind of his disciples. Jesus' reference is to the Suffering Servant and to the Shepherd, who serves and dies for the sheep (Mark 9:35; 10:42-45).

Jesus' practice of servanthood in John 13:1ff. (Jesus' washing the disciples' feet) establishes the *doularchy* directly and personally in the midst of the community of the people of God. Therefore Jesus takes the form of a servant, as it is expressed in Philippians 2:7 *(morphe doulou)*.

Thus Jesus' *doularchy* is a direct transgression of the Roman political economy of slavery and the Roman *exousia* of the caesar; his *doularchy* is being the servant of all, against all oppressive politics; and his *doularchy* is to make all people and *minjung* the sovereign partners of God in the messianic reign. In the *doularchy,* politics means making the *minjung* the political subjects.

Phase VI

Participation under *doularchy* means a connection between *koinonia* and *diakonia. Doularchy* and *koinonia* (bond) are closely connected: the *minjung* in corporate bond become subjects to serve each other so that the *minjung* become serving sovereigns and sovereign servants. In Galatians 5:13, "Serve each other through *agape*" is the order of the One Body in Christ in interlinking faithfulness (covenant) (see Gal. 3:26-29). Thus ecclesial order is the paradigmatic manifestation of the Jesus *doularchy* in the political order of humankind, beginning in the Roman Empire.

Concluding Word

God's sovereignty is for the sovereignty of the *minjung,* debunking the *arche* of the *diabolos.* Power does not have any independent ontological status; it is non-being. Only the *minjung* can erect the authority to rule; the *minjung* are sovereign; and the *arche* is *doulos. Doulos* makes *arche* (servant makes master.) The *doulos* are in common bond to establish *exousia.*

What is the polity of feminist politics? What is the polity of liberation politics in Latin America? What is the nature of the political order that is sought by black liberation theology? How should the theologies of liberation seek a common political order in the approaching twenty-first century?

The political economy of the *minjung* is mutual servanthood and a mutual bond that makes them sovereign and turns *arche* into *doulos: doularchy,* which guarantees the *minjung*'s participation as sovereign-in-bond (covenant). This is radically different from social contract theories.

Doularchy in twenty-first-century politics should mean that the *minjung* become a comprehensive sovereign in the bond of servanthood, liberated and not enslaved, erect and not bowed down. This means direct participation in authority and politics by the mutually serving community for the enhancement of all life; it means the covenant solidarity of all *minjung* and all living things throughout the earth.

Doing Theology in a Planetary Age

Bruce O. Boston

Big Blue Marble

In 1948, the astronomer Sir Fred Hoyle predicted that if a photograph of the whole Earth were ever taken, a new idea as powerful as any in history would be let loose. It took almost a generation for his prophecy to come true. Once the astronauts of Apollo 8 sent back the first picture of the "big blue marble" from space in 1968, we earthlings entered upon a new revolution in consciousness.

Before we saw the Earth whole, we could still fend off the future with a Magellanic worldview, the illusion that we inhabited a world connected only to itself. It was a large and diverse world to be sure, steeped in mysteries and overflowing with peoples, cultures, and histories. Nations were sectioned off by boundaries (invisible from space), and their inhabitants were divided into races, classes, language groups, nationalities, and power blocs. That world filled our entire horizon; our worldview was limited, literally, to what was visible from a vantage point on (or barely above) the surface.

Context

But the image of big blue marble has created a shift in consciousness we still have not come to terms with: *here, at long last, is something we all belong to.* No mere city or country or ideology, but this planet, is our home ground. And now that we have seen ourselves from the vantage point of

231

the cosmos, where the horizon is a three-dimensional 360° in all directions simultaneously, we are faced with a new human and a new theological task.

Those of us fortunate enough to participate in the Student Christian Movement received advance notice of both the universality and the radical nature of that task. There we learned at a deeply personal level to trust a bond that questioned and transcended nations, cultures, races, and boundaries. The overwhelming personal lesson for me as a junior-year-abroad student at the American University of Beirut at the beginning of the 1960s, for example, was that the cultural, political, social, and religious "truths" I had grown up with could be creatively questioned. Indeed, the fact that other peoples could construct not only nations and cultures, but entire civilizations based on totally different premises from my own, was a revelation that made it necessary for me to rethink not only my own membership in the white American middle class, but everything I believed. My Beirut experience was intensified and focused by an internship as a youth worker in Malawi in the mid-1960s. The disappointment of watching the betrayal of a promising newborn nation to a personalized despotism taught the lessons that God permits us to reap our own folly, that personal intentions for good are often powerless, and that our humanity is not a fact but a task. In the turmoil of American politics in the 1960s and 1970s — in the civil rights movement, the struggle against the Vietnam War, the "Children's Crusade" for Eugene McCarthy, and the capstone disillusionment of Watergate — those early lessons were reinforced. Dehumanization, I learned, is structural, not just something that happens as an unfortunate by-product of events.

At Princeton Seminary, I was led by Dick Shaull and others to theological insights that have equipped me to continue a process of fruitful (if sometimes frustrating!) engagement, a process that flavors the theme of this essay. God, I have learned over and over again in personal, political, ecclesiastical, and cultural contexts alike, is not in the answers business, but in the questions business. The questions change with the historical context, but the process of engagement among God, self, and world remains encouragingly constant. Faithfulness is always about trying to discern what God is doing in the world, what questions that activity poses for God's people, and what action arises from responding to those questions — however tentative or broken.

The Christian's fundamental theological task is learning how to ask better questions. Having been transfixed by the image of the big blue marble, some of the questions in which I am now most deeply absorbed theologically are these:

- What does it mean to belong to the planet *as well as* to the United States, or Malawi, or Costa Rica?
- What rights and responsibilities do all humans share, not just in respect to one another, but to Gaia herself?
- Where, now, is the City of God?
- In the context of the mathematical near-certainty of intelligent life elsewhere in the Universe, who now are "the people of God," and what is their work?
- What may it mean for Christians to amend timeless faith statements such as "God acts redemptively in [our planet's] history" or "God was in Christ, reconciling [our particular] world unto himself"?
- Indeed, how meaningful, on the cosmic scale we now must use to measure our theologizing, is the regnant theological paradigm of *history alone* as the arena of God's activity?

In short, history has brought us to a crossroads comparable to few others in our life as a species on this planet. If, as Rosenstock-Huessy teaches, each new era in human history both reorders the past and creates a future, what era are we living in? What new theological questions should we be asking?

A New Consciousness: Five Suggestive Dimensions

My hypothesis in this essay is that the emerging shift in our consciousness about our planet, suggested above, is emblematic of a shift toward a new set of issues that point to a revolution in consciousness itself. The revolution is most advantageously viewed from the speculative and cutting edges of physical and social science. While the changes in self-understanding forced on us by the big blue marble have affected us in as yet only marginally explored ways, they nevertheless demand attention — and theological attention at that. In what follows, I want first to set out five of the dimensions of what appears to be a new consciousness, with the suggestion that what is most remarkable about them is their convergence. I want then to turn to some issues of theological method, as posed by the work of Dick Shaull, as particularly fruitful in our common struggle within that revolution.

A New Physical World

Since the beginning of this century, first Einsteinian and then quantum physics have rearranged the conceptual map of the physical world, with startling implications not only for science but for our understanding of the structure of reality itself. Classical ideas in physics such as time, space, matter, energy, event, object, location, cause and effect, and others have been utterly redefined.

Paradox has moved to the center of theory. The classical concept of solid objects, for example, has simply disappeared; matter is now known to be inter-convertible with energy at the square of the speed of light. The atoms that make up garden-variety matter — whether trees or the chairs made from them or the carpenters making them — are no longer understood by physicists to "exist," but rather to exhibit tendencies to occur in locations described by the laws of mathematical probability. We are told that — at the subatomic level, at least — particles have no meaning as isolated entities, but can be understood only as different sorts of relationships within a continuous whole. At the deepest level, there are no boundaries, only intersections among wave patterns; everything is a part of everything else.

Most dumbfounding of all is the quantum truth that, at the subatomic level, the division between subject and object — i.e., the engine of discovery released by the Enlightenment — breaks down. It is the human observer who provides the final, and indeed constitutive, link in the relational chain. According to Heisenberg's Uncertainty Principle (which states that we can either determine the location of a subatomic particle or measure its momentum, *but not both at the same time*), we in some sense *create* reality at this level by our decision of what to measure or observe. The material world is continuous, i.e., the difference between a boson and a bison is one of magnitude and not qualitative. Thus, even everyday reality must be understood as somehow brought into being as our brains process sensory information. Experiments with photons (quanta of light), for example, indicate that whether a photon behaves as a particle or a wave depends on whether or not it is being observed, and in what way it is being observed. The logic and mathematics that describe the quantum world have driven many physicists to speculate that the process of creation may be infinitely diverse, giving rise to "parallel universes" on a continuous basis. Theoretical physicists with a philosophical bent now ask such questions as, "Is reality *there,* or is it just a continuous rearrangement of information?"

The Collective Unconscious

The clinical observations that Swiss psychiatrist C. G. Jung made of the dreams, fantasies, synchronicities, and hallucinations presented by his patients revealed a host of shared images and symbols that could not be explained from the patients' own knowledge or background. The discovery of inexplicable linkages between the consciousness of many individuals eventually led him to posit the existence of a "collective unconscious" — a vast pool of archetypal memory and symbol shared by the entire human race, upon which we all regularly draw to generate meaning and understanding. He uncovered a millennial world of mythological and religious symbology, inhabited by "archetypes," which he believed were psychic phenomena normally unavailable to the conscious mind, but once made available and participated in, were powerfully insightful tools for creating changes in human consciousness.

Although the concept of the "collective unconscious" is now in widespread use among therapists, our current understanding of the Universe has no way of explaining how this phenomenon works, or why, or what its true dimensions may be. We have no science of consciousness (yet!), but one of the things that makes the Jungian insight so intriguing is that it echoes, in psychological terms, one of the core realities of the new physics: namely, that at some profound level, every member of humankind is a participant in the *same* reality, that in the deepest recesses of our being, the boundaries disappear between the individuated Self and the Whole, between Me and What Is Not Me (Descartes, phone home!). By virtue of our participation in the collective unconscious, every one of us is, in some sense, a part of everyone else, just as at some deep level the entire physical world — as seen from space — is a seamless whole. Both physically and psychically we are fundamentally, in the deft characterization of Michael Talbot, "beings without borders."

The Journey East

Since the 1960s, Americans have witnessed an explosion in the popularity of Eastern religions, not only at the superficial level of yogi-groupies and kung fu TV, but also at the much deeper levels of praxis engaged in by serious students of Hinduism, Buddhism (especially Zen), the Tao, and other Eastern ways of thinking and being. In the past decade or so, this general interest has also manifested itself in an increased attraction to various forms of mysticism, whether in Islam (Sufism), Judaism (Hasidism), or Christianity, e.g., in the rediscovery of the writings and spiritual disciplines of Meister Eckhart, Julian of Norwich, Hildegard of Bingen, Teresa of Avila, and others. An interest in contemplative Christian monasticism also remains relatively constant, witness the continuation in print of the writings of Thomas Merton.

Explanations of this turn toward the East (or in other forms, the turning inward) are many and various. Many people have a genuine and deeply felt sense of spiritual hunger, especially those who are disenchanted with the spiritual desiccation and ethical indifference in American culture. Many, once they come in contact with Eastern religions, find the inclusive and universalistic perspectives they encounter there both attractive and refreshing, especially in comparison to more dogmatic and exclusive religious traditions in the West. Others have been so buffeted by moral outrages and political injustices that they seek alternatives; often exhausted by the search, they opt out of worldly concerns altogether to burrow deeply into a womb of personal religiosity. For those to whom depth psychology speaks more cogently, Eastern religions seem a more direct route to the true Self; Taoism and Zen Buddhism, for example, are strongly oriented in this direction. Still others are attracted to Eastern religions in reaction to the lack of depth they experience in much of American denominational Christianity, which leaves them frustrated, unenlightened, and spiritually malnourished. Another group, often alienated adolescents and young adults, seeks a meaningful community and finds it in an enthusiastic and rebellious adoption of minority religious cultures. And, as does anything that comes from a foreign realm, Eastern religions attract "day-trippers" who flock to exotic gurus, but who often fall aside once the novelty wears off and they discover that the Eightfold Path is no trip to the beach.

But however the Eastward or inward turning may be explained, or whether the attractions there are superficial or profound, they are real. There is, in short, growing evidence of restlessness in the consciousness of the West. More and more, mainstream Christian ideas are experienced as restrictive, culturally arrogant, and theologically imperialistic — a narrow gate. Increasing numbers seem far more attracted to the mind-expanding, breakthrough potential of "enlightenment," to the tempting amalgam of transcendence and immanence inherent in Eastern religious praxis, and (curiously) to the intellectual frustrations and satisfactions of paradoxical theologies (e.g., "The Tao is before conception and beyond comprehension, yet it has always been known"). Eastern religions, like quantum physics and Jungian psychology, rearrange consciousness and break the bonds of old conceptual models.

The Sweep of Evolution

Looked at long-term (i.e., from the Big Bang onward), the sweep of evolution moves from the initial creation and stupendous release of energy to the creation of matter; to the creation of life; and finally within living things to the production of the highest (thus far) evolutionary stage — self-reflective consciousness. But new views of the evolutionary process have only begun to be cast in thought forms and language that can take that new consciousness into account. When the Jesuit Pierre Teilhard de Chardin published his *The Phenomenon of Man* in the United States in 1959, his idea that matter would finally evolve into a "noosphere" made up of mind/consciousness, and which would ultimately culminate in an "Omega Point" and be reunited with the Creator, was treated as theologically interesting but irrelevant to the political theologies of the 1960s. Now, he's back.

Interestingly, many of Teilhard's ideas have found a home in the thinking of scientists and writers who have become interested in questions of evolution on the grand scale. One core idea that has gained widespread currency is the "Gaia Hypothesis," most notably put forward by the British chemist James Lovelock. Proceeding from the scientific bedrock of physical chemistry, Lovelock and others have traced an evolutionary development that eventuates in the Earth's being an independent, living, self-regulating system — Gaia. James Miller, the father of modern systems theory, postulates nineteen subsystems that characterize all living systems, whether biological or sociocultural; Gaia exhibits them all. In sum, from the standpoint of systems theory, Gaia exhibits a key characteristic: the ability to maintain a self-regulating order in the midst of change. Miller's and Lovelock's ideas are accompanied by the analogical speculation by many that the human race may be something like the planet's "nervous system," a kind of global brain of which persons are individual cells — but which are obviously capable of collaborating to kill Gaia herself.

The now dominant model for understanding evolution says that it does not proceed gradually and evenly, but by revolutionary leaps. Moreover, the intervals between major leaps is shortening dramatically; put differently, evolution is accelerating. Consider the following timetable, drawn from Peter Russell's fascinating exploration of these ideas in *The Global Brain Awakens* (1995), in which the fifteen-billion-year lifespan of the Universe is compressed into a single year:

- Big Bang — sufficient cooling occurs to allow stable atoms to appear in a gaseous cloud: by first 25 minutes of January 1
- Cooling of the gaseous cloud into galaxies and stars: by February or March
- Formation of our solar system: by September
- Simple algae and bacteria appear: by October
- Sufficient atmospheric oxygen (as a product of photosynthesis) is present to support life: by early November

- Cells with well-defined nuclei evolve, making sexual reproduction possible: by mid-November
- First multicellular organisms appear: by early December
- First vertebrates crawl out onto land: by the second week of December
- Dinosaurs rule from Christmas until noon on December 30
- Ape-like human ancestors appear around noon on December 31; they begin to walk upright by 11:00 p.m.; they begin to become self-aware
- Human language develops: Dec. 31, 11:59:30 p.m.
- Buddha achieves enlightenment: Dec. 31, 11:59:54 p.m.
- Christ appears: Dec. 31, 11:59:55 p.m.

Most of us have seen "gee-whiz" calendars like this before. What is mind-boggling, however, is the leaps and the acceleration rate that these evolutionary data exhibit. In biology, our DNA-altering capabilities have made it possible today, for the first time, to *deliberately* shape the evolutionary process itself, not only among plants and animals, but among ourselves. This event, says Russell, rivals the acquisition by lifeforms of the ability to reproduce sexually — two billion years ago. We today routinely create new physical elements (Einsteinium, Fermium, Nobelium); the last time any new physical element was created happened when new elements were synthesized in the formation of our Sun. We now stand on the threshold of the colonization of space. When we cast off from Earth, it will be (so far as we know) the first time any lifeform conquered a new environment since amphibians crawled onto land four billion years ago. All these developments, *together with their synchronicity in our own century,* Russell suggests, intimate that we are in a phase of evolutionary development utterly without precedent. Even more to the point, these developments are what he calls "cross-catalytic," i.e., progress in one scientific area now accelerates progress in the others.

What must not be lost in this parade is the notion that consciousness, i.e., the self-awareness of the dominant lifeform on the planet, has now moved to the core of evolutionary change. That means a new equation: evolution + self-conscious direction = revolution. With the exception of perhaps only a few "fringe" theologians (e.g., Teilhard de Chardin, Matthew Fox, Wendell Berry), we have not begun to come to terms with any of this theologically.

A Holographic Universe?

Among the most fertile books for theological speculation — and perhaps for genuine theological work — that I have read in the past five years has been Michael Talbot's *The Holographic Universe* (1991). Drawing chiefly on the brain-function studies of neurophysiologist Karl Pribram and the work of quantum physicist David Bohm, Talbot presents to a lay public Bohm's daring thesis: Reality is a giant hologram, collectively projected in some as yet not clearly understood way by the human mind itself. Put differently, the most basic substructure of "all that is" is consciousness itself; or, in Talbot's phrase, "consciousness is a subtle form of matter."

Using the holographic paradigm in true Thomas Kuhn fashion, Talbot offers possible explanations not only for puzzling and anomalous phenomena in physics itself, but for a diverse range of "off-the-wall" experiences, including the paranormal, near-death experiences, psychic healing, and experiences of numinous and mystical phenomena usually considered at best to belong to the domain of religion and theology, or at worst, as a part of the "wacko fringe."

As a matter of physics, Bohm flatly rejects the Cartesian premise. Like dividing reality up into parts and labeling them, he says, the subject-object dichotomy is merely a convention. Bohm also pushes one of Einstein's basic insights — that time and space are part of the same continuum — to a new level. *Everything, he says, is part of the same continuum.* This does not mean the Universe is a giant, undifferentiated mass; things can be part of the whole yet retain their distinctive characteristics. He merely wants us to be aware that the Cartesian premise of observer and observed is, at bottom, fundamentally false. Everything in the Universe, Bohm seems to be saying, is ultimately some form of consciousness.

New Agenda

I am suggesting that the most profoundly significant new datum we need to deal with theologically is the remarkable convergence being produced by the factors and disciplines I have been discussing.[1] Taken together, these and other relatively new ideas are creating a force field which has the development of consciousness both at its center and on the periphery. This force field can, and in my view should, be seen as the illimitable arena of God's activity. It is not bound by human history, but includes history as part of a cosmic agenda. This convergence, of which there are other constituents in social and cultural dimensions not discussed here, acts as a

---

1. I do not mean to suggest these are the only such factors. They simply draw together a number of developments that seem to me to point in the same direction.

lens, focusing theological attention in unexpected ways.[2] Here is where the God of history goes before us, the new arena and era of the Spirit for which we must now construct a new theological agenda.

The pace of evolutionary change, which we are accustomed to thinking of in glacial and millennial terms, is now accelerating as *evolutionary processes begin to work with consciousness as their raw material,* not just the physical world, and as we begin to plumb the human meaning of the interconvertibility of matter, energy, and consciousness.

Only within the last decade, for example, have we become accustomed to thinking of ourselves as living in an Information Age. But the Information Age will be even shorter-lived than the Industrial and Technological Ages that preceded it. Russell, for example, plots a "consciousness curve" that predicts:

- exponential growth in the numbers of people attracted to and practicing consciousness-expanding activities and disciplines;
- explosive membership expansion in organizations active in the area of inner-directed transformation (e.g., holistic health, psychic healing, the "wellness" movement, meditation, the search for ecstatic religious experience), in which the doubling rate of growth even now is less than five years; and
- the commensurate development of an international literature (books and magazines) in these fields.

A recent Stanford Research Institute survey has found, for example, that as much as twenty percent of the U.S. population falls into the class of "cultural creatives" whose core personal values relate to improving human relationships, green politics, idealistic causes, and the expansion of personal consciousness. There seems to be no abatement in sight.

This reach-for-the-stars "consciousness curve" has led a number of observers to suggest further that sometime early in the next century the number of people employed in information processing (in societies where basic needs are being met for the majority) will be overtaken by the number of people employed in some form of "consciousness processing," i.e., people whose working lives are devoted to exploring their inner frontiers — both personal and collective — and helping others do the same. In short, we may be on the brink of a transformation more radical than any we have

2. For a provocative exposition of the dimensions and directions of this convergence of the scientific and spiritual, see Ken Wilber, *A Brief History of Everything* (Boston: Shambhala Publications, 1996).

yet experienced: a Consciousness Age which incorporates and advances the changes now converging and coalescing on fronts such as those discussed above.

If this were to happen, the awakening of self-awareness on the part of Gaia might itself be accelerated; indeed, if these potentialities are anywhere near the mark, some of us may live to see the convergence of cosmology, psychology, physics, "consciousness studies," and theology into something like a mega-discipline. I believe this is possible. The question is, how may we begin to prepare for it?

A Case for Theological Method

I want to suggest here that there is a way to begin preparation for the revolution in consciousness in the theological method of Dick Shaull. Shaull has always been far more concerned about the process of doing theology *in situ* than with any enduring product that might emerge from that process. He has never been a system builder. For him, theology is something like the set of directions you jot down on the back of the envelope while you try to keep up with God's walk through history. The issue (and the fun) lies in the engagement, the praxis, not in producing a finished body of thought or map.

Shaull's *Encounter with Revolution,* written in Brazil, was certainly the first book published in this country that tried to come to terms theologically with political and social revolution as a dynamic force driving the history of the Third World. Later, as a seminary professor, he sought to understand theologically the revolutionary ferment of the 1960s, both in his articles and in *Containment and Change,* written with Carl Oglesby. In his most recent books, *Heralds of a New Reformation* and *The Reformation and Liberation Theology,* he has both broadened his scope and narrowed his focus. In the former, he has provided a primer for Americans seeking to understand the broad theological underpinnings of liberation theology in Latin America. In the latter, he has mined the rich ore of the Reformers' theology and brought it to the forge of the struggle for justice for the poor. Thus, throughout Shaull's theological life, he has seen the fundamental human and theological task as articulating a theological response to the revolutions he has both participated in and observed. As an integral part of that response, he has consistently pointed to injustice as that over against which the forces of revolution are arrayed, while speaking the prophetic truth of the Word to the power of oppressive structures.

That general introduction aside, I want to turn now to two of the main structural elements I see in Shaull's theological method that point to a way ahead. They are by no means all the elements that could be discussed, nor, perhaps, are they the most fruitful to discuss, although I believe they will yield some insight.

First, begin with the human situation and proceed dialectically. Shaull has never abandoned the dialectical theological method in which he was trained, though he has amended it when the need arose. He proceeds from the real events and circumstances of the human situation where ordinary people find themselves, and where, most importantly, they must create change to humanize their lives. Shaull works by bringing these events and circumstances into a critical engagement with the Christian tradition, trying to uncover signs of God's presence and action within. For him, I believe, *analogiae fidei* give us the most important clues to what those signs might be. Like his mentor Paul Lehmann, Shaull's first theological question is always: "What is God doing here to make and keep human life human in the world?" From that point on, the primary theological task is thus always one of *discernment,* then taking the *risk* demanded by that discernment. In Shaull's repeated, off-handed characterization: "Let's try it and see what happens."

For Shaull, the unredeemed human situation is universally dominated by the power of institutional structures and their drive to self-perpetuation. Over against these structures stand the forces of liberation and humanization (for him often the same thing), which are at once God's gift and presence. The theologian's task is to understand the dynamics of dehumanizing power, to look for the thin wedge of God's action, and to align one's own action with the forces of liberation and humanization. The Quaker admonition to "speak truth to power" is one of Shaull's sharpest methodological tools.

In this context, the dialectical program of "conscientization" *(conscientização),* developed by Paulo Freire, provides a valuable complement to Shaull's theological method. Conscientization is Freire's name for what happens at those points where action and reflection intersect. There, a kind of force field of *critical consciousness* is created, which, for Freire, is the foundation for human liberation in political, social, and cultural contexts. Shaull has adapted this dynamic to his own training in dialectical theology and put it to good use for doing both political and theological work.

It is at precisely this point that Shaull's theological method can be valuable in understanding and abetting the revolution in consciousness of which we are now becoming aware. In this new environment, the struggle to claim and expand our humanity — "to make and keep human life human in the world" — continues and indeed, accelerates. But because new consciousness and false consciousness are not mutually exclusive categories, we need the tools of discernment.

One point at which such tools are critically important — there are surely others — is in sorting out the process of convergence among so many disciplines as they all wrestle with and advance the revolution in consciousness from their own perspectives. Because of its explanatory power, for example, the scientific paradigm already provides, virtually by default, the dominant categories of thought and the universal mode of discourse adopted when disciplines encounter one another. But a critical consciousness, deployed dialectically, can continually insist on grounding the dialogue in the human situation, and not just the scientific. From it, we can learn to trust what we learn from the human side of the equation, then use what we learn to stand over against the pretensions of any totalizing paradigm. That may mean laying aside the scientific model, for example, to adopt the mystic's; or to abandon purely logical rigor for the bumpier terrain of intuition — in spite of the evidence or lack of it.

At the same time, the rootedness of Shaull's theology in the human, and his insistence that every way ahead is found dialectically by creating alternatives, can prevent our getting too locked-in, dogmatic, or systematic. Only then can we begin to see the points where the revolution in consciousness is shaping the future, and discern where God may be.

Second, history is the arena of God's activity. This is a common assumption in theological methodology that Shaull shares with mainstream Christian theology. God's self-revelation and intentionality are delivered in the historical arena primarily; they are corroborated personally in and by the life of faith that is lived in response to that revelation and intentionality.

The most prominent methodological connection with this theological truth is *anamnesis,* the act of remembering and retelling the story of what God has done, both as a way of identifying oneself with that activity and of appropriating its meaning for one's own life and for the life of the Church. But history stretches only as far back as we can remember, about four thousand years — a feather on the evolutionary scale. The next revolution calls for a new frame of reference for *anamnesis* and a new direction for God's activity.

Theologically, the revolution in consciousness must now be seen as part of a continuum that reaches back to the instant of Creation and forward to the realized Integration of matter, energy, and consciousness, in a form yet to be understood. Like Abraham of old, we seek a land that is not yet our own. But nothing is lost. A revolution in consciousness will simply require us — as it always does — to reinterpret our history in the light of our new experience.

The new venue of human liberation may have not history, but Creation, as its point of origin and organization, with Integration as its Omega Point. As Matthew Fox has argued in *Original Blessing* and *The Coming of the Cosmic Christ,* the Augustinian historical paradigm of fall/redemption has run out its string. History as the battleground of the struggle between sin and salvation is now part of a cosmic frame of reference, a perspective not at all unfamiliar to the Bible, it should be noted. It is not only humanity that is redeemed, but the Creation itself, as it works its way through the transforming development of an awakened consciousness toward what Fox calls the "Original Blessing."

Perhaps in this light we can begin to understand harmony, beauty, and justice itself as cosmic energies, part of the wave pattern of the Universe itself, and not simply as human artifacts. Perhaps that new understanding will enable us to unleash those energies in different ways. Perhaps history recast is no longer salvation history but Creation history. If so, we can expect entirely new starting and ending points for our theologizing.

For the most part, Shaull's theological concerns have been dictated by what happens for God's great project of humanization in political, social, and cultural arenas. With Charles Norris Cochrane, he has held up the energy of the Christian faith in its ability to move beyond the limitations of classical culture. With Rosenstock-Huessy, he has affirmed that the history of the West has been the history of its revolutions. This plastic frame of reference can and must now be expanded, not only to the global context (where Shaull has already moved with it) but to the cosmos itself.

Shaull's use of history can still be instructive here. The most recent case in point is his *The Reformation and Liberation Theology,* in which he points to Luther's (re)discovery of grace as the basis for justification, the availability of Scripture to all believers, the Calvinist understanding of *ecclesia reformata semper reformanda,* and the Anabaptist critique of Christendom, grounded in radical discipleship. His method is one of re-articulation, i.e., restating basic principles in a form that enables them to be used in a new (often alien) historical context, without either violating their intrinsic meaning or mechanically applying them, like some wooden template from the past, to current realities.

The possibility this way of proceeding opens up lies in its flexibility. A methodology of re-articulation, which Shaull uses, for example, to bridge the gap between the communitarianism of sixteenth-century Anabaptists and Central American base communities, reestablishes continuity in an environment rent by radical discontinuity. In such circumstances, the need for theological agility is paramount. Propositional and systematic theology won't work because their abstraction from new circumstances renders them incapable of a truly sympathetic understanding of the human situation. Such theologies remain tied to the categories of thought that created them. But close historical and biblical study begins to reveal empowering correspondences, analogies, and insights that can be brought to life in the present.

Exactly *how* this process works, in operational detail, remains something of a mystery; as in so much theology, description outruns explanation. One learns to trust the process as a matter of faithfulness. Part of making it work, surely, is this: by engaging the story of the people of God in history, and by learning the kinds of questions they have struggled with in the past, *we learn what our own questions truly are.* What was once empowering in the face of one set of oppressive or alienating circumstances can provide the energy for transformation in wholly new circumstances — *once those circumstances are rightly discerned.*

If we but have the eyes to see it, as the revolution in consciousness takes hold, history moves to another level as well. At that level, we will once again have to rearticulate our faith by asking new questions. It's a process Shaull has faithfully modeled and taught in his own life and theological work.

Toward a Revolution of the Sun:
Protestant Mayan Resistance in Guatemala

MARK MCCLAIN TAYLOR

THE MOST EFFECTIVE and dramatic poor people's uprising in the world today, with organized intercontinental support, may be led by the Mayan Zapatistas in Chiapas, the southernmost state of Mexico. Although this uprising has taken several turns, and Mayan communities supporting the Zapatistas remain surrounded in 1997 by some 60,000 U.S.-supplied Mexican troops, Mayan resistance remains creative and seemingly indefatigable.[1]

Mayan cultural groups, which also spill south of the Mexican border into Guatemala, possess a distinctive mythic vision of revolutionary practice. By "mythic vision," I mean the Mayans' "practiced set of beliefs about spirit, god and gods, nature, humanity, and life." I argue that Mayan mythic visions are distinctive because they promote a set of revolutionary practices that I call "a revolution of the sun." Unfolding this argument will help identify some distinctive Mayan approaches to resistance and revolutionary change.

I will not here rehearse the well-known accounts of the Mayan uprising in Mexico, which was unleashed by the Zapatistas on January 1, 1994

---

1. For just three English-language accounts of the uprising, see John Ross, *Rebellion from the Roots: Indian Uprising in Chiapas* (Monroe, Maine: Common Courage Press, 1995); Elaine Katzenberger, ed., *First World, Ha Ha Ha! The Zapatista Challenge* (San Francisco: City Lights, 1995); and George A. Collier, *Basta! Land and the Zapatista Rebellion in Chiapas* (Oakland, Calif.: Food First, 1994). For the necessary historical and cultural backgrounds, see Antonio Garcia de Leon, *Resistencia y utopia: Memorial de agravios y cronica de revueltas y profecias acaecidas en la provincia de Chiapas durante los ultimos quinientos anos de su historia,* Tomos 1 y 2 (Mexico, D.F.: Ediciones era, 1984).

(the day of the planned implementation of NAFTA),[2] and then sustained by their ingenious cultural and political maneuvering for more than three years now. This essay, instead, presents my argument in the milieu of Mayan Guatemala, where conquest, repression, and resistance have thrived as long as in neighboring Chiapas.

My window onto such a mythic vision is made possible by interviews I have had with Antonio Otzoy, a Protestant Mayan leader in the Western highlands of Guatemala. I have shared common practical and theoretical concerns with him, because he is a revolutionary activist who is also a Presbyterian and theologian. Yet, unlike me, he is Mayan in Guatemala, and challenges all who would be in solidarity with him to practice a respect for that difference. I will be "stepping across the border" from Chiapas, Mexico, then, into Guatemala and seemingly away from the site of Zapatista resistance. Yet, with this essay, I am still working within the mythic milieu of Mayan peoples' suffering and resistance.

Antonio is a Kakchiqel-speaking Mayan in the Chimaltenango region of Guatemala's Western highlands. Age thirty-eight, he has served as a pastor in the Presbyterian Church of Guatemala, and now works full-time as coordinator of an organization that unites Mayan Christians from seven indigenous Presbyterian units (called *presbiterios*). This organization also participates in pan-Mayan movements in Guatemala and in pan-Indigenous congresses throughout the Americas. Its theology is unusual among the massive numbers of Protestants, in Guatemala and throughout Latin America, because it seeks to embrace Mayan traditions and to do so in ways that can critically accommodate both ecumenical and liberationist movements.[3] Its abilities to transcend the often provincial visions of missionary Protestantism is due in significant part to its Mayan vision.

Antonio's organization is called *La Hermandad,* translatable as "the brotherhood," or "the fraternity," even though women form the majority of its council and of its seminars, workshops, and social activities. *La Hermandad's* primary purpose is to meet the distinctive needs of Mayan communities, especially those posed by the large numbers of widows and orphans produced by recently experienced violence in Guatemala. Special attention is given to socially productive projects such as handcrafts, health, care of domestic animals, housing, and land-purchase. All this is crucial,

2. The North American Free Trade Agreement between Mexico, the United States, and Canada, which would have had a decimating impact on indigenous peoples' livelihoods in Chiapas. See Ross, *Rebellion from the Roots,* 20-21, 45-48, 241-42.
3. On the rise of Protestantism, see David Stoll, *Is Latin America Turning Protestant? The Politics of Evangelical Growth* (Berkeley: The University of California Press, 1990).

life-sustaining work in a country like Guatemala, where Mayans make up over sixty percent of the total population of nine and a half million, and suffer by far the greater proportion of the extreme poverty borne by eighty-seven percent of the country's people.[4]

His organization also has a conscious commitment to the needs of what anthropologist Barbara Tedlock has referred to as "the Mayan diaspora" — the dispersion of Mayans from their communities since the late 1970s and 1980s. Five hundred thousand have been displaced internally within Guatemala. Some 20,000 were still hiding in the mountains in 1995.[5] One hundred fifty thousand fled to Mexico, with some 40,000 or more still there in 1994 as refugees afraid to return. Over 200,000 have fled to other countries. These together form what Tedlock calls an increasingly transnational ethnic identity or pan-Mayan communal culture which includes not only Mayans but also those supporters in other countries who work in regular solidarity with them.[6]

Antonio's organization, steeped in the trauma of Guatemala and with its burgeoning transnational consciousness, has developed a distinctive "mythic vision." Before describing the context and nature of this vision, a brief meditation on my methodology is crucial.

Mandate, Academic Voice, and Desire

I have long found daunting the presentation of an academic paper from my research on Guatemala, and not only because of the intellectual challenge of exploring the full theoretical implications of my intermittent fieldwork experiences there since 1987. More daunting is navigating the ethical problem.

These ethical problems emerge from the likelihood of co-optation by a white, relatively-privileged male in North America who stands ready to make of Mayans an object of academic research. Mayans are prime examples of "subaltern" peoples, i.e., peoples both made "other" and subordinated as other. How North American academics love to commodify

---

4. On the recent figures, see Suzanne Jonas, *The Battle for Guatemala* (Boulder, Colorado: Westview Press, 1992), 1-3, 178.

5. The existence of these mountain communities, the *CPRs (Las Communidades populares en resistencia),* is contested by the Guatemalan government, although international communities have visited and verified their existence and the fact of their continual bombardment by the government's military forces. Jonas, *The Battle,* 149.

6. Barbara Tedlock, *Time and the Highland Maya,* rev. ed. (Albuquerque: The University of New Mexico Press, 1992), 211.

otherness these days! As postcolonial critic and feminist Gayatri Chakravorty Spivak warns, "the subaltern cannot speak"; not because he or she lacks fortitude or ability to do so, but because almost always their concerns are lost in the voices of us benevolent, maybe even emancipatively inclined, intellectuals.

Contemporary Mayans themselves have frequently honed this suspicion in talk with U.S. linguists and anthropologists who routinely study their peoples and then build scholarly reputations in the U.S. by doing so. The simple objectification of a people for study often is an exercise in control, and as control is only slightly removed (if removed at all) from the imperialisms that have devastated indigenous peoples.[7] Only from this perspective can we understand one Mayan's question to U.S. linguists: "Doesn't foreign study of Mayan language support Mayan subordination?" Or, again, another Mayan queried: "Gringos are interested in Mayan culture. Out of pity, as a mockery, as a joke?"[8] These Mayan queries are a 1990s version of the critique of anthropological research that Native Americans have long resisted, expressed most clearly, perhaps, by Vine Deloria, Jr., who discussed "Anthropologists and Other Friends," in his famous *Custer Died for Your Sins: An Indian Manifesto.*[9]

If I proceed to risk co-opting a Mayan voice with this essay, it is because I understand there to be an obligation and request to do so, a mandate surging from subaltern Mayans themselves. Antonio and his community insist that advocates relay their story and mobilize solidarities with them in the United States, one of the nations most responsible for their suffering.

So I begin with their testimonies, their stories. In doing so I do not just comply with their mandate, I also tap into my own desire, a desire to respond to my own sense of disturbance about the brutality they have suffered, which is connected to the white racism, ecological destruction, and psychic numbing afflicting peoples in my own nation, the United States. The mythic vision being forged by these resisting peoples is one we all

---

7. For one such study of imperialism in the Americas, see Kirkpatrick Sayle, *The Conquest of Paradise: Columbus and the Columbian Legacy* (New York: Plume, 1991); and Walter La Feber, *Inevitable Revolutions* (New York: W. W. Norton, 1984). On the notion of imperialism among "benevolent Western intellectuals," see Gayatri Chakravorty Spivak, "Can the Subaltern Speak?" in *Marxism and the Interpretation of Culture,* ed. Cary Nelson and Lawrence Grossberg (Urbana and Chicago: University of Illinois Press, 1988), 292.

8. Unpublished lecture by linguist Nora England, summarizing questions from Mayan linguistics students in a seminar in Quetzaltenango, Guatemala.

9. Vine Deloria, Jr., *Custer Died for Your Sins: An Indian Manifesto* (New York: Macmillan, 1968), 78ff.

need to find our ways toward for our own survival, as well as for others, in the U.S. dominated continents of the Americas.[10]

I first wrote this essay in Spanish for submission to Antonio for his critical reading. In this English version, I have not incorporated his corrections and critique into either the text or the endnotes, but into several substantial footnotes. Simply presenting a corrected text, even while acknowledging Antonio's critical help, would gloss the dialogical character of this writing task — a task that I insist must remain open. Rather than clean up my text, and thereby hide my first misunderstanding on certain issues, I have left those parts of the text in my original, misunderstood form. The footnotes that feature Antonio's correcting words, help call attention to the kind of critical position Antonio's voice occupies in relation to mine.

Mayan Testimonies to Institutionalized Violence

I begin with Antonio's testimonial voice out of my notes from conversations with him.[11] Then, in order to better dramatize the effect of all this on

---

10. For my own articulation of this vision for citizens of North America, see Mark Taylor, *Ghosts of the American Land: How Amerindian and African Spirits of the Dead Work Revolution in the U.S.A.* (forthcoming, 1998), and Mark Taylor, *Remembering Esperanza: A Cultural-Political Theology for North American Praxis* (Maryknoll, N.Y.: Orbis Books, 1990).

11. A word is in order about my relation to Antonio, from which this essay emerges. I have been interviewing him over a period of several years, during 2-3 month stays in Guatemala each year since 1987. The most focused interviewing occurred in the summers of 1991 and 1992. He does not speak English, nor I his native Mayan language of Kakchiqel. The interviews were thus in Spanish. I have heard him in a number of special seminars he was leading, in delegation settings, and in ecumenical church services for Mayan Christians in his Chimaltenango region of the central Western highlands.

Antonio's worries about security in militarized Guatemala made impossible my use of a recorder and tapes in interviewing him. He requested there be no taping. All my notes were handwritten during and immediately after our face-to-face conversations. In this essay, I also develop his position by making use of several essays he has authored on behalf of *La Hermandad* and/or his participation in other indigenous movements.

A much longer and detailed version of this essay was written in Spanish and submitted to Antonio for his evaluation. I have incorporated his responses, after he reviewed the original essay, into my writing, in the form of several important endnotes. This use of the footnotes is made to preserve something of the otherness of his voice, forestalling, it is hoped, some of the inevitable merging (co-opting?/losing?) of his voice in mine, which tends to happen in an essay format like this. Antonio's responses in my footnote apparatus will be in quotations prefaced by the designation "ANTONIO:".

Antonio and contemporary Mayans, I will supplement Antonio's words with the lengthier, written testimony of Rigoberta Menchu Tum, another Mayan (Quiche-speaking) who, like Antonio, is also from the region that between 1978 and 1982 experienced the displacement of eighty percent of its citizens from their communities.[12] What would cause this? Let Antonio's voice set the scene.

> I want to say that always *la violencia* has been upon us. There is the violence of the poverty. This, too, is a daily assault. But in 1979 the "armed violence" began.[13]
>
> My area of Chimaltenango suffered this violence most intensely between 1979 and 1985. This time of repression was horrible. The people that were killed were men, women, children, aged and, all were innocent. All of them were innocent! [*¡Todos son innocentes!*] Now our community has many widows, displaced persons, orphans, and populations in resistance in the mountains.
>
> It began with members of my own family. The first person to be disappeared from our areas was a member of my extended family. This occurred in 1979. But within two weeks, three community leaders were also disappeared. These disappearances continued through 1980 and 1981. It wasn't until 1982 that we discovered the first clandestine cemetery in San Juan Comalapa.
>
> There are too many stories to tell, and it is painful. From the home of my grandparents, three women were disappeared together with my grandfather. The women's bodies were later found, naked and with many signs of torture; their underwear scattered in different places over our land.[14] Another man was found in a ravine.
>
> My grandfather was found, and found alive. But after the torture he had received from the army, he couldn't speak or do anything. Finally, one day he simply went away into the country and never came back. He was never found. After the actions of repression, my mother wrote the names of her loved-ones on a paper and put it on her door with a question: "Why? What have we done to deserve this?"

12. Tedlock, *Time and the Highland Maya*, xiii-xiv.

13. ANTONIO: "Yes, I want to emphasize the cycle here: the armed violence intensifies and reinforces the existing structural poverty. And the structural poverty then leads the people to resort to resistance that brings more armed violence."

14. ANTONIO: "You have the facts right, but you have underplayed the significance for us of these women's nakedness. The army knows our whole culture's respect of the body. The nakedness of the women was a premeditated assault on our peoples' ways. It was not just a humiliating torture for these women, it was also an attack on their and our culture."

From this day onward my mind was in confusion. I and my people needed a place to be secure and to help each other out. There didn't seem to be any. I noted especially that neither the Protestant nor the Catholic churches gave any space to the people for their security. Especially, the Presbyterian churches were indifferent to the situation. All this made me desperate, desperate for some kind of organization for the people in crisis.

I turn now to Rigoberta Menchu Tum's recollection of the torture and death of her younger brother. This segment is taken from her book, *I Rigoberta Menchu: A Guatemalan Indian Woman's Story,* which brought her international attention and the 1994 Nobel Peace Prize.

Well, a few minutes later three army lorries came into the village. . . . The lorry with the tortured came in. They started to take them out one by one. . . . Each of the tortured had different wounds on the face. But my mother recognized her son, my little brother, among them. . . . My brother [age 16] was very badly tortured, he could hardly stand up. All the tortured had no nails and they had cut off part of the soles of their feet. . . . There was a squadron of soldiers there ready to do exactly what the officer ordered. And the officer carried on with his rigmarole [*su rollo el oficial*], saying that we had to be satisfied with our lands, we had to be satisfied with eating bread and chile, but we mustn't let ourselves be led astray by communist ideas. . . . If I remember aright he must have repeated the word "communist" a hundred times. He started off with the Soviet Union, Cuba, Nicaragua; he said that the same communists from the Soviet Union had moved on to Cuba and then Nicaragua, and that now they were in Guatemala. And that those Cubans would die a death like that of those tortured people. Every time he paused in his speech, they forced the tortured up with kicks and blows from their weapons.

No one could leave the meeting. Everyone was weeping. I, I don't know, everytime I tell this story, I cannot hold back my tears, for me it's a reality I can't forget, even though it's not easy to tell of it. My mother was weeping; she was looking at her son. . . . Somewhere around half-way through the speech, it would be an hour and a half, two hours on, the captain made the squad of soldiers take the clothes off the tortured people, saying that it was so that everyone could see for themselves what their punishment had been and realize that if we got mixed up in communism, in terrorism, we'd be punished the same way. . . . The Captain devoted himself to explaining each of the different tortures.

. . . I found it impossible to concentrate, seeing that this could be. . . . You could only think that these were human beings and what pain those bodies had felt to arrive at that unrecognizable state. All the people were crying, even the children. I was watching the children. They were crying and terrified, clinging to their mothers. We didn't know what to do. During his speech, the captain kept saying his government was democratic and gave us everything. What more could we want . . . ?

The captain said, this isn't the last of their punishments, there's another one yet. This is what we've done with all the subversives we catch, because they have to die by violence. The problem is that the Indians let themselves be led by the communists. Anyway, they lined up the tortured and poured petrol on them; and then the soldiers set fire to each one of them. Many of them begged for mercy. . . . Some of them screamed, Many of them leapt but uttered no sound — of course, that was because their breathing was cut off. . . . You could see that even the children were enraged, but they didn't know how to express their rage. . . . The people raised their weapons and rushed at the army, but they drew back at once, because there was a risk of a massacre. The army had all kinds of arms, even planes flying overhead. . . . The bodies were twitching about. Although the fire had gone out, the bodies kept twitching. It was a frightful thing for me to accept that. You know it wasn't just my brother's life. It was many lives, and you don't think that the grief is just for yourself but for all the relatives of the others. . . . Anyway they were Indians, our brothers.

And what you think is that Indians are already being killed off by malnutrition, and when our parents can hardly give us enough to live on, and make such sacrifices so that we can grow up, then they burn us alive like that. Savagely. . . . My mother was half dead with grief. She embraced her son, she spoke to him, dead and tortured as he was. She kissed him and everything, though he was burnt. I said to her: "come let's go home." . . . It was as though we were drunk or struck dumb; none of us uttered a word.

A Mythic Vision of *Lo Material*

"None of us uttered a word." A word. Rigoberta's mother could not utter one. Antonio long sought for his own word or words for his family's experience of torture. Then, amid his own and others' stories of torture and fear, a word from his grandmother (his *abuelita*) "flew into his mind." It came unexpectedly, after the repression, and provided the essential name for all the suffering with which contemporary Mayan mythic visions and practices work.

She invented her word to name not only the five hundred years of Mayan suffering since the conquest, but also the suffering that was to come to Antonio, Menchu, and others. The term is a Spanish term, not in the dictionaries: *desencarnacion.* I might translate it with an English invention: "disincarnation." While these are inventions, their opposites do exist in the dictionaries: *encarnacion,* or incarnation, derived from *encarnar,* to incarnate, i.e., to be in the form of, or in connection with, the body and with the material world. Antonio's *abuelita* had named her people's violation with a term signifying the absence of incarnate, fleshed-out existence. It is the deprivation of life from the body, and the extraction of blood and bone from existence.

Antonio and his religious association, *La Hermandad,* see Mayan peoples' struggles as occurring in the context of this *desencarnacion,* this defleshment. This notion is not only a negative opposite to classical Mayan valorization of materiality, but now at the five-hundred-year mark of post-conquest America, it becomes for this group a crucial term for understanding evil — an understanding that motivates a reassertion by Mayans of the claims of the material.[15]

The effort to forge a mythic vision of *lo material* in this context, is much more the concern of Antonio and his community than the issue of interreligious dialogue between his Protestant Christianity and his traditional Mayan religion. Although some religion scholars and many North American Christians may be intrigued or troubled by these issues, for Antonio and his *Hermandad,* "interreligious dialogue" (here, between Protestant Christian and Mayan traditions) seems stripped down to certain bare essentials and readily embraces a vital, life-centered syncretism.

Focusing on such life-centered syncretism, the crucial questions are not how one religious tradition is or is not similar to the other, but how both can make life when all around there is death. "Jesus is life, and wherever there is life," says Antonio, "there is Jesus." The legacy of Jesus in Christianity, he stresses, has "turned the Jesus of life and the Creator of all life into an insensitive perpetrator of destruction." Time and again, Antonio strikes the theme that the West has set the Creator against life.

---

15. Some Mesoamerican scholars have informed me that the term reminds them of some descriptions of the Mayan "underworld," and that Mayan mythologies of that underworld might, therefore, be productively searched for notions similar to the grandmother's idea of *desencarnacion.*

Western Christianity has fostered a dematerialized "spiritualism" as distinct from a true spirituality.

All this has been especially true of Protestantism, he emphasizes, which excels in "closing its eyes in front of every earthly problem while issuing passports to heaven." It is the distinctive contribution of Mayan thought and practice, and of America's indigenous peoples generally, he claims, to "restore the connection between the Creator and *material* creation."

This contribution involves developing and nurturing a mythic vision that has two key foci: first, a full interpretation of *desencarnacion;* and second, the crafting of a vision of political and religious struggle that places a cosmology of the sun at the heart of revolutionary change. The rest of this essay elaborates these two foci and their significance.

Desencarnacion

The notion of *desencarnacion,* as used by Antonio's *abuelita,* is laden with a wide array of meanings. It refers not only to the literal defleshment of torture so extensively experienced by Mayan peoples, but also to every system that drains the life out of Mayan peoples. Antonio reports, in fact, that the term became a kind of motivator for his own study of the life-denying ways of international capitalism and its connections to his peoples' suffering.

How can it be that defleshment and transnational capital can be yoked together as *desencarnacion?* To answer, we have to traverse a number of complex spheres within the Mayans' cultural and political life. We need to follow the logic of Antonio's grandmother, to note the enormity and extent of *desencarnacion* as not only the literal defleshment, but also as a complex network working against the flesh of Mayan peoples and against the flesh of any who act in solidarity with them in recent and contemporary Guatemala.

Note, first, that both the stories of Antonio and Menchu implicate the Guatemalan army in the direct war against their people's flesh. Analyses of torture in Guatemala make it clear that the army has been the major sustainer of such practices. The army trains its enlistees by readying them to inflict pain upon their own peoples. As noted by Jose Garcia, who is a former member and instructor of basic infantry training in the army, the aim of Guatemalan military life is to destroy the cultural identity, indeed

16. Jose Garcia, "Notes on the School of Torture," in *"Make It Stop!" A Campaign to End Torture in Guatemala* (Washington D.C.: Guatemala Human Rights Commission — USA, 1991).

any kind of self-esteem or collective pride that might rival "the pure air of the military base."[16] The assault on military conscripts' selves and cultural identities is achieved through beatings on almost every part of the recruit's body. Ever more refined exposure to human pain increasingly creates the torturer's character. Garcia concludes that the army and national security apparatus, which extends from a palace guard to clandestine death squads, are the major practitioners of torture in Guatemala.

In the time of Antonio's and Menchu's suffering, the army annihilated, by its own admission, 440 or more Mayan villages, destroying men, women, and children. It did so in villages, streets, churches, fields, and woods — with tortures that played out the theme of massacre in many hideous variations.[17]

This "disincarnating" army has dominated Guatemalan peoples, in its present form, since 1954, the year in which the CIA, with President Eisenhower's approval, destabilized and then toppled the only authentic democratic government Guatemalan peoples have had since the conquest.[18] After 1954, there have been only repressive, corrupt, military governments or military-dominated ones. Periodic guerrilla movements among Mayans and the poor have kept going a thirty-year civil war since the 1950s, which finally resulted, in late 1996, in a tentative cease-fire, a "peace." The United States supported the military regimes with economic and military aid, or if that was not possible, encouraged Israel, Argentina, and others to give that aid. Even in 1992, when violations and the abusive power of the military was again on the rise, President George Bush's Secretary of Defense, Dick Cheney, offered to increase U.S. military aid.[19] The virulent attacks against Mayan flesh by the Guatemalan army, then, were a means to reinforce an internationalized system of death, i.e., a veritable war against any Mayan organization that could sustain their peoples' flesh, the complex material conditions necessary for their life. This is again to follow the logic of Antonio's grandmother; for, intrinsic to the notion of *desencarnacion*

---

17. Torture and genocide were even more intense in the late 1970s and early 1980s. For earlier periods, see, for example, an Americas Watch Report, *Messengers of Death: Human Rights in Guatemala, November 1988–February 1990* (Washington, D.C.: Human Rights Watch, 1990).

18. Richard Immerman, *The CIA in Guatemala: The Foreign Policy of Intervention* (Austin: University of Texas Press, 1982); and Piero Gleijeses, *Shattered Hope: The Guatemalan Revolution and the United States, 1944-1954* (Princeton: Princeton University Press, 1991).

19. Richard Cheney, "Richard Cheney intenta fortalecer democracias," in *Siglo Veintiuno,* Viernes, 14 de Febrero, 1992, p. 71; and "Richard Cheney elogia politica del Presidente Jorge Serrano," *Siglo Veintiuno,* Martes, 18 de Febrero, 1992, p. 3.

was what she termed the *"desencarnacion del estado"* ("disincarnation of the state") — the "state" that by multiform means perpetuates political and social practices that take the life out of her Mayan people.

In fact, the aforementioned military coup of 1954, a covert military action by the U.S. that led to many antidemocratic, military governments, also protected the rights of the U.S.-based United Fruit Company to own large tracts of land (often lying fallow) in Guatemala. It was the pre-1954 democracy's confiscation of part of that fallow land, held by United Fruit, which provoked U.S. businessmen to denounce these confiscations to the U.S. government as "communist insurgency" in Guatemala.

This denunciation had great impact not only because of the Red-scare in the 1950s, but because a lawyer with United Fruit had access to the government through his brother, John Foster Dulles, the Secretary of State, and to Allen Dulles, head of the CIA, both in the Eisenhower administration. (Both Dulleses, I might add, were respected Presbyterian laymen at the time.) Thus, the struggle for land reform in Guatemala was quickly caricatured as "communist subversion." This, in turn, was used to justify the overthrow of elected government in Guatemala, the subsequent militarization of that country, and the exposure of its people to the genocide that was to follow in the 1970s and 1980s.

Through the 1980s and early 1990s, this mutually reinforcing triangle between the Guatemalan army, Guatemalan elites, and U.S. economic interests continued. The first two points of this triangle have over the past two decades come closer together, i.e., more and more the army does not simply support the elites, they are themselves among the land-owning elite. Moreover, the U.S. economic connection remains significant.

This ongoing connection is evident in that after the 1954 coup, in the 1960s, various operations of US AID virtually created the bourgeoisie in Guatemala, without altering the racist domination of Mayan peoples in that country by the "Ladinos," i.e., the "white," non-Indian citizens in Guatemala who are of European cultural descent and privilege. Further, the Guatemalan business elite was organized and structured in a way that furthered U.S. business interests.[20] The alliance of U.S. business with Guatemalan elites[21] was further cemented by various shared projects be-

20. Suzanne Jonas and David Tobis, eds., *Guatemala* (New York: NACLA, 1974), 143-50.

21. Since 1970, the local Guatemalan elite has become quite heterogeneous, made up of not only U.S.-connected businesses, but also of wealthy military figures, industrialists, and the agricultural export sector. The recent strife between these shows that the economic elite in Guatemala today is far from a homogeneous block. (I am grateful for the counsel of Dennis A. Smith on this point.)

tween the Guatemalan branch of the U.S. Chamber of Commerce and Amigos del Pais, a "chamber of commerce" for Guatemalan businessmen.

The director of the U.S. branch of the Chamber of Commerce in Guatemala was Fred Sherwood, a former pilot in the 1954 U.S.-led coup that overthrew democracy, and a businessman who made his fortune during the subsequent corporate growth of the country. He has said in print that the right-wing death squads were not active enough. They were needed, he said, to protect private enterprise from communists who take advantage of Mayan workers, whom he termed "dumb savages" who "don't know how to run anything."[22]

The connections between U.S. business interests and recent Mayan suffering became uncomfortably clear when the 1980 transition team for the Reagan-Bush administration, the self-proclaimed restorer of private enterprise, visited with numerous business elites in Guatemala, announcing support of unrestricted development of capitalism, even supporting groups like Amigos del Pais, which are known to finance death squads.[23] Moreover, the extreme right party, the MLN, which almost all Guatemalans knew had connections to "The White Hand" death squad, gave funds to the Reagan-Bush campaign. A leader in this party, Mario Sandoval Alarcon (the so-called "Godfather of the death squads") attended Reagan's inauguration.[24]

It is no accident, then, that the same speech Antonio and Rigoberta Menchu heard from their torturers, about how communism was taking advantage of the poor and spreading from the Soviet Union to Cuba to Central America, was also heard in the 1980s in U.S. living rooms from the lips of President Reagan addressing television audiences.

Today in Guatemala, the defense of private enterprise takes the form of structural adjustment policies of the International Monetary Fund (IMF), World Bank, and other lending agencies. These policies, first formally accepted in 1986 by the previous president, Vinicio Cerezo, are currently intensifying *desencarnacion,* by imposing draconian austerity measures that cause primary travail for the Mayan poor. This violence of poverty and "war on the poor" continue, even while guerrillas and the government sign peace accords in 1996 to end formal fighting.

U.S. economic interests are implicated in and reinforce this Mayan suffering, too. To be sure, IMF structural adjustment policy is not only the

---

22. Allan Nairn, "To Defend Our Way of Life," in Jonathan L. Fried, Marvin E. Gettleman, Deborah T. Levenson, and Nancy Peckenham, *Guatemala in Rebellion: Unfinished History* (New York: Grove Press, 1983), 90-91.

23. Jonas, *The Battle,* 209.

24. Jonas, *The Battle,* 198.

result of U.S. actions. Other nations are involved. On the IMF Board, however, the U.S. commands the most voting power, and exercises that power efficiently on the scene of the IMF's offices in Washington, D.C. In addition, the U.S. exercises a special vigilance in supporting IMF policies in countries along its doorstep in the American hemispheres.

Let us not lose sight of the basic point amid all this political and economic complexity. *Desencarnacion,* the term of Antonio's grandmother for all that sucks the lifeblood from Mayan peoples, includes not only the literal defleshment of torture and organized military genocide, but also the structuring of social, political, and economic processes, which routinely plunge Mayan peoples deeper into poverty by extracting labor and wealth from them. The wealth that is extracted is then kept on high, as it were, in the sparkling, skyscraper worlds of elite and increasingly transnational corporate culture.[25]

Some readers, understandably, may be suspicious that such a notion of *desencarnacion* is here constructed in too complex a fashion to really be part of the culture and mythic vision of the Mayan poor themselves. This, though, underestimates the sophistication of suffering peoples' knowledge and critique. Mothers of suffering children tend to understand the policies of the IMF and World Bank in Latin America better than do college-educated affluent classes in the North.[26]

Antonio's own daily practice in the 1990s shows how close discussions of transnational capital occur amid his peoples' concrete suffering. I remember one occasion when Antonio had set up a video on a dirt-floored dwelling with a tin roof to lead discussions with a group of Mayan *campesinos* about corporate development projects that were destroying indigenous lands. All during the discussion a Guatemalan soldier paced intimidatingly at the entrance. The surveillance had its effect. The meeting, which surely smelled like "leftist spirit," occurred under a sense of threat.

Mayans know well, therefore, the connections between mandated economic plans called "development," and the guns carried outside their doors whenever they question the privileged persons who enforce those plans. Such ever-present demonstrations of power remind the Mayan cam-

---

25. For further studies of this dynamic of corporations' extraction of wealth from the Guatemalan poor, see Mark Taylor, "Transnational Corporations and Institutionalized Violence: A Challenge to Christian Movements in the United States," in David Batstone, editor, *New Visions for the Americas: Religious Engagement and Social Transformation* (Minneapolis, Minn.: Fortress Press, 1993), 101-24.

26. For an effective dramatization of this, see the film, "Hell to Pay," on Bolivian mothers' explanations of IMF policy and the international debt crisis. Available from Women Make Movies, Inc., 225 Lafayette St., Suite 211, New York, N.Y. 10012, 212-925-0606.

pesinos, daily, of the practical threats to Mayan flesh. From those reminders amid repression, arise powerful critiques of the complex systems of *desencarnacion.* A college education in economics is not necessary to forge such critiques.

Toward a Revolution of the Sun

Given these realities of *desencarnacion,* involving discrete events of horrific suffering and complex processes of political-economic oppression, we might expect Antonio and his organization to develop a mythic vision that employs the theories and beliefs of liberation theology. Such theology offers critique of institutionalized violence, of the First World's "war against the poor," and the nurturing of liberation movements for the poor. Although Mayan mythic visions of resistance often overlap with those of liberation theology, that theology is often found wanting by Mayan activists and communities.

In truth, liberation theology never really caught on in Guatemala, even during some of the most repressive times, and this is true even when many priests, catechists, and base ecclesial communities grew up in the 1970s and 1980s to support and foster protest and even armed resistance. Antonio is emphatic when he says that neither impressive liberation theology movements nor Marxist strategists ever really mobilized the Mayan majority. To be sure, Mayans had and still have much in common with liberationist rhetoric and movements. Solidarity with them, therefore, cannot be avoided. This does not mean, however, that the mythic vision will place liberation theology as the most important resource for effective political resistance to the deeply entrenched and well-supplied military.[27] When the military governments unleashed their almost unprecedented ruthlessness in the early 1980s, the progressive movement in Guatemala was devastated. It is indeed true that now the grassroots left is again impressively organized, but it is working in different, less oppositionalist ways. Especially Mayan leaders are forging an approach to revolutionary change that takes account of Mayan *cultural* approaches to political resistance. It is precisely this that was often missing in the Latin American liberation theology that one might otherwise expect to succeed among Mayan communities of resistance. What was missing?

One might respond, first, by referring to something like "cultural

27. On this problem, see the recent work by David Stoll, *Between Two Armies in the Ixil Towns of Guatemala* (Boulder, Colo.: The University of Colorado Press, 1993).

sensitivity" and awareness of Mayan cultural difference. Antonio often notes that little thought was given by leftist strategists, among religious or political liberationists, about how the struggle for political change would include Mayan concerns to preserve their traditional religious rites or their respect for nature. In spite of occasional efforts by liberationist Christians or leftist Marxist political leaders to address "ethnic issues" of Guatemala, the tendency was to subsume these Mayans' concerns into a class-based analysis that simply saw poor Mayans as part of a Marxist proletariat that needed liberating into freedom.[28]

I discovered early in my interviews with Antonio, however, that the very notion of "freedom" is differently understood than among many liberationists — whether religious or Marxist. This contrasting construction of freedom or liberation also leads to a distinctive kind of vision of social transformation and of political strategy. I can illustrate this by referring to the ways Antonio's Kakchiqel-speaking community weaves references to a cosmology of the sun into its understandings of political freedom.

Even in the Kakchiqel language this is evident. Antonio was quick to point out that the term for "the sun" *(k'ij)* is integral to any notions of freedom, liberty, or liberation. In fact, the phrase Antonio gave me for the notion of "freedom," which is as close as possible to the meaning of what Antonio understands as "liberation," is *taya k'ij che.* Note that in this phrase, the term for the sun *(k'ij)* is positioned at the center of the whole phrase needed for signifying liberation.

Moreover, Antonio interprets this *linguistic* centering of the word for sun as consistent with the way Mayans *culturally* center their vision of revolutionary political change around the sun. For Antonio and *La Hermandad,* a liberation theology that is not sun-centered, would, in spite of

---

28. ANTONIO: "In light of these problems, I want to say three more things about liberation theology from my perspective as a Mayan Protestant engaged in cultural and political struggle.

"First, liberation theology as a revolutionary concept is compatible with Mayan culture in its focus on *change.* Thus, it is valuable if it mobilizes Christians to participate in life-giving change.

"Second, I do have to say, still, that liberation theology is not and will not be much appreciated by those of us who want to respect and practice the Mayan rites.

"Third, there is an economic relevance of liberation theology for Mayans, I believe. Because economics and money are not Mayan ideas, it is hard for us to grasp the connections between money and power. Liberation theology, especially its class analyses, helps us understand this. In so doing, we are helped to see how life is taken away by the means by which the Western cultures have joined power and money. For us Mayans, life is the essence of our economy — not money. But we can learn from the liberation theologians that it is otherwise for those who oppress us."

all its emancipatory intentions, simply reinforce the further *desencarnacion* of indigenous peoples. It would be an "emancipatory" practice that would only deprive them of their cultural identity, and hence not be emancipatory in the full sense. It is therefore essential to this Mayan community's mythic vision that political change revolve around the sun. The mythic vision is a "political revolution of the sun."

This mythic vision can be further elaborated as inspiring and reinforcing three kinds of revolutionary practice: a revolutionary materialism, a revolutionary comprehensiveness, and a revolutionary patience.

1. Revolutionary Materialism

If the mythic visions emerging from recent Mayan struggle privileges a notion like *desencarnacion* for the comprehensive suffering and entrenched oppression suffered, it is not surprising that revolutionary change would entail a countervailing restoration of material existence, i.e., a reconstruction of every resource that nurtures flesh, that refurbishes incarnate/carnal life. Thus, as Antonio claims, echoing his grandmother, it is the Mayan contribution "to save substance, to restore *lo material*."

When Antonio speaks of liberation theology's failings, he regularly cites its neglect of Mayans' distinctive cultural orientation to nature and to care of the earth that is nurtured by the sun. Of course, a frequently registered reminder is in order here: we need not romanticize indigenous peoples' connection and valorization of nature, raising again the specter of European talk about the "noble savage's" closeness to, or harmony with, nature. That talk is often more an expression of European fantasies and alienation from nature, and less serving of real understanding of indigenous peoples. Notwithstanding such reminders, careful analysis, and indigenous peoples' own comparative observations, testify to the functioning of their cultural logics and their practices, which value material existence in ways European legacies traditionally have not.

The Mayan traditions, which Antonio seeks to recover, express their valorization of *lo material,* or material existence (nature, cosmos, land, corn, human flesh), by understanding these as loci of sacred presence and activity. There are many examples of this. The human body itself, even when acted upon in the bloodletting rituals of early Mayan history, was important because of its connection to the sacred. The earth, too, is often "holy earth."[29] We might recall, also, the syncretistic subsumption of

29. Benjamin N. Colby and Lore M. Colby, *The Daykeeper: The Life and Discourse of an Ixil Diviner* (Cambridge, Mass.: Harvard University Press, 1981), 41-42.

Christian traditional trinitarian beliefs within a larger Mayan vision that links each "person" of the trinity to Mayan "trinity" of earth, mountain, and the bones of ancestors.[30] Each "transcendent" and "divine" figure of the Christians' living God was referred to an aspect of the living land. Moreover, the religiously significant sun is regularly yoked by Mayans to such creative material processes as the birthing of children and to the sprouting of seeds.[31] Nature, sun, earth, childrens' bodies, birthing and sprouting of seed — these aspects are all examples of Mayan valorization of the material.

This is not a simple reversal, i.e., the sacralizing of matter against spirit. In Barbara Tedlock's terms, the Mayans employ a "dialectical" logic of spirit *and* matter that is internal to their encompassing religious vision. This logic works in a countervailing way against the many religious visions infused into Latin America from Europe and North America (Catholic and Protestant) which hold themselves to be "spiritual" over and against a nonreligious, or sometimes "evil," matter.

Antonio and his Protestant community are highly conscious of this valorization of the material because the fastest growing groups of Protestants in today's Guatemala (the neo-Pentecostals, and the diverse *evangelicos* nurtured by decades of missionary Protestantism) often assume a spirituality opposed to being material, even though many of these zealous spiritualisms teach a "health and wealth Christianity" that ends up being in love with the "materialism" (accumulating capital) spawned by elite corporate cultures.

In contrast to this, in Antonio's community, the ideal for being spiritual is resident in a material existence. This is not a vision of accumulating material wealth, but of sustaining a practiced relation to cosmos and nature, to corn and flesh, and to a sharing of material resources with those who suffer without them. Especially in this latter communal sharing of material goods, the Mayan valorization of *lo material* becomes a life-affirming, spiritual resistance to the spiritualistic religions that promote a "health and wealth" materialism among Protestants enamored with capitalist cultures of accumulation. In so doing, the whole Mayan cultural practice of finding spirit *in* matter becomes a revolutionary celebration of tangibility and of the material.[32] This is revolutionary because change is sought through

30. Tedlock, *Time and the Highland Maya,* 41-42.

31. Robert Carlsen and Martin Prechtel, "The Flowering of the Dead: An Interpretation of Highland Mayan Culture," *Man* (n.s.) 26:33-42.

32. ANTONIO: "Yes, and I want to stress again that the incarnation we oppose to *desencarnacion* is 'life itself.' This life is always in process, changing. That is, again, the

resistance to the de-materializing, de-fleshing systems of *desencarnacion* that are often reinforced by the spiritualistic Christian communions (again, Protestant or Catholic).

2. Revolutionary Comprehensiveness

The process of a struggle against *desencarnacion,* the struggle for a "revolutionary materialism," does not yield a narrow or constrained mythic vision. It does not, for example, focus on "the material" as if it focused on some region marked off from other regions of life. To the contrary, there is an accompanying "revolutionary comprehensiveness." It is here that material existence's impressive power, the sun, becomes especially central to Mayan life and political struggle.

In all Mayan languages, the sun is not simply a singular figure (celestial body or deity), but rather also defines the totality of both space and time.[33] The movement of the sun defines the directions that situate the human community, not only the East and West traced by the sun's course, but also the North and South that are to the right and left, respectively, of that solar movement. Moreover, as Tedlock and others stress, these directions should not be seen as "discrete cardinal or intercardinal compass points frozen in space, but rather are sides, lines, vectors or trajectories that are inseparable from the passage of time."[34] Antonio and members of his community often travel to Mayan sites to better inhabit such ritual space/time. Antonio goes to the Guatemalan city of Momostenango, for example, to nurture and recover his Mayan senses of time and space, which Protestant communities have often repressed.[35]

In so doing, the sun is continually acknowledged as that which defines and traces out an encompassing whole, orienting mythic vision toward comprehensiveness. This function of the sun is so comprehensive, that students of Mayan cosmologies of the sun regularly find themselves taken into not only horology, but also into notions of "the timely" (the "opportune"), of divination and destiny, of ritual, healing, epistemology, politics, and economy.

---

moving quality of life. Life is, indeed, in *lo material,* but this life is also always *in motion,* a process of transformation. *Desencarnacion,* therefore, not only dematerializes, but also stops life's movement. By contrast, our spirituality must celebrate the material *and* keep life moving. Ours is a spirituality of material transformation."

33. Tedlock, *Time and the Highland Maya,* 173.

34. Tedlock, *Time and the Highland Maya,* 178. Cf. John Watanabe, "In the World of the Sun: A Cognitive Model of Mayan Cosmology," *Man* (n.s.) 18 (1983): 710-28.

35. Unpublished paper distributed by Antonio's organization, *La Hermandad: Estudios sobre los Ritos y ceremonias Mayas,* 12ff.

To place the sun at the heart of political struggle, therefore, is to orient struggle to a totality of life and being. It is not only to resist what needs to be resisted (here *desencarnacion* of Mayan peoples), but also to resist any fragmentary or unidimensional strategies of resistance. Hence, Mayan revolution of the sun becomes, as Antonio repeatedly notes, a resistance to any liberationist movements and ideologies that fixate, for example, on only class issues.

Because Mayans are victims of classism and of labor exploitation, Marxian theories and liberationist analyses of class will, indeed, always be relevant. These, however, will always be insufficiently revolutionary to members of Mayan culture unless the politics of class struggle are related to a politics of natural process, i.e., of the healing of human bodies, of kin and of communal life, of the cycles of seasons and time.

On this topic Antonio becomes emphatic. It was primarily an Occidental mind that presented to Mayans a notion of liberation focused narrowly on the themes of classism. By contrast, Mayans' political revolution of the sun is multidimensional, and comprehensive. In fact, given the complexity and comprehensiveness of forces of *desencarnacion,* any political struggle worthy of the name will have to be, for Mayans, equally complex and comprehensive. It will have to resist not only military assault and literal defleshment, but also the cultural racism against Mayans, the social practices that routinize oppression, and the political powers and their transnational development plans.

In short, nearly everything "under the sun" needs to be resisted in some fashion, and in the context of their many relations, in, so to speak, their many "directions of East, West, North and South." Antonio's sphere of thinking and practice, then, is understandably *both* local *and* global. He will head for the mountain town of San Juan Ixcoy, in one month, to practice Mayan ritual, then to Quito, Ecuador, the next month, to participate in pan-American indigenous congresses.[36] In such activities, Antonio exhibits a revolutionary comprehensiveness that demands what Stefan Varese has called for: a new sociology of the native peoples of Latin America — transnationalized, urban, proletarian, border crossing, bilingual and trilingual, professional."[37] The comprehensive nature of the oppression of in-

---

36. Obviously, not all Mayans have access to funds for this kind of travel. Antonio's funds come from the Guatemalan Presbyterian Church, which, in turn, stem from sources in the Presbyterian Church, U.S.A. Availability of these funds for such travel is the result of Mayan organizing and actions of solidarity in Guatemala and the United States.

37. Stefano Varese, "Think Locally, Act Globally," *The First Nations 1492-1991,* in *Report on the Americas* (NACLA), vol. xxv, no. 3 (Dec. 1991): 12.

digenous peoples calls forth nothing less than a mythic vision and practice that is equally comprehensive.

3. Revolutionary Patience

The materialism and the comprehensiveness, which are essential to Mayan mythic visions of political struggle, mix to produce still another distinctive trait: "revolutionary patience." Ritually observing the dialectics of spirit in matter and the sharing of material life (revolutionary materialism), respecting the cycles of time and the interpenetrating spheres of space under conditions of *desencarnacion* (revolutionary comprehensiveness), have an important additional result. They yield no simple oppositional strategies of revolt, nor any expectations of rapid political change. Instead, there is this "revolutionary patience" (or "impatient patience" as another has said).[38] As I use the term, here, it means first, Mayans' moving between a variety of survival techniques as opposed to using only outright oppositional approaches, and second, Mayans' capacities for being in revolution for the long duration.

Concerning the first, we may note that a Mayan abstinence from simple oppositional strategies is rooted in that comprehensive vision that identifies a multiplicity of spheres in which political change must be sought. Correspondingly, as anthropologist Carol A. Smith has noted, Mayans feature a strategy that moves on many fronts simultaneously. This is not only to respect an agenda of comprehensiveness that envisions many agendas requiring careful, experimental, and complicated orchestration. It is also crucial to survival. The outright oppositional strategies proposed by Western revolutionaries and liberationists are often destructive to survival, especially within a ruthless military setting.

As a result, Mayans exhibit a strategy for revolution that often seems to step back from seeking victories that other revolutionaries often advocate. As with other subaltern peoples, the approach is not simply to counter and reverse hegemonies of racism, classism, and militarist aggression, but instead to absorb and transform them. To more traditional revolutionaries, this may appear to be selling out or compromising the revolution. The Mayan approach is not unlike that of another Mesoamerican group, the Zapotecs, whose women especially employ what Lynn Stephen has called a "dialectical dynamic" by which they *absorb* and *rework*" oppressive material conditions, ideology and culture imposed upon them by dominant

38. Conversations with Dennis Smith, Coordinator, CELEP, Guatemala City, August 1992.

groups.[39] Bell Hooks has suggested something similar as the better paradigm for African American women in resistance, noting that outright heroic resistance rarely generates hope-creating practice for African American women.[40] Without this strategy, Mayans are easily exposed to disaster by European visions of revolutionary conquest that press prematurely for opposition. Anthropologist David Stoll has suggested that such premature oppositionalism amid ruthlessly repressive environments, as in the Ixil triangle region of Guatemala, were partially responsible for the devastating violence endured there by the Quiche Maya.[41]

All this culminates, then, in the second sense of "revolutionary patience": a Mayan respect for the timely. Tedlock and others have commented on the Mayan search for the timely, or "the opportune."[42] The "right time" cannot be determined simply by whether or not there is opposition strong enough to overthrow dominant hegemony. The right conditions for such a transformation must be in motion, i.e., some cultural experience of the spirit/matter connection, an articulation of the various sites of political struggle (nature, family, community, nation, international solidarities). Rapid transformation and outright rebellion may, and have, occurred in Mayan history.[43] Many times, however, revolution means settling in for the long duration, respecting the revolutions of the sun and cycles upon cycles of time that place transformation well beyond present-day Mayans' own, and often their childrens,' generations.

In this connection, Antonio notes his own and his peoples' "cultural psychology," one that orthodox Marxists and liberation theologians find difficult to accommodate, but which Antonio insists needs integrating into a new theology of liberation. He discusses, therefore, a "Mayan temperament,"[44] which may opt for either violent revolt or intentional passivity. "When the repression is *not* very hard," he says, "Mayans then use demonstrations, actions, even violent rebellion. But when it *is* very hard they

39. Lynn Stephen, *Zapotec Women* (Austin, Texas: The University of Texas Press, 1992), 14.

40. Bell Hooks, "Revolutionary Black Women: Making Ourselves Subject," in *Black Looks: Race and Representation* (Boston, Mass.: South End Press, 1992), 51ff.

41. Stoll, *Between Two Fires*.

42. Tedlock, *Time and the Highland Maya*, 3.

43. Victoria Reifler Bricker, *The Indian Christ, the Indian King: The Historical Substrate of Mayan Myth and Ritual* (Austin, Texas: University of Texas Press, 1981), 11-52 and 85-126.

44. ANTONIO: "I wish you had used the word 'capacity' *(capacidad)* instead of temperament or inclination. What we are talking about here is not a problem of Mayan passivity. I am talking about a gift or strategy with which we are culturally equipped for struggle."

become more tranquil and passive."[45] From the perspective of some Western revolutionaries who expect the most intense oppositional rebellion during the most ruthless repressions, this seems like Mayan submission to tyranny. As Antonio suggests, however, the Mayan capacity is to even out the revolutionary impulse, relaxing it during the most severe genocidal periods and — perhaps unexpectedly — quickening it when repression begins to abate.

This Mayan strategy entails a rhythm of revolution appropriate to a comprehensive and multidimensional revolutionary agenda among a people for whom struggle and survival are the everyday, long-term realities. Carol A. Smith, who appreciates the Mayans' own initiated rhythms of change, their "revolutionary patience," wonders how this temperament and fluctuating action could become a strategy actually to transform the oppressive conditions suffered by the vast majority of Mayans.[46] Indeed, repressive forces in Guatemala may be able to perpetuate "eternal tyranny" by calibrating rhythms of genocide and repression with this "even" Mayan temperament, such that the repressor temperament and Mayan temperament simply lock together to systematically and regularly cancel out real change. This might serve only to perpetuate the "eternal tyranny" for which Guatemala has become famous. Although there is this risk that Mayan "revolutionary patience" will lead to a kind of inertia in struggles for overall transformation, this patience must be understood as an essential trait of Mayan cultural approaches to political change, i.e., to a political revolution that is "of the sun."

Antonio tells me that his community will for long, if not always, be a martyr community. The relatives, kin, and companeros of Antonio and Rigoberta Menchu are still dying, half their children slipping into death from the preventable diseases born from poverty and neglect, while the gun, bayonet, and even fire from U.S. Bell helicopters, for example, keep helping to rain a savage "de-fleshment" upon their peoples.

This has gone on among Mayan populations in Guatemala, and it continues among Mayans in present-day Chiapas where the Zapatista uprising continues its maneuvers. Only with a revolutionary patience, supplementing revolutionary materialism and comprehensiveness, amid the repression that Antonio's grandmother termed unrelenting *desencarnacion,*

45. ANTONIO: "Yes, I did say this, but recall that I am talking about a different mode of tranquility and passivity, i.e., one that honors the primacy of *life,* not one that just bows to repression."

46. Carol A. Smith, "Mayan Nationalism," *The First Nations 1492-1992* in *Report on the Americas* (NACLA), vol. xxv, no. 3 (Dec. 1991): 32-33.

can Mayans go on affirming the words of Guatemala's famous revolutionary poet of the 1950s, Otto Rene Castillo, who was tied by the army to a tree with his companera, before both were tortured and burned alive. His affirmation of revolutionary patience:

> It is beautiful to love the world with
> the eyes of those who have
> not yet been born.[47]

---

47. Jonas, *The Battle,* ix.

Reclaiming Liberative Trends: Owning Asian American Women's History of Struggle

Nantawan Boonprasat Lewis

IN MARCH 1997, I was invited to participate in the twelth annual conference of PANAAWTM (Pacific Asian North American, Asian Women in Theology and Ministry) as a faculty advisor to the group. The conference was held at Candler School of Theology, Emory University, in Atlanta, Georgia. We spent the first two days of the conference engaging with each other on various topics that are relevant to members of the group who are working in graduate degree programs in seminaries and theological schools in Canada and the United States. This theological engagement with members of the group left me with a particular challenge. This challenge emerged from an awareness of a necessity to produce knowledge about ourselves as Asian American, Asian Canadian or Asian women — whichever our geographical, cultural, and racial identity is — and what this means for us and our community of struggle theologically. I have become increasingly aware that the production of knowledge about ourselves is critical to our activity and practice of "naming the Divine."[1] This is especially important concerning how methodological and theoretical assumptions influence the way we generate our scholarship and propose theological strategies towards the struggle for liberation.

In addition, as a feminist scholar of color, I realize that I have a responsibility and accountability to the way particular knowledge about ourselves, i.e., women of color, is recorded, framed, articulated, disseminated, and read as it becomes a body of self-knowledge of Third World

1. Elisabeth Schüssler-Fiorenza, ed., *The Power of Naming* (Maryknoll, N.Y.: Orbis, 1996), xxxiii.

women and women of color. This is a kind of knowledge that has a tremendous impact on our theological work and clearly serves as a critical resource for our acts towards emancipation. Emancipation here is understood as a state of being free and liberated from all encompassing and systemic power of domination spiritually, intellectually, and materially.

The Politics of Producing Knowledge About Ourselves

In suggesting that the production of knowledge about ourselves is critical to our theological understanding and articulation of emancipation, I acknowledge that this is not an easy task. Furthermore it poses a great challenge to the way in which we, in this case Asian American women, have been acculturated and conditioned to think and theologize. Nonetheless, it is a required step for the task that needs our immediate attention and energy.

Reflecting on my experience, I am inclined to suggest that for us, Asian American women theologians, to be contributive to our own struggle and to a movement toward collective praxis for liberation, we need to produce a body of knowledge about ourselves and our struggle that goes beyond mere criticism and assessment of white feminist theologies and theories and strive toward analyses, both social and theological, that lead to a deeper understanding and a broader vision of our struggle and the collective struggle. Just as in Audre Lorde's famous statement that the master's tools will not dismantle the master's house, we too must realize that we cannot perpetuate our scholarly practice of using white feminists' theological paradigms as methodological frameworks for our situation and our theological articulation. (Nor is it commendable for white feminists to produce their knowledge about us and appropriate it to frame their theological interpretation of our struggle.) This is difficult because of a long history of intellectual domination that we have internalized. As an Asian American theologian has observed, scholars (both Third World and Western) are still not free from the illusion that the Western is universal. Third World scholars who are trained in the West and scholars of color are certainly not immune from a belief that a Eurocentric canon is the canon of our scholarship. We need to come to terms with this captivity and seriously evaluate and assess our long intellectual habit of existing under this condition. This is particularly the case when we become increasingly aware of and politically sophisticated in articulating about space and location from which the knowledge of colonized and postcolonized people is produced. As a result, it affects the way we address our struggle and speak theologically and communally about it.

Knowledge About Ourselves as Emancipatory Resistance

Thus in this essay, I propose a theological attempt toward a task of producing knowledge about ourselves as a resource for our struggle for liberation, which in itself signifies an act of resistance — a fundamental gesture and a tool of struggle toward emancipation from social-historical and spiritual domination. My discussion will center around the theological and spiritual meanings and interpretations of resistance as taken place in the context of the history of struggle of Asian American women, and which I hope will generate some understanding of ourselves, our struggle in history, and our spirituality for liberation. This exploratory and analytical discussion is drawn from stories, memories, and social and theological writings by and about Asian American women which provides a portrait of their social and spiritual biography as they, with their families and community, labor to survive and reach out to spread their dream of achieving social and economic opportunities and being free.

Naming Our Experience

In order to understand the context of the history of struggle of Asian American women, it is critical to come to terms with what has been their experiences in this continent and to allow these women to name them in their own voices. This is because in naming them they become subjects of their situation, not mere victims of their historical condition. And it is because, out of these experiences, they witness to us their spirituality of liberation as embodied in their lives and as expressed through their love of life, their commitment to justice, peace, and healing in communities and society. However, it is important to also acknowledge the diversity of experiences among these women. These diverse experiences indicate the specificity of their situation in which they anchor their particular struggle and from which they are engaged with other struggles.

Celebrating Our "Singular Plurality"

Recent discussion in communities of feminists of color, womanists, mujarista, white feminists, and feminists of working class brought out the significance of differences or diversity of experiences impacted by (to name a few) race, class, sexual orientation, faith tradition, and nation of origin as key factors in feminist theory and praxis. As Chandra Mohanty correctly points out, because women live in diverse realities, we do not function as a social and united category. Nor can we be categorized as a class. This communal acknowledgment also applies to Asian American women's situation. No one agrees that because we are of Asian descents, we represent a coherent interest group. Neither are we an automatic unitary group because we share the same ethnicity. Gale A. Yee succinctly affirms this position when she states: "The construction of an American identity for a Hmong woman growing up in Minnesota, or a Korean woman adopted as a child by a Southern white couple, will be completely different from that of a Taiwanese woman growing up in San Francisco or New York's Chinatown."[2] Asian Americans are a multiethnic group with many cultures, languages, and histories. This reality is further complicated by different patterns, chronologies, and histories of their migration to the United States. Issues and concerns facing the first and second generations are quite different from those of the third and fourth generations. For instance, while the first generation, or early immigrants, perceived themselves as sojourners, the second, third, and fourth generations see themselves as settlers and as Americans. Thus Shirley Geok-lin Lim correctly proclaims, "Asian American women" are exemplars of living in difference — "We are not single but plural."[3] To know ourselves as Asian American women is to acknowledge and celebrate this remarkable plurality.

Dismantling Our Victimization

Despite the above-mentioned differences in Asian American women's lived situation, there are similar patterns of experiences which have been expressed and articulated mostly in social and political terms in Asian American women's writings. These patterns, to name just a few, are invisibility (Mitsuye Yamada), otherness and difference (Trinh Minh-ha), alienation (Elaine Kim), exclusion (Kim Yuen Quan), marginalization and in-betweenness (Diana Chang). All of them represent and reflect a communal experience of Asian American women who, as members of their ethnic group, share with their men a history of victimization caused by racism, classism, colonialism, and imperialism. In addition, because of their gender,

2. Gale A. Yee, "The Impact of National Histories on the Politics of Identity," *Journal of Asian and Asian American Theology* 1:2, forthcoming.
3. Shirley Geok-lin Lim, "Introductions," in *The Forbidden Stitch,* ed. Shirley Geoklin Lim and Mayumi Tsutagawa (Corvallis, Ore.: Calyx Books, 1989), 10.

these women also experience gender prejudice and discrimination from their communities — both within and without.

In an article entitled "Invisibility Is an Unnatural Disaster," Mitsuye Yamada, a Japanese American poet describes her experience as "the visible minority that is invisible."[4] Yamada, who had a career teaching English in a community college, felt that she had long lived a life that contributed to her own stereotyping as a middle-class woman who is content just to bring an extra income to her family and as such she fitted nicely in the world of men's work. As she explains:

> I had created an underground culture of survival for myself and had become in the eyes of others the person I was trying not to be. Because I was permitted to go to college, permitted to take a stab at a career or two along the way, given "free choice" to marry and have a family, given a "choice" to eventually do both, I had assumed I was more or less free, not realizing that those who are free make and take choices; they do not choose from options proffered by "those out there."[5]

In her consciousness-awakening Yamada recognizes that she, the poor, and other women live in a state of "conditioned invisibility." As she puts it:

> Not only the young, but those who feel powerless over their own lives know what it is like not to make a difference on anyone or anything. The poor know it only too well, and we women have known it since we were little girls. The most insidious part of this conditioning process, I realize now, was that we have been trained not to expect a response in ways that mattered. We may be listened to and responded to with placating words and gestures, but our psychological mind-set has already told us time and again that we were born into a ready-made world into which we must fit ourselves, and that many of us do it very well."[6]

Having come to terms with this situation, Yamada was concerned that Asian American women still mostly remain in the background of women's and minority movements. Thus, she cautioned women in her

---

4. Mitsuye Yamada, "Invisibility Is an Unnatural Disaster: Reflections of an Asian American Woman," in *The Woman That I Am,* ed. D. Soyini Madison (New York: St. Martin's Press, 1994), 539.

    5. Yamada, "Invisibility," 540.

    6. Yamada, "Invisibility," 542.

community that "to finally recognize our own invisibility is to finally be on the path toward visibility. Invisibility is not a natural state for anyone."[7] In fact being invisible is a disastrous state of being for anyone.

Other women such as Kit Yuan Quan, a working-class feminist who migrated to the United States when she was seven and has lived here for over twenty years, views her experience as oppressive because of language and class (economic and social) barriers. As a result, she feels excluded from being a participatory and free member of American society. From early on, she was terrified to learn anything new that involved words or writing. She expressed her internalized oppression in the following:

> I get this overwhelming fear, this heart-stopping panic that I won't understand it. I won't know how to do it. . . . So I tuned out or nod my head as if there is nothing wrong. I've had to cover it up in order to survive, get jobs, pass classes and at times to work and live with people who do not care to understand my reality.[8]

The difficulty to express herself in English traumatized Quan during her childhood and kept pace with her until adulthood. As an adult, she found herself an outsider even in a feminist community because of class attitude and the use of sophisticated and theoretical languages in the community. As Quan articulates: "Even though feminist rhetoric does give me words to describe how I'm being oppressed, it still reflects the same racist, classist standards of the dominant society and of colleges and universities."[9] This frustration led her to comment at a women's meeting that the behavior and values of those at the meeting felt "middle class" to her and their "political vision" did not include people like her.

Quan's situation and her frustration is not unique, as many Asian and other immigrant women will testify. Many of them went through the same experience with Quan, only in varying degrees, and many still struggle in a similar situation. Her following words serve as a good reminder of the multiple elements of oppression that at times are neglected even in a feminist movement:

> Those of us who feel invisible or misunderstood when we try to name what is oppressing us within supposedly feminist or progressive groups

---

7. Yamada, "Invisibility," 543.

8. Kit Yuan Quan, "The Girl Who Wouldn't Sing," *Making Face, Making Soul,* ed. Gloria Anzaldlua (San Francisco: Aunt Lute Books, 1990), 213.

9. Quan, "The Girl," 215.

need to realize that our language is legitimate and valid. It comes from our families, our cultures, our class backgrounds, our experiences of different and conflicting realities. . . . Because our experiences and feelings are far too complex to be capsized in abstractions like "oppression," "sexism," "racism," etc., there is no right combination of these terms which can express why we feel oppressed.[10]

Chinese American women, with a one-hundred-and-fifty-year history of discrimination which includes at least fourteen pieces of legislation written by both state and federal governments, including antimiscegenation laws, understand and have a long memory of the meaning and consequences of "exclusion."

Another commonly and painfully shared experience of Asian American women is that of being marginalized and being in-between. Diana Chang says it well in her poem called "Second Nature."

> How do I feel
> Fine wrist to small feet.
> I cough Chinese.
> . . . .
> I am the thin edge I sit on.
> I begin to gray-white and black and in between
> My hair is America.[11]

Nellie Wong describes her "second nature" of trying to "fit in" as follows:

> I know now that once I longed to be white
> How? you ask
> Let me tell you the ways.
>
> > When I was growing up, people told me
> > I was dark and I believed my own darkness
> > in the mirror, in my soul, my own narrow vision
> > . . . .
> > When I was growing up, I was proud
> > of my English, my grammar, my spelling
> > fitting into the group of smart children
> > smart Chinese children, fitting in,

10. Quan, "The Girl," 216.
11. Diana Chang, "Second Nature," in *The Woman That I Am,* 13.

> belonging, getting in line
> When I was growing up, I hungered
> for American food, American styles,
> coded: white and even to me, a child
> born of Chinese parents, being Chinese
> was feeling foreign, was limiting, was unAmerican[12]

The shared experience of Asian American women, namely a condition of being invisible, excluded, and in-between as they articulate them, also points to a shared goal of their struggle — resisting domination — and a desire to be visible, included, and the same or part of. It is on a personal level a struggle of postcolonial women on the issue of identity and on the issue of difference. Yet there is a structural implication. These are issues of identity and difference caused, to a large extent, by factors outside the personal self of these women — a struggle against the multiple and systemic (socioeconomic, cultural, political, racial, and patriarchal) power of repression and domination that has a profound impact on their own well-being and the well-being of their community.

Living the Spirit of Liberation:
From Margins to Potential Sites of Resistance

Viewing their communal experience in the above, Asian American women have thus historically lived a life of being on the margins. From the beginning of their arrival in the United States, they have struggled alongside their men, be they Chinese, Japanese, Filipino, Asian Indian, Korean, Taiwanese, Malaysian, Thai, Burmese, Cambodian, Vietnamese, Laotian, Hmong, etc., against legal and political barriers that systematically discriminate or exclude them from becoming lawful and contributive members of U.S. society. Asian women were brought here as prostitutes, picture brides, mail-ordered brides, wives, daughters, and relatives of male immigrants. Some came as wanted professionals and some as political refugees. Nonetheless, since the time of their arrival in the U.S., these women have entered and worked their way into all stratums of American society, as prostitutes, produce growers, farmers, laborers, waitresses, seamstresses, launderers, cooks, live-in house maids, intellectuals, nurses, physicians, scientists, artists, activists. They have also worked, in the words of Diana Chang, "to dismantle the myth of the docile, submissive Oriental and to challenge the stereotypes that Asian Americans

---

12. Nellie Wong, "When I Was Growing Up," in *The Woman That I Am*, 151-52.

are the 'model minority.' They are creating new identities for themselves that are more empowering."[13] In their struggle, they do not completely surrender to become mere victims of historical and social circumstances. Being invisible, excluded, marginalized, and in-between as they describe their experience, they have a choice of succumbing to despair due to the state of oppression and repression, or creating strategies for survival. Many Asian American women choose life. The state of Asian America today reflects to a large extent the commitment of its women to this choice, a choice that implies actions which are channeled through ethnic solidarity and women solidarity. It is a choice inspired by their spirituality of liberation which in turn generates the spirit of resistance that has transpired into a way of being and a way of living in the world for them.

The Spirit of Resistance As the Spirit of Liberation: Transforming the Wilderness Experience to a Journey into the Promised Land

The term "resistance" in recent times has become a code word and a key concept in liberative struggles. Asian American women's literature that addresses issues of struggle in their own community speak volumes of "resistance." Although there is not much difference in white feminist, womanist, mujarista, Asian, and Asian American feminists' understanding of "resistance," the context of the history of struggle of Asian American women provides additional meaning to the term. This is discernible through the way they have lived out the spirit of resistance during the one hundred and fifty years of their history as Asian America. Such lived experience has theologically transformed the spirit of resistance into the spirit of liberation — one that generates life, justice, and compassion for women, children, and men in their own ethnic communities and in the larger society.

Existing literature on Asian American women reveals that their struggle has featured a spirit of resistance which is in itself informed by their moral vision of liberation. This is a spiritual resource from which they draw meanings of their experience and at the same time implement it as a key strategy for survival. More importantly, resistance as a main force of Asian American women experience reflects the nature of the struggle to be spiritual, social, and political. As such, the struggle has been understood and articulated in this term.

Understanding their existence as a mode of resistance offers Asian

13. Chang, "Second Nature," 17.

American women an alternate condition of being, another way of existing in the world that is different from that of the dominant pattern and norm. As Asian American literature critic Elaine Kim argues, affirming our "otherness" as American "others," as Asian American writers have done, is considered part of the resistance to domination. Resistance as inspired by the spirit of liberation is consequently being interpreted as a theological concept which transforms Asian American women's struggle from the wilderness experience into a journey to a promised land. This journey, as one similar to that of the Israelites, has historically been accompanied by temptations, challenges, and hardship. However, inspired by strong determination to reach the promised land, those committed to this journey persevere. Such transformative journey bears a spiritual, social, and political understanding of what it takes to reach the destination. The spirit of resistance informed by the spirit of liberation of Asian American women is expressed in the forms of ethnic solidarity, women solidarity, community healing, community teaching, and community activism. All reflect the struggle to be intrinsically three-dimensional, namely spiritual, social, and political.

Ethnic solidarity as lived out in the history of Asian American women's struggle signifies their love of and commitment to justice and the survival and well-being of their ethnic group. From the beginning of their arrival in Hawaii and on the mainland, Asian women from China, Japan, the Philippines, Korea, India, etc. were well aware that their survival was closely linked with the survival of their men and their ethnic group. Chinese, Japanese, Filipino, and Korean women who either accompanied their husbands to Hawaii and the mainland or who were brought here as prostitutes or picture brides, which was mostly the case for early Asian immigrants, were faced with hardship and hostility when they first arrived. As Asian men were brought to the United States to work as plantation laborers, miners, railroad workers, farmers, and rice growers, they were subjected to regimented work and harsh treatment by the lunas (foremen), plantation owners, and the like. So were their wives and children. Historian Ronald Takaki provides some detail of the situation as follows:

> After the 5:00 a.m. plantation whistle had blown, the lunas and company policemen strode through the camps. "Get up, get up," they shouted as they knocked on the doors of the cottages and barracks. "Hana-hana, hana-hana, work, work." A Korean remembered the morning her mother failed to hear the work whistle and overslept: "We were all asleep — my brother and his wife, my older sister, and myself. Suddenly the door swung open, and a big burly luna burst in, screaming and cursing, 'Get

up, get to work.' The luna ran around the room, ripping off the covers, not caring whether my family was dressed or not."[14]

Numbers of women also worked in the plantations and camps in Hawaii doing laundry, cooking, and sewing. Takaki, a third-generation Japanese American, recalled his grandmother managed a boarding house feeding her husband, her eight children, and fifteen men everyday. But women's hardest work was in the canefields, cutting canes, hoeing weeds, stripping leaves, and harvesting. One Japanese woman recalled the lunas riding horses carrying whips as they patrolled the field. The women were very afraid of them and felt that they had to work harder or else they would be fired. Historian Sucheng Chan notes that "women treated this way determined to do everything possible to enable their families to leave the plantations as soon as possible. They took in laundry, grew vegetables, and undertook whatever additional work they could to help save up money to open their own stores, boardinghouses, bathhouses, or restaurants in Honolulu."[15] She also remarks that those who persevered were "physically tough and emotionally resilient."

The tradition of being in solidarity with their own ethnic group continues to affect younger generations. A Sansei woman tells about ethnic solidarity in her community and what this has meant to her.

I have a place on the West Coast where my relatives still farm, where I heard the stories of feuds and backbiting, and where I saw that people survived and flourished because fundamentally they trusted and relied upon one another. A death in the family is not just a death in a family; it is a death in the community. I saw people help each other with money, materials, labor, attention, and time. I saw men gather once a year without fail, to clean the grounds of a ninety-year-old woman who had helped the community before, during, and after the war. I saw her remembering them with birthday cards sent to each of their children.

I come from a people with a long memory and a distinctive grace. We live our thanks.

And we are Americans. Japanese Americans.[16]

14. Eun Sik Yang, "Korean Women of America: From Subordination to Partnership, 1903-1930," *Amerasia* 11:2 (1984): 5, as quoted in Ronald Takaki, *Strangers From a Different Shore* (New York: Penguin Books, 1990), 134.

15. Sucheng Chan, *Asian American: An Interpretive History* (New York: Twayne Publishers, 1991), 110.

16. Kesa Noda, "Growing Up Asian in America," in *Making Waves,* ed. Asian Women United of California (Boston: Beacon Press, 1989), 248.

Being members of a racial group, Asian American women learn by heart that their struggle is beyond gender oppression and women's rights. Who they are and what they will become depends a great deal on the well-being of their group. Given this acknowledgment, they also know that they have commitment to women.

Women Solidarity signifies Asian American women's commitment to justice, survival, and the well-being of women. Existing Asian American women's literature reveals a trend of strong relationships among women. In some cases it is a relationship between mother and daughter and in others a connection with women of other race and ethnicity.

For example, early Asian women immigrants who survived the hardship of life caused by the systemic power of oppression, exclusion, and domination which is operated through racism, capitalism, patriarchy, and colonialism understood that they were survivors because they were strong. They wanted to make certain that their daughters also survived and were strong. One resource that was available to them was their own lives. Thus they modeled it to their daughters and other women. Poet Janice Mirikitani wrote about lessons a daughter had learned from her mother's life.

You gotta be a Survivor,
Fumiko. They'll try to whip
you down, but don't you flinch.
Never let them see
you're hurt
or afraid.
Just keep standing straight
turn your back,
let the latch fall
without twitching.

I gotta tell you, Mama.
You're pretty hard on me . . .

Mama, I gotta give it
to you. You were a
Survivor.
You turned that rock farm
into strawberries.
And when they took us
to the camps,
you didn't look back once.

Eyes dead ahead,
dripping big like berries.
The sun
that day
was like no other
rotting in an orange sky.
It dried up the world
like an apricot pit
hard . . . bitter . . .
The world they sent us to
Amache Gate
A gate slammed shut
one way.
The ground there was ungiving
No dirt, no sand
just dust that blew
into our pores.
I can't forget, Mama
The guards were making bad jokes
at our backs
about low built barracks
for low built japs.
Those barracks —
mocking us, row after row
in the dust.
. . . .
God, Mama, I really miss you.[17]

Younger generation women, like Kesa Noda, searched for some model of strength in black womanists and white feminists. However, she discovered that her identity and model of strength lies instead within the relationship she has with her mother and how she lives her life. In her own words: "My mother is a woman who speaks with her life as much as with her tongue." She concludes: "I am my mother's daughter. And I am myself."[18]

In addition, lessons learned from other women's struggles also serve as a source of strength and a reservoir of life for Asian American women. Poet Merle Woo writes:

17. Janice Mirikitani, "The Survivor," in *The Things That Divide Us,* ed. Faith Conlon et al. (Seattle: The Seal Press, 1985), 163-65, 169.
    18. Noda, "Growing Up Asian," 248, 250.

Karen, comrade and sister poet, sends me this news article
about a woman warrior.
She includes a note that says:
 "We've got her philosophy and her strength, too.
 We'll get them all by the ears and let them have it."
The article is one I've been wanting
to slip into speeches, talks, poems, conversations.
The images we get from reality . . .
Those fighting-back images in the face of great diversity.
. . . .
Beijing

A crippled grandmother caught a leopard by the ears, dragged it to
the ground and then helped kill it with her bare hands, official reports
said Tuesday.

Qi Deying, who can barely walk because her feet were bound from
birth, was gathering herbs with her niece and grandchildren on a mountain in North China's Shaanxi Province when the six-foot leopard attacked her and sank his teeth into her arm.

The 77-year-old Qi grabbed the leopard by the ears, wedged its jaw
shut with her right shoulder and forced it to the ground, the Shaanxi
Daily said.

Their bodies locked in combat, the grandmother and the leopard rolled
more than 120 feet down the mountainside, bouncing off rocks before
coming to rest in a wheatfield.

Qi called out to her grandchildren, who were hiding behind a boulder,
to come to her aid. They tore branches off a tree and helped her beat the
animal to death.

Qi, only bruised, told the paper: "Whenever you're cornered, the only
way out is to fight."[19]

Some see the importance of connecting with other women of color
who share similar struggle as feminist socialist scholar and community
activist Esther Ngan-Ling Chow insists:

Asian American women must unite with other women of color who, for
the most part, share similar life circumstances, experience multiple oppression, and struggle for common goals. Unless the whole social struc-

19. Merle Woo, "Whenever You're Cornered, the Only Way Out Is to Fight," in *The
Forbidden Stitch,* 133.

ture is uprooted, many institutional barriers in law, housing, education, employment, economics, and politics that are deeply embedded in the stystem will remain unchanged. Only when different groups work effectively and strategically together as a political force will all women achieve a new political consciousness and gain collective strength, to supersede the race, gender, sexual, class and cultural differences that now divide them.[20]

It is obvious that the Asian American women whose opinions of the struggle are mentioned in the above share a view that there are other factors, social and historical, that are integral to the context of their lives. An awareness of a systemic and encompassing power of domination compels them to see the intersection of their specific struggle in light of other struggles.

Community Healing and Community Teaching

There is another strategic mode of action besides ethnic solidarity and women solidarity that expresses Asian American women's "spirit of resistance" as informed by their "spirit of liberation." It is the so-called community healing and community teaching. This is perhaps the most pronounced social and political consciousness emerging from their struggle. Seeing the significance of healing and teaching the community as a strategic tool for change demonstrates a communal recognition among Asian American women that in the midst of injustices, a constructive solution lies in addressing them in the community and as a community. This understanding is provocatively articulated through two theological themes, namely reconciliation and healing. These themes prominently appear in various writings — autobiographical, poetical, social, and theological — by Asian American women.

Community healing as discussed in Asian American literature is understood in relation to reconciliation. Exploring the concept of reconciliation in Asian American literature, Elain Kim concludes that Asian American writers' interpretation of reconciliation lies in three contexts of relationship. This includes reinventing or reconciling one's identity as American, reconciling the relationship between men and women, and reconciling the relationship between oneself and the community.

20. Esther Ngan-Ling Chow, "The Feminist Movement: Where Are All the Asian American Women?" in *Making Waves*, 377.

The work of reinventing one's identity as American by Asian American writers is being done in coalition with other people of color, in particular blacks and Native Americans. As people of color, Kim argues, our identity is mostly and firstly defined by race. To connect our struggle with others who also fight against domination, is first to claim our identity as Americans and reconcile this identity with our past, which may have been repressed, distorted, or neglected by racism. In her words: "Claiming America requires reconciliation with our father and forefather in this country."[21]

Kim also sees reconciliation in the context of gender. As she explains,

> Claiming America also means reconciliation between men and women. Racism has created a haunting distance between the sexes in our literature and culture. Certainly the absence of significant female characters in Asian American men's writing reflects the harsh realities of the bachelor life created by exclusion and anti-miscegenation laws. Carlos Bulasan, for example, wrote at a time when Filipino men outnumbered women in some American cities by as many as forty-seven to one.[22]

Jade Snow Wong adds another perspective to this understanding. In her internationally acclaimed autobiography, *Fifth Chinese Daughter,* she details her upbringing experiences as a Chinese girl living in Chinatown of San Francisco as being affected by both race and gender. In Wong's experience, gender prejudice exists in her family and her Imperial China culture. Claiming her Americanness from her Chinese ethnicity and Chinese history, Wong's autobiography makes aware the need for gender reconciliation from within the Asian American community as well.

Yet, there is also a call for the reconciliation between the self and the community. As Kim warns, "Without the reconciliation of the self to the community we cannot reinvent ourselves."[23] Here Kim understands "the community" to mean the community of struggle — one that goes beyond one's family, clan, ethnicity, and race. To Kim, the community extends to "wherever resistance to domination is taking place." Reconciling oneself to the community, even when that community is one that hates women, people of color, and others who are on the margins and excluded, appears to be a recurring understanding among Asian American

---

21. Elaine H. Kim, "Defining Asian American Realities Through Literature," in *The Woman That I Am,* 614.

22. Kim, "Defining Asian American," 615.

23. Kim, "Defining Asian American," 616.

women.[24] This is because they see it as a primary step towards an authentic resistance in the state of domination. But as Kim insists, this reconciliation shall be directed towards claiming one's identity from one's racial, ethnic, cultural, and national origin as American. It is to assert one's own otherness as American "others." As she and others see it, the claiming of America is part of their resistance to domination and part of reinventing a new historical situation for the oppressed community.

Reconciliation in the context of Asian American women's struggle also relates to healing. Speaking out of her Japanese American experience that is informed by her Christian faith tradition, Diana Akiyama calls the community's attention to the need for healing. Recalling the encounter she had with her father when she broke the news that she wanted to go into the Christian ministry, Akiyama felt her father's resentment and bitterness toward the church for its silence and inaction toward Japanese American internment during the second World War. As he remarked:

> I don't have much need for the Christian church. Why should I? Where were they when we were relocated? They weren't there. If what they say is true — all this stuff about love and compassion and justice — then where were they when we were in the relocation camps? They didn't do anything for us Japanese back then. I don't feel like they are anything special.[25]

Akiyama disagreed and insisted that her wish resulted from her belief in the Christian message of justice as one that must also address racism and because she wanted to be part of the justice movement. She saw the necessity for community healing in the justice-making process.

> Embracing the gospel message of justice and liberation requires courage and love, forgiveness and healing. For Japanese American women, healing is the first component in moving towards embracing justice and liberation. Our wounds are bound up in a complicated historical, cultural, sociological knot, the untangling of which seems exhausting and frightening. But we must untangle the knot. We must move forward to heal our wounds because any effort to "do theology" — to tell our stories of

24. See, for example, Maxine Hong Kingston, *The Woman Warrior* (New York: Vintage, 1985) and *China Men* (New York: Alfred A. Knopf, 1980).

25. Diana D. Akiyama, "Doing Theology Towards Healing and Freedom: A Japanese American Woman's Perspective," in *Sisters Struggling in the Spirit,* ed. Nantawan Boonprasat Lewis et al. (Louisville: Presbyterian Church USA, 1994), 161.

living in and with God — will not be honest or whole if we cannot face our own wounds and patiently cleanse and close them.[26]

Indeed, Akiyama's words heal. Her story is significant in reminding the community of struggle of the real motivation behind their movement of resistance. It also affirms Elaine Kim's invitation to those in the struggle to take heed of a fundamental step of resistance, namely to reconcile themselves to the community that hates them. This step is crucial so that the healing process can begin and the message of liberation can be proclaimed with integrity and honesty. Such understanding in itself is a powerful testimony to the liberating spirit of women.

Community Teaching: In Remembrance

No, we will not forget
    Amache gate, Rohwer, Poston, Heart Mountain,
    Minidoka, Jerome, Gila River, Manzanar, Topaz
    Tule Lake.
Our tongues are sharp like blades.
We overturn furrows of secrecy.
Yes, we will harvest justice.
    And yes,
The struggle continues on
with our stampede of voices.

                Janice Mirikitani, "In Remembrance"

In the spirit of the struggle for liberation, Asian American women remember. They remember their history, the injustices done to them, their family, their ancestors, their community, and their women. Their resistance to this history of domination is channeled through engaging the community with memories of what have been done to them, their ancestors, their community, and their women. Despite a direct warning from her mother — "You must not tell anyone what I am about to tell you" — Maxine Hong Kingston wrote *The Woman Warrior* in memory of her "No Name" aunt who committed suicide under the Imperial China culture. This is an aunt she never met but felt connected to because of her plight as a woman. Kingston wrote *China Men* in part to be a remembrance of the struggle

---

26. Akiyama, "Doing Theology," 162.

and the contribution of her ancestors who came to Hawaii and California to work in the canefields and to build the railroad in the Sierra. Jade Snow Wong remembered her childhood growing up in Chinatown of San Francisco and the limitations she encountered as a female child and later a Chinese woman who aspired to a professional career outside Chinatown. Yet her defiant spirit continues. Mary Paik Lee, an eighty-six-year-old Korean immigrant, in her autobiography entitled *Quiet Odyssey* recognizes "subversive remembrance." In her own words, "Oh, I am so old now that I often forget what I did last week. But these things I've written down, what I am telling you now, I remember them because they made me suffer so." These women writers and ordinary storytellers model their resistance through their writings and memoirs, which in turn help to educate the community and keeps the community's memory of their history alive. Memory of one's suffering and triumph is not a passive activity when it is told and retold from generation to generation. It is the individual's and the community's subversive tool for change and for hope for freedom. Owning this history of struggle is what is required of us, women on the road to liberation.

Conclusion

There are indeed liberative trends manifested in the history of struggle of Asian American women. These trends are, as I argued, informed by the spirit of liberation of women which is expressed in various forms of resistance. This history of struggle in itself bears witness to the message of liberation that can serve as a powerful resource for Asian American feminist theology of liberation. In claiming this history and in remembering this collective act of resistance as guidance for their liberative journey, Asian American women join those in the struggle in reinventing, reconciling, and healing the wounded world. They are living and exemplifying "naming the divine."

Biography of Richard Shaull

ANDREW W. CONRAD

THOSE OF US WHO KNOW Dick Shaull are regularly amazed when we pause to remember his age. Millard Richard Shaull was born seventy-seven years ago on November 24, 1919, the firstborn child of Millard Shaull and Anna Brenneman on a small farm in southern York County, Pennsylvania. He grew up there with the two sisters and one brother who came along later. He attended a one-room school for his primary education. His family has been marked by extraordinary longevity, a genetic advantage Dick seems to have inherited to the advantage of us all.

In the background of everything in those early years was the Great Depression and the threat that posed to the very survival of the family. Dick's father worked, and the family survived, because of a WPA job; he later continued to work for the government in the Department of Public Assistance of York County. Life was hard, and Dick learned about the futility of labor when the assumptions of the civil arrangement leave no room or context for rewarding work. The experience of poverty is never far from Dick's consciousness nor from his commitments. Dick's confidence in the possibilities of transcendence pushed him forward, first to Elizabethtown College, from which he was graduated in 1938, and on to Princeton Theological Seminary, from which he was graduated in 1941, the year he left for Colombia as a Presbyterian missionary.

In Colombia, he became more and more convinced that the work of the church, in order to be part of the work of God in history, must be a work of identification with and the search for transcendence alongside the poor, the disenfranchised, those on the margins of power and position. Here the early seeds of a continuing theological project were sewn, and Dick's faith took shape, a faith still evolving and growing. In 1950, Dick returned to the U.S. to do graduate work with Paul Lehmann, a project he pursued enthusiastically, completing his residence in 1952 when he went to Brazil in a new role. This time his focus in Brazil centered around training young people for ministry at the Presbyterian seminary in Campinas, near the city of São Paulo.

In 1957, Dick again returned on furlough to Princeton to work on his dissertation with Paul Lehmann. In January 1959, at the beginning of the last semester of his graduate study, Dr. Mackay, Princeton's long-time President, invited Dick to teach a course in Ecumenics. That was a busy semester. The course led eventually to Mackay's invitation for Dick to assume the chair in Ecumenics. But Dick refused the appointment at that time, and immediately after receiving his doctorate in June of 1959, he returned to Brazil to take up his work there. In 1962, however, he was persuaded by his friend, James I. McCord, Princeton's president, to move to Princeton where he could influence an entire generation of emerging Presbyterian ministers and missionaries. So for eighteen years, until 1980, Dick was Henry Winters Luce Professor of Ecumenics at Princeton Theological Seminary.

Those were momentous years. After more than a decade of social upheaval and turmoil in Latin America, Dick could have been excused for perhaps expecting some tranquility in Princeton in which to reflect, teach, and write. The sixties and seventies proved to be no such time. Rather the breakdown in social assumptions he had seen so vividly in Latin America in the previous decade had already begun to invade North American political and social consciousness. From the execution of Caryl Chessman and the birth of the Berkeley Free Speech Movement to the founding of the Students for a Democratic Society (SDS), the U.S. had already begun moving rapidly into a decade which would be marked by rapid change, erosion of order, assassination, and disruption at an unprecedented scale on the college and university campuses, and an accompanying reassessment of basic assumptions. In short, the time was ripe for a prophetic word to be spoken and lived in the midst of dizzying change. The time was right for Dick Shaull to begin his ministry at Princeton Theological Seminary.

When Dick came to Princeton in 1962, he came with his wife, Mildred Miller Shaull, his classmate from Elizabethtown College whom he had married in 1941. They have two daughters, Madelyn and Wendy, who today both live in Southern California. Mildred had been with Dick in Colombia, in Brazil, and during his previous stays in Princeton. Now they moved into 14 Alexander Street, and Dick moved into a period of momentous productivity and personal growth and change. Separated in 1973, Dick and Mildred later divorced.

Dick's students from those years (of which I am one) remember an extraordinary teacher, thoughtful and energetic, who distrusted the inherent power of the teacher (siding with the writer of the New Testament Book of James who warns, "Don't many of you be teachers, for you shall receive the greater condemnation.") and who questioned the authority of the institution which gave him that problematic power. He enabled students to find their own voices by being careful never to drown them out with his. He listened to his students in a way no student could miss. Such a stance kept him at a creative distance from the assumptions of seminary "training" but clearly in the center of the debate that was building momentum in American education at the time.

Dick's life and career continue to be about theological education and about how the "leading out" implied in the word education can be nurtured and fostered in ways that leave students and teacher alike liberated from the authority structures inherent in the institutions which we experience as inimical to freedom of either thought or action. Eventually, in 1980, Dick decided to take an early retirement option from Princeton to pursue his work in theological education in new and diverse settings. His connection to Latin America seems today more vital than ever. After several years at General Seminary in New York as Academic Director of an alternative program of theological education for Hispanics living in the U.S., and years of writing and travel, he is able to go freely to Brazil, ending what had become twenty years of exile. He is engaged in short-term teaching in Presbyterian seminaries in Guatemala, Mexico, and San Jose, Costa Rica. His work in Nicaragua continues, as does his active writing. Dick is once again in the midst of change, energetic reflection, and constant conversation with yet another generation of women and men committed to social change and spiritual transformation.

Married now for many years to Dr. Nancy Johns, Dick's is a familiar voice and face in many conversations around Philadelphia centering on the future of theological education and the evolutionary process through which it must go to teach new generations with new experiences what ministry can be in a new context. Dick remains committed to transformation in the church, a renewal of life in the spirit that finds meaningful context in a changing history. His has been, and continues to be, a productive life of prophetic work dedicated to calling the church to a faithful and responsible role in relation to society.

Selected Bibliography of Richard Shaull

Books

O Cristianismo e a Revolucao Social. São Paulo: UCEB, 1953.
Spanish edition, Buenos Aires: Aurora, 1956.
Encounter with Revolution. New York: Association Press, 1955.
Alternativa ao Desespero. São Paulo, Brazil: Imprensa Metodista, 1962.
As Transformaçoes Profundas a Luz de una Teologia Evangelica. Petropolis: Vozes, 1966.
Containment and Change (Carl Oglesby and M. Richard Shaull). New York: Macmillan, 1967.
Dutch edition, Utrecht: Amboboeken.
Portuguese edition, Rio de Janeiro: Paz e Terra.
German edition, Frankfurt: Suhrkamp Verlag.
Une théologie de la révolution? (Jan Milič Lochman, Richard Shaull, and Charles West). Geneva: Labor & Fides, 1968.
Uitdaging aan Kerk en Maatschappij. Baarn: Het Wereldvenster, 1969.
Befreiung durch Veranderung. Munich: Kaiser Verlag, 1970.
Oltre le Regole del Gioco. Torino: Editrice Claudiana, 1972.
Liberation and Change (Gustavo Gutiérrez and M. Richard Shaull, ed. Ronald H. Stone). Atlanta: John Knox Press, 1977.
Heralds of a New Reformation: The Poor of South and North America. Maryknoll, N.Y.: Orbis Books, 1984.
Responding to the Cry of the Poor: Nicaragua and the USA (Richard Shaull and Nancy Johns). Philadelphia, Penn.: Omega Press, 1984.
De dentro do Furação: Richard Shaull e os Primordios da Teologia de Libertação. São Paulo: Sagarana Editol, 1985.
Naming the Idols: Biblical Alternatives for U.S. Foreign Policy. Oak Park, Ill.: Meyer-Stone, 1988.

The Reformation and Liberation Theology: Insights for the Challenge of Today.
Louisville, Ky. Westminster/John Knox Press, 1991.
Portuguese edition, São Paulo: Petropolis, 1993.
Spanish edition, San Jose: DEI, 1993.
A Reforma Protestante e a Teologia da Libertação: Perspectivas para os Desafios da Atualidade. São Paulo: Livraria e Editora Pendao Real Ltda., 1993.
La Reforma y la Teologia de la Liberacion. San Jose: DEI, 1993.

Pamphlets

The New Revolutionary Mood in Latin America. New York: Committee on Cooperation in Latin America, Division of Foreign Mission, National Council of the Churches of Christ in the U.S.A., 1962.
Vida e astructura da Igreja em relação com o seu testemunha na sociedade latino-americana (The Present Life and Structure of the Church in Relation to Her Witness in Latin American Society). Background Information, 1962.
Cadernos da UCEB. São Paulo, 1964.
Humanizção e Politica. São Paulo: UCEB, 1964.
Consumers or Revolutionaries? (Josef Smolik and Richard Shaull). Geneva: Foyer, and Atlanta: John Knox Press, 1967.

Chapters in Books

"Vocação da igreja na Evolução Politica de um Povo." In *Estudos sobre a Responsabilidade Social da Igreja.* Rio de Janeiro: Sector de Responsabilidade Social da Igreja, 1960.
"New Forms of Church Life in a New Society." In *Raise a Signal: God's Action and the Church's Task in Latin America Today,* ed. H. Converse. New York: Friendship Press, 1961.
"Ashbel Green Simonton, A Calvinist in Brazil." In *Sons of the Prophets,* ed. Hugh Kerr. Princeton: Princeton University Press, 1963.
"The New Challenge before the Younger Churches." In *Christianity and World Revolution,* ed. E. H. Rian. New York: Harper & Row, 1963.
"La Iglesia y la Situacion Politica-Ideologica de America Latina." In *La Naturaleza de la Iglesia y su Mission en Latinoamerica.* Bogotá: CCPAL, 1964.
"Christian Participation in the Latin American Revolution." In *Christianity amid Rising Men and Nations,* ed. Creighton Lacy. New York: Association Press, 1965.
"The Form of the Church in the Modern Diaspora," In *Theology No. 2,* ed. Martin Marty and Dean Peerman. New York: Macmillan, 1965. Also in *Princeton Seminary Bulletin* 57 (March 1964): 3-18.
German translation in *Appell an die Kirchen der Welt.* Stuttgart: Kreuz Verlag, 1967.

"The New Revolutionary Mood in Latin America." In *Readings and Essays in Latin American History,* ed. Harold Bierch. Boston: Allyn & Bacon, 1965.

"Una Perspectiva cristiana del desarrollo historico y social." In *Hombre, Ideologia y Revolucion en America Latina.* Montevideo: ISAL, 1965.

"Revolutionary Change in Theological Perspectives." In *Christian Social Ethics in a Changing World: An Ecumenical Theological Inquiry,* ed. John Bennett. New York: Association Press, and London: SCM Press, 1966.

"Technology and Revolution in Theological Perspective," and "The Context of Personal Freedom and Maturity," In *Challenges of Change to the Christian College.* Washington: Council of Protestant Colleges and Universities, 1966.

"Y un Dios que actua y Transforma la Historia." In *American Hoy, Accion de Dios y Responsabilidad del Hombre,* ed. Luis E. Odell. Montevideo: ISAL, 1966.

"Confronting the Power Structures: Cooperation or Conflict." In *Proceedings of College Theology Society.* 1967.

"A crise nas igrejas nacionais." In *Protestantismo e Imperialismo na America Latina,* ed. Waldo Cesar. Petropolis: Vozes, 1968.

"The Rehabilitation of Ideology." In *Religion and International Affairs,* ed. Jefrey Rose and Michael Ignatieff. Toronto: House of Anansi, 1968.

"Toward a Reformation of Objectives." In *Protestant Crosscurrents in Mission,* ed. Norman A. Horner. Nashville: Abingdon Press, 1968.

"Christian Faith as Scandal in a Technocratic World." In *Theology and Revolution (New Theology 6),* ed. Martin Marty and Dean Peerman. New York: Macmillan, 1969.

> German translation: "Der Christliche Glaube als Skandal in einer Technokratischen Welt." In *Diskussion Zur 'Theologie der Revolution,'* Ed. E. Feil and R. Weth. Munich: Chr. Kaiser Verlag, 1969. (French edition: *Discussion sur "La théologie de la révolution."* Paris: Ceri-Mame, 1972.)

> French translation: "La foi chrétienne, scandale dans une civilisation technocratique," *Bulletin du Centre Protestant d'Etudes* 20, no. 3 (1968): 17-27.

> Also printed in *Consumers or Revolutionaries.* Geneva: Foyer John Knox, 1968.

"Resistance and the Third World." In *Delivered into Resistance.* Milwaukee: Milwaukee Fourteen Defense Committee, 1969.

"Church and Theology in the Vortex of Revolution." In *Projections: Shaping an American Theology for the Future,* ed. Thomas O'Meara and D. Weisser. Garden City, N.Y.: Doubleday, 1970.

German translation: "Kirche und theologie im Kontext der Revolution." In *Zur Ethic der Revolution.* Stuttgart: Kreuz Verlag, 1970.

"The End of the Road and a New Beginning." In *Marxism and Radical Religion: Essays toward a Revolutionary Humanism,* ed. John Raines and Thomas Dean. Philadelphia: Temple University Press, 1970.

"American Power and the Powerless Nations." In *What the Religious Revolutionaries are Saying,* ed. Elwyn Smith. Philadelphia: Fortress Press, 1971.

"A possibilidade da Fe." In *Credo para Amanha,* ed. Raimundo Cintra. Petropolis: Vozes, 1971.

"Iglesia y Teologia en la Voragine de la Revolucion." In *De la Iglesia y la Sociedad.* Montevideo: Terra Nueva, 1971.

"Grace: Power for Transformation." In *Liberation, Revolution and Freedom: Theological Perspectives: Proceedings from the College Theological Society,* ed. M. M. Thomas. New York: Seabury, 1975.

"Carter: su religion y su presidencia." In *Capitalismo,* ed. E. Tamez and S. Trinidad. San Jose: DEI, 1978. Also in *Sojourners* 7 (1978): 12-14.

"The Inclusive Christian Promise of New Life." In *Empowering Ministry in an Ageist Society.* New York: Program Agency, United Presbyterian Church in the U.S.A., 1981.

"A Theology of Sanctuary from a Calvinist Perspective." In *Sanctuary: A Resource Guide for Understanding and Participating in the Central American Refugees' Struggle,* ed. Gary MacEoin. San Francisco: Harper & Row, 1985.

"Testimonio." In *Nicaragua y los Teologosm,* ed. Jose Maria Vigil. Mexico: Siglo Veintiuno, 1987.

"The Church and Revolutionary Change: Contrasting Perspectives." In *The Church and Social Change in Latin America,* ed. H. Landsberger. Notre Dame: University of Notre Dame Press, 1988.

"Responding to the Challenge: Renewal and Re-creation." In *Freedom and Discipleship: Liberation Theology in an Anabaptist Perspective.* Maryknoll, N.Y.: Orbis Books, 1989.

"The Redemptive Suffering of the Poor." In *Suffering and Healing in Our Day,* ed. F. Eigo. Villanova: Villanova University Press, 1990.

"New Church, New Ministries." In *Struggles for Solidarity: Liberation Theologies in Tension,* ed. Lorine M. Getz and Roy O. Costa. Minneapolis: Fortress, 1992. Also in *Ministerial Formation* (January 1988): 9-14.

"The Christian Base Communities and the Ecclesia Reformata Semper Reformanda." In *Christian Ethics in Ecumenical Contect,* ed. S. Chiba. Grand Rapids: Eerdmans, 1995. Also in *Princeton Seminary Bulletin* 12 (July 1991): 201-13.

"Toward the Recovery of the Prophetic Power of the Reformed Heritage." In *The Future of Prophetic Christianity,* ed. D. Carmody. Maryknoll, N.Y.: Orbis.

Articles

"Politica e Revolucano." *Mocidade* (September 1953).

"O Evangelho e o Homem Rural." *O Puritano* (25 December 1953): 10.

"O Cristao e a Politica." *Mocidade* (December 1953): 11.

"Evangelism and Proselitism in Latin America." *Student World* 46 (1953): 14-20.

"A ACA como uma comunidade Missionaria." *Testimonium* II, no. 3: 54.

"Dos anos de un MEC en Revolucion." *Testimonium.*

"Challenge of Student Work in Brazil." *International Review of Missions* 44 (July 1955): 323-28.

"Church and Culture in Latin America." *Theology Today* 13 (April 1956): 37-44.

"The Devotional Life of Brazilian Protestantism" (Richard Shaull and Rubem Alves). *Student World* 49 (1956): 360-66.

"Protestantism in Latin America: Brazil." *Religion in Life* 27 (Winter 1957-1958): 5-14.

"Influencia de Karl Barth." *Suplemento Teologico d'O' Caos* (1958).

"John Alexander Mackay as Missionary Statesman." *Princeton Seminary Bulletin* 52 (May 1959): 22-26.

"O Servico da Igreja." *Suplemento Teologico d'O Caos* (October 1959).

"Reflexoes sobre o Papel do Ministro e do Leigo na Igreja." *Revista Teologica* (November 1959).

"A Fe Crista e a Ordem Economica." *Testimonium* VII, no. 4 (1959).

"A Actualidade de Calvino para o Pensamento Protestante Centemporaneo." *Suplemento Teologico d'O' Caos* (October 1960).

"Palestras em um Seminario sobre o Calvinismo." *Suplemento Teologico d'O' Caos* (1960).

"O Desafio Comunista." *Suplemento Teologico d'O' Caos* (October 1961).

"A Igreja e Eu." *Revista da Mocidade Batista Brasilei* (1961).

"New Revolutionary Mood in Latin America." *Christianity and Crisis* 23 (1 April 1963): 44-48. Reprinted in *Motive* (October 1963): 19-23.

"O Comunismo do Rev. Richard Shaull." *Brasil Presbiteriano* (July 1963): 1-15.

"Depoimento da Semana." *Brasil Urgente* no. 30 (October 1963): 6-12.

"The Church in the World." *Theology Today* 20 (1963): 401-11.

"Church in the World: Impatience in Latin America." *Theology Today* 21 (October 1963): 307-23.

"De nieuwe revolutionaire gezindheid in Latijns-Amerika." *Wending* 33 (1963): 226-45.

"Recientes estudios sobre el desarrollo politica en Asia, Africa y America Latina." *Cristianismo y Sociedad* 1, no. 2 (1963): 43-50.

"Südamerika im Umbruch." *Zeitwende Die Neue Furche* 34 (1963): 185.

"Military Coup in Brazil." *Christianity and Crisis* 2 (27 April 1964): 70-72.

"Community and Humanity in the University." *Theology Today* 21 (October 1964): 307-23.

"Ideologia, Fe y Revolucion Social." *Testimonium* X, no. 2 (1964).

"Latin Ferment: Challenge to the U.S." *Christianity and Crisis* 25 (9 August 1965): 175-77.

"Christian World Mission in a Technological Era." *Ecumenical Review* 17 (July 1965). Reprinted in *Cross Currents* 15 (Fall 1965): 461-72.

"Latin Ferment: Challenge to the U.S." *Christianity and Crisis* 25 (1965): 175-77.

"Van Leeuwen Thesis: A Review of Christianity in World History." *Study Encounter* 1, no. 2 (1965): 68-71.

"Christian Initiative in Latin American Revolution." *Christianity and Crisis* (10 January 1966): 295-98.

"The Struggle for Economic and Social Justice." *Social Action* 32 (January-February 1966): 27-30. Also *Social Progress* 56 (January-February 1966): 27-30.

"The Second Latin American Church and Society Conference." *Christianity and Crisis* 26 (2 May 1966): 89-91.

"Special Report on Dominican Elections." *Christianity and Crisis* (16 May 1966): 103-4.

"Technology and the Christian Faith." *Union Seminary Quarterly Review* 21 (May 1966): 417-25. Abridged reprint in *Theology Today* 23 (July 1966): 271-75.

"Berdiaev: Perspectiva Crista da Revolução Social." *Paz e Terra* (1966): 180-94.

"Revolutionary Challenge to Church and Theology." *Princeton Seminary Bulletin* 60 (October 1966): 25-32. Reprinted in *Theology Today* 23 (January 1967): 470-80.

"Presence of God and the Human Revolution." *McCormick Quarterly* 20 (January 1967): 97-103.

"Next Stage in Latin America." *Christianity and Crisis* 27 (13 November 1967): 264-66.

"Response to President Bennett." *Theological Education* 3 (Winter 1967): 291-93.

"Confronting the Power Structures: Cooperation or Conflict?" *Proceedings of the College Theology Society* (1967): 92-97.

"Christian Theology and Social Revolution." *Perkins Journal of Theology* 21 (Winter-Spring 1967-68): 5-12.

"New Latin Revolutionaries and the U.S." *Christian Century* 85 (17 January 1968). Reprinted in *Current* 93 (March 1968): 13-15.

"The Guerrillas — Next Stage in Latin America?" *Worldview* 11 (April 1968): 15-16.

"The Political Significance of Parabolic Action." *Motive* 28 (April 1968): 27-29.

"Theology and the Transformation of Society." *Theology Today* 25 (April 1968): 23-36.

"Christian Realism: A Symposium." *Christianity and Crisis* (5 August 1968): 175-90.

"He Who Lives, Can Die." *Presbyterian Survey* (November 1968): 15-17.

"A Theological Perspective on Human Liberation." *New Blackfriars* 49 (July 1968). Reprinted in *Listening* 3 (Fall 1968): 170-79.

"Realism and Celebration." *Christianity and Crisis* 28 (11 November 1968): 272-73.

"Failure of a Mission." *Tempo* (15 December 1968): 5, 12.

"A Theological Perspective on Human Liberation." *New Blackfriars* 40 (1968): 578, 509-17.

"Crisis in the Churches." *World Encounter* 6 (1968): 1, 9-11.

"Desarrollo nacional y revolucion social." *Cristianismo y Sociedad* (1968): 31-41.

"La Liberacion Humana desde una Persectiva Teologica." *Mensage* 168 (1968).

"Theology and the Transformation of Society." *Theology Today* (1968): 21-25.

"University Education for World Responsibility." *Federation News* (1968): 21-25.

"The New Latin Revolutionaries and the U.S." *Christian Century* (17 January 1969): 69-70.

"National Development and Social Revolution." Parts 1, 2. *Christianity and Crisis* (20 January, 3 February 1969): 347-48, 9-12.

"The Challenge to the Seminary." *Christianity and Crisis* 29 (14 April 1969): 81-86.

"Repression Brazilian Style." *Christianity and Crisis* 29 (14 April 1969): 198-99.

"Does Religion Demand Social Change?" *Theology Today* 26 (April 1969): 5-13.

"Une Communauté Chrétienne Subversive." *Tribune de Geneve* (Supplement) (11 December 1969): 290.

"A New Look at the Sectarian Option." *Student World* 64 (1969): 294-99.

"Crisis in the Young Church." *National Christian Council Review* 89 (1969): 22-26.

"Liberal and Radical in an Age of Discontinuity." *Student World* 62, no. 3/4 (1969): 350-58; and *Christianity and Crisis* 29 (5 January 1970): 339-45.

"Liberation through Transformation." *Communio Viatorum* 14, no. 2 (1971): 85-106.

"Response to G. Williamson Jr." *Christianity and Crisis* 32 (1 May 1972): 108-9.

"From Somewhere Along the Road" (with Barbara Hall). *Theology Today* 29 (April 1972): 86-101.

"The WSCF: A Crisis of Vocation." *IDOC Internazionale* 49 (1972): 29-34.

"Ainda o Comunismo." *Mocidade* (May 1975).

"Symposium on the Hartford Declaration." *Theology Today* (July 1975): 188-89.

"Leaven in the Loaf: The Nicaraguan Difference." *Christianity and Crisis* 42 (12 July 1982): 208-12.

"Reflexioes Sobre os anhos que Passei no Brasil." *Revista de Sociologia* 9 (1983): 47-58.

"The Prophetic Challenge to Imperial America: What Would the Old Testament Prophets Have to Say About Our Central American Policy?" *The Other Side* (February 1984): 14-16.

"Aportes de la Biblia al Desarollo de la Democracia." *Amanecer* (March-April 1984): 24-25.

"Christian Faith and the Crisis of Empire." *Witness* (January-February 1984). Reprinted in *Monthly Review*, (April 1984): 36-42.

"La Conferencia Juzgada." *Testimonium* 3-4 (1984): 48-58.

"The Call of Moses." *Church and Society* (March-April 1985): 25-31.

"A Personal Reflection." *Church and Society* 77 (May-June 1987): 51-56.

"What Does the Lord Require of You?" and "Theological Reflections." *Church and Society* (May-June 1987): 37-46.

"Liberation Theology and Karl Barth." *North-South Dialogue* (Fall 1987): 4-6.

"The Witness of the Holy Spirit in the Sanctuary Movement." *Pacific Theological Review* (Winter 1987): 8-14.

"Liberating Ourselves: Recovering the Gospel for North America." *The Other Side* (September-October 1989): 42-46.

"Teologia de la liberacion y Reforma protestante: Continuidad y nuptura." *Vida y Pensamiento* vol. 10, no. 1 (1990): 5-13. Also in *Amanacer* 63 (1989): 20-24.

"Solidarity in the Risk of Struggle." *Sojourners* 20 (October 1991): 25.

"La participacion de los Protestantes en la lucha por la transformacion social." *Revista de Historia del Protestantismo Nicaraguense* 2 (April 1992).

"Latin America: Three Responses to a New Historical Situation." *Interpretation* 46 (July 1992): 261-70.

"Rediscovering the Power of Our Spiritual Heritage." *Whisperings* 1, no. 3 (October 1992): 2-3.

"La Iglesia, Crisis y Nuevas Perspectivas." *Vida y Pensamiento* vol. 15, no. 3 (1995): 8-48.

"New Voices, New Visions: Liberation Theology is Alive and Well." *The Other Side* 32 (January-February 1996): 48-50.

"The Pentecostal Appeal to the Poor." *Church and Society* 86 (March-April 1996): 49-55.

"The Story of Salvation: Experiencing the Good News in Latin America." *The Other Side* 32 (May-June 1996): 30-32.

"The Third Conversion." *The Other Side* (March-April 1997): 32-34.

"Discord in the Americas: Naming the Roots." *CALC Report* 13, no. 2: 4-6.

"The Latin Phoenix." *Colloquium* (North Adelaide, Australia) XIV, no. 2 (May 1982): 5-12.

Forewords and Prefaces to Books

Jose de Broucker. *Dom Helder Camara: The Violence of a Peacemaker.* Maryknoll, N.Y.: Orbis Books, 1970.

Paulo Freire. *Pedagogy of the Oppressed.* New York: Herder and Herder, 1970.

Charles Antoine. *Church and Power in Brazil.* London: Sheed and Ward, 1973.

William R. Coats. *God in Public: Political Theology Beyond Niebuhr.* Grand Rapids: Eerdmans, 1974.

Rubem Alves. *Protestantism and Repression.* Maryknoll, N.Y.: Orbis Books, 1985.

Dominique Barbe. *Grace and Power: Base Communities and the Churches of Brazil.* Maryknoll, N.Y.: Orbis Books, 1987.

Philip Wheaton and Duane Shank. *Empire and the Word.* Washington: EPICA, 1988.

Philip L. Wickeri. *Seeking the Common Ground: Protestant Christianity, the Three-Self Movement and China's United Front.* Maryknoll, N.Y.: Orbis Books, 1988.

Bill Cane. *Circles of Hope: Breathing Life and Spirit into a Wounded World.* Maryknoll, N.Y.: Orbis Books, 1992.

Reviews

W. M. Ryburn, *Christ and Society.* In *International Review of Mission* 47 (1958): 108-09.

Harry R. Boer, *Pentecost and Missions.* In *Student World* 53, no. 3 (1962): 376-78.

Johannes Blauw, *The Missionary Nature of the Church: A Survey of the Biblical Theology of Mission.* In *Theology Today* 20 (January 1964): 566-67.

D. T. Niles, *Upon the Earth: The Mission of God and the Missionary Enterprise of the Church.* In *Theology Today* 20 (January 1964): 566-67.

Dietrich Bonhoeffer, *The Communion of Saints: A Dogmatic Inquiry into the Sociology of the Church.* In *Interpretation* (October 1964): 493-98.

Paul Lehmann, *Ethics in a Christian Context.* (Charles C. West and M. Richard Shaull) In *Princeton Seminary Bulletin* 58, no. 1 (October 1964): 44-50.

Alan Geyer, *Piety and Politics: American Protestantism in the World Arena.* In *Review of Religious Research* 6 (1964): 51-52.

Georg F. Vivedom, *The Mission of God: An Introduction to a Theology of Mission.* In *Theology Today* 22 (January 1966): 560-62.

Leonard J. Swidler, *The Ecumenical Vanguard.* In *Princeton Seminary Bulletin* 59, no. 3 (June 1966): 88-89.

Dom Helder Camara, *The Church and Colonialism.* In *The Christian Century* (5 November 1969): 1421-22.

Daniel B. Stevick, *Civil Disobedience and the Christian.* In *Religious Education* 64 (1969): 404-6.

Jürgen Moltmann, *Religion, Revolution and the Future.* In *Union Seminary Quarterly Review* 25 (Winter 1970): 235-39.

Michel Schooyans, *Chrétieneté en contestation: L'amérique latine.* In *Journal of Ecumenical Studies* 8 (1971): 327.

Paul E. Pierson, *Younger Church in Search of Maturity*. In *Journal of Presbyterian History* 54 (Summer 1976): 277-78.

Leonardo Boff, *Jesus Christ Liberator: A Critical Christology for Our Time*. In *Theology Today* 36 (July 1979): 292-94.

Severino Croatto, *Exodus: A Hermeneutics of Freedom*. In *Theology Today* 38 (January 1982): 542.

Jon Sobrino, *The True Church and the Poor*. In *International Bulletin of Missionary Research* 10, no. 2 (April 1986): 84-85.

Carlos Mesters, *Defenseless Flower: A New Reading of the Bible*. In *Princeton Seminary Bulletin* 11, no. 3 (1990): 175.

Justo González, *Mañana: Christian Theology from a Hispanic Perspective*. In *Theology Today* 48 (July 1991): 184.

Enrique Dussel, *The Church in Latin America*. In *Princeton Seminary Bulletin* 14, no. 2 (1993): 501.

Stephen Bevans, *Models of Contextual Theology: The Struggle for Cultural Relevance*. In *Theology Today* 50 (January 1994): 634-36.

Gustavo Gutiérrez, *Las Casas: In Search of the Poor of Jesus Christ*. Trans. by Robert Barr. In *Theology Today* 51 (October 1994): 442-44.

Mysterium Liberationis: Fundamental Concepts of Liberation Theology. Ed. Ignacio Ellacuria and Jon Sobrino, trans. Robert Barr. In *Princeton Seminary Bulletin* 15, no. 3 (1994): 310-11.

Cecilia Loreto Mariz, *Coping with Poverty: Pentecostals and Christian Base Communities in Brazil*. In *International Bulletin of Missionary Reserach* 19 (April 1995): 195.

Elsa Tamez, *The Amnesty of Grace: Justification by Faith from a Latin American Perspective*. Trans. H. Sharon. In *Interpretation* 49 (July 1995): 295-97.

Dorothee Sölle, *Stations of the Cross: A Latin American Pilgrimage*. In *Interpretation* 49 (July 1995): 295-97.

Contributors

María Marta Arís-Pául, an ordained Episcopal priest, has served as a prison chaplain for the New York State Department of Corrections, and as the Executive Director of the Instituto Pastoral Hispano. She received a B.A. from Smith College, and an M.Div. from Union Theological Seminary.

George Armstrong is an ordained Anglican priest who for many years served as a lecturer in systematic theology at St. John's Theological College in Auckland, New Zealand. He holds educational degrees from schools in New Zealand as well as a Ph.D. from Princeton Theological Seminary. Throughout his life he has been active in working to establish a nuclear-free and independent Pacific.

Bruce O. Boston was educated at Muskingum College and Princeton Theological Seminary, where he received his Ph.D. Presently he is serving as president of a writing and editorial consultant business. In addition, he is a lay preacher in the Episcopal Diocese of Virginia and an active participant in church and community affairs.

Waldo Cesar has for over fifty years served as a journalist, sociologist, and theologian in Brazil. He has directed and performed numerous studies and research on pentecostalism, the suffering of the poor, liberation theology, and social and religious problems in Brazil. Although retired, he remains an active member of the Lutheran Church in Brazil.

Andrew W. Conrad currently serves as Dean of the Liberal Arts Division at Mercer Community College. Although beginning his Ph.D. studies at Princeton Theological Seminary, he transferred to Princeton University, which granted him a Ph.D. in linguistics. He is actively working on issues of sociolinguistics and issues of spirituality in the gay and lesbian community.

Nancy A. De Vries holds academic degrees from Hope College and Princeton Theological Seminary, as well as a Doctor of Divinity degree from Coe College. Presently she is the university chaplain at Colgate University, Hamilton, New York. In addition to serving as pastor to Colgate's ecumenical Protestant community, she is also a lecturer in religion.

Nantawan Boonprasat Lewis is currently an associate professor of religious studies and ethnic studies at Metropolitan State University in Minneapolis/St. Paul, Minnesota. She holds degrees from Chiang Mai University, Payap University, and Princeton Theological Seminary, where she received her Ph.D. She has authored many articles on the themes of the struggle of Asian women, in particular the situation of sex tourism and AIDS in Thailand and southeast Asia, and recently served as co-editor of the book *Sisters Struggling in the Spirit.*

Alan P. Neely is the Henry Winters Luce Professor of Ecumenics and Mission, Emeritus at Princeton Theological Seminary. He holds degrees from Baylor University, Southwestern Baptist Theological Seminary, and a Ph.D. from the American University, Washington, D.C. He has authored many books and articles and most recently completed the English translation of Enrique Dussel's *History of the Church in Latin America* and *Christian Mission: A Case Study Approach.*

Timothy Njoya, a holder of a Ph.D. from Princeton Theological Seminary, serves as pastor in Nairobi, Kenya. He is the author of many books and articles concerning the plight of the Kenyan people and was a recent recipient of the E. M. Johnson Human Rights Award.

Joseph C. Nyce, a recipient of a Ph.D. from Princeton Theological Seminary, is currently involved in the integration of theology with day-to-day business practices. Serving as a general contractor, he is confronted daily with the tensions of political agendas, the needs of workers, and the message of the gospel.

T. Richard Snyder is Academic Dean and Professor of Theology and Ethics at New York Theological Seminary. An ordained Presbyterian minister, he was granted both an M.Div. and a Ph.D. from Princeton Theological Seminary. He has authored several books, including *Once You Were No People: The Church and Social Transformation* and *Divided We Fall: Moving from Suspicion to Solidarity.*

Douglass Sullivan-González is an assistant professor in the Latin American History Department at the University of Mississippi. He studied at Samford University, Princeton Theological Seminary, and was granted a Ph.D. from the University of Texas, Austin. He has authored several articles on church and society in Latin America.

Elsa Tamez is president of the Seminario Biblico Latinoamericano in San Jose, Costa Rica, where she also is a professor of biblical studies. She holds a Th.D. from the University of Lausanne, Switzerland; and a Licda in literature and linguistics from the National University, Costa Rica. She has authored and edited several books including *Bible of the Oppressed, The Amnesty of Grace,* and *Through Her Eyes.*

Mark Taylor, an ordained Presbyterian minister and holder of a Ph.D. from the University of Chicago, is an associate professor of theology and culture at Princeton Theological Seminary. He has authored numerous articles and books, including *Ghosts of the American Land: A Spirituality of Revolutionary Social Protest* and *Remembering Esperanza: A Cultural-Political Theology for North American Praxis.* In addition to his academic work, he is also involved in AMAJ — Academics for Mumia Abu-Jamal, a group which advocates a new trial for the award-winning journalist who has been on Pennsylvania's death row since 1982.

Philip L. Wickeri is serving as the Overseas Coordinator for China's Amity Foundation in Hong Kong. He holds a Ph.D. from Princeton Theological Seminary. He is a frequent writer on mission, ecumenism, and development. Beginning in January 1998, he will serve as the Hewlitt Professor of Evangelism and Mission at San Francisco Theological Seminary.

Kim Yong-Bock holds a B.A. from Yonsei University and an M.Div. and Ph.D. degree from Princeton Theological Seminary. An ordained minister of the Presbyterian Church of Korea, he currently serves as president of Hanil University and Theological Seminary in Seoul, South Korea. He has written many books and articles in both English and Korean, including *Minjung Theology* and *Healing God's World.*